Global
Communications

Global Communications

Toward a Transcultural Political Economy

Edited by
Paula Chakravartty and Yuezhi Zhao

ROWMAN & LITTLEFIELD PUBLISHERS, INC.
Lanham • Boulder • New York • Toronto • Plymouth, UK

ROWMAN & LITTLEFIELD PUBLISHERS, INC.

Published in the United States of America
by Rowman & Littlefield Publishers, Inc.
A wholly owned subsidiary of The Rowman & Littlefield Publishing Group, Inc.
4501 Forbes Boulevard, Suite 200, Lanham, Maryland 20706
www.rowmanlittlefield.com

Estover Road, Plymouth PL6 7PY, United Kingdom

British Library Cataloguing in Publication Information Available

Library of Congress Cataloging-in-Publication Data
Global communications : toward a transcultural political economy / edited by Paula
Chakravartty and Yuezhi Zhao.
    p. cm. — (Critical media studies)
Includes bibliographical references and index.
ISBN-13: 978-0-7425-4044-6 (cloth : alk. paper)
ISBN-10: 0-7425-4044-8 (cloth : alk. paper)
1. Communication in politics. 2. Mass media—Political aspects. 3. Communication,
International. I. Chakravartty, Paula. II. Zhao, Yuezhi, 1965-
    JA85.G56 2008
    327.101'4—dc22

                                                        2007005570

Printed in the United States of America

♾ ™ The paper used in this publication meets the minimum requirements of American
National Standard for Information Sciences—Permanence of Paper for Printed Library
Materials, ANSI/NISO Z39.48-1992.

For Aisha and Linda

Contents

Acknowledgments   ix

1 Introduction: Toward a Transcultural Political Economy of
   Global Communications   1
   Paula Chakravartty and Yuezhi Zhao

**Part I: The State and Communication Politics in
         Multiple Modernities**

2 Neoliberal Strategies, Socialist Legacies: Communication
   and State Transformation in China   23
   Yuezhi Zhao

3 Media, State, and Responses to Globalization in
   Post-Communist Russia   51
   Olessia Koltsova

4 Regional Crisis, Personal Solutions: The Media's Role in
   Securing Neoliberal Hegemony in Singapore   75
   Soek-Fang Sim

5 Regulating the Consciousness Industry in the European Union:
   Legitimacy, Identity, and the Changing State   95
   Katharine Sarikakis

6 Media, Democracy, and the State in Venezuela's
"Bolivarian Revolution"   113
Robert Duffy and Robert Everton

Part II: Embedded Markets and Cultural Transformations

7 Cultures of Empire: Transnational Media Flows and Cultural
(Dis)Connections in East Asia   143
Koichi Iwabuchi

8 Local and Global Sites of Power in the Circulation of
Ghanaian Adinkra   163
Boatema Boateng

9 Critical Transculturalism and Arab Reality Television:
A Preliminary Theoretical Exploration   189
Marwan Kraidy

10 Rethinking the U.S. Spanish-Language Media Market in an
Era of Deregulation   201
Mari Castañeda

Part III: Civil Society and Multiple Publics

11 Gender and Empire: Veilomentaries and the War on Terror   219
Sunera Thobani

12 Neoliberalism, Nongovernmental Organizations, and
Communication in Sub-Saharan Africa   243
Arthur-Martins Aginam

13 Move Over Bangalore, Here Comes . . . Palestine? Western
Funding and "Internet Development" in the Shrinking
Palestinian State   263
Helga Tawil Souri

14 Labor In or As Civil Society? Workers and Subaltern Publics
in India's Information Society   285
Paula Chakravartty

References   309

Index   343

About the Contributors   357

Acknowledgments

Paula Chakravartty and Yuezhi Zhao

This book is a project that we have been thinking about and talking through over the last seven years. Seven years is a long time for a book in the field of communication, and as a result we have many people over the years to thank. The idea for a collaborative project grew out of our short but productive time together at the Department of Communication at the University of California, San Diego, between 1999 and 2000, and our colleagues there at the time played an important role in shaping and sharpening our ideas. Andrew Calabrese's interest in and support of the project as series editor at Rowman & Littlefield was crucial in moving our ambitious plans onto tangible pages. The professionalism of the staff at Rowman & Littlefield, especially the patience and persistence of the book's acquisitions editor, Brenda Hadenfeldt, has been instrumental in the book's completion.

We are very grateful to our authors for their faith in this project and their patience with us throughout the process. We have also been fortunate over the course of several years to have had feedback on the broad theoretical framework put forth in the book, as well as on specific drafts of chapters, including several presented at various conferences, beginning in 2003. In both direct and indirect ways, the following people have played an important role in shaping and challenging the logic of this project: Amin Alhassan, Mari Castañeda, John Downing, Daniel Hallin, Lawrence Liang, Toby Miller, Sujata Moorti, Manjunath Pendakur, Katharine Sarikakis, Hemant Shah, Dan Schiller, and Ellen Seiter.

Paula Chakravartty would like to acknowledge support from the UMass Lilly Fellowship and the research assistance of Fida Touma, who played a crucial role in the stages of putting the manuscript together. Elana Khatskevitch and Sophia Checa also helped with the final stages of the book's production. Iris Baiocchi translated a chapter that did not ultimately make it into the volume, but we very much appreciate her hard work. Sabah Baxamoosa, Sreela Sarkar, and Thanu Yakupitiyage have been stimulating students and played an important role in shaping some of the arguments in the book. She would also like to acknowledge the productivity of an ongoing collaboration with Anita Gurumurthy and colleagues at IT for Change in Bangalore. She would like to thank Ravina Aggarwal, Nerissa Balce, Sangeeta Kamat, Stephanie Luce, Anca Romantan, and Srirupa Roy for scholarly and social sustenance throughout the writing and editing of this volume, and also her family across Toronto, Kolkata, and Bangalore—Arun, Gopa, and Dolon Chakravartty; Laila and Piyush Gandhi; Vivek Benegal and Saswati Chakravartty; and Chinmoyee Mukerji—for their love and patience. Most of all, Paula would like to thank Aisha Baiocchi for making everything better always and Gianpaolo Baiocchi, equally for his humor, politics, and intellectual good judgment.

Yuezhi Zhao would like to acknowledge support from the Canada Research Chair program and Martin Laba, the director of the School of Communication at Simon Fraser University, and research assistance from Rob Duffy. She is grateful to Arthur-Martins Aginam, Abu Jafar Bhuiyan, Andy Hu, Greig de Peuter, and Rob Prey for inspiring her and challenging her to keep up with them. As always, she owes immense personal debts to members of her family for completing yet another of her projects: Jianxing and Linda for their unconditional support, understanding, and love; and her mother, Yujiao Qin, whose quiet support and tireless contribution to household work made a whole world of difference.

While we are grateful to all the authors of our volume, we would like to specially acknowledge Robert Everton and Rob Duffy. For many years, Robert Everton carried the load of teaching the undergraduate curriculum in the political economy of communication at Simon Fraser University. As a political activist, Everton's passion for social justice carried him from revolutionary Chile in the early 1970s to the global justice movements of the twenty-first century. As a precarious academic laborer, Everton taught courses in communication and Latin American studies not only in different departments at Simon Fraser University in British Columbia, but also in Ontario. When he was invited to contribute a chapter for this volume in late 2003, he had just completed his long-sought PhD degree and started to apply for jobs. Sadly, Bob Everton passed away in late 2004 while still teaching courses, and after having produced a promising first draft of his paper for us. Subsequently, we invited Robert Duffy, an MA student studying with Yuezhi Zhao, to continue Bob's unfinished job. Rob did an admirable job in bringing the chapter to its current shape while working as a teaching assistant and doing research for his own thesis. There was no money for field research, let alone hiring research assistants. However, while institutional support matters profoundly, in this case, it is human agency—that is, the sheer passion for knowledge, the intellectual capacity to grasp the world beyond our immediate experiences through theoretical reasoning and secondary material, and in the end, the quest for a more just global order and more democratic communicative relationships—that has made their contributions possible. We are proud to have all of these individuals as our authors.

Introduction: Toward a Transcultural Political Economy of Global Communications

Paula Chakravartty and Yuezhi Zhao

Let us begin with some snapshots of the "global" in January 2007, both mediated and through our personal transnational experiences. The Bush administration in the United States escalated its four-year occupation and war in Iraq, a nation thrown into yet another civil war in the "Third World," while Iran's nuclear aspirations cast a long shadow on the future of Western dominance in the region. Venezuela's president Hugo Chávez, winning a third popular mandate after famously surviving the April 2002 coup that aimed to oust his left-leaning government, was granted "extended powers" by the national assembly and promises "Socialism or Death," raising new hopes and fears. Epitomizing its strategy of amassing "asymmetrical power" in the post–Cold War global political economy, China shocked the Western world and scored victory in its determination to contest U.S. military supremacy in space by quietly launching a ballistic antisatellite missile. Bollywood star Shilpa Shetty's racist encounter on the British hit reality show *Big Brother* became an international diplomatic incident between the UK and India—two nations that speak of renewing a "special relationship" in the new century. Meanwhile, the *Times of India*, one of the major English-language national newspapers, splashed headlines that announced "India's global takeover" featuring a campaign titled "India Poised: Make 2007 the Year of India." As an editorial from the Sunday edition on January 21 mused that the "mindset" of India taking on the globe is firmly in place, a middle-class India composed of *lathi*-charged doctors and fasting students waged regularly televised battles against expanding caste-based reservations in universities and the private sector.

We were consuming our daily dose of news and popular culture from our temporary vantage point in Bangalore, as participants of a workshop studying information societies in the South, organized by IT for Change, a progressive nongovernmental organization (NGO) based in the city.[1] For one of us, this was a first trip to India, an opportunity for a Chinese Canadian scholar to compare experiences across the South without the point of reference always being mediated through the North American or European experiences. For the other, India was home, along with Canada and the United States. Although it is virtually impossible to see the "real" Bangalore, much less India, in a few days, we faced some restriction in our mobility on our one day "off" from the meeting rooms of the workshop when a partial curfew was called because of localized incidents of communal violence in response to protests against Saddam Hussein's execution in Iraq.

The workshop that we were attending was meant to stimulate a research agenda around the specificities of the fractured information economies *and* societies in the South, with an emphasis on greater "South-South" collaboration. We spent several days discussing the political economy of e-governance; the respective roles of the state and the market in ensuring digital inclusion; and the role of NGOs and social movements, across India's varied regional information economies, and also between Brazil, China, Ghana, and South Africa. However, the discussions were constantly inflected with the pressing reality of the wider and more urgent political world in which we lived. Our discussions with fellow participants included, among many other tangents, debates about what explained the local demonstration and counterdemonstration nearly three weeks following Saddam Hussein's execution, how to make sense of new left populism or pragmatism, whether embodied by Chávez in Venezuela or the Communist Party of India (Marxist) (CPIM) fending off months of local protest against its plans to establish West Bengal's first export processing zone (EPZ).

The fact that there was greater direct foreign investment in India through the NGO sector, as opposed to through the manufacturing sector, made us wonder if China's authoritarian political structure and its continuing suppression of an independent civil society meant that India might maintain a "comparative advantage" in NGO funding. Would exploitative sweatshops remain as part of the "world's workshop" in China, while civic-minded NGOs with transnational presence flourish in India? Meanwhile, what are the global political economic and cultural implications of China's increasing economic presence in Africa? Can there be a true "partnership in development" between China and Africa, as China's official discourse champions? Over dinner conversations, our colleague Amin Alhassan, a Ghanaian Canadian scholar based at York University, Canada, expressed a welcoming attitude toward the flow of Chinese capital into Africa to the extent that Chinese capitalism provides a new option for African countries that have long felt the stranglehold of the World Bank and the International Monetary Fund (IMF) regime. U.S. and British media discourses, perhaps betraying a not-so-subtle double standard about the political role of global market expansion, point to a new form of Chinese colonialism in Africa. Both Chinese and Western discourses, however, are less likely to pay attention to the fact that along with Chinese capital, the Chinese male workers who help to build the new temples of African modernity—new highways, conference centers, and mobile phone networks—have become part of everyday gossip, as related by a Southern African official, about how many more "children with Chinese characteristics" are likely to be born to African women. This, perhaps signals a sense of local uneasiness about the profound racial and cultural implications of a continental shift in the transnational flows of capital, labor, and culture.

We use this particular vantage point in January 2007 as a point of entry to help contextualize our specific framing of global communications and its necessary omissions. Any scholarly work on globalization that attempts to provide a transnational or translocal analysis attentive to difference is doomed to fail without some clear recognition of the limited conceit of the global. Here, the proliferation of ethnographic and historically situated studies of everyday people and their relationship to modern state and nonstate actors, communication technologies, and mass-mediated culture (Abu-Lughod 2004; Appadurai 1996; Ferguson 2006, García-Canclini 1995; Ong 2006; Rajagopal 2005; Yúdice 2003), has considerably influenced our understanding of the utility and resonance of an overarching political economic analysis of global communications.

We also locate this volume within an expanding body of literature on global communications and media studies in the following three broad categories: works that attempt to historicize and critically interrogate the shifting boundaries and trajectories between local and global flows of information and culture (Chan and McIntyre 2002; Artz and Kamalipour 2003; Ginsburg et al. 2002; Kraidy 2005; Miller et al. 2005; Sreberny-Mohammadi et al. 1997; Thussu 2006; Wang et al. 2000); works that attempt to decenter the conceptual parameters of global information and media studies (Abu-Lughod 2004; Alhassan 2004; Curran and Park 2000; Downing 1996; Iwabuchi 2002; Martín-Barbero 1993; Mattelart 1994; Semati 2004); and finally works that attempt to address normative debates underpinning global communications in the context of neoliberalism (Bailie and Winseck 1997; Calabrese and Sparks 2004; Chakravartty and Sarikakis 2006; Hackett and Zhao 2005; Herman and McChesney 1997; Hills 2002; Mattelart [1996] 2000; Morris and Waisbord 2001; Mosco and Schiller 2001; D. Schiller 1999a, 2007; Thomas and Nain 2004; Vincent, Nordenstreng, and Traber 1999).

As the first decade of the twenty-first century quickly draws to a close and as neoliberal globalization reaches a critical juncture, we build upon this body of research by offering a theoretically driven and empirically grounded discussion of global communications as understood through key vectors of state, market, and societal power and multiple sites of domination and contestation.

Before introducing the book's overarching transcultural political economy framework and its organizational logic, it is necessary to briefly expand on our understanding of both globalization and neoliberalism.

NEOLIBERAL GLOBALIZATION:
INCLUSIONS, EXCLUSIONS, CRISES, AND RESPONSES

Thomas Friedman, "court-philosopher" of information technology (IT) and financial capital–driven globalization (Žižek 2006), has already written "a brief history of the twenty-first century" as early as 2005, with the best-selling book *The World is Flat*. Friedman relied extensively on "techno-gurus" from both China and India as native informants for his technologically deterministic arguments about the leveling effect of IT-led development, reducing differences instantaneously between emerging and advanced economies. Back in Bangalore in January 2007, as we waited to make our way to the workshop from the airport in a spectacular traffic jam that was an everyday part of life, we assumed that Friedman must have been parachuted into the gated IT corridor, therefore avoiding the decidedly "unflat" wait in snarled traffic criss-crossing the unplanned and unorganized spaces of life and work for most of the city's workforce. As the problem of getting from one part of an emerging "global city" to another makes apparent, we are compelled to understand a globalizing and globalized world as multifaceted, fractured, and hotly contested political and social spaces. In fact, Held and McGrew have gone so far as to identify no less than six major paradigms on the politics of globalization: neoliberals, liberal internationalists, institutional reformers, global transformers, statist/protectionists, and radicals (Marxists, communitarians, anarchists) (2002, 98–117). Despite the frequency with which the term *globalization* has been invoked in the media and academic literature, Chinese official discourse, for example, continues to refuse to use the all-encompassing term "globalization." Instead, it prefers to use the more specific term of "economic globalization," signifying the Chinese state's attempt to integrate with the global market system on the one hand, and resist political and cultural assimilation into the American-dominated global capitalist order on the other.

This book foregrounds a conception of globalization as not only multifaceted and extremely uneven, but equally importantly, lived and experienced through new modes of both citizenship and exclusion. We identify neoliberalism as a political philosophy rooted in a claim that the market is more rational than the state in the redistribution of public resources and is based on a "return" to individualism animated by the modern notion of consumer sovereignty (Ong 2006, 11). As in the work of Harvey (2005), Ong (2006), and Robison (2006), among others, we argue that the institutional imposition or adoption of neoliberalism must be understood in the Polanyian tradition of market embeddedness in society. In *The Great Transformation*, Karl Polanyi ([1944] 1957) argued not only that markets were part of the totality of society as a political economy approach would insist, but "[f]or markets to be sustainable they must also be capable of at least staking a claim to furthering the ethical basis of social life" (Jenkins 2006, 307). In the post–Washington Consensus era, when the economic architects of neoliberalism like Jeffrey Sachs and Joseph Stiglitz invoke an urgent need to temper the excesses of "free trade,"[2] Polanyi's attention to the symbolic legitimacy of market transformation seems especially prescient. Throughout this book, we examine how neoliberal transformations of information, communication, and culture industries are embedded within historically specific political cultures, across legacies and ongoing processes of state formation and transformation, and across distinct trajectories of civil society organization/disorganization. Neoliberalism conceived in this framework is thus more dynamic and complicated than the caricaturized ideas of market fundamentalism because it not only sustains and creates repressive political economic conditions and deepens extant inequalities, but also provides new and often unintended possibilities for negotiation, incorporation, and contestation.

Throughout the book, the authors examine the inherent tensions of neoliberal reform across market societies embedded in shifting local, national and transnational contexts. These include Yuezhi Zhao and Olessia Koltsova's chapters on China and Russia's very different trajectories of reintegration with global capitalism, and Katharine Sarikakis's chapter examining the ideological and cultural configuration of the European Union. In the same section, we have Soek-Fang Sim's analysis of Singapore's own quiet negotiation of neoliberal reform as the poster child for globalization, compared with Robert Duffy and Robert Everton's chapter on Venezuela's more dramatic and vocal rejection of neoliberal globalization. The next section features chapters by Koichi Iwabuchi and Marwan Kraidy, who survey the new parameters of liberalized regional media markets in East Asia and the Arab world respectively, while Boatema Boateng traces the gendered transnational production and circulation of "local" *adinkra* cloth and Mari Castañeda considers the possibilities of Spanish-language broadcasting targeting the growing migrant working classes of the United States. In the final section, Sunera Thobani analyzes the challenges of the venerated public service documentary representing the interests of multiple publics in the politically charged post-9/11 discussions of Islam and gender within and beyond Canada, while Helga Tawil Souri focuses on the expansion of informational capitalism against the shrinking if not absent Palestinian nation-state. Arthur-Martins Aginam critically engages with the "NGO-ization" of the political landscape in sub-Saharan Africa and Paula Chakravartty considers the relationship between workers and civil society within emerging and deeply unequal information societies like India.

In their studies of the above variegated cases, the book's authors go beyond both alarmist and celebratory approaches by grounding their analyses of communication and globalization in specific spatial and temporal terms and multifaceted realities. We recognize as conventional wisdom that it is no longer adequate to simply invoke the epochal defining terms that have been associated with globalization, that is, "the age/era of globalization," in the delineation of the temporality of our experiences. However, we do not accept at face value the opinion that some scholars expressed at the 2006 International Association for Media and Communication Research (IAMCR) conference in Cairo, that is, that globalization is dead.[3] Even if globalization is indeed dead—and some would argue that the 9/11 assault on the symbols of American military and financial power marked the exact moment of this death—capitalism, the socioeconomic system driving the current phase of globalization, and the related, but not necessarily parallel, processes of modernization and modernity are moving on, not forward, at full speed.

Historical continuities of developments prior to the current era of globalization therefore figure prominently in our work. Locating current global transformations in a longer history of modernity is apparent in Olessia Koltsova's contextualization of the Soviet era of glasnost (1985–1991) in relation to imperial Russia's embrace of Western European modernity under Peter the Great, whose desire to modernize Russia led him not only to be a student in western Europe, but also move imperial Russia's capital from Moscow to St. Petersburg, so that Russia could be closer to western Europe both spatially and temporally. Elsewhere in the volume, historical continuities are emphasized in Koichi Iwabuchi's attention to the role of Japanese colonialism in the shaping of popular cultural affinities in East Asia and in Arthur-Martins Aginam's consideration of the legacy of the violence of the colonial state in Nigeria and South Africa in relation to current celebratory discussions of civil society and human rights. Yuezhi Zhao focuses on how the Maoist search for a Chinese socialist alternative to either Western capitalist modernity or Soviet bureaucratic socialism casts a long shadow on the contemporary Chinese program of neoliberal economic development and global reintegration. Similarly, Paula Chakravartty analyzes the historical shifts from the Nehruvian to the neoliberal postcolonial Indian state as the backdrop against which to make sense of the ongoing politics of access to the much-prized information technology sector.

While we draw upon and contribute to a now well-established body of literature that has analyzed the astonishing developments in global communications in the last two decades of the twentieth century, the book's time frame is distinctively set in the post–Washington Consensus period. That is, building upon existing work that has documented neoliberal developments in a whole range of communication industries and described the formation of "electronic empires" (Thussu 1998), the rise of "global Hollywood" (Miller et al. 2005), "the globalization of corporate media hegemony" (Artz and Kamalipour 2003), or the expansion of informational or digital capitalism both globally (Herman and McChesney 1997; D. Schiller 1999, 2007) and regionally (Mosco and Schiller 2001), we move on to analyze the aftermath of these developments, that is, responses to and revisions of neoliberalism, both in and through the realm of global communications.

Moreover, rather than taking 9/11 in 2001 as the definitive beginning of what might be seen as a "postneoliberal" era, we identify the global economic crises that occurred in Russia, Brazil, Argentina, and most significantly, in a number of East and Southeast Asian "tiger economy" nations and regions—including Thailand, Malaysia, Indonesia, Singapore, Hong Kong, and Korea—in 1997 as the beginning of a new phase of globalization. Although this worldwide economic crisis was commonly known as the "Asian Financial Crisis," it was actually a "global contagion" as even the *New York Times* acknowledged (Kristof et al. 1999, cited in Calabrese 2004, 4). This worldwide economic crisis, and global financial capital's attempt to overcome it, which ironically contributed to the making of the subsequent telecommunications crisis and the Internet bubble in the United States at the turn of the new century (D. Schiller 2003), marked the beginning of the internal readjustment, if not the unraveling, of the "neoliberal revolution" (Robison 2006).[4]

What is significant is the extent to which many of the authors writing about different parts of the world in our volume recognize the importance of this crisis and discuss the variegated ways in which this global contagion has shaped subsequent developments both nationally and regionally.

In Russia, as Olessia Koltsova describes, the economic crisis of the late 1990s led to a profound disillusionment with the "shock therapy" approach in the transition from communism, with many among the Russian citizenry experiencing a deep sense of betrayal by Western capitalism and a rising nostalgia for the order, security, and national unity of the Soviet era. This led to a new dynamic of state, society, and media interaction and the rapid reconsolidation of state power under Putin's more authoritarian regime.

In Singapore, through and together with the media, the ruling People's Action Party (PAP), which Soek-Fang Sim characterizes as the exemplary neoliberal nation with its unique combination of economic liberalism and a strong "soft authoritarian" government, legitimized further neoliberal restructuring of the economy and refashioned its hegemony over Singaporean society by framing economic hardships in terms of "regional crisis, personal solutions." Marwan Kraidy's chapter considers the possibilities for hybrid cultural transformation of a pan-Arab commercial television market in the current context, while Iwabuchi shows how the celebratory discourse around East Asian cultural industries conceals uneven power relations between nations, classes, and communities. Iwabuchi's chapter therefore shows that the dialogic potential of intra-Asian popular cultural flows cannot erase the memory of Japanese colonialism and imperialism in the region, nor can it transcend the real limits of exclusion that are constitutive of neoliberal urban consumer culture.

In contrast, across much of Latin America, where neoliberal governance took hold much earlier than in many other parts of the global South, the crisis of neoliberalism led to the electoral victories of left-leaning governments in many countries and the rise of new forms of popular as well as populist democratic politics. In Brazil, the Workers' Party has been pushing for greater South-South collaboration challenging intellectual property rights norms in multilateral arenas and crafting participatory digital inclusion programs based on open-source software (Chakravartty, forthcoming). In Venezuela, as Robert Duffy and Robert Everton's chapter demonstrates, Chávez's leftist government has not only been able to hold on to power but also has tried to consolidate new forms of communication politics and media structures despite the dominance of private media conglomerates and their right-wing instrumentalism, which played a key role in staging the April 2002 coup.

In the African context, broader political economic analyses are brought to the forefront in the chapters by Arthur-Martins Aginam and Boatema Boateng, in challenging the racially plagued discourse of "failed" and corrupt African states blamed in a conceptual vacuum for the continent's place in the world. The "good governance" doctrine proposed by the economists and technocrats who designed the now discredited Structural Adjustment Policies (SAPs) faced a profound crisis of legitimacy across Africa in the last decade,[5] and we would highlight this fact and not solely the mass protests in Seattle and Genoa in offering an explanation for the institutional shift toward the post–Washington Consensus global order. In India, as Paula Chakravartty notes, the mass popular opposition to and discontent with the narrow gains of globalization has both fueled the resurgence of Maoist Naxalite insurgencies across thirteen of the nation's poorest twenty-nine states and led to a series of unexpected losses for politicians and parties too closely associated with this new development mandate, including the ousting of the chauvinist Bharatiya Janata Party–led (BJP) coalition from national power in 2004.[6] In the aftermath of the discrediting of the BJP government's "India Shining" campaign featuring the beneficiaries of "high-tech" India, the new centrist government under Prime Minister Manmohan Singh has tried to define its administration as addressing the growing inequalities of global India.

For its part, China, the fastest-growing economy in the post–Cold War period, not only escaped the 1997 "Asian" financial crisis thanks to its still relatively closed financial system, but also helped to prevent a further running down on other Asian currencies by not devaluating the Chinese currency. This contributed to the containment of the crisis, but hurt Chinese exports and caused further layoffs of Chinese workers, leading some domestic commentators to muse that "only China can save capitalism," in an ironic reference to the official slogan that "only socialism can save China" (Huang, Yang, and Yuhai 2006). Moreover, the party leadership does not have to subject itself to the test of electoral politics, and its tight grip on the media makes the articulation of oppositional voices and the organization of popular contestations extremely difficult. Nevertheless, as Yuezhi Zhao emphasizes in her chapter, growing inequalities and mounting social unrest resulting from the leadership's two-decade-long embrace of neoliberal strategies of economic development, coupled with Chinese society's deeply rooted normative expectations for the long-propagated socialist values of equality and justice for all, have compelled the Hu Jintao leadership, which came to power in late 2002, to foreground the issue of redistributive justice and to strengthen the ideological mantra of socialism under the slogan of "building a harmonious socialist society."

Finally, in the North, the impact of global economic instability and precarity alongside the "war on terror" has manifested itself most obviously in the ferocious debates over immigration, national identity, and security. Within the European Union (EU), as documented by Katharine Sarikakis, the arrival of postcolonial migrants, as well as more recent economic migrants from the semiperiphery of Europe, has created new tensions between supranational and national governance over cultural policy. Across the Atlantic, Sunera Thobani examines how Canadian liberal feminism and multiculturalism embodied through its public broadcasting and independent documentary film production traditions reproduces Orientalist narratives justifying national security policies. In the United States, Mari Castañeda calls attention to the rapidly expanding Spanish-language media markets and the contradictory consequences of neoliberal developments in the U.S. and Latin American media industries. Her more optimistic assessment of the centrality and use of Spanish language media for the expanding Latino communities is offered against the backdrop of a mounting civil rights movement for undocumented Latino migrants facing a xenophobic English-only backlash across the country.

TOWARD A TRANSCULTURAL POLITICAL ECONOMY OF GLOBAL COMMUNICATIONS

As the preceding discussion illustrates, our book deliberately avoids "media centrism" (Downing 1996, xiii) or "communication essentialism" (Mosco

1996), which tend to "decontextualize communication from the social framework" (McChesney 2000, 113). Instead, we follow a long tradition in critical media studies that places communication within broader political economic and cultural processes and treats communication research as an inherently integrative exercise that cuts across disciplinary lines (Garnham 1990; Golding and Murdoch 1978; Hills 2003; Martín-Barbero 1993; Mattelart 1994; D. Schiller 1996). Our expansive definition of "global communications" not only encompasses "old" and "new" media and the related issues of the public sphere, meaning-making, and identity formation, but also includes telecommunication networks and information technologies that are deeply integrated into the processes of economic production, social development, and community formation. Furthermore, we engage with global knowledge systems, intellectual property rights regimes, and forms of material culture that epitomize the inseparability of and interpenetration between the economic and the cultural, or the material and the symbolic. Whether it is community television in Venezuela or *adinkra* cloth in Ghana, public service documentaries from Canada, reality television in the Persian Gulf, or Internet cafés in the Gaza Strip, our focus on a particular medium or dimension of global communications is not arbitrary in relation to our respective research agendas. However, neither are we preoccupied with achieving comprehensiveness in the inclusion of all media across all regions or, for that matter, focusing exclusively on particular moments in the production, circulation, and consumption loop.

Underlying the chapters is a common intellectual engagement with the long-standing theoretical and methodological affinities and tensions between the political economy and cultural studies approaches to communication. Much ink has been spilled over the respective merits and inadequacies of each approach. Numerous calls have been issued for a creative synthesis between the two approaches—the widely used text *Media in Global Context: A Reader* (Sreberny-Mohammadi et al. 1997), for example, articulated an explicit agenda to bring these two traditions together a decade ago. Since then, many more attempts have been made toward just such an objective (e.g., Calabrese and Sparks 2004; Mosco 2004; Meehan and Riordan 2002b; Artz and Kamalipour 2003; Semati 2004). Building on these works, we anchor our attempt at a theoretical and methodological synthesis around what we call a "transcultural political economy" framework. We conceptualize this analytical framework as one that enables us to integrate institutional and cultural analyses and address urgent questions in global communications in the context of economic integration, empire formation, and the tensions associated with adapting new privatized technologies, neoliberalized and globalized institutional structures, and hybrid cultural forms and practices.

In developing this framework, we firmly ground ourselves in the tradition of critical political economy in communication studies. We take as our starting point political economy's overriding concerns with communications and power in a global market economy and the generative insights of this tradition, including the formative role of ownership and regulation of communications industries and processes and the asymmetric structures of power within the world system. Following Mosco, we define political economy broadly as "the study of the social relations, particularly the power relations that mutually constitute the production, distribution, and consumption of resources" (1996, 25).

Consistent with our expansive conceptualization of global communications, we draw from what we can identify as both the North American and European traditions of political economy in communication research—the former with its emphasis on the relative power of capital over contemporary communicative practices and the ascending status of communications industries in "informationalized global capitalism" (D. Schiller 1999b, 90) and the latter with its greater attention to the complex relationship between symbolic and material practices (Bourdieu 1999, 2007; Garnham 1990).

As with previous scholarship that has tried to reformulate what are seen as core tensions between the political economy and cultural studies perspectives within the North American academy (Alhassan 2004; Chakravartty and Sarikakis 2006; Zhao 2003a), this volume deliberately tries to decenter developments in the political economy of North American communication. We therefore refer back to our previous discussion of Polanyi's careful attention to the embeddedness of markets in social practice or the renewed relevance of Pierre Bourdieu's (1999, 2007) framework of symbolic power and social practice, when we consider the negotiation of neoliberal communications reform on the ground. It is perhaps for this reason that critical scholars of global communications studying Latin America like Jesús Martín-Barbero (1993), analyzing some of the earliest experiences in the South with the hegemony of liberalized and commercialized cultural industries, have focused on the fragile connection between the state and the nation, and the violence and contradictions of mass cultural modernization. Similarly, Koichi Iwabuchi's (2002, 18–19) innovative analysis of popular culture through Japan's encounter with the rapidly industrializing and modernizing Asia (East and Southeast Asia) of the early 1990s emphasizes the telos of the modernization narrative about the nation's place in the world and human history.

For many of our authors, political economy at its most basic level is "the study of control of and survival in social life" (Mosco 1995, 26)—a level that is many layers removed from a caricaturized understanding of political economy as merely the study of media ownership. Although the emphasis may differ in each chapter, our authors address global communications as both processes of meaning making and identity formation and as means of production and livelihood. As with earlier works, including Martín-Barbero

(1993), Mattelart (1994), Pendakur (1991, 2003), and Sussman and Lent (1991) among others, many chapters in this volume engage directly with the problematic of communication and modernization or the "media's role in national development" (Golding 1974), an issue that used to be at the center of theoretical debates in the field (e.g., Lerner 1958; Schramm 1964; H. Schiller 1976, 1992; Nordenstreng and Schiller 1979; Smythe 1981) but has become a subfield of communication studies of "developing countries," disconnected from the Anglo-American and Eurocentric core of media or cultural studies.

In so doing we integrate insights from cultural studies and postcolonial theory to enrich our political economic analysis. We are particularly influenced by the transnational and ethnographic turn in cultural studies (Abbas and Erni 2004; Chen 1998; García-Canclini 1995; Yúdice 2003), and the unflinching criticism of essentialist theories of cultural formation and "tradition," offering instead nuanced studies of globalized cultural mediation and practice. Just as we understand political economic analysis to mean much more than ownership studies, we thus locate cultural studies as going well beyond audience reception or consumption studies, especially as the critical tradition is appropriated in the larger field of communication studies within the U.S. academy. As Mosco (1996, 262) points out, "the very term 'audience' is not an analytical category, like class, gender, or race, but a product of the media industry itself, which uses the term to identify markets and to define a commodity." The transnational turn in cultural studies shows an engagement with poststructuralist and postcolonial theories of modernity and national identity as well as gender, racial, and ethnic differences. National identity and modernity, often relegated to the ghetto of "development communication" within the U.S. academy, figure prominently both as categories and focal points of analysis in this volume.

More specifically, we draw from recent postcolonial political and anthropological research in our attempts to make sense of the particulars and multiple realities within the universal of neoliberal capitalist modernity. Against arguments about cultural homogenization, the term "transculturation" has been deployed by media and cultural studies scholars to describe how an unequal encounter between cultures—colonial and colonized, imperial and globalized—creates new social and cultural forms, styles, or practices (Hall 1995; Iwabuchi 2002, 40; Chan and Ma 2002). This then allows us to consider the centrality of gender, race, and national differences in shaping political struggles over globalized information and cultural flows.

For example, in her chapter, Boatema Boateng examines the multifaceted transcultural transformations and multiple sites of power that operate around the commodified production and globalized circulation of *adinkra* cloth as folk cultural artifacts. At the local level, the accelerated pace and increased scale of commodification of *adinkra* cloth has opened a space for women producers, leading to a reversal of gender roles in its (re)production, which was traditionally controlled by men. At the global level, while *adinkra* producers are largely marginalized in the globalization of their cloth designs, consumption choices made by African Diasporic communities in North America are bound up with their struggles over symbolic identity, which look to Africa as a source. These struggles not only raise questions about the complicated symbolic and political relationship between Diasporic and continental Africans but also point to the racial politics of consumption in global markets. Meanwhile, Sunera Thobani's powerful critique of Anglo-American liberal feminism and Canadian public service multiculturalism is advanced through the analysis of two independent documentaries about Afghan women produced by Canadian women filmmakers and human rights activists. As Thobani argues, by depicting the lives and images of Afghan women as pitiable and abject victims in need of "saving" by the West, these critically acclaimed and widely circulated documentaries, one of which was produced by an Afghan Canadian woman as a native informant, contributed to the hegemonic construction of Western women as civilized and emancipated subjects, which serves as an ideological trope informing U.S. foreign policy.

Although we find the term transculturation productive, we acknowledge the limits of the concept of hybrid transcultural forms (Kraidy 2005) or "happy hybridity" referencing the celebration of novel forms of globalized niche marketing (Pinney 1998). For us, the value of a transcultural approach to political economy is captured more accurately by the metaphor of friction rather than through the concept of hybridity, as identified by anthropologist Anna Lowenhaupt Tsing in her astute study of the globalization of Indonesia's rainforests. For Tsing, the metaphor of friction is the process of diverse and conflicting social encounters that make up transnational capitalist integration—challenging the "seamless" and "flexible" logic of globalization. Tsing's discussion of the friction that results from unequal encounters is useful to our project when she writes,

> Capitalism only spreads as producers, distributors, and consumers strive to universalize categories of capital, money, and commodity fetishism. Such strivings make possible globe-crossing capital and commodity chains. Yet these chains are made up of uneven and awkward links. The cultural specificity of capitalist forms arises from the necessity of bringing capitalist universals into action through worldly encounters. (2004, 4)

We insist that these "awkward encounters" producing friction are constitutive both for non-Western modernities and for the articulation of dominant Western political economic and cultural power. In our volume, this is clearly underscored across many chapters, from the ways in which China's self-initiated neoliberal-oriented development strategies feed into the maintenance of global capitalism and American consumer capitalism on the one hand, and create anxieties about national identity and a place in the world both in China and in the United States on the other, as discussed in the chapter by Yuezhi Zhao, to the ways in which liberal and highly racialized feminist and human rights discourses might enable the mobilization of public support for the United States–led "War on Terror," as argued in the chapter by Sunera Thobani.

Furthermore, consistent with postcolonial scholars of culture and political transformation from Jesús Martín-Barbero (1993) to Chun Lin (2006), a number of authors in this volume challenge the Eurocentric conflation between capitalism and modernity that allows "no distinction between development and capitalism, or between modernization and capitalist transformation" (C. Lin 2006). As Lin argues, "lost in the conflation" is the reality that "capitalism is not required for a society to be or become modern" and that anticapitalist regimes could foster both social achievements or equally "visible non-capitalist forms of exploitation, repression and destruction" (2006, 22). The historic specificity of modernization and the legitimacy or the lack thereof for the current mode of neoliberal governance within market societies are explored in contexts ranging from the exemplars of globalization like Singapore, China, and the European Union to the "exceptional" cases of Venezuela and Palestine.

Across many of our chapters, the authors examine transcultural encounters through new challenges to national sovereignty and citizenship associated with the redefinition of state power, the strategic mobility of capital, and the often forced dislocation of workers and communities within and across national borders. It is in this broadest of contexts that we would locate current debates about cultural diversity versus homogenization in the context of globalization. "Cultural diversity" has been widely appropriated in corporate speech, as evident in the plenary speeches at the 2005 Tunis phase of the World Summit on the Information Society. Most evidently, it was the CEO of media giant Vivendi Universal, and not the heads of state or, for that matter, civil society representatives, who most passionately championed "cultural diversity" in his plenary address to delegates by celebrating the company's achievements in promoting multicultural talents around the globe in music production.[7] Similarly, many of the academic and policy studies of "cultural globalization" and the cultural industries have centered on a geocultural and mediacentric "reverse flow" argument, which celebrates, affirms, and promotes the ability of non-Western countries and regions to "make it" in the global cultural marketplace and increase their shares in transnationalized multicultural media production (Straubhaar 1984, 1991; Sinclair 1992; Sinclair, Jacka, and Cunningham 1996; Keane 2006).

Political economists have challenged these arguments (H. Schiller 1991; D. Schiller 1996; Sussman 2001), and here we reengage with this debate on the basis of a non-Eurocentric understanding of the relationship between modernity and capitalism. We would therefore reemphasize that a more radical version of the "cultural imperialism" thesis, initially articulated against the backdrop of international socialist and decolonization movements, was predicated on the possibility of transcending capitalist social relations (D. Schiller 1996). As Zhao (2003a, forthcoming) has argued elsewhere, rather than depoliticize the "cultural" and reduce it to local favors and differences within capitalism, it is necessary to insist on the inseparability of the political and cultural and the possibility of "imagining outsides to a globalized capitalism" (Dirlik 2004, 289), that is, alternatives to, not within the "cultures of capitalism" (Dirlik 2004, 265).

Although political economists have also challenged the structural logic of modernization theories, which substitutes time for place—regions and nations are not exploited by unequal market integration, but are rather "not yet" developed (Chakrabarty 2000)—they have generally failed to recognize the violence associated with these teleological assumptions that place "poor people and poor nations" not only at the "bottom" but also at the "beginning" (Ferguson 2006, 178). Postcolonial and cultural studies scholarship unhinges modernity from telos and therefore opens up the possibility of recognizing cultural difference through multiple modernities. However, as anthropologist James Ferguson has insightfully argued in his recent study of the political economic crisis in globalized Africa, a focus on pluralist cultural difference risks deemphasizing the looming socioeconomic inequality and relative low global rank of the African poor. This is a concern not only in the context of Africa, but also, as Chakravartty (2007) has argued elsewhere, for excluded publics across the variegated neoliberal global order. James Ferguson (2006, 192) contends that for critical scholars,

> key questions are no longer temporal ones of social belonging (development, modernization), but spatialized ones of guarding the edges of a status group—hence, the new prominence of walls, borders, and processes of social exclusion in an era that likes to imagine itself as characterized by an ever expanding connection and communication.

Rejecting teleological assumptions, the authors in our volume instead focus on awkward and uneven global encounters, new modes of citizenship and exclusion, and the aspirational logic of modernity, which is so viscerally embodied through the lure and promise of the global information and culture industries. Helga Tawil Souri drives this analysis home in her chapter about the hopes and follies of technocratic development through the Internet in the spatially segregated and violent confines of Palestine's market society. It is precisely in such an exceptional neoliberal space that the promise of new communications technologies as an integral part of Palestinian state building and development assumes its fragile mythic power, with its "dreamlike promise of Palestine one day becoming a new Bangalore—the Bangalore of a capitalist's dreams, where everyone is happily employed behind a computer screen, and cultural, religious, gender, socioeconomic inequalities are nonexistent." Returning to our initial remarks about the ways in which the "global" is mediated through one's particular vantage point based on our own recent experiences in the "real" Bangalore, we hope that such a transcultural approach to the political economy of global communication offers perspectives that engage equally with the questions of modernity and inequality, and consider with some humility questions of repression and emancipation.

REFLECTIONS ON THE TRANSCULTURAL POLITICAL ECONOMY OF ACADEMIC PRODUCTION

This book is intentionally not organized by geography or medium. Moreover, in contrast to previous works that tend to juxtapose the forces of domination and forces of resistance and treat them in distinctive sections—typically with the last (and often thinner) section being on "resistance and alternatives" anchored in civil society and social movements—the organization of this book underscores a more complex and relational understanding of the state, market and civil society as conventionally conceptualized in media studies. As the chapters demonstrate clearly, the state and the market can both be sites of contestation and empowerment, just as civil society can be a site of governance and exclusion. In this way, we have drawn from the substantive arguments in the chapters to inform our theoretical framework. In doing so, we hoped to avoid the accepted practice of presenting chapter summaries in the last section of the introduction, which in this case would diminish connections between the chapters within each section and across the volume.

As discussed above, this volume attempts to draw from empirical research that decenters the locus of political economic theories of global communications away from the Anglo North American experiences. The first section of the book, "The State and Communication Politics in Multiple Modernities," reformulates questions about the shifting role of the state in relation to discussions about media and processes of political communication and cultural identity formation across "multiple modernities." This section features five chapters exploring theories of state power, governance and legitimacy in relation to information and culture institutions, processes and practices in China (Yuezhi Zhao), in Russia (Olessia Koltsova), in Singapore (Soek-Fang Sim), in the European Union (Katharine Sarikakis), and in Venezuela (Robert Duffy and Robert Everton).

The second section, "Embedded Markets and Cultural Transformations," is made up of four chapters that examine the societal embeddedness of national, transnational, and regional markets and processes of cultural transformation in East Asia (Koichi Iwabuchi), between Ghana and the United States (Boatema Boateng), across the Arabic Middle East (Marwan Kraidy), and in the Spanish-speaking United States (Mari Castañeda). The final section, "Civil Society and Multiple Publics," closes with four chapters on the formation and limits of civil society in addressing often contradictory claims made by multiple publics: between war-torn Afghanistan and a multiracial Canada (Sunera Thobani), across an increasingly NGO-ized sub-Saharan Africa (Arthur-Martins Aginam), within the confines of a debilitated Palestinian state (Helga Tawil Souri), and across the deeply "uneven information society" in India (Paula Chakravartty).

Instead of soliciting work from senior scholars, or at least a combination of senior and junior scholars, we experimented with an unconventional process of intellectual production by deliberately selecting a group of transnationally located, racially and linguistically diverse junior and midcareer scholars. In a field that has traditionally attracted a much higher proportion of male scholars, we also sought out women colleagues whose research shapes current discussions of global political economy.

As newer voices in the field, our authors have built our scholarship on the contributions of existing conceptual categories, while simultaneously trying to transcend and enrich existing categories and frameworks of analysis. Almost all the chapters draw from either recently completed or ongoing empirical research. The academic backgrounds of this book's contributors cut across political economy, cultural studies, policy studies, media sociology, feminist studies, and postcolonial scholarship.

Our common first academic home, the Department of Communication at the University of California, San Diego (UCSD), hired us one after another in the late 1990s, and gave us the opportunity to know each other and to work together briefly as colleagues. Although familial ties pulled us away from UCSD, we have been privileged to be able to continue our respective academic careers elsewhere in North America. As immigrants from China and India to Canada, and at least temporarily "legal aliens" in the United States, we have both been beneficiaries of scholarly support from the Canadian government as well as from U.S. public institutions and Chinese state education. However, just as unevenness in access to resources and institutional positions is a defining feature in the production, circulation, and consumption of communication goods and services, the same is the case in the academy. In the North American context where we teach, numerous tenure-track professors carry out research with heavy teaching and service loads, while at the same time balancing personal and familial obligations of various kinds. Still, there are many more individuals who have yet to enter the tenure track and still carry a heavy load in holding up the ivory towers by working on increasingly precarious terms as sessional instructors and teaching/research assistants. Many pursue their own academic work with few resources and limited access to academic networks.

Although the lack of funding and organizational resources made it impossible for us to bring together all our authors in a conference setting, which would have promoted more dialogue and allowed various authors to make cross-references to each other's work, we are grateful to all our contributors, who worked diligently on their chapters over a lengthy period of time and generously received our editorial interventions in our attempt to achieve some degree of overall coherence in the volume, despite the fact that a book chapter is often not evaluated as highly as a journal article in a tenure file.

In particular, we want to pay tribute to Robert Everton, coauthor of chapter 6 on Venezuela. Bob Everton was a long-time graduate student and sessional lecturer at the School of Communication, Simon Fraser University, Canada who, very sadly, passed away one year after he received his PhD and while writing his chapter for this volume. Rather than hiding the materiality of intellectual production in the acknowledgements, we have tried through this introduction to set a tone that is both critical and self-reflexive, offering what we hope is grounded (political economic approach to communication and culture in the following chapters.

NOTES

1. For more details on the ITfC-organized workshop in Bangalore, see itforchange.net/mambo/content/view/156/1/.

2. Economist Jeffrey Sachs is now the director of the Earth Institute at Columbia University, where he has become a leading critic of neoliberal policies; he was in the 1990s a pivotal economic advisor to the radical liberalization strategies implemented in postsocialist Eastern Europe and Russia. Nobel prize recipient and economist Joseph Stiglitz, who is credited with defining a "post–Washington Consensus" era, is today an outspoken critic of neoliberal economic reforms, but was the senior vice president and chief economist of the World Bank from 1997–2000.

3. The death of globalization was heralded by the media in the West as a result of the failure of the WTO negotiations to progress meaningfully after the Doha Rounds in 2001. More specifically, Yuezhi Zhao acknowledges her colleague, Robert A. Hackett, for relating this point to her upon his return from the IAMCR conference in July 2006.

4. Robison (2006, xiv) similarly notes "dramatic confrontations" against the "market fundamentalism" of the Washington Consensus and its central institutions. However, he remains ambivalent as to "whether such dramatic confrontations represent shifts in power within the neoliberal camp or whether they reflect a more structural challenge to the neo-liberal order."

5. Ferguson (2006) expands on the crisis of legitimacy of the SAPs in Africa, which have been abandoned by the IMF and World Bank for a new program based on Poverty Reducing Strategy Papers targeting Highly Indebted Poor Countries. There is a growing body of research and debate on the implications of this shift in terms of poverty alleviation and the empowerment (or lack thereof) of poor nations.

6. The violent Maoist insurgency had its roots in an armed peasant revolt in the village of Naxalbari in West Bengal in 1967, but has seen a dramatic resurgence and with it, state-sanctioned violence in retaliation in the last decade across the economically least developed regions in the country. In 2006, Prime Minister Manmohan Singh referred to the Naxalite movement as the biggest threat to the internal security of India since independence. See *Times of India*, April 13, 2006, http://timesofindia.indiatimes.com/articleshow/1489633.cms (accessed January 29, 2007).

7. The authors were present during the plenary session of the Tunis phase of the WSIS in November 2005. For transcripts of the speech by Jean-Bernard Levy, CEO of Vivendi Universal, see www.itu.int/wsis/tunis/scripts/archive.asp?lang=en&c_type=2%7C16&c_num=296.

I

THE STATE AND COMMUNICATION POLITICS IN MULTIPLE MODERNITIES

2

Neoliberal Strategies, Socialist Legacies: Communication and State Transformation in China

Yuezhi Zhao

Socialism on the surface appears to amount to little more than hollow rhetoric in China today. Nevertheless, Chinese socialism has a long historical legacy and the party state continues to claim allegiance to it. Indeed, as Chun Lin (2006, 1) has observed, "Chinese socialism can best be grasped as a modern project that has sought to develop by its own unique means into its own type, always conscious of the other possibilities it has refused to emulate," from diverse forms of peripheral capitalism to Soviet-style bureaucratic socialism (now Russian postcommunism) and Western capitalist modernity. During the heights of the Cultural Revolution (1966–1976), as Red Guard tabloids and big-character posters supplemented the official media as the means of popular communication, radical Maoists even sought an alternative socialist modernity with the mediations of neither the market nor a bureaucratic structure. In international communication, the postrevolutionary Chinese state, in the face of a Western capitalist blockade and aspiring to create an alternative to Stalinism, "delinked" itself with both Western capitalist consumer culture and the Soviet Union, while pursuing cultural exchanges with friendly socialist countries within an internally conflicted international socialist movement.

Since the late 1970s, however, the Chinese state has undergone a radical transformation in response to the profound internal and external contradictions of the state socialist experiment. It has not only incorporated market relations in a wide range of communication industries and processes but also pursued substantive linkages (*jiegui*) with transnational capitalism and its concomitant consumer culture. This ongoing process of state transformation, in turn, has not only generated new contradictions and tensions but also engendered intensive forms of political, ideological, social, and cultural

23

contestation at both the elite and popular levels, including the crisis of 1989, the challenges of Falun Gong, and ongoing protests by disenfranchised farmers, workers, and other subaltern social groups that have begun to make claims on the state regarding market opportunities, citizenship entitlements, and the state's capacity to define the ethical horizons of the population (Perry and Selden 2003; O'Brien and Li 2006; Y. Zhao 2003b, 2007a, forthcoming).

At the risk of making this chapter too dense, I undertake the daunting and yet urgent task of analyzing the dynamics of Chinese state transformation during the reform era through the lenses of communication and culture. Specifically, I focus on how the post-1989[1] Chinese state has embraced the new politics of neoliberal capitalist development on the one hand, and addressed class polarization, ideological and social contestation, and its socialist and anti-imperialist legacies on the other. After the first section outlines the broad context and my theoretical propositions, the chapter's remaining four sections are organized along two axes of analysis. Sections two and three provide overviews of the domestic and global dimensions of Chinese state transformation in and through a whole range of communication institutions and processes. Sections four and five focus on the internal contradictions and the socialist legacies of the Chinese state with regard to two broad issues: state policies that continue to put substantive restrictions on private media ownership, and the state's reckoning with the social justice agenda and resurgent leftist critiques of its neoliberal strategies. These issues have assumed new urgency in light of China's accession to the World Trade Organization (WTO) in 2001 and in the context of heightened elite and popular debates over the future directions of the Chinese state since the Hu Jintao leadership assumed power in late 2002. They have not only compelled the Chinese state to face the logical conclusions of its market-oriented reform processes but have also raised pertinent questions about the limits of neoliberal globalization in China.

BEYOND CENSORSHIP: CONCEPTUALIZING THE CHINESE STATE IN THE ERA OF NEOLIBERAL CAPITALIST EXPANSION

Many analysts have noted the heavy hand of the Chinese state and the fusion of state power and market rationality in the Chinese media, Internet, and even short massage services (Y. Zhao 1998, 2000a, 2004a, 2007a, 2007b; Barmé 1999; C. Lee 2000, 2003; Lee, He, and Huang 2006; Wacker 2003; Qiu 2007). Jing Wang (2000, 159) went even further to note that the literature on the Chinese state harps on a "double theme" that "highlights the oppressive nature of the post-1989 Chinese state as a policing apparatus, and emphasize its absolute collusion with capital, and thus alluding to (and wishing for) a meltdown of its sovereign power." Although this may be a somewhat outdated generalization in light of recent, more positive discussions of the role of a robust Chinese state (e.g., Stiglitz 2002; Zheng 2004), Wang is certainly quite right in pointing out the high-stakes implications of the modernizing and globalizing Chinese state. In the context of the American political right's rising fear of a "China threat" and the "coming conflict with China" (Bernstein and Munro 1998), it becomes all the more important, as Ong (2006, 79) cautions in the case of the East Asian states in general, not to allow reports of political repression to overshadow a more nuanced approach to the question of state power. Such an approach not only entails an acknowledgment of the state's active role in macromanaging China's economy and global integration but also compels us to pay attention to "the restructuring of state ruling technology and the changing stock of its ideological practices" (Wang 2001b, 37). Furthermore, it requires us to take the Chinese state's claim about its continuing search for a "socialist" market alternative to capitalist integration seriously. Although strong arguments have been made that "market socialism" is a "contradiction in terms" (Wood 2002, 196; see also Hart-Landsberg and Burkett 2005), insofar as China's search for a socialist alternative to capitalist modernity has a historical legacy, and "[i]nsofar as this collective effort has persisted, the chance of the Chinese model to succeed cannot be ruled out" (C. Lin 2006, 1).

In what follows, I account for state repression and disciplinary technologies—exemplified by the archetypical Western news story about Chinese media censorship. However, I move beyond this liberal framework to highlight the state's transformative role in pursuing the instrumentalization of market logic in the Chinese communication system and in redefining the terms of its hegemony over society. More specifically, following Ong (2006), I examine how the Chinese state has redefined its sovereign rule through the proactive and selective deployment of neoliberal strategies, or the twin modalities of "neoliberalism as exception" and "exceptions to neoliberalism," in its attempt to build a "socialist" market alternative. Within this context, neoliberalism is conceptualized not merely as an economic doctrine, that is, "the Washington Consensus" as elaborated by Williamson (1990) that champions open markets, privatization, and unregulated financial flows, but more broadly and generally as a "political rationality," or a "technology of governing" whereby "governing activities are recast as non-political and nonideological problems that need technical solutions" (Ong 2006, 3; see also Robison 2006). Drawing upon Foucault's notion of governmentality (Foucault 2000), Ong defines neoliberalism as "a governmentality that relies on market knowledge and calculations for a politics of subjection and subject-making that continually places in question the political existence of modern human beings" (2006, 13). Neoliberalism as exception is deployed to allow the state to manage sovereignty in a graduated and variegated manner, subjecting certain populations and places to neoliberal calculations to facilitate interactions with global markets. Concurrently, exceptions to neoliberalism are invoked in political decisions to "exclude populations and places from neoliberal calculations and choices" to either protect social safety nets or to strip away all forms of political protection (2006, 4).

China is not an openly committed neoliberal capitalist social formation. Nevertheless, as a number of observers have noted, neoliberal ideas have been influential in China as the post-Mao leadership embraced the market system as a means to develop the country and to ensure is grip on power, leading to the "construction of a particular kind of market economy that increasingly incorporates neoliberal elements interdigitated with authoritarian centralized control" (Harvey 2005, 120). Consequently, it is easy to speak of "neoliberalism with Chinese characteristics" (Harvey 2005) or the materialization of a particular form of "neoliberalism in China" (Breslin 2006; see also H. Wang, 2003). Without implying that the Chinese state began the economic reforms with an ideological commitment to neoliberalism, I agree with Ong (2006) that the Chinese state, like the East Asian "tiger" states such as Malaysia and Indonesia, has been very proactive in the deployment of neoliberal strategies of governance. The establishment of the "special economic zones" at the onset of China's economic reform process is the primary example of neoliberalism as exception. In fact, the defining characteristics of neoliberal governmentality, that is, "the infiltration of market-driven truths and calculations into the domain of politics," have in many ways characterized China's transition from a planned economy to a "socialist market economy." Although there are limits to this process, which I will discuss in the second half of this paper, the conceptual framework of neoliberalism as exception and exceptions to neoliberalism provide a point of entry to analyze the Chinese state's role in shaping communication policies and processes.

Instead of pursuing media centric and nation-state-centric modes of analysis, I conceptualize China's reintegration with the global market system through the communication industries as an integral part of an ongoing global political economic transformation, leading to the emergence of a new global order in which China has the potential to redefine the norms of global governance. Chinese communication has typically been analyzed from the perspective of either Chinese democratization or a national cultural industry, where the analytical focus is either on the (potential) democratizing impact of global market forces or the scope and mechanisms of foreign capital penetration in China on the one hand and Chinese media industry responses to market forces and global capital on the other (Y. Zhao 2003b). Implicit in these perspectives is at worst an Orientalizing predisposition of seeing China as an object of Western transformation and at best as a patronizing appreciation of China's capability to "catch up" with the West, that is, to make it into the global capitalist cultural market. What is missed in these analyses, however, is a fuller understanding of Chinese agency. This not only includes both the agency of China's "active audiences," who are well known for their abilities to "read between the lines" of the official media, and the ability of Chinese cultural entrepreneurs to produce films like "Hero" or Hollywood block-busters with Chinese characteristics, but also Chinese agency at a more pro-found political and cultural plane, that is, the "ambition of resisting subordi-nation to global capitalism" (C. Lin 2006, 1) and the agency of those Chinese citizens who continue to search for a "socialist" alternative to capitalist modernity.

Recognizing the global implications of China's linkages to transnational-ized "digital" or informational capitalism (D. Schiller 1999, 2007), Dan Schiller (2005) has documented China's recent outward expansionary initia-tives in communication hardware, content, and services. He argues that the significance of these developments "lies beyond any punitive zero-sum game" between the United States as the current global hegemon and China as a would-be rival, but instead in the ways such developments have contributed to the "structural reconfiguration of transnational capitalism with which China's rise is so profoundly intertwined" (2005, 86). In this way, Schiller has chal-lenged media analysts to move beyond nationcentric and mediacentric frame-works in understanding China's linkages with the global market system. His conclusion that transnational capitalism's successful exploitation of China and the information and communication sectors as the "two poles of growth" will paradoxically "contribute to a resurgence of the very economic crisis that pro-moted their own prior development" (2005, 96) remains a critical insight for understanding the political economic implications of "China's rise."

In expanding on this line of inquiry, I draw attention to recently articulated ideological and cultural underpinnings of the Chinese state's internal and ex-ternal communication initiatives, including elite attempts at promoting the "the Beijing Consensus," which I will soon explain, as an alternative to the discredited "Washington Consensus." In this way, I explore the *political* agency and the transformative role of the Chinese state vis-à-vis the overrid-ing logic of neoliberal and informationalized capitalism, foregrounding its profoundly ambiguous articulation with this logic and the ongoing struggles over the terms of this articulation within China. In particular, I engage with the multifaceted and complicated nature of the Chinese state in the context of its formal commitment to a socialist alternative. As I will show in what fol-lows, this official label has its political efficacy and popular resonance inside China. Consequently, it cannot be completely swept away with leftist de-featism or capitalist triumphism. Moreover, as Dirlik (2004, 229) has pointed out, whether to call the current Chinese system "capitalist" or "socialist" is not just a matter of description. Rather, it is a matter of prescription in the sense that such a representation is intended to shape the reality that it pretends to de-scribe, thus constituting part of "an intense struggle between two discourses that seek to appropriate its future for two alternative visions of history."

China's national state is still ruled by a powerful communist party as a so-cially penetrating organization with an explicit modernist project informed by the Marxist ideology and "a massive power base across social cleavages" (C. Lin 2006, 220). For this reason, I would not go so far as Ong (2006, 99) to treat the Chinese state "not as a political singularity but as an ever shifting as-semblage of planning, operations, and tactics increasingly informed by ne-oliberal reason to combat neoliberal forces in the world at large." However, I do accept Ong's poststructural insight at a tactical level, emphasizing the Chi-nese state as a contradictory entity and a site of struggle between competing bureaucratic interests, divergent social forces, and different visions of Chi-nese modernity (Rofel 1999; C. Wang 2003; H. Wang 2003; M. Lin and Ga-likowski, 1999; K. Liu 2004; C. Lin 2006). In the area of communication, for example, there have been bloody street battles and fierce bureaucratic turf wars between Chinese broadcasting and telecommunication authorities over the right to wire Chinese neighborhoods and the control of China's informa-tion highways, as well as raging online and offline debates between different intellectual perspectives (Y. Zhao 2000b; Zhang 2003; Gong 2003; Andy Hu 2006). Clashes between different strands of popular Chinese nationalism are a mainstay of public discourse (Gries 2004; S. Zhao 2004; Y. Zhao, 2004b; Zhou 2006). Although the Chinese Communist Party is historically and offi-cially a party of the left, it has never been a monolithic political force to be-gin with, and the "two-line struggles" between leftist and rightist tendencies[2] within it have been long-standing. With its embrace of neoliberal strategies of development in the 1990s, the party, in one cynical observation made in 2001, "looks more and more like the right-wing authoritarianism of a Suharto of In-donesia or a Franco of Spain than anything Marx might have dreamt up" (Gilley 2001, 19). By 2006, the ongoing political and ideological battle be-tween left and right trajectories of the reforms within the Chinese Communist Party, which peaked in the 1982–1984 and 1989–1992 periods and continued into the early 2000s (Chen 1999; Fewsmith 2001), had reached a new high (Li and Xu 2006). Despite the domestic mainstream media's suppression of the debate, the March 2006 meeting of the National People's Congress, China's parliament, in the words of a *New York Times* report, "is consumed with an ideological debate over socialism and capitalism that many assumed had been buried by China's long streak of fast economic growth" (Kahn 2006a). In short, the dynamic intersections between the neoliberal strategies of selective inclusion and exclusion in access to citizenship entitlements and market opportunities and the socialist legacies of equality and justice for all set in motion Chinese communication policies and politics that not only defy any linear logic and dichotomous characterization but are also fraught with complication, contingency, and compromise. The result is a fluid and in-tensely contested process with indeterminate outcomes.

COMMUNICATION AND NEOLIBERAL STATE
TRANSFORMATION: THE DOMESTIC DIMENSIONS

Samir Amin (1993, 95) wrote that the unequal development immanent in capitalist expansion has placed anticapitalist revolutions not by specific classes, but by "the peoples of the periphery," on the agenda of history. As a result, "the three tendencies of socialism, capitalism and statism combine and conflict" in postcapitalist regimes resulting from social movements that "feed on the spontaneous popular revolt against the unacceptable conditions created by peripheral capitalism" on the one hand, and have "fallen short of making the demand for the double revolution by which modernization and popular enfranchisement must come together" on the other. Institutionalized from one of the central anticapitalist and anti-imperialist revolutions in the periphery of global capitalism in the twentieth century, the postrevolutionary Chinese state embodies the tendencies and tensions that Amin described.[3] These, in turn, have cast a long shadow on the Chinese state's protracted and internally conflicted mutation during an era of unprecedented neoliberal capitalist expansion. In 1989, the Chinese party state faced a near-death experience as the political economic and social tensions of the reform and opening-up process exploded and as the intersections of elite and popular politics led to a profound political crisis. Instead of being replaced by a bourgeois liberal state, the most desirable state form for capitalist activity (Harvey 2003, 91), the Chinese state, in contrast to the Soviet Union, not only survived the crisis, but managed to consolidate its power by further embracing the market and expanding its linkages to the global market system.

Developments in the Chinese communication realm have been central to this transformation. At the institutional level, this has encompassed the well-documented changes in the political economy of the media, telecommunication, and Internet systems with a fortified regime of political control and state capacity building in the management of these systems and increasing commodification of services (e.g., Barmé 1999; C. Lee 2000, 2003; Lu and Wong 2003; Hughs and Wacker 2003; Y. Zhao 1998, 2000a, 2000b, 2007b, forthcoming). In the media sector, market rationality was initially deployed through the importation of popular commercial radio formats in Guangzhou in the early 1980s, the establishment of commercial radio and television stations in Shanghai's Pudong District in the early 1990s, and then the establishment of the News and Commentary Department at China Central Television (CCTV), the very heart of the Chinese broadcasting system, in 1994. These strategies were then gradually diffused into other domains of the media system, allowing the Chinese state to promote innovation, entrepreneurship, and relative autonomy in production, thus making the media system more responsive to popular tastes, concerns, and sensibilities (Y. Zhao 1998).

By November 2002, the party's Sixteenth National Congress had officially called for an expansion of the economic reform program to a whole range of media and cultural industries, elevating them not only as the new focal point for systematic state-led development but also as a strategic site for the growth of China's "comprehensive national strength"—encompassing both economic power and cultural power, or "soft power," in a competitive global context. Viewed through Ong's conceptual framework, this entire process of media marketization and cultural industry restructuring can be seen as the progressive deployment of neoliberalism as exception and exceptions to neoliberalism.

The transformation of the Chinese party state also encompasses significant cultural, ideological, and normative dimensions. The Chinese state, perhaps qualifying as the most powerful post-Marxist apparatus, made a decisive breakthrough at the onset of the reform process by abandoning the Cultural Revolution–era essentialist class discourse but maintaining a version of narrow but effective identity politics—that is, the politics of nationalism. The official media's historical, and admittedly partial, role in the cultivation of class-based subjectivity among the population was completely replaced with an all-out effort to promote a pan-Chinese national identity during the reform era—not only to unify the increasingly stratified mainland Chinese population but also to appeal to overseas Chinese financial and human capital in the name of nation building (B. Zhao 1998; Ong 1999; W. Sun 2002). Within this discourse of nationalism, the state's job was to fulfill the grand objective of the "Chinese nation's great rejuvenation."

Like other postcolonial nation-states, the party state endeavours to secure for the Chinese nation "a place in the global order of capital, while striving to keep the contradictions between capital and the people in perpetual suspension" (Chatterjee 1986, 168). As part of its strategy, the Chinese state champions cultural chauvinism amid the aggressive commercialization and secularization of culture. This is apparent in the state-led revival of Confucian values, traditional cultural symbols, practices, institutions, and discourses on "Chinese civilization." Most notably, the Chinese socialist state and its official media outlets, which historically privileged class solidarity over familial ties and even briefly installed a commune system that superseded the family as a unit of economic production and consumption, have been actively promoting the family as a repository of affection, organic solidarity, and responsibility as a cushion to ease the hardships of a market-oriented social transformation. From melodramatic shows promoting care and love among family members to sentimental songs urging the upwardly mobile neoliberal subject to "go home often," nowhere has this been more articulated than in the themes of CCTV's annual Spring Festival Gala since the mid-1990s (B. Zhao 1998; Lu 2006; Pan 2006).

The more explicit ideological dimension of party state transformation, meanwhile, involves the rearticulation of the terms of the party's hegemony. Notwithstanding the cynical claim that the current Chinese regime "advocates nothing at all," with its legitimacy "based wholly on performance" (Gilley 2004, 33), it remains a historical fact that the party assumed state power through leading an anticapitalist and anti-imperialist social revolution, and that it launched its reform program on the promise of developing, not abandoning, socialism. "An essential feature of Chinese alternative modernity," as Liu Kang (2004, 50) has observed, "is revolutionary hegemony, or the primacy of culture and ideology, in legitimating the modern nation-state and also in constituting the basic and core components of the new socialist country."

In fact, continuous reinvention and rearticulation of its ruling doctrines has been an integral part of the Chinese state's post-Mao transformation. Deng first stabilized the political and ideological field for post-Mao market-oriented developments by imposing "the Four Cardinal Principles"—upholding the socialist road, the dictatorship of the proletariat, the leadership of the Communist Party, and Marxism-Leninism-Mao Zedong Thought. He then glossed over the political and ideological contradictions of the economic reforms with the "no debate" decree—that is, no discussion about the political implications of the reforms—and the developmentalist dictum that "development is a hard truth." In doing so, Deng effectively left his successors to address the profound political and ideological contradictions of a reform process whereby the Chinese Communist Party, the self-proclaimed vanguard of the working class, creates the conditions for market-based social relations and cultivates a capitalist stratum in China. In early 2000, the Jiang Zemin leadership addressed this challenge by inventing the "three represents" thesis—that the party has always represented the developmental requirements of China's advanced productive forces, the orientation of China's "advanced culture," and the fundamental interests of the overwhelming majority of the Chinese people (Fewsmith 2001; G. Lin 2003). The real objective of the doctrine, of course, was to redefine the party from a supposedly working-class vanguard to a "party of all people," including the rising capitalist and managerial strata. The codification of the "three represents" in the party's constitution at its Sixteenth National Congress in 2002 officially completed the party's rightward political and ideological turn.

Facing massive social unrest from disenfranchised workers and farmers, the party's originally purported power base, the Hu Jintao leadership has tried to address the excesses of neoliberal development in the 1990s since coming to power in 2002. In addition to concrete policy and legal revisions aiming at improving social redistribution and welfare provision, this has included a whole series of new ideological doctrines and an extensive ideological education campaign to "preserve the progressive nature of Communist party members." In the aftermath of the 2003 SARS epidemic, the so-called "scientific concept of development," popularized by the media in terms of a people- and nature-friendly "Green GDP," was propagated to correct the single-minded pursuit of neoliberal economic growth at the cost of social development and environmental sustainability. In 2004, the leadership attempted to strengthen the theoretical underpinnings of its rule by launching a "Basic Research and Construction Project in Marxism." Simultaneously, it sought to address mounting social conflicts and ensure social stability by articulating the slogan of "constructing a socialist harmonious society," a society, according to party General Secretary Hu Jintao himself, that "should feature democracy, the rule of law, equity, justice, sincerity, amity and vitality" (Xinhua News Agency 2005). By early 2006, in response to economic depression and social disintegration in the rural areas, the party leadership had recycled a key slogan of the state socialist era of the 1950s, "to construct a socialist new countryside."

Despite its commercialization, the Chinese media system has been instrumental in propagating the party's new ideological doctrines of the day. Although we clearly should not take these doctrines at face value, neither should they be simply dismissed as empty signifiers in the party's already overflowing ideological dustbin. As the social contradictions of China's neoliberal-oriented development have become more acute since the mid-1990s, the party state has been increasingly compelled to elaborate its ruling ideology in a way that will still appeal to the Chinese public. Thus, even if such regime ideology is "a living lie" (Gilley 2004, 33), it nevertheless sets the basic terms of the party state's hegemony and defines the parameters of elite struggle and grassroots social contestation. Moreover, the very acts of its articulation, legitimation, and dissemination—from Jiang Zemin's maneuvers to encode the "three represents" in the party's constitution to Hu Jintao's imposition of an education campaign for party members, are essential dimensions in the exercise of power. Most crucially, to stay in power, the party must continue to articulate and rearticulate its socialist pretensions—otherwise, as I will discuss later in this chapter, socialism threatens to once again become a powerful subversive ideology against a party that has itself championed capitalistic-style developments.

Ironically, as the Chinese state has unleashed market forces, it has also strengthened the normative basis of its rule by "marketing itself as a benevolent regulator" (Wang 2001a, 93) of a chaotic and destructive marketplace. Social pressures, including moral panics often created by the media themselves among cultural elites and moral conservatives within the urban social strata, strengthen and legitimate the state's normative power in communication and culture. Developments in Internet regulation in the past few years have been most illustrative of this process. In June 2002, an unregistered Internet café in Beijing caught fire and killed twenty-five people. This led to a moral panic in the official media about the hazardous nature of unregistered Internet cafés, which were actually the by-products of draconian state regulations, including prohibitive registration fees, in the first place. Immediately, the party state launched a major crackdown on unregistered Internet cafés nationwide (Qiu 2005). Moral panics over pornography and Internet gambling have provided another powerful rationale for the state to reclaim the normative basis of its power. In July 2004, the state launched the "people's war" against pornographic content in cyberspace, with individuals who reported pornographic websites receiving cash rewards. By October 2004, some 445 people were arrested and 1,125 websites were shut down (Cody 2004).

Moreover, the normalizing impulse of the Chinese state's Internet regulation regime has been further entrenched in industry self-regulation, and in a language that transforms the objective of control into a matter of civilization, and indeed, a matter of hygiene for the Chinese body politic. For example, on April 9, 2006, the first day of Hu Jintao's visit to the United States, Sina, Sohu, Netease, and eleven other influential Chinese websites collectively issued "Proclamation to Run Websites in a Civilized Way." The next day, the "civilized Internet" campaign was launched with the slogan "run websites in a civilized way, surf online in a civilized way" (Hu 2006, 122).

Thus, even though the market opens up opportunities for media organizations to pursue economic self-interests and thus provides a potential power base for them to assert autonomy vis-à-vis the state, the excesses, or what Polanyi ([1944]1957) identified as the disruptive and polarizing effects of the market, provide the moral grounds for the state to expand its disciplinary regime and reproduce the normative basis of its power. To further complicate the matter, the bolstering of the state's normative power as a "public good regime" epitomized in its slogan of "serving the people" (C. Lin, 2006) in response to the conservative sensibilities in Chinese society has been strengthened by concurrent popular claims on the state for it to (re) assume the social redistribution, social protection, and public welfare provision functions that it has relinquished during an era of unprecedented market expansion. From emotionally charged media images of party state officials leading the national fight against the SARS virus in 2003 to the media's dramatization of a poor rural woman's appeal to Premier Wen Jiabao to help her with collecting her husband's unpaid wages—the massive phenomenon of nonpayment of wages is perhaps the ultimate expression of "exception to neoliberalism" in China— the reaffirmation of the state's positive role as a "public good regime" has deep popular resonance. Thus, Chinese state power, after having been deployed to unleash the power of the market, has been compelled to meet political demands for self-protection by an activated society in a playing out of Polanyi's famous "double movement," whereby the unleashing of market forces is met by a counterforce on the part of society to protect itself from the destructive power of the market. Most significantly, instead of positioning themselves as "the contractual, juridical, and abstract labour subject normally assumed in theories of capitalist modernity," that is, the rights-bearing subject in a liberal "civil society," Chinese workers, for example, typically construed the nature of their own political subjectivity in terms of the traditional Maoist notion of the masses constituted by "workers, the peasantry, the intelligentsia and the national bourgeoisie whose interests were harmonious with each other and also with the state" (S. K. Lee 2004, cited in Harvey 2005, 150; see also Yu 2006). In this way, workers making moral claims for state protection ended up "reinforcing the leadership and responsibility of the state to those it rules." The aim of any mass movement, therefore, would be to make the central state live up to its revolutionary mandate against foreign capitalists, private interests, and local authorities" (Harvey 2005, 150).

COMMUNICATION AND NEOLIBERAL STATE TRANSFORMATION: THE GLOBAL DIMENSIONS

The reconstitution of the Chinese state, the restructuring of the Chinese communication industries, and the rearticulation of the state's ideological, cultural, and normative underpinnings are part and parcel of the broad transformation of the global political economy in the era of neoliberal globalization. As is the case with the nature of the Chinese state, which has set off a "paradigm sweepstake" among China scholars in search of a meaningful label (Baum and Shevchenko 1999), there has also been a paradigm sweepstake in characterizing the new global order, ranging from Huntington's (1996) "clash of civilizations" on the right to various Marxist and poststructuralist formulations on the left, including Harvey's (2003) "capitalist imperialism," Panitch and Gindin's (2003) "informal American empire," Hardt and Negri's (2000) "Empire," and Ong's (2006) formulation of globalization as the spread of neoliberal governmentality.

Though some of these formulations have emphasized the role of transnational capital flows and communication networks in undermining the power of the nation-state, here again, a notion of reconstitution and transformation, rather than of a net increase and decline of state power, is a more useful analytical framework (Jayasuriya 2000, 315). In recognition of the necessity to re-evaluate the thesis of diminished state power in the study of media globalization (Morris and Waisbord 2002, ix), Chakravartty and Sarikakis (2006, 36–37), for example, have argued that the changes that are taking place in the field of communication and media policy should be seen as a kind of "re-regulation" of neoliberal governance. During this process, the nation-state loses autonomy in relation to supranational regimes and regional and local governance bodies, while at the same time reorganizing the functions of the state to include "partnerships" with parastatal, nongovernmental bodies and private capital.

The Chinese state's role in reshaping or re-regulating China's communication industries and processes to accommodate a U.S.-dominated global capitalist order is evident in several important ways (Zhao and Schiller 2001; Y. Zhao 2003b, 2004b). For example, by reconnecting the media industries with the global flow of consumer cultures and symbols, and by prioritizing telecommunications network expansion, first in the coastal regions and then on a national scale, the Chinese state made it possible for transnational capital not only to reach an expanding Chinese consuming strata, but also, more importantly, to tap into China's vast labor pool freed up from the dismantling of the commune system and expelled from a depressed rural economy. From the establishment of the very first Sino-American joint venture with the U.S.-based International Data Group in information technology publication to serve China's rising digital elite in 1980 to allow Hong Kong–based Phoenix TV, in which Rupert Murdoch was an investor, to reach a selected mainland Chinese audience just before the Chinese state reassumed sovereignty over Hong Kong in 1997, the application of neoliberalism as exception has created a particular pattern of inclusion and exclusion in media production and consumption within and beyond national boundaries, feeding into a potential process of transnational class formation (Sklair 2001; Dirlik 2003; Y. Zhao 2003b, 2004b).

Much has been written on issues relating to China's global integration through the communication and cultural industries, including the scope and pattern of foreign media penetration, market opening provisions in China's WTO accession agreements in these sectors, the Chinese state's ongoing effort in asserting its sovereignty and re-regulating these sectors in the post-WTO environment, and its ongoing attempt to assert national sovereignty over cyberspace through the Internet Domain Name System (see Y. Chin 2003; C. Lee 2003; Ermert and Hughes 2003; Sparks 2003; Downing and Yong 2004; Fung 2006; Y. Zhao 2003a, 2004a, 2004b, forthcoming). Rather than revisit these well-traversed territories, I would like to take up the much-noted Chinese censorship regime in this context. I suggest that this seemingly quintessential "Chinese" regime must be understood for its transnational significance. Indeed, it can be argued that the suppression of independent communication by disenfranchised Chinese workers and farmers and the banning of news reports on any protests by these groups have been partially responsible for low labor costs, or what Harvey (2005, 148) has called a regime of "super-exploitation of labour power, particularly of young women migrants from rural areas" as China's primary "comparative advantage" in the international division of labor, leading to the rise of China as a global manufacturing powerhouse and the number one destination for direct foreign investment among developing countries.

Similarly, the Chinese state's ongoing suppression of popular nationalist sentiments against both historical and contemporary manifestations of Japanese and American imperialism remains a key plank of its accommodation with an American-led neoliberal global order. To create a foreign investment–friendly environment and to gain the favorable international conditions for its economic development, the Chinese state has long followed Deng Xiaoping's dictum of *taoguang yanghui* in its dealings with the dominant powers in the current global order. According to this dictum, one must hide one's brightness or lay low in order to earn the time to accumulate the necessary strength for eventual greatness. In this way, the Chinese state justifies its retreat from the Maoist anti-imperialist agenda as a tactical, rather than a strategic, move. Still, such a policy has provoked leftist and popular nationalist critiques against the party leadership for its "selling" of China's national interests and its complicity in sustaining a U.S.-dominated and unjust global order. The popularity of nationalist-oriented books such as *China Can Say No* and *China in the Shadow of Globalization* since the mid-1990s, as well as the explosion of cybernationalism since NATO's bombing of the Chinese embassy in Belgrade in 1999, is a clear illustration of these nationalist and anti-imperialistic popular sensibilities (Zhou 2006).

Thus, although the mainstream Western view of Chinese nationalism as propaganda generated by the party elite for its own instrumental purpose is not wrong, "it is incomplete" (Gries 2004, 18) and risks "dangerously trivializing the roles that the Chinese people and their emotions play in Chinese nationalism" (Gries 2004, 20). Although the most vocal form of popular nationalism tends to be linked to political authoritarianism and contains neither a critique of global capitalism nor substantive class analysis, there are forms of popular nationalism that are critical of global capitalism and class domination at both the intellectual and popular levels (Y. Zhao 2004b, 212–13). A group of intellectuals who view the United States as the standard-bearer of liberal democratic values in the world and favors a closer relationship between China and the United States, for example, expressed dismay when the overwhelming majority of the Chinese public — from young faculty members lecturing to cheering university students to workers on the streets — were critical of American imperialist foreign policies and saw the 9/11 terrorist attacks as a form of blowback.[4]

Consequently, the Chinese state's censorship regime not only controls domestic dissent but also suppresses extremist comments and media reporting of popular expressions against the United States as well as news reporting of key facts that the Chinese state fears may provoke popular protests in terms of its dealings with the United States and Japan. For example, the Chinese state censored news reports of its $2.87 million compensation payment to the United States for damage inflicted on U.S. diplomatic property in China by anti-American demonstrations in 1999 (S. Zhao 2004, 160), along with both news coverage and Internet discussion of the "bugged plane incident"—when bugging devices were found in a Boeing 767 jet delivered from the United States and due to serve as the official aircraft of Chinese President Jiang Zemin in January 2002 (Zhou 2006, 208–9). The Chinese state's approach of downplaying Sino-Japanese conflicts in the media has also been consistent since the mid-1990s (S. Zhao 2004, 274; Y. Zhao, forthcoming).

But in so doing, the Chinese state risks losing its legitimacy by pursuing a single-minded project of capitalist integration. In addition to its determination to deter Taiwanese independence by contesting U.S. military supremacy through the doctrine of "asymmetrical warfare,"[5] which was underscored in the Chinese military's launching of an antisatellite ballistic missile in January 2007, recent efforts and pronouncements by the Chinese state about projecting its "soft power" onto the global stage also signal an ongoing commitment to enlarging its own place within the existing system of U.S.-led transnationalizing capitalism. As a *New York Times* report noted in relation to the CCTV's broadcast of a high-profile documentary series titled *The Rise of Great Powers* in November and December 2006, "[w]ith its $1 billion in foreign exchange reserves, surging military spending and diplomatic initiatives in Asia, Africa and the Middle East. . . . Chinese party leaders are acting as if they intend to start exercising more power abroad rather than just protecting their political power at home" (Kahn 2006b).

As the international component of the party state's rearticulation of its hegemony, these efforts and pronouncements not only have acquired a new coherence under the Hu Jintao leadership but also seem to crystallize its more conscious effort in attempting to transform the current global order. Recent Chinese official appropriation of the concept of "soft power" and concomitant discussions regarding "the Beijing Consensus" are illustrative of this new development. That is, instead of merely critiquing the penetration of American "soft power" in China, official Chinese discourses have appropriated this term and actively sought to strengthen China's own "soft power," emphasizing, among other things, essentialized Chinese cultural values such as harmony and unity between humans and nature that presumably are capable of transforming the negative dimensions of Western capitalist culture; and more specifically, presenting "the Beijing Consensus" as an alternative to "the Washington Consensus." On May 28, 2004, the party's politburo held its thirteenth routine study session, focussing on strengthening China's position in the areas of philosophy and social sciences. Situating this session within the context of the party's newly issued guidelines on enhancing China's strength in these areas and global discussions about "the Chinese Model" (as endorsed by Joseph Stiglitz [2002]) and "the Beijing Consensus" (as formulated by former *Time* magazine editor and Goldman & Sachs analyst Joshua Cooper Ramo [2004]), a Xinhua News Agency report called this study session "extraordinary" because it signalled that "the new central leadership has started to accelerate the construction of China's soft power from a strategic plane" (Yang 2004).

After the central leadership issued a call for Chinese theorists to "study and criticize" neoliberalism and reflect upon the failure of "the Washington Consensus" in the former Soviet bloc and in many developing countries, official Chinese media discourses have been more than willing to endorse "the Beijing Consensus." According to Ramo (2004), whose formulation first appeared in a report for the British Foreign Policy Center, "the Beijing Consensus" consists of "three theorems about how to organize the place of a developing country in the world": an insistence on the necessity of leading-edge innovation to "create change that moves faster than the problems change creates"; "a developmental model where sustainability and equality become first considerations, not luxuries"; and "a theory of self-determination" that aims to accumulate asymmetric power and "stresses using leverage to move big, hegemonic powers that may be tempted to tread on your toes." In November 2006, as the Chinese state held the Sino-Africa Forum summit meeting in Beijing and renewed its solidarity with "African brothers" who had played an instrumental role in helping socialist China to gain its membership to the United Nations during the Cold War, the Chinese media, with headlines such as "Africa Looks East: From the Washington Consensus to the Beijing Consensus" (B. Liu 2006), were eager to express China's global aspirations and showcase "the Chinese model" of development. Of course, they did so despite the profound contradictions of "the Chinese model" and the obvious incoherence of "the Beijing Consensus," a point I will return to in the last section of this chapter.

At the same time, the Chinese state has been extremely cautious in its international public relations. For example, the Hu Jintao leadership, after having used the idea of China's "peaceful rise" to describe its foreign policy goals in 2004, later opted for the "tamer-sounding" idea of China's "peaceful development," because the term "development" suggests that "China's advance can bring others along," whereas the term "rise" implies that others must decline in a relative sense, risked stoking fears of a "China threat" in Japan and the United States (Kahn 2006b). Similarly, Chinese media discourses have been careful not only to highlight the tentative nature of "the Beijing Consensus" but also to contrast its mode of articulation and means of promotion with those of the U.S.-sponsored "Washington Consensus." As Wu Shuqing, a former president of Beijing University, argues (Tian 2005),

> Whereas "the Washington Consensus" was advanced purposefully and systematically and its subscribers truly formed a consensus on the basis of their acceptance of neoliberalism, "the Beijing Consensus" as a perspective emerged voluntarily within the global public opinion arena . . . its content is still under

discussion, and neither its proponent nor the participants of its discussion share the theoretical basis of such a "consensus."

Wu concluded that there is not yet "an already formulated 'consensus.'" As I will show in the next two sections, this point is certainly well taken. Contradiction and contention, rather than consensus, continue to define Chinese communication policies and politics.

LIMITS TO NEOLIBERAL TRANSFORMATION IN STATE AND PRIVATE MEDIA OWNERSHIP STRUCTURE

After three decades of state-directed and market-oriented development, Chinese communication and culture are at a new threshold. The party state itself remains the dominant player in this newly elevated realm for China's political economic and sociocultural development, committing itself to maintaining the necessary regulatory and ideological conditions for domestic and transnational capital accumulation and acting as a "responsible" state within the existing global order. At the same time, it is carefully expressing its intentions to transform this order. The particular form of Chinese modernity, including the institutional and ideological legacies of state socialism and ongoing international tensions, not least of which is the current U.S. and Japanese hegemony in the Asia Pacific region, makes this a profoundly contentious and fluid process. I highlight the manifestations of these contradictions and tensions in the area of media ownership in this section, to be followed by a discussion of the political and ideological tensions and contingencies in the next section.

State ownership was a defining feature of Chinese socialism, and one of the key components of the reform program has been the phenomenal expansion of the private sector and the large-scale privatization of state-owned enterprises in the Chinese economy. Concomitant with this fundamental change has been a gradual recognition of the role of private property in the Chinese Constitution, which was amended in early 2004 to officially protect private property.[6] Yet such developments have clearly excluded the media and cultural sector, where the institutional and ideological legacies of Chinese state formation are at odds with any program of radical ownership transformation of party state media and cultural institutions, let alone permission of private media ownership.

Apart from the most sensitive question of whether it is the Chinese state or the Communist Party that has the ultimate proprietary right over the existing media—a question that immediately comes to the fore as soon as one problematizes the very structure of party state formation itself (Y. Zhao, forthcoming), there has been a profound contradiction between what Harvey

(2003) has called "the logic of territory" and the "logic of capital" in the Chinese party state's transformation of its official organs and, more specifically, in its efforts to recentralize media operations and build domestic media conglomerates. As Harvey points out, the logic of territory emphasizes the political, diplomatic, and military strategies of a state as it strives to assert its interests and achieve its goals within the global system. The logic of capital refers to the "molecular processes of capital accumulation in space and time," stressing the ways in which economic power flows across and through continuous space, toward or away from territorial entities through the daily practices of production, trade, commerce, and other market-related activities (2003, 26–27). Although these two logics sometimes overlap, they are distinctive and "intertwine[d] in complex and sometimes contradictory ways," even "to the point of outright antagonism" (Harvey 2003, 29).

In the context of China's unique form of development, in which the party state–owned media are both official political organs and units of capital accumulation, the manifestations of the accommodation and tension between these two logics have been particularly intense. The nature of the Chinese state as a complicated web of vertically and horizontally integrated administrative units covering a vast and unevenly developed territory and the party state–organ status of media organizations have necessarily led to the market fragmentation of the Chinese media industry along territorial and sectorial boundaries. Consequently, although the party state has been able to absorb the force of media commercialization by turning party and government organs affiliated with different levels of party committees and government administrations into advertising-supported and market-oriented media operations, the formation of cross-regional and cross-media conglomerates, for example, has been hindered by the media outlets' official organ status and bureaucratic and administrative boundaries. On the one hand, the market expansion imperatives of commercially successful local party media organizations such as the *Guangzhou Daily* Group, and the party state's desire to make its propaganda organs "bigger and stronger" in order to face real and imagined international competition, have compelled these media organizations to expand beyond local markets. On the other hand, under the current structure, a party media organization such as the *Guangzhou Daily* Group is subordinated to the Guangzhou Municipal Party Committee, and all its subsidiary publications are politically and administratively accountable to that body. If the *Guangzhou Daily* Group, which as a large press conglomerate publishes not only the *Guangzhou Daily* but also a dozen subsidiary newspapers and magazines catering to different readerships, publishes a new paper in Xi'an, it inevitably raises an awkward question: which party committee will be the political master of this new paper? No matter how commercially successful the *Guangzhou Daily* Group is, it has no legitimate political and administrative grounds to expand beyond its geopolitical boundaries, because "such an expansion can be interpreted as trespassing on the Chinese administrative system" (Chan 2003, 162). For the same reason, the *Guangzhou Daily* Group is not in a position to take over an existing paper in Xi'an in the way privately owned media properties are acquired in a capitalist media system. But if media conglomerates based in the economically developed regions are not allowed to expand geographically or, for the same reason, expand into other media sectors, how will they become "bigger and stronger" and where will their capital find new media markets to invest in? And yet, the reorganization of the media system from its subordination to the logic of territory to the domination of the logic of capital would mean the complete transformation of the Chinese party state from one that privileges the political nature of the media to one that prioritizes the logic of capital. This is a step the Chinese party state evidently is not yet prepared to take.

Private ownership in the media and communication sector remains an even thornier issue for the Chinese party state, which not only has historically defined public ownership—which is currently equated with party state ownership—as the hallmark of "socialist press freedom" but also has waged a protracted battle against the emergence of privately owned media outlets as a hallmark of "bourgeoisie liberalization" (Y. Zhao 1998, forthcoming). As the reform process deepens, the party state's unresolved tension over private media ownership has assumed new forms. On the one hand, tight political control and increased social division in the age of the Internet have diminished the possibility of a single and well-organized social force or movement that advocates an independent press as a political cause. In a concomitant development, private entrepreneurs, rather than political essayists, have become a social force with both the motivation and capital resources required to operate the media for profit-making purposes. In this sense, private media ownership has assumed a different meaning—it can be in the form of either sole proprietary control over a media outlet or forms of "private/public partnerships" in which a private company owns the operational right of a state-owned media outlet or acquires equity shares in the business operations of state-controlled media outlets.

Concurrent with the cultivation of the media's entertainment function, the party state has developed a complex and differentiated policy regime regarding the entry of private capital in the media and cultural industries. In the aftermath of China's WTO accession in 2001, which prompted domestic private capital to argue for a larger role in the Chinese cultural economy, the official media policies have explicitly embraced domestic private capital as a junior partner, while reaffirming areas in which foreign and domestic private capital are prohibited (State Council of PRC 2005). Full ownership of news media and broadcasting outlets and the production and distribution of news and informational content, for example, are deemed "sacred," and they continue to be monopolized by the party state. Simultaneously, full or partial ownership in the peripheral areas of media and cultural production and distribution, including the production of film, television entertainment, and the areas of advertising and audiovisual distribution, has been opened up to domestic and foreign private capital. As Mike Meyer (2005) observes in the case of Chinese book publishing, "the state ostensibly controls publishing," but it relies on private publishers "to do the heavy lifting." In this way, the state retains strategic control over the media system, but largely without engaging in the actual tasks of production.

Unlike Rupert Murdoch, who in 2005 was quick to accuse the Chinese state of "being paranoid" when it nixed a satellite television joint venture he had established with the Qinghai provincial satellite television channel without the approval of central state authorities and in clear violation of existing Chinese media ownership policies ("Murdoch Calls Beijing Paranoid" 2005), domestic Chinese private capital and their spokespeople have been acquiescent to the Chinese state's media ownership policies. Given their incorporated status within the current Chinese political economy and the fact that their voices have been fairly well represented in the media system, especially in the market-oriented business media, they do not seem to have a compelling imperative to mount a frontline confrontation with the party over this issue (author's interview with a media regulator, July 2004). Privately owned media have coexisted well with authoritarian regimes in many parts of the world, and Chinese officials, based on their experience in dealing with foreign media firms such as the International Data Group and the News Corporation in China, have come to realize that these media outlets will follow the party line out of their own business interests. Shi Zongyuan, director of the state's General Administration for Press and Publication, for example, stated that "the quality of publication has nothing to do with [the type of] capital, but with [state] management" (Peng 2003).

Nevertheless, party state officials remain wary of private capital. Their fear of foreign capital is both economic and political. Economically, limiting foreign entry is considered essential for the survival of China's national media industry. Politically, party officials assume the worst. The rationale for this fear can be paraphrased along these lines: although private media outlets may not pose a political challenge in normal times, there is no guarantee that domestic private media outlets, let alone foreign media outlets, will not turn their back against the party and support oppositional forces during the times of political crisis (author's interview with a media regulator, July 2004). Given that party-controlled media outlets turned against the party itself to advocate for "bourgeois liberalization" in 1989, when party leadership was divided and paralyzed by a power struggle, such a consideration is not surprising.

As is the case with the geographical expansion of local party organs, there is an ideological barrier to this issue as well. Media ownership by private capital undermines the very conceptual and institutional foundation of the Chinese socialist state: it means the acceptance of a media outlet both as an independent entity outside the party state and as first and foremost a private profit-making business, contrary to the party's definition of press freedom as being first and foremost freedom from private profit-making. Thus, apart from the practical imperative of maintaining control over the media, the acceptance of independent media ownership by private capital means one more step toward "capitalist restoration." And this is not a step any Chinese leader still claiming to be the heir of the Chinese Communist Revolution can take easily.[7] Herein lies the limits of the applications of neoliberalism as exception by a state that not only has a socialist legacy but also continues to claim this mantra, making the Chinese case different from that of the right-wing Singaporean state discussed by Sim in this volume. This is also a fact that Ong (2006), in failing to take the history of Chinese socialism seriously and to differentiate Malaysia, Indonesia, and China in her discussion of neoliberalism as exception, has ignored.

LIMITS TO THE ANTIPOLITICS OF NEOLIBERAL POLITICS: COMMUNICATING THE SOCIAL JUSTICE AGENDA

As I have already suggested in earlier sections, the Chinese state remains caught in the profound ideological and social contradictions of its post-1989 market authoritarian development strategy. Although the Chinese economy has grown exponentially throughout the 1990s and the reforms have increased the standards of living for a significant portion of the population, urban and rural divisions and inequalities across class, social strata, gender, regional, ethnic, and other cleavages have also increased dramatically. Today, "socialist" China is one of the most unequal societies in the world (Harvey 2005, 14). In fact, it is more inequitable than the United States, one of the world's most inequitable capitalist societies (Manthorpe 2006; Bulard 2006). As sociologist Liping Sun (2003, 2004) has noted, Chinese society since the mid-1990s has become a "fractured" one characterized by profound social divisions and imbalances. Rather than speaking of "China," it has become more meaningful to speak of many "Chinas" or "one country, four worlds": the ultramodern and high-income Beijing, Shanghai, and Shenzhen constitute the first world, large and middle-sized cities and small cities in the coastal areas and high-income rural areas the second world, middle- and low-income rural areas the third world, and minority and border areas and extremely low-income rural areas the fourth world (Hu, Ping, and Chunbo 2001, 167). Although the party state has tried to hold the different Chinas together by reinventing itself as a corporatist party claiming to represent the interests of all sectors of society and by pleading for "social harmony," it has not found a feasible answer to the challenges of reconciling social interests that are fundamentally incompatible in the Marxist framework that it officially still espouses (Madsen 2003, 109). Moreover, "poverty is intensifying among those left behind even as growth roars ahead at 9 per cent" (Harvey 2005, 144).

With profound crises in meaning, identity, and ethics, mounting social unrest, and growing ecological problems—as underscored by the Falun Gong movement, workers' and farmers' protests, and the SARS epidemic—the Chinese reform program's neoliberal turn in the post-1989 period has brought the country once again to the verge of social upheavals (Y. Zhao 2007a). By 2004, the Hu Jintao leadership had openly acknowledged that social instability had reached "the red line" (Manthorpe 2006). Although the variegated forms of resistance against the negative consequences of a neoliberal reform agenda in China do not fit in with Western-centric imaginations of "globalization from below" anchored in a liberal notion of "civil society," they have nonetheless "stimulated and shaped significant dimensions of the reform programme itself" (Perry and Selden 2003, 1).

The negative consequences of neoliberalism as exception; the fallacy and unsustainable nature of the "Chinese model," including its increasing economic dependency on foreign markets; and the incoherence of "the Beijing Consensus" thus have become apparent. In fact, in formulating the "Beijing Consensus," Ramo conflates the two descriptive theorems of "innovation" and "self-determination," which can be claimed to have characterized the developmental strategy of the Deng and Jiang eras, with the Hu Jintao–era prescriptive theorem of "sustainability and equality" as development priorities. In this way, Ramo ignores the fact that it was Deng who officially institutionalized inequitable development through the slogan of "letting some people get rich first." It is this enduring reality, rather than the newly rearticulated ideals of sustainability and social justice, that has actually characterized "the Chinese model" up through the early 2000s.

One of the core normative underpinnings of Chinese socialism, the social justice agenda, has returned to haunt the Chinese state, compelling the Hu Jintao leadership, which consolidated its power after leading a campaign against the SARS epidemic in 2003, to take its socialist rhetoric more seriously and foreground its redistributive capacities. More importantly, popular struggles for social justice accentuate elite struggles over the control and even the very nature of the Chinese state—a process that has been central both to the very founding of the post-revolutionary Chinese state and the launching of the reform program.[8] Despite the official media's embrace of nationalism, the anti-capitalist and anti-imperialist legacies of the Chinese state expressed themselves throughout the 1980s, leading to the crisis of 1989, in which the socialist agenda of justice and equality and popular demand for social protection against the polarizing impact of the market loomed large (H. Wang 2003; C. Lin 2006). Although the suppression of elite debates about the political implications of the reform program by Deng after 1989 paved the way for China's explosive growth under a neoliberal governmentality that recast governing activities as nonpolitical and nonideological problems, covert and even overt debates about the political and ideological nature of the reform program have persisted. "Old" leftists (i.e., aging communist revolutionaries within the party), for example, have persistently attacked the party's reform program as de facto "capitalist restoration."

Just as communication has been central to the Chinese state's neoliberal turn in the post-1989 era, it has also been central to the process of elite contestation and the potential formation of counterhegemony. Confrontation between the central leadership and marginalized "old leftists" within the party, together with fear that leftist critiques of the reform program could inflame the Chinese working class, for example, led to the Jiang Zemin leadership's suspension of two leftist periodicals, *The Pursuit of Truth* and *Midstream,* in the summer of 2001. By then, these "old leftists" had begun to "gain adherents among millions of disenfranchised workers and farmers" (Gilley 2001, 18) and their journals had already become "vital to the labour activists' propaganda efforts" (Jiang 2001, 74). Although it is difficult to substantiate these foreign journalistic observations, widespread popular sayings such as "after thirty years of hard struggle [to build socialism from 1949 to 1979], overnight it is a return to the pre-liberation era"[9] underscore the popular resonance of leftist critiques of the party's betrayal of socialist values and a concern about the returning of unacceptable prerevolutionary social conditions.

Ironically, political censorship, officially sponsored nationalism, the Internet, and global intellectual and cultural flows—the very forces that the party state mobilizes to propel China forward—are carrying China, as it were, backward to its future by reviving and stimulating the production of various leftist discourses. For example, as official censorship, together with marketization and concerted marginalization efforts on the part of neoliberal intellectuals, left no space for leftist discourses in the mainstream media, "old leftists" within the party—some of them in their nineties—discovered the Internet, which had just taken off as a new medium in the early 2000s. In this way, "old leftists," defying the dictum that the Internet is a medium of young people, unwillingly coalesced with and strengthened a multiplicity of online popular leftist discourses, which, unlike the "old leftists," have never had print media access to begin with. In 2003, when the editors of *The Pursuit of Truth,* seeing little hope in resuming the journal's publication, collaborated with nearly a hundred retired party members in launching the website Mao Zedong Flag (*Mao Zedong qizhi*), it prompted a rapid alliance of existing leftist forums and became a major site for the circulation of online leftist discourses, threatening to turn leftist voices into the dominant tenor on Chinese Internet chatrooms (Hu 2006, 87–88). Even the *People's Daily*'s "Strengthen the Nation Forum," an online forum launched by the central party organ in 1999 in the aftermath of the NATO bombing of the Chinese embassy in

Belgrade so that Chinese netizens could vent their nationalist anger against the United States in an officially contained cyberspace, was dominated by left-leaning participants (Hu 2006, 132–35). Because "old leftists" are retired revolutionaries and the founders of the Chinese state, they are "still located at the periphery of the party-state's center of *political* influence" (Hu 2006, 80). Consequently, they function as the living embodiments and the speaking subjects of the Communist Revolution, rather than the empty symbols and caricatured images of the invocation of the revolutionary legacy of Mao that the party state relies upon for its continuing legitimacy. Their presence in a broad leftist discursive formation is thus particularly threatening to the dominant neoliberal agenda.

A similar dynamic is unfolding in China's external communication. Deng Xiaoping disparagingly characterized undesirable global cultural flows into China as "flies" that will unavoidably get into the country as it abandoned its "delinking" strategy and opened up to the Western world. However, the transnational flows of capital, culture, and people not only have mobilized Chinese modalities of neoliberalism and but also have allowed the circulation of new ideas and the empowerment of social agents that may contribute to the transcendence of the dominant neoliberal reform agenda. In late 2004 and early 2005, Lang Xianping, a Taiwan-born, U.S.-trained, and Hong Kong–based economist, made an effective intervention into Chinese public discourse by initiating a debate on the nature and consequences of China's fundamentally flawed and corrupt process of privatization. In this way, Lang contributed to breaking Deng's "no debate" curse about the political nature of the reform process and lent support to domestic leftist economists in their effort to challenge the ideological hegemony of neoliberal intellectuals over the directions of China's economic reforms. As the debate took off, the State Asset Management Bureau, which, like other Chinese state agencies, has seen its policy objectives influenced by neoliberalism and its proclaimed public interest mandate undermined by corruption and bureaucratic self-interest, undertook a series of policy and administrative initiatives to tighten up its supervision of the privatization process and limit its scope, so that the coalition of local bureaucrats, private capitalists, and neoliberal economists was prevented from seizing the entire agenda of state enterprise reform. Although a bureau official denied that these actions were prompted by the debate, it was clear that the debate had put pressure on the state agency and created a favorable media environment for it to pursue actions in this direction (Y. Zhao, forthcoming). That Lang was able to launch an effective public policy intervention through the mobilization of market-oriented media and the Internet is a testimony to the multifaceted and contradictory nature of globalization. Marginalized local leftist economists, who have long articulated similar critiques, not only considered the debate initiated by Lang as too little and too late, but also viewed Lang's success in stirring up the controversy as a sign of

American intellectual hegemony and the Chinese media's continuing worship of an outside authority. It is clear, however, that domestic leftists had nothing to gain by adhering to an old mode of nationalist thinking. They had no choice but to seize the discursive space opened up by Lang as a cosmopolitan intellectual.

Although arguments have been made that the Chinese Communist Revolution, in fighting against both a repressive native ancient regime and foreign domination, was historically "liberating" (Madsen 2000) and even substantively "democratic" (C. Lin 2006, 237), the official "project of Chinese socialism turned conservative and was forced by threats and the party's own making to let its opponents take away the lofty banner of liberty" (C. Lin 2006, 238). Moreover,

> As long as the global liberal ideology with an open or unspoken anticommunist (and racist) influence continued to be (perceived as) destablizing, with the collapse of the Soviet Union in the background, official fear and public caution readily joined forces in China. If historically the weak and vaguely proposed liberal solution fell through in revolutionary China because of the liberal-colonial alliance, the constant economic and political "China bashing" at the present had a similar impact. The cold war survived in hot globalization to keep the concept of imperialism alive. (C. Lin 2006, 238)

To stay in power, the Chinese party state has tried to suppress inflammatory comments by both the political left and right, with grassroots leftists who dare to claim autonomy from the party facing the harshest repression (Y. Zhao, forthcoming). Meanwhile, He Weifang, a Beijing University legal scholar and an outspoken right-wing party member who has argued that the Chinese Communist Party is an unregistered and therefore illegal organization in China, provided an interesting description of the political, ideological, and above all, communicative constraints on a liberal democratic capitalist prospect in China. According to He, who spoke at a high-profile strategy forum on March 4, 2006, designed to articulate a right-wing agenda for the party state, the leftists are "rampant" online because they hit the party state's "soft ribs" and are empowered to utilize the socialist discourse in critiquing the reform without risk. Rightists, on the other hand, have always felt that they have something to hide. As a result, although they all have clear aims, that is, liberal political objectives such as a multiparty system, press freedom, democracy, and individual rights, they have been constantly hesitant to respond to the leftists "because some words can't be articulated." That is, as He put it, these political objectives "are in fact currently unspeakable" ("He Weifang Xishan huiyi fayan jilu" 2006).

He Weifang had apparently omitted the neoliberal economic objectives of further privatization and more economic freedoms for private capital as part of the political agenda of some Chinese right-wing thinkers. Moreover, it can be argued that a genuine socialist discourse must first and foremost embrace liberal political objectives such as press freedom and political democracy. Nevertheless, he has certainly captured the ultimate impasse in the communication politics of "socialism with Chinese characteristics."

CONCLUSION

Slavoj Žižek, in a statement that perhaps exemplifies leftist cynicism, saw in post-Mao China "an ideal capitalist state" of world historical proportions: "freedom for the capital, with the state doing the 'dirty job' of controlling the workers," and "everything subordinated to the ruthless drive to develop and become the new superpower" (2002, 146–47). The primary purpose of this chapter, however, has been to question such cynicism and challenge any hasty conclusion about the nature and future direction of the Chinese state. Meanwhile, inside China, a revitalized "new left" has articulated a democratic socialist alternative to neoliberalism. Instead of trying to apply the boilerplate of capitalist liberal democracy to China, "new left" intellectuals are seeking alternative sources of inspiration for the democratic renewal of Chinese socialism, including drawing lessons from Chinese socialism itself, from the economic and workplace democracy embodied in the Angang Constitution (1960) to indigenous and participatory notions of "people's democracy" (C. Lin 2006). Huang Jisu, a "new left" playwright, expressed this renewed "self-confidence" in the project of alternative socialist modernity in the dedication to his new play "We Walk on a Broad Road": "the Chinese nation, which has long engraved 'the heavenly way [dao]' and 'the great common' in its soul and whose martyrs have long dedicated themselves to these ideas, has lofty inspirations: . . . to use the power of the tigers and wolves to subvert the way [*dao*] of the tigers and wolves, to chart a new course for humanity, and to open a new page in history."[10]

Although the progressive deployment of neoliberalism as exception by the Chinese state in the 1990s and early 2000s has indeed made it in many ways "an ideal capitalist state," its socialist legacies and ongoing rearticulations of socialist principles make this not only a highly contested, but an unfinished project. Despite the absence of a well-organized "civil society" in a liberal polity and the existence of a fortified censorship regime, Chinese society, especially members of subaltern social groups who have regained a new appreciation of the socialist values of equality and justice in the wake of neoliberal excesses, are being activated, making redistributive and social justice claims on the state on the one hand, and calling for political protection against the destructive impact of the market on the other. If "socialism is the subordination of market and state to the self-regulating society" (Burawoy 2003, 198), *then perhaps it is not so much the party's official socialist slogans per se, but their reappropriation by various Chinese social forces and the unfolding societal processes of subordinating both state and market to social needs, is what the struggle for socialism in China is about.* Thus, although I must express caution in accepting Chun Lin's (2006, 5) conclusion that the "emergence of a 'Beijing consensus,' the introduction of a 'green GDP,' and the pledging of attending 'social harmony' by bettering the plight of peasants and migrant workers are among the signs of a resumption of reform socialism," which she believed was derailed in the post-1989 reforms, I do agree with her that the Chinese transformation is still an open-ended process. How the Chinese state will address its internal tensions and redefine the global order will depend not only on the intersections of domestic elite and popular contestations and the decisions it subsequently makes but also on its external structural and symbolic environments, most notably what Chalmers Johnson (2007) has recently characterized as the "Republic or Empire" choice for a United States that now counts China as one of its main creditors. It is clear that China's state transformation is reaching a critical historical juncture.

NOTES

1. Although there is continuity between the pre-1989 and post-1989 phases of the reform process, the suppression of the 1989 pro-democracy movement ushered in a more radical neoliberal-oriented reform agenda (see C. Lin 2006).

2. The political labels of "the left" and "the right" are admittedly confusing and complicated in contemporary China. In very broad strokes, the rightists advocate more market-oriented economic reforms and view state interference as the source of China's problems. The leftists, on the other hand, tend to defend state ownership and argue for increased state capacities in regulating the market.

3. Writing from a different framework, Chun Lin (2006) posits the triad of nationalism, socialism, and developmentalism as the defining features of China's socialist modernization.

4. See, for example, articles by Wang Dongcheng, Yang Zizhu, Zhi Xiaomin, Yu Jie, Zhang Yuanshan, Sha Lei, and Ge Hongbing in *Dangdai Zhongguo yanjiu* 76 (November 2002), 117–56.

5. This doctrine means that, instead of engaging in a full-scale arms race with the more powerful United States, the Chinese military intends to rely on relatively inexpensive but highly disruptive critical battlefield weapons as "deterrence to those forces [that support] Taiwan independence or oppose unification" (Stephens 2007, 13). The U.S. military's heavy dependence on satellite communications has made it logical for China to develop antisatellite technologies.

6. The property rights law, which has been the subject of intense contestation among different political forces within the Chinese state for many years, was finally approved by the National People's Congress in March 2007.

7. Of course, privately owned and profit-oriented media outlets do not have to be the only alternative to state-owned and state-controlled media, let alone media owned and controlled by the party. Not-for-profit community or cooperative ownership, for example, can be possible al-

ternatives. However, current Chinese debates seem to have been caught in the binary logic of party state ownership versus private ownership, while the distinctions among public ownership, state ownership, and party ownership remain extremely murky and sensitive.

8. The reform program was inaugurated in the aftermath of a popularly endorsed military coup that saw the suppression of the "ultraleftists " of the "Cultural Revolution" era within the party soon after the death of Mao in 1976.

9. "The preliberation era" refers to the period before 1949, the year the Communist Party came to power in China.

10. I attended the premiere of the play on the evening of October 27, 2006, in Beijing.

3

Media, State, and Responses to Globalization in Post-Communist Russia

Olessia Koltsova

News media are usually seen as agents of globalization in academic discourse on global change. While globalization would hardly be possible without the media, Russia exemplifies not only the ways in which historical context and the particular process of state (trans)formation shape the media's contradictory roles in society, but also the extent to which society's response to globalization overdetermines the courses of state and media (trans)formation. This chapter examines the complicated intersections between the Russian media system and major challenges of postsocialist development: state transformation, globalization, and rapid changes of popular opinion. For this purpose, I draw upon primary research on the Russian news media between 1997 and 2001, secondary literature on Russian media developments since 2001, and public opinion polls conducted by VCIOM—the All-Russia Center for Public Opinion Research, the leading polling organization in Russia.[1] My primary research, which provided the bulk of the main data for this chapter, included over seventy interviews with media officials, journalists, media sources, and other external agents of influence on the media as well as large-scale secondary data analysis (for more details see Koltsova 2001, 2006a, 2006b).

My goal here is not to give final answers, but to contribute to the debate on state and media roles in relation to globalization, and present some evidence that may challenge traditional visions of this relation. I will adopt broad and relatively simple definitions of the media, democracy, and globalization. Although here I draw most of my examples from television, the media in general are understood as institutions that carry out centralized production of symbolic goods and disseminate them to anonymous dispersed audiences.

Democracy as an auxiliary concept is defined as the ability of all people to take part in making the most important decisions concerning the development of their society. Globalization is seen as the increasing role of those social phenomena (institutions, networks, groups, processes) that transgress national boundaries and make previously relatively isolated entities (societies, states, nations) more interconnected and interdependent.

The central and the most problematic concept of this chapter is the state and its multifaceted roles and constitutive dimensions. Too often scholars who have written on media and globalization within the liberal framework tend to view globalization as opening new opportunities for processes of democratic transformation, while positing the state as the last fortress of resistance to these democratic processes, and national identity as an ideological mechanism used by national political elites to retain power (Price 2000, 51, 72–73, 91). Cultural imperialism theorists, beginning with Herbert Schiller (1976), have a differentiated approach to states: while Western states are seen as agents of imperialism, all the rest are analyzed in terms of their potentials and limits to protect their citizens from cultural intrusion. However, as Curran and Park (2000, 3–11) have convincingly shown, the relationship between the state and the global forces is more complicated. The Russian state has traditionally been the major agent of modernization and global integration, and it surely cannot be seen as the only agent of post-Soviet neo-isolationism and nostalgia for a romanticized past. The latter trends reflect the popular reaction to the intensity of globalization of the 1990s. In this context, the mass media have supported an isolationist perspective as much as they have promoted globalization.

I believe that the ambivalent role of the Russian state in globalization can be explained if two propositions are accepted. First, the state must be seen as a constitutive element of globalization: global integration can only exist as long as there remain boundaries between states, nations, and societies, making possible the distinction between the global and the local, the foreign and the domestic, the external and the internal. Second, we must recognize that the state is not one concept, but a "family" of related concepts describing a range of social phenomena, each of which may have a different contribution to globalization. Roughly, approaches to the state may be divided into two broad groups. A first one, which I will here conventionally term institutional, stems from the Weberian definition of a state as "a group that has managed to gain the monopoly for legitimate violence over a given territory" (Weber 1968, 53). This particular term has, of course, become insufficient: modern states have a range of functions much wider then just the exercise of violence; in a globalizing environment they also have to compete for legitimacy with various local and global groups. But what is central for this cluster of approaches is that it places the state within a society among its other institutions and foregrounds its coercive element in its integrative activity.

A second group of approaches, on the other hand, sees the state as a framework within which society operates and underscores the symbolic component of its integrative function. These approaches are centered around the notion of the nation-state. Though sometimes this understanding of the state is in fact close to the "lay" word *country,* most of the time these theories presuppose the coincidence of the territorial, political, ethnic, and cultural boundaries of the entity they seek to describe. However, this is a predominantly Western European phenomenon and this particular notion of the nation-state has proven too narrow to account for modern state formations. In much of the "non-first" world (Africa, South Asia, the Middle East, Central Asia—and Russia), there is no necessary correlation between the nation and the state. In fact, the Russian language—either spoken or academic—does not have the term of nation-state. The word *nation* (*nazia*) mostly means a group of people of the same "nationality/ethnicity," which is united by common language, traditions, and "blood." Thus, *nazia* includes the Russian diaspora outside contemporary Russia but excludes, for example, Turkic peoples living within the Russian Federation. Of special importance here is also the word "Russian," which in fact has two translations in its native tongue: *russky* and *rossiysky.* The first refers to ethnicity, and it would be used together with the word *nazia* to mean "Russian nation" as defined above. *Rossiysky* is an attribute of Russia as a country or a state (*rossiysky* citizen, economy, president, etc.). Since the closest Russian equivalent to "nation" as community united by common citizenship and territory is *narod* (the people), "Russian nation" in its nonethnic meaning is spoken as *rossiysky narod,* which has no linguistic connection with anything national. It is also not surprising, then, that the word *nazionalism* in Russian is very close to ethnocentrism and, implying belief in the superiority of one's *nazia* over others, is usually associated with Nazism and racism. It is in this context that Russian (*rossiysky*) intellectuals raise concerns about the rise of nationalism in Putin's Russia.

Besides the listed above "individual" limitations, both approaches also share some common shortcomings. The point most relevant for my work is that, based on the experience of stable Western societies, these approaches have seen states as static, coherent, and operating within formal institutional frameworks. This is absolutely inapplicable for periods of state transformation, of which recent Russian history is a vivid example. But, once we recognize the difference between the two groups of approaches and their different roles in globalization, both turn out to be equally important in accounting for the complicated processes of media, state, and social transformation in Russia.

In this piece I will first show how the disintegration and later reconsolidation of the Russian nation-state and "institution-state" influenced the "size of the window" through which global winds could blow into the country, and what cultural and social tensions it produced. Then I shall demonstrate how popular reaction (reaction of the "nation") to these tensions had an impact on institution-state formation and the changes in the media system. In particular, I will show how the euphoria surrounding open markets and global integration in the 1990s gave way to what former presidential advisor Andrey Illarionov called the "Iranization" of Russian society (Sokolov 2005).

WESTERNERS VERSUS SLAVOPHILES: GLOBALIZATION IN RUSSIA

Even after the collapse of the USSR, Russia remains a vast country with eleven time zones, ten climatic zones, and disparate socioeconomic realities. Industrial and postindustrial enclaves centered around megalopolises contrast with economically depressed rural areas that suffer from high unemployment and the remnants of gigantic Soviet farms and heavy industrial enterprises. Urban Christian (or rather post-Christian) postmodern lifestyles of Russian-populated cities, rural Muslim societies in northern Caucasus, and indigenous communities in the tundra—all coexist within one state. This diversity is one of the reasons why the modern state has historically reinforced the symbolic work of sustaining a unified national identity, that is, creation of an "imagined community" (Anderson 1991) out of disparate cultural experiences. However, centralized Soviet propaganda failed in promoting the socialist "melting pot." National identity always had to compete with local and later with global, or more accurately transnational identities.

This competition, along with the broader globalization of Russia, did not begin with Mikhail Gorbachev's accession to power in 1985. In fact, awareness about the growing impossibility of ignoring international changes and foreign pressures came to Russia quite early and is usually connected with the name of the famous reformist czar Peter the Great, who ruled in the late seventeenth and early eighteenth centuries. Peter's radical reformism divided the political elite, and later the whole class of intellectuals, into "Westerners" and "Slavophiles." The latter's heated discussions about "the Russian way" have not ceased in today's world but appeal to increasingly larger parts of the nation's citizens. Despite this simple binary opposition, what unites the two groups is the obligatory reference to Western influence, which should be either absorbed and assimilated, or resisted, but cannot be ignored.

Soviet leaders did not avoid this agenda either. In fact, the first generation of revolutionaries, led by Vladimir Lenin, ascribed Russia a central role in the global history: the victory of the formerly exploited working class over its oppressors was to catalyze similar revolutions worldwide. When these hopes failed, both Soviet policy and rhetoric became focused on the idea of constructing a socialist alternative modernity to outrun the West. The obligations of the state-owned media, then, were twofold: First, the media were just one of the spheres of national development in which the USSR was to outrun the West; they thus had to become an exemplary institution of enlightenment, "cultured leisure," and press freedom in a particular understood way. Second, at the same time in this outrunning game the media were to visualize Soviet victories and Western failures along with the struggle of the oppressed foreign workers against capitalists. Thus, although Soviet media of course filtered, carefully measured out, and reinterpreted global influences, they tirelessly kept them on the agenda. In the Soviet symbolic universe the individual was placed not only into his or her immediate environment but also into the global space organized in a certain way by various state propaganda agencies (Grushin and Onikov 1980; Hopkins 1970).

Ironically, even the so-called epoch of *glasnost* ("openness," "publicness," 1985–1991) started as a policy planned "from above." Moreover, the Soviet elite did not seem to foresee the globalizing consequences of this policy: the party-government's intention then was to promote internal glasnost, as opposed to opening up to global information flow. But the doctrine of glasnost, once introduced, immediately made the situation uncontrollable: the society was already "cultured" and "enlightened" enough to demonstrate the unplanned level of criticism and to engage in unforeseen activities. The causes of glasnost are still much debated in scholarly accounts. Some writers (Rantanen 2002, 50–55; Hopkins 1983; Alexeyeva 1983) underscore the role of various alternative (and often Western-provoked) media during the Soviet time, but the impact of these media is questionable. Others point to the fact that the social change in the USSR owed more to general global competition than to "free global flow of information" and dissident media (e.g., Shlapentokh 2000). Most agree, however, on the significance of international factors in the late Soviet change and the eventual collapse of the USSR. More generally, the development of local-to-global relations in Russia may be seen as a pendulum-like or, perhaps, spiral movement in which periods of more or less intensive absorption of international influences were followed by times of relative isolation or even political, military, and cultural expansion. The Russian history of the last two decades is a good illustration of this. In this period both the Russian state and Russian national identity have passed through two clear phases: disintegration/opening to the global (late 1980s–late 1990s), and reintegration/closure (since the late 1990s). Mass media institutions, and the television industry in particular, have had to respond to these dramatic changes.

"PARADE OF SOVEREIGNTIES": MEDIA AND THE SPATIAL DISINTEGRATION OF THE RUSSIAN STATE

The disintegration of the Soviet state was more than the mere geographical decomposition of the USSR. First, the latent spatial disintegration of the post-Soviet Russian nation-state continued after the collapse of the USSR, dividing the country into "89 different political regimes" corresponding to the number of Russian provinces (Yakovenko 2000). Second, and perhaps, more importantly, Russian society kept going through a painful structural disintegration that affected all of its major institutions, with the state undergoing the most dramatic decomposition. The media entered this situation mostly as junior partners of more powerful institutional actors.

Eighty-nine (since 2005, eighty-seven) post-Soviet "subjects of federation" are the messy heritage of Soviet and Imperial Russia: their establishment was arbitrary and combined ethnic and territorial principles of province formation, while the contemporary legislation and practice of federative relations are contradictory in terms of provinces' rights and obligations. In the early 1990s many regions, from Chechnya[2] to "inland" Russian-speaking provinces, declared their sovereignties (this phenomenon is known as the "parade of sovereignties"), so the federal elite had grounds to fear that Russia would soon follow the pattern of the Soviet Union. However, the events in Chechnya became a "bloody vaccine"[3] against radical separatism, and most regions preferred to make deals with the federal center, exchanging personal loyalty of their leaders with the president for various benefits. The terms of these deals depended on regional resources, including the potential mobilization of ethnic, national, or other local identities. In turn, the central role of the local media in such mobilization stimulated regional leaders to gain control of these media while simultaneously cutting local inhabitants off from discrepant messages from the "central" (federal) media. Many regional leaders used to block out the signals of federal TV channels during unfavorable broadcasts. Discriminative price policies in delivery service for federal newspapers were also a common practice. Provinces where non-Russian-speaking populations prevailed experienced an outburst of media in local languages, lavishly supported by regional elites and promoting regional identities (Petrulevich 2004, 5). Some republics—first of all, Chechnya—tried to carry out autonomous foreign policies, to integrate into the external world aside from the federal center and to develop transboundary identities—for example, of Chechnya as a natural part of the Islamic world, bypassing Russia.

Thus the spatial-political disintegration of Russia, often called the "feudalization" of the Russian state, promoted the disintegration of Russia's common informational/media space, making some regions quite isolated. Furthermore, since the styles of political leadership varied greatly from one region to another, a great variety of local media landscapes emerged. As Yakovenko et al. (2000, 107) have put it, "Traveling through contemporary Russia, one also travels in historical time: from year 2000 one can get into 1930s and 1950s. Within one state medieval *khanates* neighbor Chicago of gangsters' times." While the metaphor of "khanate" in the 1990s applied mostly to the northern Caucasian traditional provinces, Russian-speaking regions dominated by one agent of power increasingly resembled the classical Soviet media system with its institutionalized paternalism and diversified propagandist approach to various target audiences. In both cases the "state," in its local embodiment, experienced much less disintegration than the Russian state on the federal level. In other regions, however, as at the federal level, the state went through a dramatic decomposition into a number of competing actors, supplemented with the formation of entirely new centers of power (the majority of which were cross-institutional groups that are discussed further below). In these regions media content became much more diverse and resembled, in the words of one of my interviewees, "free competition of unfree media" (Interview with "Nikolai," editor in chief of a national newspaper, Moscow, January 2001).

GIANTS' FIGHTS: MEDIA AND INSTITUTIONAL DISINTEGRATION OF THE RUSSIAN STATE

While the spatial disintegration of the state is a relatively easily grasped process, its institutional disintegration is a less obvious and a less visible phenomenon. When the Soviet state developed to its maturity, it became institutionalized so profoundly that it started to resemble a gigantic corporation: a well-consolidated institution of party-state was the only owner, employer, distributor, and decision maker, while the people were subordinate employees, and the media—one of the corporation's departments (for such a vision see, e.g., Zassoursky 1999, 20–21). It is not difficult to imagine, then, what a dramatic change this all-embracing corporation had to go through with the introduction of private property and a multiparty system, the abolishment of centralized distribution and price formation, and the dismantling of official censorship. First shrinking from an omnipresent entity to an institution whose size was to be comparable to Western states, the corporation then split into a number of relatively autonomous agents and groups. In the case of the media, some of them were entirely new players, such as advertisers (advertising hardly existed in the USSR and had no impact on media survival); others, such as private owners, for the first time emerged as actors separate from the state. Still others, such as journalistic sources, were for the first time left face to face with their media counterparts without any state mediators. Finally, both rank-and-file journalists and media executives became autonomous enough to exercise their own power (Koltsova 2006).

All of these diverse actors suddenly found themselves in an unpredictable environment without any clear rules of interaction and without relevant skills. Thus this period, between 1990 and approximately 1996, became a time when these new actors themselves got a chance to create and introduce their own rules, and many did not hesitate to do so. It is not surprising then that the level of conflict in all spheres of social life, including the media industry, became quite high. Since resources were far from being evenly distributed among various actors, and since each actor tended to possess only one or a few types of resources, strategic alliances between actors were quickly formed.

When a leading actor(s) managed to unite agents with different resources and effectively coordinate their interaction, such groups grew into large and internally complex entities. Typically, they included individuals from different social institutions. Since different institutions tend to produce different kinds of resources, if one seeks to combine resources, then it makes sense to look for partners in a multitude of institutions: that is why I have termed such teams "cross-institutional groups" (CIGs). They consolidated by cutting across traditional institutions, and cleavages between CIGs sometimes were deeper than boundaries between formal institutions (Koltsova 2006). The struggle and cooperation between CIGs against the background of weakened formal institutions (especially those of the state) constituted the life of the Russian politico-economic elite in the 1990s, while relations with the rest of society and with the outside world receded into the periphery of institutional attention.

A typical CIG was usually centered around a personality of any institutional affiliation, but it necessarily included state representatives with their access to public resources, economic actors with enterprises or other economic capital, enforcement bodies—whether "legal" (corrupted police members or registered private "security" businesses) or "criminal" (unregistered "gangs")—and propaganda tools embodied in journalists, producers, or media organizations. For example, in a well-known case from the city of Krasnoyarsk the leading local CIG, headed by a former racketeer and centered around the Krasnoyarsk Aluminum Plant (*KrAZ*), also included its "security" service, several dozen legal business units, and a leading regional TV channel and other media, working together to support a weak candidate for governor by censoring competing candidates from airtime on local television.[4]

Thus, what often looked like repression of independent media/journalists by the state or by "bandits" at a closer look turned out to be an attack of one CIG on the media resources of another. However, it would be misleading to conclude that CIGs were using bandits just to get rid of rivals and their media—rather, CIGs, acting in the situation of state failure, included their own quasi–police enforcement bodies and thus became protostate entities competing with what was left of the "official" state for all its power. Additionally, although for most CIGs media resources were an auxiliary concern, some CIGs were centered around their media industries. The most prominent example was Media-MOST holdings—a giant media empire that grew from the first and the most successful private national television company, NTV. Despite its media-centric character, Media-MOST seemed to have no other choice than to include all other CIG components: it was strongly supported by the mayor of Moscow and police bodies controlled by him (later also by its own powerful security department); it cooperated with Yeltsin's team and had a strong business component from the banking sector which had been central at its initial stage.

At that stage it looked as if Media-MOST leader Vladimir Gussinsky, unlike most of his "oligarchic colleagues," viewed his media resources not as tools to support other activities but as a primary source of income. Therefore, he needed a vast loyal clientele (audience), and in the first half of the 1990s perhaps the most demanded media product was "objective" news—or rather a discourse of news objectivity, freedom of the press, and criticism of authorities. In this respect NTV's timing was propitious, as its launch in 1994 coincided with the start of the first unsuccessful military campaign of the federal center against the separatists in Chechnya. However, later events, such as Media-MOST's initial close collaboration and subsequent electoral rivalry with Yeltsin's team and other cross-institutional groups meant that it would still be a CIG struggling for power rather than for normative goals. Nevertheless, Media-MOST was a somewhat unusual CIG that unintentionally contributed to more pluralistic and, as we shall see further on, more global media content in Russia.

MEDIA WARS: INTRA-ELITE COMMUNICATION VERSUS MASS COMMUNICATION

Why would CIGs buy or establish new media outlets and why would established media "surrender their freedom" to them? While there are multiple explanations, the predominant ones are economic. The period of "euphoria,"[5] when production costs were low and old levers of state power were no longer in place, was very brief and covered approximately the years 1989–1991. But from 1992 until the end of the decade the economic situation changed so much that the media's expenses grew dramatically, while "legitimate" sources of media revenues—advertising, sales/subscriptions, and foreign investments—were virtually unavailable.

In place of "legitimate" clients (audiences and advertisers) media time and space were purchased retail and wholesale for hidden interests or open propaganda by various "wrong" sources, ranging from individual businessmen and "bandit groups" to full-size CIGs. Strictly speaking, these players can also be seen as advertisers, but advertisers of a specific kind, whose objective was not to increase sales of their goods and services but instead to gain access to symbolic capital that could later be converted into political capital. The first type of capital was needed to influence arbitrary decision making on the large-scale privatization of huge state properties launched in the early and mid-1990s. The second, targeting volatile post-Soviet voting, brought loyal congresspeople, mayors, and governors to power, again strengthening CIGs' ability to influence decision making.

As a result, a typology of sociopolitical media that had emerged by the mid-1990s could not be conceptualized as private versus state/public, or as independent versus state, or as commercial versus public interest, or in any other commonsense Western terminology. The criterion that really mattered and that could help observers separate media into meaningful groups was their proximity to these less-than-"legitimate" clients, which was related to permanency of cooperation, number of clients, and the ability to voluntarily change their composition. The most successful were the media that were established, legally owned, or informally supported by CIGs and other external agents on a permanent basis. I have termed this formation "domesticated media," since having once sold out to a client who they could not maintain editorial autonomy. It is important that the success of such media did not presuppose profitability, as their masters valued them not for their profitability but for propaganda effectiveness. Another group of less sustainable but slightly more autonomous media were those that would change their main "strategic partner" (backer/wholesale hidden advertiser) from time to time—either because their former partner had refused to cooperate, or because media executives tried to preserve some degree of autonomy. Since this autonomy was limited by the constraints of having to choose between CIGs with hidden agendas, I would call these media organizations "nomadic." Finally, there were what I call the "disposable" media outlets, that is, media organizations that published or broadcast any propaganda material that "flowed" to them by anyone who offered money—that is, they traded their time and space retail.

According to the estimates of the Russian Union of Journalists, in 2000 only about 30 percent of the aggregate income of the Russian media came from legitimate sources (advertising, sales/subscriptions, and legal state funding). The other 70 percent came from those hidden agents of power who used media to wage political battles. In this context, the role of the audience turned out to be that of a silent witness of the media wars between the consortia of private-public backers. In other words, the "mass" media became the means of intra-elite communication. As one of my interviewees put it, the media wars were a precaution "to avoid a real war, with bloodshed, shooting rivals in the streets" (Interview with "Galina," head of department of work with clients at a PR agency, November 2000, Moscow). It is thus not surprising that, neglecting mass audiences, media organizations paid only secondary attention to content aimed at them. For example, according to Kachkaeva (2001), the CIG backing of the leading national TV channel ORT did not invest a penny into its development during the whole period from its privatization in 1995 to its renationlization in 2001.[6] Because of the Russian audience's poverty and the resulting low interest of advertisers in the media, domestic TV production was modest and mostly consisted of in-studio talk and quiz shows, while cheap foreign products were imported in abundance to fill air time. This explains why, for instance, the 1979 Mexican telenovela *The Rich Also Cry* was extremely popular in Russia in the early 1990s.

Thus, the disintegration of the state that resulted in the media's CIG-orientation and the audience's impoverishment led to both the unregulated inflow of "secondhand" international media products into Russia and the absence of international media investors. The forgotten silent audience, fed on a mixed menu of media wars and cheap foreign entertainment, had little influence on this situation in this period. But very little time would pass until the public's irritation and fatigue, coupled with high oil prices, would lead to very important changes in media policy and the broader processes of state and nation rebuilding.

"VERTICAL OF POWER": MEDIA AND RECONSOLIDATION OF THE RUSSIAN STATE (1999–2006)

Changes since the beginning of the new millennium show that in the era of globalization, states may reconsolidate as rapidly as they disintegrate. By reconsolidation I mean the return of the ability of the state to create coherent policies, formulating laws and implementing decisions over the claimed territory. Conventionally the start of this new period may be ascribed to the accession to power of the new prime minister and later president, the former secret police (KGB) officer Vladimir Putin, in mid-1999. The president himself termed the process "construction of the federal vertical of power."[7] Putin started a large-scale reconfiguration of power, using support within enforcement bodies and the contradictory character of Russian legislation. First, he forced out the two CIG leaders who owned Russia's largest media networks, including Media-MOST, and in effect nationalized all three national TV channels. This led to a weakening of the CIGs in general and to the strengthening of all kinds of more traditional formal institutions, including first of all state enforcement bodies and more generally the state itself.

Second, Putin put an end to regional "feudalism" by removing governors from the upper chamber of the Russian parliament and by abolishing gubernatorial elections. A central part of his regional policy also included the military suppression of separatism in Chechnya. Putin's team did not reach social or economic stability in this province, but it managed to eliminate separatists' slogans from official Chechen media and forced separatists underground by bringing to power a Chechen clan loyal to the federal center. Although these moves led to the launch of several illegal newspapers and TV stations, the situation was a radical departure from the earlier period when the separatist regime had the whole Chechen media system at its disposal. Thus Putin effectively removed all official rivals challenging the state's monopoly of power. These radical changes, which have had profound implications for the role of the media in Russian society, met very little resistance anywhere, with the exception of Chechnya.

In this second (post-1999) time period, I characterize the changes in the Russian media industry as marked by centralization, standardization of structure, and selective isolation from global influences. I use the expression "selective isolation" to avoid the impression that Russia firmly cut itself off from the rest of the world; rather there was more control over the inflow of global media content. Thus the term presupposes not decrease in content importation but its more deliberate filtering out and adaptation. It also means the ability to decide which world players can participate in the domestic media game. Earlier I mentioned that scant presence of foreign players in the Russian media market had been its constant trait throughout the entire post-Soviet period. While in the 1990s it happened spontaneously without the insiders' deliberate effort, later, in mid-2001, the Russian parliament adopted an amendment to the Law on Mass Media prohibiting legal entities with more than 50 percent of foreign capital as owners of media organizations in Russia.[8] This decision might appear redundant, but the event took place at the peak of the battle between Putin's team and the Media-MOST CIG. While the new political elite was struggling to replace the owner of Media-MOST, which owns the popular NTV, Gussinsky, the head of Media-MOST, began hastily looking for a foreign company that could buy his share of NTV and thus secure some independence from the authorities. As soon as U.S. media mogul Ted Turner expressed interest in the deal, the restrictive amendment was introduced and quickly passed. It is revealing that in practice this has never hindered the activity of some other media organizations such as Russian MTV, but in the end neither Turner nor any other foreign company bought NTV. In this way, just as economic interest in the Russian media industry by foreign investors started to grow, a political barrier was implemented to anyone targeting the nonentertainment media, especially the public affairs and news sector. At the same time, high costs for satellite TV and Internet access meant that the majority of Russian audiences continued to have access only to domestically produced news and sociopolitical commentary.

The *standardization of the structure* of the media industry means that the typology of domesticated, nomadic, and disposable media gave way to less exotic and more recognizable structures such as are found in many other countries. Private domesticated media conglomerates were partly expropriated from their backers by the state, and partly shifted to the new sector of entertainment media. Media nomads either ceased to exist or (mostly) settled with state bodies of different levels and thus, together with previously domesticated media, formed the core of the new media system. The always modestly successful retail propaganda traders (disposable media) were pushed to the margins of the system and turned into its "underclass." The peripheral position was also now occupied by a few small oppositional media and by relatively independent high-quality analytical periodicals for intellectuals. This latter group was successful but reached a very small proportion of the overall population. Between the political core and the margins, we can trace the emergence of an enormous media sector that closely resembled U.S.-based commercial entertainment media—catering to specific audiences and sold to advertisers—posing almost no challenge to the Putin regime. This outcome was possible because of the improvement of the general economic situation[9] and was speeded up by the regime's deliberate effort to push the media out of the sociopolitical niche earlier occupied by the CIG model.

The *centralization* of the media system was a part of a broader consolidation process described above. In addition to gaining control over all three national TV channels, the state reunited the regional subsidiaries of one of them (Channel 2), widely used in the 1990s by regional leaders for their interests, into one state holding company; a system of terrestrial transmitters able to carry their signal was included in the holding as well. Furthermore, regional media conglomerates controlled by the governors also became centralized as local "feudals" were replaced by figures loyal to Moscow. The general decline of the CIGs and the predictability of elections at all levels also cut the budgets of informational wars, depriving the nonnationalized media of a significant part of their income. The federal political elite increasingly controlled sociopolitical media, especially at the national level. At this point, as the mass media were less and less a forum of intra-elite communication, their vector became directed from elite to mass. Mainstream media now carry less material advertising the interests of particular groups or discrediting these groups' political opponents and were therefore now able to provide public support to the president. Unlike its Soviet predecessors, Putin's team understood that, to mobilize public support, it needed to appeal to a wider mass media audience by going beyond the mere provision of pro-regime news and commentary to include more human interest stories, soft news, and infotainment. Thus the Soviet policy of propaganda plus enlightenment was replaced by post-Soviet propaganda and entertainment.

In public discussions in Russia, this period of Russian media development is often perceived as an authoritarian backlash, as compared with the relatively democratic situation that existed during Yeltsin's time. I would be cautious about this conclusion. It is questionable that the new media system with its rapidly developing commercial sector and relatively diverse oppositional margins is farther from democratic ideals than the media of competing CIGs alien to ordinary citizens. In fact, the new media structure is closer to that of so-called developed democracies.

Furthermore, it is important to note again that Putin came to power not by a military coup but through elections at which people voted for him. He then met only very limited public resistance when he unconstitutionally reduced the governors' authorities, or jailed leading CIG leaders, or when a protest by ten thousand people against the capture of NTV was ignored by the government. In contrast to his predecessor Yeltsin, Putin did not lose public approval ratings because of the start of a Chechen war; quite the opposite, the war *made* Putin's rating.[10] It is true that Putin had not initially been the public's favorite—actually, not a public figure at all—and could not have emerged as a candidate without the help of the leading CIG, closest to Yeltsin (the so-called "Family"). And it is true that the 1999 parliamentary elections were not fair, as they were shaped by the last of the fiercest media wars. But why did the Family choose Putin? Before appointing him prime minister and declaring him his official successor, Yeltsin had changed three prime ministers because all of them were rejected. The answer is that the Family had found Putin to be the most likely to gain enough support—which was confirmed by the rapid growth of his rating in 1999. The next question is, of course, why would people who strongly opposed the anti-reformist coup in 1991 and supported "liberal-democrat" Yeltsin ten years later become ready to vote for the representative of the most notorious ministry, known for enforcing Stalin's repressions back in the 1930s? Let me return to the early 1990s to trace some processes that then were not central, but later played an essential role in these puzzling political shifts.

MEDIA GLOBALIZATION AND WOUNDED NATIONAL IDENTITY

Back in the euphoric period of late 1980s and early 1990s the hopes of the active part of the population for improvement were connected with reforms and associated with Westernization. According to VCIOM polls, even though the vast majority of Russians met the collapse of the USSR with regret, they were adamantly critical about the Soviet regime and society and largely welcomed demilitarization, withdrawal of the Soviet army from Eastern Europe, glasnost, disintegration of the Party, and retreating from "communist ideals" (Gudkov 2004, 147, 538–39). Based on their previous experience people knew that the media had lied to them about Soviet victories and Western failures, and they merely assumed that the situation was quite the opposite. Many people in Russian society believed that all one had to do to achieve a better life was just to copy Western models, particularly economic models. The enthusiasm with which Soviet reformist leaders were accepted in the West created a feeling that the change was not only welcomed but would be vigorously assisted—this was not only a popular belief, but partly a belief of the political elite as well. Everything labeled Western suddenly became prestigious and aroused interest; imported goods were consumed as hungrily as people could only afford to buy them (see also Rantanen 2002, 113–15). "West" was a sign of higher quality; such expressions as "Eurostandard" or "truly American" were enough to advertise a good or a service. Russian words or earlier borrowings from different languages were replaced by newly borrowed English equivalents, or even pseudo-equivalents; in the sphere of the media, for instance, *boyevik* turned to "blockbuster" (*blokbaster*), *film uzhasov* to "thriller" (*triller*), media "genre" (*zhanr*) to "format," *plakat* to "poster," *listovka* to "flyer," and so on.

Therefore, imported content and formats were assumed to increase media popularity, although, of course, the spread of imported products owed much to the economic crisis that affected domestic media production along with other branches of the economy. Moreover, Western media products, unlike other consumer goods, not only meant a higher degree of quality but also implied greater truth and more information about the previously unknown. Solemn news announcers slowly reading from their papers were replaced by Western-style energetic anchors reading from teleprompters, thereby creating an atmosphere of up-to-date-ness and truthfulness (Mickiewicz 1997, 79). American movies and shows copied from American TV filled the screens. First Latin American, and then U.S. soap operas aroused nearly hysterical attachment; the whole villages stopped working when popular serials began (Dubitskaya 1998, 101). The discrepancy between beautiful Western images and everyday painful experience also made everything labeled Russian or Soviet the synonym of poor quality with a sense of general failure. It not only produced a phenomenon that may be called a national inferiority complex but was coupled with the rapid delegitimization of old Soviet rules, symbols, and values. This led to a sense of deprivation of the cultural symbols required to build a new national identity, creating what can be thought of as a "symbolic deficit" (Oushakine 1999). Russian ethnic (or national?) identity in this period was reconfigured to evoke a notion of Russians as passive, patient, and nonefficient (Gudkov 2004, 136). In the first years of the reforms both symbolic deficit and negative identification were almost fully compensated by hopes for rapid "recovery" from the Soviet "disease."

The engagement of the media into intra-elite communication and their decrease of interest in the wider audience left media producers with the above described vision of audience interests; however, these interests kept changing and, upon a closer look, had never been so straightforward as they seemed at first glance. First, some viewers watched imported serials out of pure curiosity about something they had never seen before; since such motivation gets exhausted quite quickly, they soon became critical of and estranged from this type of programming (Dubitskaya 1998, 85–92). Second, the new reliance on advertising also increasingly aroused irritation as people saw their favorite movies interrupted by stories about detergents and other banal consumer goods during the most dramatic scenes. Furthermore, TV commercials intruded quite brutally into the spheres of life that in Soviet culture had been considered private, such as topics connected with the human body — sweat smell, constipation, and especially menstruation (Levinson 2000, 58–62).

Economic hardship, which generally diverted people from any leisure activity, including media consumption, also invoked the public's irritation with glossy images of the rich West presented in ads following imported movies (Levinson 2000, 52–57; Rantanen 2002, 119–24). Moreover, the economic crisis had a deeper effect that brought disenchantment with the ideals of the market and democracy associated with the West and thus disappointment with the West itself. According to VCIOM polls, the percentage of respondents expressing "rather bad" and "very bad" attitudes to the United States grew from 8 percent in late 1991 (collapse of the USSR) to 23 percent in late 1998, a figure that, despite some fluctuations, has virtually never gone below the 1998 level (Gudkov 2004, 506). Anti-Western sentiments reflected the fact that hopes for a quick recovery were gradually vanishing and giving way to frustration and hopeless envy. As opinion polls demonstrated, throughout the second half of the decade respondents with negative attitudes to life prevailed over "optimists" (Gudkov 2004, 277), and the wider social situation was mostly perceived as catastrophic both in public opinion and news.

FROM NATIONAL INFERIORITY COMPLEX TO *NAZIONALISM*

By the mid-1990s, the thirst for national symbols was so immense that President Yeltsin created a special commission of scholars to "elaborate the national idea"—which ultimately failed to accomplish this goal. Meanwhile more spontaneous explorations of identity were taking place in the media and in the broader context of popular culture. First, the emptiness of the category of *rossiysky narod* and the dominance of ethnic Russians led to the merging of Russian ethnic and national identity. Public opinion firmly associated the inhabitants of Russia with ethnic Russians, and the idea of "Russia for [ethnic] Russians" was increasing in popularity at the turn of the new century (Gudkov 2004, 193). Second, given the deficit of positive symbols, the search for identity took the form of negative self-identification in contrast to an alien and hostile other, and this identity itself was constructed not as a set of particular features, but in binary opposition between universal categories of "us" against "them." Along with the domestic power elite, the obvious other became the West. Western media formats by no means were an obstacle to anti-Western content. This merging—a case of what Robertson (1995, 29–31) called glocalization—was manifest in some media forms more than in others. And below I consider two of the media forms that have been touched on before—news and commercials.

Throughout the 1990s advertisers in Russia were mostly foreign. It was they who, acting through their associations and advertising agencies, gave a start to Russian commercial audience research and the rating system on TV.

In the late 1990s, standardized polls conducted by the advertising industry showed that the most highly rated products were, along with news, old Soviet comedies and songs. Media-MOST was the pioneer in recognizing this trend by introducing Soviet movies and music into its schedule—as energetically as it had been introducing Western-style news and imported movies in the mid-1990s. The discovery of interest in Soviet-made media led professionals to attempt domestic production, and producers of commercials to hurriedly seek domestic images. Initially, attempts to introduce "authentic" Russian images were clumsy in their ironic use of Soviet historical characters and ideological clichés. Very quickly, however, a nostalgic use of symbols associated with Soviet everyday life became a great and stable success. Brands with Russian names, including archaic ones, had broad appeal as well. Moreover, the opposition between Russian and foreign became a marketable symbolic mode of address. In one TV ad for domestic juice, a grandfather in a traditional Russian setting preaches to his grandson: "What's good of *their* apples? Only chemicals. Have you ever seen me fertilizing *my* apples with any trash?" This change in public opinion led to a radical and almost overnight swing in the strategies adopted by foreign advertisers. Siemens launched the slogan "Going the way of progress together with Russia." But perhaps the champion was Philip Morris, with this slogan for its Peter the Great cigarettes: "Return blow—our reply to America" (Gudkov 2004, 797).

This change in popular media taste might not have appeared without a brief wave of political mobilization in the late 1990s in response to NATO's campaign against Yugoslavia,[11] an event that was quite global in its origin. This military action coincided with Yeltsin's first attempt to try a candidate with both journalism and KGB experience as prime minister, which brought about important changes to Russian news production. Yevgheny Primakov, an elderly candidate associated with the Soviet Union when it was one of the world's two superpowers, tried to play an active role in the Yugoslav conflict after many years of passive Russian foreign policy. It was perhaps this sharp contrast that made many media organizations join those controlled by Yeltsin's team to form a patriotic chorus. As one could judge from media coverage in 1999, especially at the very beginning of the bombings, the heroes of the conflict were the Russian prime minister and his assistants bravely defending a helpless Slavic victim-state from a shameless aggressor. Although such "home-centered" coverage of international issues is typical, for instance, of American news, for post-Soviet Russia it was a novelty. Images of victims in Russian and Western media also resembled inverted mirrors of each other: Europeans and Americans were shown images of the endless sufferings of Yugoslav Albanians (including stories on concentration camps and mass murders, later questioned by many scholars, journalists, and public figures [see, e.g., Collon 2002, 24–79]). Russian viewers saw destroyed buildings in Belgrade and stories about Albanian terrorism against Kosovar Serbs; "pro-Yugoslav" stories outnumbered "pro-NATO" items by three to four times (Liberman 1999). The rise of hostility in public opinion in Russia and the United States to each other was also quite symmetrical.[12] Public opinion polls showed that the proportion of those critical of the United States in Russia had grown from 8 to 23 percent during the 1990s; in May 1999 (the period of the NATO bombings) criticism reached its peak with 54 percent; the proportion of those regarding the United States "rather well" and "very well" dropped from the 65 to 71 percent it had comprised in the previous decade to unprecedented 32 percent (Gudkov 2004, 506). Although later Russians' attitude to the United States improved, it never reached the level of the 1990s.

Thus the Yugoslav story had a number of important consequences for the articulation of Russian national identity. Despite the failure of Primakov's policy, the political elite learned a useful lesson: the event showed how mobilization against an external enemy could become a basis for national consolidation. It is not surprising that in mid-1999 Putin's presidential "pre-electoral" campaign began with a military action in Chechnya similar to the one which five years earlier had ruined Yeltsin's public approval. Although Putin's first steps were cautious, the scale of the operation gradually grew from the withdrawal of armed Chechen separatists from the neighboring province of Dagestan to the advance of the federal troops deep into Chechnya, to heavy bombings of its capital in early 2000. The increasing violence was not spontaneous: the deeper into the campaign, the more the Russian population supported a military solution to the conflict increasing Putin's popularity in polls (Zadorin 1999).

This evolution of public opinion can be partially explained by changes in the structure of the media. First, the decisiveness of the pro-Putin team revealed itself in its ability to mobilize resources in all spheres, not only in the Chechen conflict, but also in its struggle against competing CIGs, most notably Media-MOST and its partner presidential candidates. Therefore, by fall 1999, Media-MOST was significantly weakened and could not offer large-scale oppositional coverage. What is more interesting is the fact that public opinion shielded itself from nonofficial viewpoints. Thus, although at that time stories about atrocities of the federal troops in Chechnya still could find their way to national media, about two-thirds of the population refused to believe in them. The resonant story of Russian colonel Budanov, who had raped and murdered a Chechen girl, aroused the disbelief of about a third of the respondents; the majority of the rest thought he deserved at least leniency (Gudkov 2004, 337). This defensive reaction revealed the depths of the nation's fatigue with the negative national images that bombarded audiences during the 1990s. This fatigue in its turn was used by political elites in their policy to reduce critical coverage of all spheres of contemporary Russian life and to substitute it with stories of success and infotainment. Along with economic improvement, this fatigue is one of the major factors that explain the growth of entertainment production in the next decade.

Second, the Yugoslav conflict gave political elites grounds to accuse the "West" of double standards when it criticized Russia for its brutal intrusion into Chechnya. Furthermore, the West was regarded as hypocritical on a more general level: it is now blamed for not assisting Russia in its sincere attempts to build a market economy and, moreover, for imposition of models that were inappropriate in Russia. From a teacher and missionary the West reverted back to its earlier role of an agent of economic and cultural imperialism, responsible for Russia's internal problems. Conversely, the Soviet past turned from a historical mistake to an object of nostalgia. It is now associated not with goods shortage, bureaucratic stagnation, and absence of truthful news, but with "order," stability, paternalistic protection, modest well-being, and egalitarian justice. By the end of the millennium, opinion polls registered that Russians increasingly believed that their country was under the threat of being robbed by hypocritical foreigners and that, instead of Westernizing, it should seek its own path to development. In this context it is very important to recognize that Putin offered an image of a leader to the nation that was not completely negative. In contrast to the aged and sickly Yeltsin, the young, energetic Putin was associated with long-expected "order," paternalistic protection, stability, and, as the world oil prices went up,with economic well-being. In fact, Putin fulfilled the Soviet-nostalgic expectations of the Russian people. For these reasons, Putin's KGB background not only was seen as non-threatening but symbolically confirmed the probability that such expectations would come true. However, Putin was much more polysemic and offered Russians a skillful blend of symbols of past and present: thus, he approved Yeltsin's choice of the new national flag (the tricolor borrowed from pre-Bolshevik imperial Russia), restored the melody of the Soviet anthem, and supplied it with new post-Soviet lyrics. Reclaiming its (mythologized) historical past along with the good news about the (mythologically) improving present, the nation regained an abundance of material for the creation of its identity, symbols, and other cultural goods, including media products. In 2004, the proportion of domestic serials on national TV exceeded 50 percent and a Russian-produced film outperformed all its foreign competitors in terms of revenues for the first time since 1991.[13]

CONCLUSION: LESSONS FROM RUSSIA

When in 2005 Andrey Illarionov talked about the "Iranization" of Russia, he pointed, in an alarmed manner, at some commonalities in people's reaction to globalization in both countries. Whether the Iranian case should be necessarily viewed as a danger is beyond the scope of this article, but the intention to compare Russia to others and to find its place in the external world is important both as a new tendency of the Russian public discourse and as a question for comparative media studies. Generally, we may discern several levels of the relevance of international (media) experience for Russia and, correspondingly, the significance of Russia's experience for the rest of the world.

First, the feeling of humiliation connected with the loss of high international status may be found in all postimperial societies as a potential source of nationalism. More broadly, *nazionalism* may emerge from any feeling of deprivation or defeat, and here Russia displays many similarities to Germany's frustrations after World War I that resulted in the rise of fascism. While the fear of such an outcome led the international community to cushion the consequences of deprivation for Germany, Italy, and Japan after World War II, half a century later Russia's hopes for such interventionist policies were in vain. Perhaps a reason is that Russia's contemporary weakness is thought to guarantee the world from its expansionist ambitions, forcing it to remain in a state of defensive isolation.

Second, a wary attitude to globalization combined with the desire to import Western economic success is typical for many "developing" countries, because of their history of modernization as external "intrusion." Virtually everywhere in such countries attempts to resolve this tension lead to what in Russia is called the "Westerners-Slavophiles" dispute and to searches for the country's "own way." Given these tensions, it is not surprising that many countries make pendulum-like movements to and from openness to international influences: both the Russian and Iranian cases fit into this scheme. The striking difference in Iran is, however, that the sources of its traditionalization and isolation were global in origin and literally came from abroad with illegally imported small media (see, e.g., Sreberny-Mohammadi and Mohammadi 1994), while Russian nationalism more trivially emerged from within the Russian media mainstream. However, the general path of both countries indeed has much in common. So it is not a unique Russian trait that after opening a new media market to global winds a country becomes flooded with imported media production, but after a while domestic products return supported both by revived popular interest and protectionist barriers. To be fair, Russia's 50 percent limit for foreign ownership in the media is relatively mild—milder than in such countries as France, Greece, and Japan.

Third, the most general anxiety about national identity and fear of external threats may be found everywhere, not only at the margins of the globe, but also at its core; for example, Schlesinger (2002, 644–46) points at the spread of such phenomena in Europe. The study here does not provide enough data to decide whether this is a universal effect of globalization or a tendency only remotely connected with globalization. What is more obvious from the Russian example is that a popular feeling of threat does not necessarily mean that globalization threatens nation-states and/or the institution of statehood. Rather, the Russian experience shows that only certain types of states fail to adapt to changing conditions, and even they may return very quickly in a better-adjusted form. As long as the legitimacy of the state's monopoly on rule making and violence is not questioned by people within given territories, states may enforce their will without much resistance. Furthermore, although the initial push toward the collapse of the Soviet Union might have been global, the first post-Soviet decade demonstrates that major threats to the state have been rather domestic than international. In the geographical dimension the Russian state was threatened by the loss of loyalty of certain local elites and/or populations. In the institutional dimension it was threatened by privatization of the state, as an extreme form of clientelism and corruption. The chaotic inflow of foreign influences was thus not a cause of state disintegration but its by-product, which later was not stopped but taken under domestic control.

Fourth, different dimensions of a country's development (globalization-isolation, state disintegration–consolidation, and authoritarianization-democratization) appear to be not necessarily closely connected, and again here Russia is a vivid, though not a unique example. As I have tried to show in this chapter, an analysis of Russia's movement along the first two axes explains Russian transformation much more adequately and profoundly than the conceptualization of recent Russian history in terms of democratic theories. Despite the widespread clichés about Putin, the characterization of his regime as more authoritarian than Yeltsin's is disputable. Understanding the changes in the degree of state consolidation and of the country's integration into global systems reveals a much richer picture of the ongoing social change. Finally, another "independent" dimension here is that of the media, which have played an absolutely ambivalent role in this multifaceted development. Depending on the situation, media could contribute to diversification and unification of public discourse, play to the hands of those subverting the state or those struggling for its consolidation, and promote international influences or nationalism. After all, the media are equally necessary to construct both national and global identities, as well as loyalties both to the state and to separate interest groups—all of them are bases for different types of imagined communities that should be maintained across space and time.

NOTES

1. VCIOM is the oldest (and therefore state-owned) research polling institute in Russia, founded in 1987; its reliability is confirmed by correspondence of its major results to those of other (nonstate) leading polling organizations, such as FOM, ROMIR, and Levada-Center. In its regular poll system, Omnibus, VCIOM uses multistep stratified territorial random samples ranging from 1100 (in the early 1990s) to 1600 (in 2006) respondents. VCIOM was chosen here because it is the only polling organization that covers the period of the early 1990s. Results of its numerous polls concerning Russian national identity and attitudes to key issues of Russian life are collected and analyzed in the volume *Negative Identity* by a well-known VCIOM expert, Lev Gudkov (2004), on which I rely in later sections of my chapter.

2. Chechnya is a rural Moslem republic at the Russian-Georgian border; with few of its own oil beds left, it has a crucial significance as a transit region that links Caspian oil with the Black Sea and Europe. It is the only Russian region that on the way to its sovereignty went as far as having its own military forces, ignoring federal taxes, and introducing Shariat law. As a result it was almost completely destroyed during the two wars with the "Federal Center" (1994–1996 and 1999–?).

3. A Russian journalistic expression, often used in reference to Chechnya.

4. The governor got rid of his criminal promoter two years after his victory, although in another year he himself perished in a strange helicopter catastrophe.

5. As many media professionals I interviewed termed it.

6. In 1995 Boris Berezovsky, the leader of the CIG closest to President Yeltsin's family, or, more precisely, a CIG merged with the family, lobbied a plan for the privatization of Russia's best national channel according to which 49 percent of it would be distributed among a narrow number of private shareholders, while 51 percent would stay with the state. Later Berezovsky acquired the whole privatized stock, but independently of his official share he was the one who determined all policies at the channel, which, though, were nearly identical or at least quite close to those of the Kremlin.

7. The Russian word *vlast* used by Putin, besides "power," also means "authorities."

8. The "Law of the Russian Federation On Mass Media," N 2124-1, December 27, 1991, was amended by the law "On amendment of the Law of the Russian Federation 'On Mass Media,'" N 107-??, April 8, 2001, after its passage article 19.1 reads: "A foreign legal entity, as well as a Russian legal entity with a foreign participation, wherever the share (input) of the foreign participation in the stock (joint) capital equals or exceeds 50 percent, a citizen of the Russian Federation with a dual citizenship, may not act as founders of television, video programs." To understand this clause correctly it is necessary to know that notion of "founder" is the only substitute for "media owner" in Russian legislation on media, and television and video programs are the only possible kinds of broadcast visual mass media.

9. While from 1990 to 1998 the Russian GDP dropped by approximately 45 percent, from 1999 to 2006 it almost returned to its initial level, comprising, by the preliminary estimates of results of the year 2006, about 96 percent of the GDP of year 1990. See numerous materials of the Ministry of Economic Development and Trade of the Russian Federation at its website, www.economy.gov.ru: for example, the extended interview of the minister of economic development and trade with RIA Novosti, June 5, 2006, at www.economy.gov.ru/wps/portal/!ut/p/.cmd/cp/.c/6_0_3T1/.ce/7_0_92P/.p/5_0_7DH/.pm/H?helpMode=Detail_default.jsp&documentId=1149588523406.

10. During the second half of 1999, when the second Chechen war started and reached its culmination by the New Year, Putin's rating grew from 2 percent in July, when he was appointed, to 48 percent in December—an unprecedented level for any politician of that time (see e.g., Zadorin 1999). It happened against the background of overwhelming popular support of the Chechen campaign, which contrasted so much with negative attitudes to the first war (see, e.g., Gudkov 2004, 328–38). Many social scientists, including Zadorin, directly connect these facts.

11. Expressing discontent with the human rights of the Albanian population of the then Yugoslav province Kosovo, the U.S. administration insisted on military interference that culminated with bombings of Belgrade in May 1999 and with international occupation of Kosovo. Russia was against this plan, which led to extreme tension between it and the United States, actually, the first serious tension after the Cold War. Russia lost, and Yugoslav president Milosevic was overthrown the same year.

12. The general level of hostility of Americans toward Russia was higher both before and after the crisis, but its maximum during the conflict was nearly equal, so the rise was not as sharp as in Russia (Gudkov 2004, 504).

13. The fact that the Russian fantasy movie *Night Guard* became an absolute post-Soviet box office best-seller, outperforming in Russian cinemas such films as *The Lord of the Rings: Return of the King, Spiderman 2*, and *Troy*, was widely reported—see, for example, stories on the leading online daily Utro.ru at www.utro.ru/news/2004/08/03/336352.shtml or on the fantasy website Olmer at http://olmer.ru/book/2004filmkom.shtml.

4

Regional Crisis, Personal Solutions: The Media's Role in Securing Neoliberal Hegemony in Singapore

Soek-Fang Sim

THE CHALLENGE OF GOVERNING NEOLIBERAL SOCIETIES: WHY IDEOLOGY (AND THE MEDIA) MATTERS

The fundamental challenge of governing a neoliberal society has been variously articulated. For Hall (see Tamney 1996, 184), the basic contradiction within capitalist society is that "if you drive the notion of enterprise far enough, you undermine any sense of tradition, or organic belongingness to society." Elsewhere, I (Sim 2001) described the contradictions of late capitalism as the emergence of welfare demands in a context where capitalism generates intense social inequality. This contradiction typically engenders "third way solutions" (Giddens 1994), which involve the weakening of capitalistic impulses and the affirmation of some form of collectivism. In the United States and Europe, these are illustrated in the various degrees of compromise between the left and right in the form of welfare states or the provision of social security.

This challenge—of balancing competitiveness and its consequence of intense inequality—is well understood by the People's Action Party (PAP), the one-party government in Singapore. Terming this as "the price of success," the PAP considers the challenge of governing advanced capitalism as a question of how to "maintain social cohesion and manage growing income differences between the highly educated . . . and those who are less skilled and less mobile" (*Straits Times,* June 7, 1997). The challenge is then, in creating a globally competitive society, how is it possible to get losers to accept that competition is not only fair but necessary so that there is mass support and social cohesion behind the ideology of competitiveness?

In responding to this contradiction, the "Western" path of compromise was seen as an inferior solution, not least because its legitimacy often depended on economic growth generated by foreign investments, which could be secured only if societies remained extremely capital friendly and nonprotectionist. If neoliberalism denotes a mode of global market capitalism based upon free trade and where the fewer hindrances there are to it (e.g., protectionism of domestic labor or commodities), the closer an economy can be said to be enshrining neoliberal values, then Singapore, as the world's freest economy with the best workforce (including "worker attitude," according to Business Environment Risk Intelligence 2002), is indisputably the best model of neoliberal governance and serves as an excellent case study for neoliberal hegemony.

In this introductory section, I will explain some of Singapore's neoliberal features and how the PAP has been able to create "welfare" without compromising competitiveness. Given the complex challenge involved, its response is necessarily also complicated, which has led some scholars to describe Singapore as "capitalism with socialist characteristics" (Vogel cited in Tamney 1996, 69).

Invoked in praise of a public housing scheme that allows 88 percent of the population to "own" their own homes (for 99 years), Vogel's description ignored the historical context that triggered the need for state housing in the first place—that is, the use of the highly coercive Land Acquisition Act (1966) inherited from British colonial rule that allowed the PAP to acquire any land deemed necessary for national development at a rate of compensation determined by the state (B. Chua 1995, 130). By destroying traditional communities and land-based subsistence and by inflicting housing debts, the scheme compelled many to sell their labor to have a home. Along with health and pension schemes that work on the principle of forced contributions and savings, these schemes sought to make proletarians out of autonomous subjects (Sim 2005) rather than to redistribute wealth. Furthermore, these schemes do not provide universal benefits but are available only to those who work. Within popular discourse, this so-called socialism has been dubbed "Singapore Inc."—where benefits accrue not from citizenship but from employment within the national economy.

More importantly, what makes Singapore's model of capitalism superior is its ability to ensure that those who need welfare get it, but not from the state or corporations. Here, I will examine the two instances when welfare demands arose and how the PAP dealt with them. The late 1980s and early 1990s were periods of unprecedented competitiveness, prosperity, and social inequality. Alarmed by the problem of "abandoned elderly," the discourse of the Westernized, overcompetitive *kiasu* (local slang for "afraid to lose out") Singaporean emerged and became constructed as a social problem, the antidote to which was "Asian Values." In particular, filial piety was invoked to justify the Parents Maintenance Bill (which was copied by Taiwan, China, and India). In this way, Asian values allowed for the emergence of "Asian Capitalism" (unlike Western welfare capitalism), in which welfare was organized through the family.

In 2001, during the Asian economic crisis, when Singapore was experiencing its worst recession since independence, the PAP's strategy of organizing welfare transformed significantly. As part of an election strategy to "sweeten the ground," the "New Singapore Shares" (sums of money) were distributed to all Singaporeans, with lower-income citizens given more shares. Given that this was the first time public funds were used to help the unemployed, some have upheld it as a socialist gesture (Seah 2001). However, it is important to note that this compromise was a one-off measure rather than a social contract based on a new consensus or ideological compromise. The question has never been how to institute schemes to protect workers from the hardship and vagaries of the market; competitiveness has long been considered the backbone of national survival for a country that imagines itself as a small city-state with no natural resources.

What makes Singapore a model of neoliberalism then is not only its miraculous economic growth or its relatively uncompromised model of capitalism but its success in "embedding market values and structures not within economic, but also within social and political life" (Rodan 2004, 1). The PAP's immense success in persuading citizens to accept an economic and social order based on neoliberal principles has been praised by world leaders and is an object of envy among its rivals. President Bush called Singapore "an example for . . . the world of the transforming power of economic freedom and open market" (White House 2003), while British prime minister Blair considered it "the best illustration of the parallel achievements of economic success and social cohesion" (*Financial Times*, January 10, 1996). Faced with workers' protests at home, officials in Taiwan and Hong Kong expressed envy that the PAP was able to get Singaporeans to "tighten their belts" and accept austere policies (e.g., a wage freeze, retrenchment, welcoming foreign talents to compete for domestic jobs) aimed at making the economy more competitive.

It is my argument that it is this social cohesion—the successful universalization of elite perspective or hegemony—that is the basis of the PAP's one-party legitimacy. Contrary to theses that argue for the affinity between free markets and liberal democracy (cf. Fukuyama 1992), not only does the PAP's successful blending of neoliberalism and authoritarianism in the form of neoliberal hegemony offer a vital counterexample and model that is admired by authoritarian and democratic countries alike, but its unparalleled success also suggests that neoliberalism may best be administered by (hegemonic) authoritarian states. Elsewhere, I (Sim 2001, 2005) called this the logic of one-party dominance: a one-party government can only legitimately claim to represent a consensual/cohesive nation since an ideologically fragmented nation would require multiparty representation; that is, ideological fragmentation (e.g., different definitions of the causes and solutions to the economic crisis) must be averted at all costs. To the extent that subjects share rather than challenge the PAP's vision and definition of reality (what *is* the crisis and *thus* what is the solution), what is precipitated is consensus or a common sense of the situation.

If my thesis—that the PAP's success rests on ideology—appears self-evident, it is something that is far from evident in terms of theory since scholars continue to trace the basis of the PAP's power to coercion or economic performance. Even while acknowledging that Singapore is a "classic example" of hegemonic electoral authoritarianism (Diamond 2002), scholars ignore the factor of ideology (and the role of the media). Focusing on its authoritarianism, political scientists devote their attention to making lists of the coercive regulations that abound in Singapore (cf. Thompson 2001; Means 1996). Alternatively, political economists trace the PAP's legitimacy to Singapore's miraculous economic performance and seek to identify the causes (e.g., its "vassal state" status to the United States during the Cold War or historical and contemporary United States trade subsidies; see Castells 1988 and Wade 2004 respectively).[1] While there is no denying that Singapore is "an offshore center for foreign capital" (Yoshihara 1988, 71) and "a stable and efficient vehicle for the Western exploitation of Southeast Asia" (Mirza 1986, 73), what is problematic is that the net effect of both perspectives is the suggestion that citizens comply with PAP policies out of fear or bribery, rather than because they consent to the PAP's definition of reality.

There are two problems with such analyzes. Firstly, historical evidence suggests that these theses are either inaccurate or increasingly obsolete. Coercive laws exist, although they are seldom used and never invoked without ideological justification, for example, the arrest of Jemaah Islamiyah members for terrorism in 2002 and the detaining of six persons for espionage in 1997–1998 under the Internal Security Act (which allows the government to detain without trial) was generally seen by citizens as legitimate and necessary for national security; otherwise, the act had not been invoked since 1987, when it was used to curtail what was termed as "a Marxist conspiracy." Additionally, the PAP appears to be less reliant on coercion upon the realization that rather than censoring dissent, it needed to "respond decisively, convincingly, and stylishly," such as by sending members of the PAP Youth Wing into cyberspace to debate, "correct and convince" discussion groups (Rodan 1997, 79).

There are also problems with the economic legitimacy thesis—there is a lack of correspondence (and even an inverse relationship) between economic performance and legitimacy. In the late 1980s, when Singapore was at the height of its miraculous economic growth, the PAP was confronted with "the price of success"—a liberal middle class accustomed to consumerist choices began demanding political choice, which led to the end of the PAP's parliamentary monopoly. In November 2001, when Singapore was experiencing its worst recession in history, the PAP improved its electoral popularity by 10 percent to 75.3 percent.

That political legitimacy can strengthen in face of an economic crisis nicely illustrates the incongruity between economic performance and economic legitimacy; an economic crisis does not necessarily trigger a political crisis, nor does an economic miracle translate directly into strong legitimacy. If ideology "expresses a will, a hope or a nostalgia, rather than [describes] a reality" (Althusser 1969, 234), then legitimacy is less about sustaining double-digit growth than an ideological question of keeping citizens' dreams alive. It is problematic to assume that material realities such as economic growth or crisis are ontological, prediscursive entities; the case of Singapore suggests that realities such as "economic performance" and "economic crisis" are themselves ideologically mediated. The PAP embarked on a long and hard media project to ensure that citizens understood that the crisis was "Asian" and thus not to be blamed on the PAP.

This essay examines the PAP's project to persuade journalists and citizens that the many highly viable alternative ways of perceiving the crisis were irrelevant and that its definition of the crisis and (neoliberal) solution was the only alternative. I first set up a theoretical framework to think about who/what determines common sense, focusing on the debate between media power and active audience. I then illustrate the hegemonic process by identifying the strategies used by the state to control the media and shape public discourse and contrast the official framing of the crisis with those in the media and popular discourse. Arguing that popular consent to the PAP's representation of reality owes as much to its ideological sophistication as to its strategic control of the means of representation (media), I offer an enfolded argument (via ideological analysis) in the conclusion as to why political economy still matters.

THE SOURCES OF COMMON SENSE:
BETWEEN POWERFUL MEDIA AND ACTIVE AUDIENCE

To reject the coercion and economic legitimacy theses and to take ideology seriously requires three fundamental shifts in the way we theorize the relationship between subjects and power—that subjects have agency, that agents are not only guided by the "dull compulsion of the economic" (Abercrombie, Hill, and Turner 1980), but that what constitutes economic necessity and success is shaped by a shared system of meanings, and that this common sense is experienced as organic and natural even if it is only "the people's sense of itself" as reflected by the political elite (Nowell-Smith 1977, 13). In this section, I address the questions of where common sense comes from and how to identify it.

The debate about the origins of common culture has been polarized into two camps—one emphasizing media power and effects, and the other emphasizing the active audience. While theories about elite domination of the media and ideology abound, their credibility has been challenged by criticisms from a very potent source—studies that examine these media effects empirically. In the face of waves of criticisms from audience studies, some theories have undergone revision in the attempt to take "the popular" seriously.

Among the theories of media power, political economy has been especially dominant. Following Marx's observations that the ruling ideas in each epoch are the ideas of the ruling class, political economists have focused on the study of media ownership and regulation. However, the significance of these studies is based upon the assumption of economic determinism. If we do not accept that those who own the means of production also shape our symbolic universe, why should we be concerned about who owns the media?

While few would challenge the facts of media conglomeration, these facts rely on audience research to give them meaning and significance. In the founding years of audience studies in the United States, where researchers "found" strong and direct effects of TV violence (Gerbner 1976), there was hardly any need for political economists to reflect on its assumptions of media effects, which were then considered self-evident.

Subsequent waves of audience studies presented serious challenges to theses of media power. The first challenge centered on the problematique of structure and agency, with scholars critiquing "hypodermic" models of audience effects (Morley 1980) and insisting that while "preferred meanings" may be encoded into media products, there is no guarantee that these will be the meanings decoded by an active audience (Hall 1980).

A more serious challenge came from the poststructuralist criticisms of essentialism. Deriving ever more nuanced insights into everyday life, researchers emphasized the unsystematizable and contradictory nature of popular discourse and rejected the possibility of making any generalizations about "the audience" or even about "the individual" as if it is a cognitive, coherent individual with ready-made "opinions" inside its head. Some theorists situated meaning intertextually as a product between the various media and social texts encountered by subjects; Fiske (1986) went so far as to declare the existence of a "semiotic democracy," directly challenging theories of media effects. Others situated meaning contextually, arguing that meaning depends on the questions asked (Zaller 1992). Still others argued that subjects contradict themselves because of the dilemmatic nature of ideology (Billig 1991) and the fragmented nature of common sense (Gramsci 1971).

By inserting ambivalence and contradiction into the heart of its analysis, audience studies arrived resolutely at the end of sociology and its privileged category of analysis—the individual—and entered decisively into a discursive epoch. This criticism goes far beyond the structure-agency project to salvage the individual as an active agent; it amounts to the deconstruction of (and rejection of the possibility of knowing) the very categories of "individual," "popular," and "audience."

It is in this context that we can appreciate contemporary attempts to rearticulate theories of media power without reconstructing the audience or the popular, not even as sociologically fragmented or contextually fragmented. One particular persuasive attempt comes from hegemony theory as interpreted by Hall (1997). Fusing poststructuralist and Marxist theories, meaning is seen to be intrinsically arbitrary and any fixity of meaning or coherence is achieved through acts of power. That meaning is temporary and fragile implies first that the project of hegemony is hard ideological work on an everyday basis to privilege one arbitrary association of signs (e.g., crisis = economic = Asian) over others (e.g., crisis = moral = corruption as in the case of Indonesia). Second, it neatly solves the question of agency by distinguishing an active audience from a powerful one (Ang 1995, 247). Subjects might question or doubt certain constructions of reality, but they have little control over which constructions circulate in public discourse.

While hegemony provides us with a theory to connect media power with an active audience, it does not provide us with ready analytical concepts for identifying hegemony empirically. At least, we know that the media power/effects method of seeking a match between elite and individual opinion would not suffice because everyday discourse is rarely without contradiction and not easily classifiable, and that a method based on hegemony theory would need to foreground the heterogeneity, incoherence, and contradictions in common sense. Here, I propose two ways of identifying hegemony. Minimally, hegemony could be understood as limits to variations. Leys (1990, 127) argued that "for an ideology to be hegemonic, it is not necessary that it is loved, merely that it has no serious rivals"—a description that succinctly captured the "not lovable, but electable" (*New York Times,* June 4, 2001) Tony Blair during the British elections. Maximally, hegemony could be indicated by the presence of shared values or even identification with leaders' visions. For instance, citizens' emotional identification with PAP leaders as "the Fathers of Singapore" can transform ordinary authoritarianism into "popular dictatorship."

In the next three sections, I examine official strategies of securing hegemony—in terms of both limiting discursive variations and building consensus—and evaluate whether and how they are reproduced in media and popular discourse.

In terms of data sources, official discourse is gleaned from speeches and policies initiated during the Asian economic crisis and its proposed antidote, the Singapore 21 project. Data for media discourse was generated by a Lexus-Nexus search for "Singapore 21" in the *Straits Times* (*ST*) between 1997 and1998, which generated thirty-seven articles (twenty-four news, thirteen nonnews). The *ST* is the most widely read daily in Singapore and has a circulation size of 398,248. Founded in 1845 and printed in English, it is regionally recognized as a credible newspaper and was named Newspaper of the Year by the Australian-based Pacific Area Newspaper Publishers' Association in 2002.

Data for popular discourse were collected through field research. Heeding Mattelart's (1994, 234) criticism of audience studies' tendency to reify consumer sovereignty and "leav[e] . . . no place for other issues than those related to consumption" and guided by my interest in longitudinal ideological effects rather than reactions to specific campaigns, I spent eight months in 1997–1998 interviewing citizens of different generation, race, gender, and class for at least two hours each, with thirty-two citizens selected based on a combination of the snowball and skip methods (in the skip method, individuals who recommended others were "skipped" in the hope of diluting whatever ideological proximity might exist). Although the focus of the fieldwork was not the economic crisis, it was a subject that interviewees chose to talk about extensively. Since my conceptualization of hegemony requires that I foreground heterogeneity and discursive variations as much as limits and consensus, my field research focused on citizens' dilemmas and hesitations as these seemed to be the best illustrations of the "structures of feelings" that are negotiated in everyday life, allowing us to see ideological contestations in "live" and embodied contexts.

CAPTURING THE MIDDLE GROUND: FROM REGULATING THE MEDIA TO CHANGING MIND-SETS

The PAP's strategies of managing dissent have shifted away from direct control of the media to the subtle project of ideological domination. This by no means suggests the obsolescence of political economy perspectives (that focus on means of direct control such as regulation and ownership); however, it does raise an urgent question about the continued relevance of political economy and compel us to explain *why* political economy matters. It is my argument that where political economy *really* matters is its impact on ideological processes; however, since this is an argument that is better made after some discussion of how ideology works, I will make this argument only in the conclusion. Here, I will focus on the PAP's strategies of managing dissent and securing consensus, or in its own words, the project of "capturing the middleground."

The Singapore media operate in an environment that is highly structured by the state, not only in terms of regulation of the degree of liberalization of the media industry, but also ideologically, through government projects to influence journalistic practices and mold public discourse. Unlike the situation in many "dependent-integrated" Third World countries such as the Philippines or Mexico (Sussman 1995, 2001) where domestic media are largely influenced and even owned and operated by transnational media, the PAP is careful to put constraints on foreign ownership to ensure that social morality and public discourse are not hijacked by Western values but guided by its own unique interpretation of Asian values. This care to not cede ideological control to transnational media is clear in its strategy of liberalizing the local media—rather than invite global media to compete with domestic media (which is generally the case in non-media industries), the PAP's Media 21 policy (to restructure the media industries for the twenty-first century; see below) sought to make domestic monopolies compete with each other.

In terms of regulation, the Newspapers and Printing Press Act and the Undesirable Publications Ordinance allow the government to refuse the annual renewal of the license to practice journalism and to censor or ban publications that are "likely to cause ill will or misunderstanding between the government and the people of Singapore" (Borkhurst-Heng 2002, 566). Media technologies are also regulated. Rodan (1997) observes that the PAP goes to extraordinary lengths to demonstrate its technical capacity to monitor usage of the Internet by scanning public Internet accounts and argues that such practices have a chilling effect on local politics.

The PAP exerts tremendous influence on the newspaper industry through its decisions to selectively centralize and liberalize. In 1978, there were eleven dailies and by 1985, there were only seven despite a significant increase in readership. Today, Singapore has eight dailies in four languages serving a population of four million. This has been the direct consequence of a series of mergers and closures during the mid-1980s that created a controlled newspaper monopoly under the Singapore Press Holdings (SPH) with government endorsement. In 2000 under the "Media 21" initiative (to strengthen local media industries to compete globally in the twenty-first century), the SPH's monopoly was broken with the approval of a government-owned Media Corporation of Singapore to publish newspapers; in turn, the SPH was granted the right to compete in broadcasting. By September 2004, this project of liberalizing the media had clearly failed; economically, the Singapore market did not generate sufficient advertising revenue to sustain competitive corporations while politically, scholars observed that the period of liberalization had only generated tabloids "devoid of critical content" (Borkhurst-Heng 2002, 564) and argued that liberalization ought to be understood as a strategy to shore up the credibility and popularity of a government-controlled media industry (Rodan 2003, 509).

Besides regulating the media, the PAP also undertakes ideological projects to influence journalistic practices. During the 1990s, Southeast Asian journalists were encouraged to imagine an Asian model of journalism (also called "development journalism") based on "nation-building" rather than Western "watchdog" journalism. For instance, President Aquino (Philippines) exhorted journalists to build up rather than tear down, while Malaysian prime minister Mahathir argued that media are not elected but privately owned and thus have no business criticizing the government.

Besides targeting journalistic beliefs with occasional campaigns, the PAP also targets citizens' common sense by ensuring that official framings of reality monopolize the public sphere, with no credible space being available for alternative discourses. Here, I will focus on one particularly important moment — the economic crisis that was looming during the election year in 1997 and the PAP's neoliberal solution in the form of the Singapore 21 project.

The way the crisis is represented directly impacts the types of policies pursued. In Malaysia and South Korea, strong anti-West and antiglobalization movements compelled governments to introduce some degree of currency or labor protectionism. Meanwhile, all over Southeast Asia, a regime-threatening discourse prevailed. On a daily basis, Singaporeans were exposed to recurring media coverage of anticorruption discourses in neighboring countries such as the KKN discourse (corruption, cronyism, nepotism) in Indonesia. What was there to stop Singaporeans from thinking the same?

The material reality in 1997 could have been experienced in a variety of ways. Had it been perceived through a historical frame that contrasted the present with the nation's earlier miraculous performance, citizens might have been led to ask, "If the government is so good, why did the crisis happen?" Instead, the crisis was framed as a regional-geographical or "Asian" one, where comparison with worse-off neighbors made the crisis less severe and even made citizens feel, in their own words, "lucky" to have a " "non-corrupt" government. This is a remarkable feat that is tantamount to an ideological short-circuit: if the crisis is beyond the control of the state, how could the PAP convince citizens that it could lead them out of the economic storm?

The PAP's solution came in the form of the Singapore 21 election slogan (S21). S21 originated as an election slogan to describe the PAP's vision for Singapore in the twenty-first century. Upon the prime minister's reelection, the slogan was transformed into a nationwide project to mobilize "people from all walks of life to give their ideas of what kind of Singapore they want" (*Straits Times,* October 20, 1997).

More than an exercise in democracy, S21 was a sophisticated project to promote a particular definition of the problem (and thus solution) and delegitimize other definitions. According to the S21, the "five dilemmas" confronting the nation were as follows:

1. Internationalization/regionalization versus Singapore as home
2. A less stressful life versus retaining drive

3. Attracting talent versus looking after Singaporeans
4. The needs of senior citizens versus the aspirations of the younger generation
5. Consultation and consensus versus decisiveness and quick action

These five dilemmas were presented by the PM as the response of a small fragile nation to the challenge of surviving in a competitive global economy. In a speech launching the S21 project (*Straits Times,* June 7, 1997), a neoliberal frame was clearly present: the global economic system was presented as an unchangeable and universal condition facing "all countries" and it was declared that national survival depended on the resilience and determination of its citizens to "not let [our] work ethic weaken," rather than on the state interfering with the free market and serving as a bulwark against the effects of globalization. The task of S21 was, in the PM's words, to "prepare Singaporeans for [the] unknown future" by making them understand why Singaporeans need to

1. be willing to travel overseas and globalize national brands;
2. rely less on government and take "responsibility to keep [themselves] employable and productive through continuous learning" rather than opt for leisure;
3. accept foreign talents competing for local jobs;
4. take responsibility for maintaining and caring for aged parents; and
5. accept that consultative government is a luxury that must be sacrificed in periods of crises.

What is noteworthy is that while challenges were defined as national and global in scope, solutions were framed as personal dilemmas. There were no discussions of policies (what the government needs to do), and politics becomes reduced to personal choice (what individuals ought to do). The ministers spoke explicitly of the need to "step away from the existing reliance on top-down government initiations to address national issues" (*Straits Times,* October 20, 1997): "We do not want to generate a list of things which the Government and other government agencies have to do . . . but for the community, voluntary organizations and even the individuals and families . . . reflecting attitudes which they should hold on various national issues."

The S21 project illustrates the Singapore regime's "hegemonic authoritarianism." By encouraging citizens to articulate popular concerns and then rearticulating these anxieties within the context of global challenges that require specific (neoliberal) solutions, the PAP cleverly encourages mass participation without allowing it to have policy and political consequences. Having identified the neoliberal features of the PAP's framing—namely presenting reality in terms of "regional crisis, personal solutions"—I will proceed to examine whether these frames are reproduced or challenged in media and popular discourses.

REPRODUCING DISCURSIVE LIMITS AND BUILDING CONSENSUS: JOURNALISTS' PERSONALIZATION OF NEWS

The PAP's frame dominates the ST's coverage of S21. Twenty-three out of twenty-four news, and nine out of thirteen non-news articles were focused on identifying the right mind-set. Only one news article featured policies in the form of a report of policy recommendations to the government; however, in this last article (*Straits Times,* November 22, 1998) for the years of consultation, these policies were presented as decisions rather than as topics for public debate. This method of covering S21 news illustrates the government's position that "what we can do is try to understand, . . . flesh out ideas and suggestions on how the apparent conflict can be resolved, and submit it to the government. If those changes warrant a change in policy, that would be left entirely to the government. But we should not begin by saying let's examine policy" (*Straits Times,* November 1, 1997).

Given that the government saw S21 as a project to bring about "a mindset change" (*Straits Times,* July 5, 1997), it was not surprising that news was framed around what Singaporeans (rather than the government) ought to do, ranging from reigning in emotions (jealousy), becoming less dependent on government, and complaining less, to managing paranoia:

> "Singaporeans are quite worried about the influx of foreign talent. They have to compete with them and foreigners are paid more than Singaporeans, so there is a bit of jealousy," said Mr Wong Fook Soon from the Central youth executive committee. (*Straits Times,* October 20, 1997)
>
> Mr Lee Beng Shaw, a fourth-year engineering student, said: "It seems to me that if we could somehow make Singaporeans less dependent on the government for everything, there would be no dilemmas." (*Straits Times,* March 8, 1998)

Frame, unlike opinion, is a sophisticated discursive structure that permits controversy and criticism to be articulated within it, giving off an illusion of democracy. Journalists covered S21 as an issue of legitimate controversy, using nongovernmental sources (in fourteen out of twenty-four news articles) and even reporting fierce criticisms. However, what constitutes criticism within the pre-defined PAP frame is criticism of Singaporeans, not criticism of the government, as can be seen in the above examples.

So far, I have only described instances when the journalists play a relatively passive role (of citing sources) in reproducing the government's personalizing frame. Journalists' role in personalizing issues is more active and systematic and goes beyond the contingency of the sources they happen to come by. Here, I will illustrate a few journalistic routines that reproduce and even intensify the government's personalized frame.

Firstly, because journalists rely on the S21 frame of "what Singaporeans need to do" to pose questions, they limit the types of replies that can be articulated. In the following examples, journalists' quest to find answers to what they regard as *the question* renders impossible any articulation of governmental responsibility:

> The challenge: how can *the individual* deal with the competing needs between the young and old in his family?
> What students say: Instill a greater sense of responsibility in youngsters so that the older generation will be cared for by their children.
> The challenge: How can we re-define our *notion of success* and *an individual's self-worth,* yet retain the drive?
> What students say: Singaporeans want perfection. More emphasis should be placed on community service and enjoying the arts. (*Straits Times,* March 8, 1998)

A second routine—contextualizing—can work together with framing. In the next excerpt, journalists define certain "realities" as unchangeable, leaving the solution to be limited to changing Singaporeans' mind-set to adjust to these "realities":

> The problem: Life in Singapore is too stressful. But there are so many countries waiting to catch up. And being so small, we cannot afford to stop and rest on our laurels.
> The solution: There are many things in life which make for success. You don't have to be rich to be happy.
> The problem: Foreign talent creates jobs and brings in fresh ideas. But people are anxious that more foreigners would mean greater competition for jobs.
> The solution: Singaporeans must develop a big heart and welcome foreigners. (*Straits Times,* September 18, 1998)

The previous two examples also illustrate a third routine of editorializing or summarizing—diverse opinions of students and citizens are simplified into unidimensional representations of "what students say," or "what Singaporeans think."

Fourth, journalists sometimes paraphrase citizens' opinions into statements that are more personalizing than in the original quoted form. In the following excerpt, what is problematic for Miss Boey is prejudice, which she fears may trigger the perceptional side effect of a glass ceiling. When her opinion is summarized by the journalists, the *perception* rather than the *existence* of prejudice becomes what is problematic:

> Students were concerned that they would come up against a glass ceiling at the workplace.
>
> Miss Lynette Boey, a communication student at Ngee Ann Polytechnic, said that diploma-holders were only considered for technical support positions, middle management and assistant roles.
>
> She said: "Prejudice against polytechnic graduates creates a glass ceiling. There is only so far you can rise, especially in statutory boards." (*Straits Times,* November 28, 1997)

In a feature article, a housing problem (that the wait for public housing is too long) was presented by the journalist as the *perception problem* of greedy Singaporeans:

> It is all too easy for Singaporeans to complain . . . and demand to know what the government is going to do about it while seemingly oblivious to the land and resource constraints that prevent the government from granting all of them that cash windfall which they will get when they sell their existing flat. (*Straits Times,* July 5, 1997)

The routine personalization of social issues in media discourses contributes vitally to the PAP's neoliberal hegemony in two ways—not only does it perform the minimal hegemonic work of shutting out alternative frames, but it also performs the maximal hegemonic work of building consensus.

By accepting the PAP's perspective of what the question is (what Singaporeans, not the government, should do), journalists' complicit use of personalizing frames sufficiently filters out alternative articulations, without the PAP having to intervene coercively. By successfully defining and limiting the question and controversy to the personal, the PAP can be said to have achieved the minimal standard of hegemony in the form of limits to discursive heterogeneity in media discourses.

The maximal work of building consensus can also be glimpsed in news discourse through the construction of "society" and what it thinks—a notion that is ubiquitous in popular discourse. However, this common sensibility should not be understood as a consensus that reflects what citizens actually think but rather as a media construct that is deeply entwined with individuals' perception of what society thinks. In the case of news discourses around S21, reports of survey findings and especially journalists' routine of editorializing contribute vitally to shaping people's imagination of "society."

What then, in news discourses, is the nature of society—what does "society" consider to be good or bad behavior and values? Good values certainly include filial piety; good citizens do not expect state welfare but find morally satisfying balances with regards to the needs of the young and the old. Good values can also be glimpsed through thinking about what constitutes bad values. While it is understandable that individuals may be anxious about competition, it is a bad thing to be "jealous" of foreign talents. What is even worse is individuals drop out of competition or, in the language used by journalists, "self-disqualify" themselves by imagining the existence of a glass ceiling (since they *really* do not exist except as figments of individuals' imaginations). What is clear in this psychologization of social problems into personal, imaginary ones is that what begins as a crime against the economy transforms into a crime against society and even against the self. The maximal work of hegemony in this case is the construction of a particular representation of society (as subscribing to competitiveness) that, in popular discourse, translates into an organic entity that is delinked from state imperatives, becoming a gaze that disciplines.

PERSONAL DESIRES AND THE BURDEN OF SOCIAL EXPECTATIONS: HOW OFFICIAL IDEOLOGY BECOMES ORGANIC IN POPULAR DISCOURSES

The PAP's framing of the crisis and solution appears to be very entrenched in popular discourses—not only does it set limits to what is thinkable, but it has also transformed into something organic and detached from the state through being fused with personal desire or social expectations. In this section as in others, I first illustrate the discursive limits in everyday talk before exploring the existence of shared values or common sense.

That there is much heterogeneity in everyday talk is hardly surprising. The substantial dissatisfactions that interviewees expressed conform to the stereotypes in popular culture and songs that Singaporeans are "famous for complaining." What is exceptional though is that despite all disagreements and even criticisms of the current system, none of my interviewees—not even those who were educated overseas and who have some knowledge of welfare states—considered there to be any alternatives.

Complaints abounded about the competitiveness and cost of living in Singapore, especially with reference to health costs. Jimmy, a factory worker, told me that it is common to hear the phrase "it's better to die than to be hospitalized" (since hospital bills can kill, so to speak) in coffeeshop talk. There were also many complaints about the government's stance on foreign talent. Teo commented directly on the S21 call for citizens to "develop a big heart and welcome foreigners" (*Straits Times*, September 8, 1998):

Teo: Why are we always discussing how to cope with foreign talents, to welcome them? Of course, it is hoped that we will welcome them, but it is human nature. If they are here to snatch your rice bowl, you will feel unhappy. You will surely not want them here!

It is interesting to contrast the fierce anti-immigrant discourse in Europe and to a lesser degree in the United States with the way it is trivialized as jealousy and insecurity in Singapore. Notice that Teo does not argue that the government should stop foreign talents from coming in—since that would be a policy debate—what he is arguing instead is that the government should not ask citizens to repress what he considers to be a very natural and human reaction. Here is a clear limit to discursive heterogeneity: protectionism (of domestic labor) as an option is not unthinkable but unarticulatable.

A stronger limit can be seen in how welfare is an unthinkable option. Despite complaints about the high cost of living, interviewees dismiss welfare on the grounds either of morality or logic:

> Mohammad: I wouldn't go so far as to say we need a welfare system because I don't agree with it.
>   Interviewer: Why not?
>   Mohammad: Many people will get dependent on handouts, not working for themselves. Singaporeans will take just advantage of it, because they will take the opportunity to get what freebies they can get.

Mohammad's association of welfare with handouts harks back to the media's association of welfarism with Thatcher's failure, vividly communicated by photographs of lines of people waiting for handouts. This is also the image invoked by a reader's letter to the *ST* criticizing "young Singaporeans" who would gladly trade in a job to get "on the dole" (*Straits Times,* August 22, 1998). In another case, it is interesting that a student who has recently returned from graduate studies in the UK would nevertheless have a fundamental misunderstanding about the logic of the welfare system: "Melati: How can we afford health and education bills if we are taxed 50 percent!"

In the above examples, what is clear is that *despite intense anxieties* about unaffordable health care and job loss, there are no alternative visions; indeed subjects *proactively argue against the alternative* of state welfare. If these ideological limits appear strong, the strength of the PAP's neoliberal hegemony becomes even more impressive when we take into account that these interviews took place in 1997–1998, in the midst of an economic crisis of unprecedented proportions in Singapore's history. If faith in the PAP's neoliberal system seems unshakable during a period when it is most likely to be called into question, what potential is there for the emergence of a counter-hegemonic alterative? It is this seemingly unshakable hegemony (despite Hall's reminder that hegemony is always fragile) that makes O'Leary and Coplin's (1983, 21) prophetic insight that the PAP regime is "likely to continue indefinitely" as relevant as today as it was in 1983.

While it is clear that the PAP passes the minimal test of hegemony with flying colors, its score on the maximal test (of consensus) is more complicated, although no less impressive. It is indicated generally by a layer of consensus that is based on a shared understanding—regardless of whether individuals personally desire it or conform to it merely out of social pressure—of what constitutes success and a good life. What is vital here is that this consensus, while resonating with the PAP's neoliberal values, is freed from its official antecedents and appears to citizens as relatively autonomous and organic. That this layer of consensus exists and that it is perceived as real and autonomous is vital—dissatisfactions and criticism against the political system are easily deflected to this layer of social morality so that complaints against the system are translated into criticisms of people's greed, their jealousy, or their reliance on government, or simply submerged into the Chinese culture of "face."

In trying to make sense of the extent and depth of PAP hegemony, it is useful to examine the degree to which this consensus not only exists as a social morality but also penetrates deeper to fuse with personal aspiration so that social expectations are no longer something that citizens need to reluctantly comply with, but something that is wholeheartedly consented to.

Let us turn to those instances when neoliberal ideology is translated not only into society's expectations but also into personal desire. In the above examples, complaints often reflect failure to achieve the Singapore Dream rather than a rejection of such a dream. The stress that citizens complain so much about is often induced by their desire to acquire a luxurious lifestyle that can be achieved only by succeeding in a competitive society. In the following two instances, interviewees describe instances when society's expectations and personal expectations have fused into personal desire for success in society's eyes, so much so that individuals are not led by their "heart" but by where success could be found:

Lee: On TV, children were asked whether they wanted to study EM1 [English and Mandarin as first languages] or EM2 [English as first, Mandarin as second language]. The child said EM1. Why? The child replied: "Because my mother says it's better." The child was then asked if he knew what EM1 meant. The child said: "I don't know, but I know it's better."

Tang: The government said we needed more engineers. . . . Suddenly, everyone wanted to be an engineer. They didn't consider, "what is it that I want, is this really me? . . . This takes conformity to an extreme, [they want] a comfortable lifestyle at the expense of personal integrity.

There are also instances where neoliberal ideology is translated only into social morality and *not* personal desire. In such instances, since society has not been collapsed with the self, the dialogue between self and society becomes visible. A Malay-Muslim (the lowest-achieving ethnic group)

professional woman, Rashida was concerned about how "others" will inte -
pret her decision to work part time instead of full time during the economic
crisis:

> Rashida: If I decided I don't like the medical profession, and I want to quit to
> become an artist, do you know what kind of flak I will get? . . . I will tell peo-
> ple not to think of it as a loss. It's not as if I am leaving and staying at home. . . . I
> appeal to their sense of good family—I have family and children and they are
> priority. I am contributing to the community at large too!
>   Interviewer: [laughs]
>   Rashida: [laughs] always have to be justifying. I cannot do it because I want
> to. People will talk. And I have to say I am working half-time because of the
> children.

In a situation when social expectations are not fused with personal desire, citizens clearly feel tremendous disciplinary pressures to comply. Rashida's reason for wanting time off was to have more time for leisure. However, she was
aware that this reason would not be "acceptable" in the eyes of those around
her. The only reason that "society" would deem legitimate would be that she
wanted to devote more time towards being a good mother, wife, worker, and
Malay. Ironically, she took the morning off—the time when her son was in
school—which makes her an active complicit subject rather than a passive
compliant one.

Rashida's case illustrates how ubiquitous and interfering the disciplinary
arm of "society" can be, such that its rod is not even spared on an issue as private and trivial as personal leisure. Common sense tells Rashida that there is
such a thing as a right or wrong response. She knows that the default expectation of society is that a "normal" person would try to hold her job during an
economic crisis. Recognizing her decision as a deviation from the norm, she
knows that her deviation has to be accounted for, preferably voluntarily. On
an everyday basis then, subjects like Rashida rely on common sense to navi-
gate the demands of social interactions and to select, organize, and discipline
discursive heterogeneity into order. In this way, common sense is crucially
tied to subjects' imagination of what society thinks and expects.

Finally, the most powerful testimony to the strength of the PAP's hegemony is not citizens' attraction to or reluctant compliance with it, but their
semi-awareness of the inorganicity of this consensus. The PAP's hand in
shaping this consensus is not invisible and citizens often exhibit moments of
extreme lucidity about the PAP's social engineering of Singapore's economic
culture:

> Tan: The government didn't want complacency. Instead of welfare, they think of
> other ways of caring for people. . . . This develops the hardworking attitude of
> Singaporeans to look for jobs and support their families. Everyone must stand

on his own. . . . If you do not improve you will earn [little], you cannot face people, you develop an inferiority complex. . . . If you cannot provide for yourself, you cannot provide for your family or get married; you cannot have children. No children mean you cannot pass down the generation. Then you keep having inferiority complex.

What is so impressive about the PAP's hegemony then is the ideological short-circuiting that happens on a regular basis. Despite sharp awareness of the PAP's hand in constructing society, citizens continue to perceive it as having an aura of organicity *nonetheless* and what is criticized and complained about in public discourse is the values of society rather than the policies and vision of the government. Coupled with the strong limits to options that are articulatable or thinkable in public discourse, the organicity of this consensus and the immunity it lends to the PAP speak of the strength, breadth, and depth of the PAP's hegemony.

DEMOCRACY AND COUNTERHEGEMONY: POLITICAL ECONOMY AND IDEOLOGY

I have argued that the PAP's hegemony can be seen minimally in the absence of viable ideological alternatives in public discourse and maximally in its success in embedding in neoliberal values onto the social construction of society, whose perceived organicity deflects criticisms of the negative consequences of neoliberalism as criticisms of Singaporean society rather than as criticisms of state policy.

To fully comprehend the hegemonic process, it is necessary to examine why no alternatives are available in public discourses. Alterative articulations certainly exist in the margins of public discourses—for example, opposition parties and fragments of everyday talk (e.g., describing the problem as prejudice rather than glass ceilings, complaints about costs of health care). However they are not articulated into a coherent alternative in public discourse, for two reasons.

First, there exists a strong consensus on the moral superiority and technical necessity of a society where individuals are self-reliant. Insofar as this perspective is privileged over other considerations, there are few ideological resources and little discursive space for alternatives to emerge. Second, those groups who are able to articulate coherent alternatives are often barred from participation in the public sphere. For instance, in the S21 project, a PAP minister justified the noninclusion of opposition politicians: "I do not want to see the discussion become political debates where each person has a particular ideological point of view. I do not think we will have a very productive discussion this way" (*Straits Times,* October 20, 1997).

The way these two obstacles work together in the Singapore context offers us interesting insights into the role of the material and the ideological for the purpose of democratization and counterhegemony. It is clearly insufficient to focus merely, as political economists do, on the elite's direct control of the media; ideological projects such as the S21 project are embarked on precisely to decrease the elite's reliance on regulation, ownership, and censorship. In the case of Singapore, where elites have secured a relatively firm consensus, it is unlikely that decreased state regulation or increased market liberalization of the media would contribute much to ideological diversity. (Recall that previous media liberalization in Singapore generated only tabloids devoid of critical content.) At the same time, it would be naïve to dismiss the importance of political economy to understanding ideological processes, especially the ideological effects that result from the relationship between the elite and the media. The emergence of a coherent viable alternative in public discourse cannot happen without a network that allows for the dissemination of ideas, an infrastructure that allows for dialogue, and a space where popular concerns can be expressed and rearticulated by organic intellectuals into a viable and genuinely popular-national alternative.

NOTES

1. An essay about hegemony requires considerable breadth since the argument cannot be convincingly made without examinations of official, media, and popular discourses. Thus, arguments that have been made elsewhere will be summarized here. For the full review and critique of the absence of ideology in theories of authoritarianism, see Sim (forthcoming).

5

Regulating the Consciousness Industry in the European Union: Legitimacy, Identity, and the Changing State

Katharine Sarikakis

THE CHANGING POLICY AND MEDIASCAPES IN EUROPE

This chapter will explore the ways in which the regulation of communication and culture in the European Union reflects some of the most significant changes in policy in the last part of the twentieth and early twenty-first centuries, which are common across industrialized nations. The chapter draws attention to the centrality of the "consciousness" industry[1] in the shaping and legitimating of contemporary European Union (EU) governance. Throughout, the tensions, questions, and concerns surrounding the structural and cultural transformation of the European polity are discussed, while special attention is paid to the changing relationship among citizens, the media, and the state, exploring the EU's governance processes and their impact on questions around identity, social cohesion, and the very legitimization of the polity.

The regulation of communication and culture industries has undergone significant changes in the past quarter of a century. Indeed, analysts and observers speak of the *de-regulation* and *re-regulation* of the industries, pointing to the withdrawal of the state from their close regulation and their "entrustment" to the free market. It may sound archaic to younger ears, but up to twenty years ago, public service broadcasters (PSBs) in Europe, Canada, and in a majority of countries across the world were considered to rightfully hold a monopoly over broadcasting or to be at the core of a public service ethos, even in those nation-states where private and public broadcasting systems coexisted, as in the case of the UK. The characteristics of this transformation can be summarized as follows: a process of liberalization—and consequently, privatization—of communications and the airwaves,[2] particularly promoted through neoliberal politics in Europe; the subsequent lifting of PSB monopolies and their normative centrality in national media-scapes; and the withdrawal of proactive intervention on behalf of the nation-state in what was understood to be the economic affairs of the media indus-tries. On an ideological, normative level, the aforementioned policy trajecto-ries were based on three arguments: first, the media are industries (like any other); second, the free market promotes spontaneous social order, as per ne-oliberalist economics, thereby allowing for individuals to compete freely and make decisions about their consumption "choices"; third, "consumer sover-eignty" is claimed to be the ultimate value standard that underlies the organ-ization and production of media and culture industries. This normative frame-work, necessary for the legitimization of policies that transformed the media across Europe, redefined the public in its relation to the media, as consumers of media services and accumulators of cultural goods, rather than as members of an informed and active citizenry. This redefinition of the public assisted in and acted as the basis for an assault against public service broadcasting, state subsidization, and the raison d'être of cultural protectionism.

These changes have long been accompanied by a change in the role of the state, and in particular of the nation-state, as seen through the lenses of the media and culture industries. Although the exact nature and intensity of this transformation are debated, it is safe to say that certain factors are commonly considered important in this process. For one, the processes of economic globalization seem to accelerate the transformation of the role of the state in international relations. Second, the emergence of a world polity through in-ternational and supranational organizations, such as the EU or the African Union, world summits, or the highly controversial Group of Eight (G-8) and World Trade Organization (WTO), constructs a political architecture that makes new demands on the state. Third, increased, forced, or otherwise, hu-man mobility across borders creates the conditions for the mobility of cultural practices,[3] ideas, and norms but also raises questions of structural polariza-tions, social cohesion, and cultural diversity. Underscoring the processes of globalization is the understanding that technological development and the use of communications technologies enable the continuation of the financial and trading markets across the globe on a twenty-four-hour basis. Compounding its importance as a facilitator of round-the-clock business and speedy human interaction, the two most visible effects of globalization, communications has come to occupy a special place in the relationship between state, market, and citizenry. Though not new, the role of communications as a "consciousness" barometer and compass is attaining a special significance, in particular in the ways in which this role is at its closest to the changing role of the state: through policy and regulation.

THE SHIFTING PARADIGMS OF IDEOLOGICAL
LEGITIMACY AND THE CHANGING STATE

The "state-in-question" is predominantly the European nation-state and the European Union polity, as they interact to form new constellations of jurisdiction and accountability—or lack thereof. The political architecture of the European Union presents a particularly interesting case in the project of rethinking the state. Through an incremental, albeit not stable, development in the last half century,[4] the EU has grown to become one of the most economically integrated areas in the world, while at the same time it has promoted a new definition of citizenship and political integration. This latter function of the polity seems to be the object of contestation between Eurosceptics and supporters of the EU project, especially because this new form of polity, or superstate, is seen by the former to undermine national sovereignty. These positions have their roots in various, often irreconcilable ideologies.[5] Analyses bringing together the development of the EU and its role in media and culture policy often emphasize the democratic deficit of the polity that is exacerbated by its neoliberal agenda in deregulating the media, thereby privatizing public communicative spaces and failing to address the problem of media ownership concentration (Kaitatzi-Whitlock 2006). Moreover, the historical tendency of the EU to support policies with an economistic aim and based on the least common denominator results in an overall negative integration (Humphreys 2007). The EU is also understood as a polity influenced by and interacting with the international system: these interactions result in policy directions that have far-reaching influence not only within the EU countries but also in other countries. One such example is the consistent resistance of the EU, led by France, to allowing the inclusion of cultural products in the GATT/GATS (General Agreement on Tariffs and Trade/General Agreement on Trade in Services) negotiations for several years, opposing in this way the United States–led initiative for the liberalization of audiovisual services. The EU has maintained quite successfully the argument for the protection of culture and the culture industry and achieved the famous "cultural exception" from the trade discussion rounds.[6] The argument of cultural protection has at its heart the much-discussed "content quota" policy provision in the Television Without Frontiers Directive (TVWF), according to which half of the broadcast content has to be of European origin (therefore significantly reducing the Hollywood-originated material shown on European screens).

The EU presents us with an interesting set of paradoxes: on the one hand, its overall tendency is toward economic integration through the privatization of culture goods and services, facilitated first and foremost by the TVWF, which effectively created a single audiovisual market. On the other hand, due to its construction, and in particular due to the existence of a representational institution (the European Parliament [EP], the only one in international policy regimes), there is considerable resistance and counteraction in the EU that promotes social and political priorities. EP provides a democratic space for positive political, and sociocultural European integration through its campaigning for issues such as the protection of journalists' independence, protection of cultural diversity, protection of media pluralism, content quotas, and the protection of the PSB system (Sarikakis 2004, 2005). Perhaps symbolically, the most significant achievement of the EP and one of the most important decisions of the EU was the Public Service Broadcasting Protocol to the Amsterdam Treaty, clearly stating that the protection of PSBs in the EU is the cornerstone of democracy and culture in European societies. The gravity of the statement can be better understood if we consider that it is the only such provision available in any kind or form of international agreement.

Overall, most significant studies are taken from the history of broadcasting and audiovisual policy in the EU. The TVWF Directive was first established in 1989, after a decade of deliberation and conflicts in the EU. The contrasting tendencies of negative and positive integration are evident in the directive, and they resurfaced again through its recent revision throughout 2005 and 2006. On the one hand, there are policy claims in the recently revised draft aimed at a more comprehensive policy framework that encompasses communications as a concept and not only as technologies, through general principles of cultural protection, protection of human dignity, protection of consumers and restrictions to advertising, regulation of hate and discriminatory speech, public service ethos and "must carry" principles, and protection of pluralistic ownership structures. On the other hand, there are conflicting tendencies that pull away from proactive, socially centered claims, toward further liberalization of audiovisual services that emphasizes consumer "choice" and undermines the role of European PSBs. These tensions express conflicting visions about the EU and its governance, which range between an administrative response to the integration of global markets through the creation of the pan-European market, and the drive toward a political union that needs at its forefront public policies addressing questions of the public interest.

The relationship between the EU structure and the nation-states is similarly not straightforward: Parliamentarians represent the peoples of Europe and are elected within national boundaries but by any residing EU citizens. The Council of Ministers consists of representatives of nation-states who are not directly elected but rather appointed by the national governments. So on one level, the decisions made for communication and culture policy (and any issues) involve a mixture of supranational governance and intergovernmental interaction. This seemingly *multilevel governance* of the EU is thought to offer more platforms for citizens' involvement in supranational decision making in communications and culture (e.g., Ward 2005), whereby multiple levels of government and actors *share* power in policy making (Majone 1996; Marks, Liesbet, and Kermit 1996). This presupposes a partial loss of control of the nation-state. State-centric analyses argue, however, that ultimately national sovereignty and autonomy are the primary sources of integration according to *"Intergovernmental Institutionalism"* (Milward 1992; Moravcsik 1991). Supranational institutions are important in "cementing" existing agreements, but it is the interest of nation-states that provides the wheels for further integration. Supranationalist approaches, largely developed by Sandholtz and Stone Sweet (1998), point to the institutional organization of the EU that can be found in the political and decision-making activity of institutions at the supranational level: the construction of policy regimes that constitute some of the most central areas of national economies, such as the monetary union, but also "second-level" regulation, such as the telecommunications regime; the very process of legitimization of policies through citizens' direct participation, as in election periods; or in more general and admittedly more-difficult-to-measure areas of cultural citizenship.

From an economic institutionalist perspective, Milward suggests that integration meant survival for the nation-state, especially given the conditions of political instability and economic depression in postwar Europe.[7] In this process, economic interdependence became a core element in the "rescue" of the nation-state: according to Milward, social and political consensus were crucial in the revival of European economies in which income and growth were unachievable targets without a larger (outside the domestic sphere) recovery plan (Milward 1992, cited in van Kersbergen 1997). Along similar lines, French regulation scholars approach the institutional and broader political changes in the EU as a response to the need for a reformed system of administration and regularization that derives from the establishment of a new accumulation system on a global scale (Aglietta [1979] 2000, 414). Characteristics of the system are the increased scope of economic integration, the internationalization of the division of labor, and the expansion of wage societies. As Aglietta observes,

> In these [wage] societies, social rights are a constituent element of citizenship; they are the cement of social cohesion. . . . [T]he need to formulate regulatory principles that can guide the accumulation of capital into a new era of wage societies calls for changes in many institutions. ([1979] 2000, 415)

Economic expansion and legitimation of political structures are seen as the driving forces behind European integration by other scholars as well. For Cocks, an early account of the EU points to the long history of similar integration processes in the European territory, which are characterized by the development of a capitalist economy accompanied by state regulation and economic freedom. Regardless of whether state analysis is based on the assumption that capital *dictates* state evolution or whether one ascribes more autonomy to the state, Cocks's overview of the parallel development of economic integration, state transformation, and regulatory reform, coupled with ideological dominance, provides a historical background largely absent in most analyses and descriptions of the European polity. The unification of territorial space that began to emerge in Western Europe as early as 1500 (Cocks 1980),[8] has sustained permanent bureaucracies, standing armies, codified law and taxation systems, and unified embryonic markets. Support for the consequently evolving system was obtained from the traditional ruling classes (Anderson 1991; Wallerstein 1974). Ideological components of these processes of legitimization were the justification for the breaking down of barriers, political unification, and the use of colonies as the suppliers and consumers of goods (Cocks 1980, 17).

However, the function of integration has not been restricted to economic aims, even if this may have been the primary goal. Beside trade and the market, a parallel set of complex, sometimes subtle, and sometimes profound demonstrations of identity building have taken place. While on one level, economic integration allowed for the simplification of trade regulation, on another, the construction of nation-states and empires utilized the "consciousness" industry to foster an ideological safety net. Be it the press, literature, the church, or later early forms of broadcasting, these means have carried the "message" of national identity but also European "superiority" vis-à-vis the colonies. Indeed, colonization has taken place within Europe as well and has left its own cultural, administrative, and political legacies.[9] In a postcolonial era, the constructions of otherness are most vividly present in immigration and securitization policies. As Hardt and Negri argue,

> Colonialism and racial subordination function as a temporary solution to the crisis of European modernity, not only in economic and political terms, but also of identity and culture. . . . The negative construction of non-European others is finally what founds and sustains European identity itself. (2000, 124)

Again, the complexity of Europe creates interesting paradoxes: multiculturalism has been heralded as a top priority in the EU agenda, with a number of initiatives that actively foster dialogue between EU and its "others" on the one hand, and through strong antidiscriminatory and antiracist legislation at the EU and also national levels. So for example, there is a great range of media spaces created for the diverse immigrant and minority communities of the EU in countries such as the Netherlands or Germany, and mainstreaming media programming policies in the UK. A number of cultural initiatives on an EU level include education and culture campaigns. Moreover, through the well-established structural programs, peripheries in the EU are supported in building their regional economies through cultural enterprises. The result is that cultural and structural solidarity is being actively constructed at a grass-roots level, by focusing on the integration of migrant populations into the economic and social life of the regions.

Nevertheless, at the same time, the resurfacing of xenophobia and moral panics about migration and the "influx" from the "East" is very vivid in a populist press pendulum between cultural relativism and cultural "clashes" and populist, disorientating governmental policies. Currently, the controversial "War on Terror" wave of policies arriving from the United States is creeping into national legislations. In the UK, for example, a systematic campaign to devalue human rights as the ultimate standard for civil liberties is being taken to the EU level, with the most dangerous implications not only for the viability of human rights legislation in the UK, but also for the fundamental, constitutional declarations of the EU as a polity, as well as those values claimed to be associated with EU citizenship.

EUROPEAN IDENTITY, CITIZENSHIP, AND THE QUESTION OF "CULTURE"

As the historical development of communication and culture policies in the EU demonstrates, EU governance has evolved to address questions that are hardly answered by market integrationist policies. Indeed, the inclusion of "culture" in the legalistic repertoire of the EU has not been uncontested: the European Parliament has insisted since the early 1980s—when it had no legislative powers in the administrative structure of the EU—that the question of "culture" and that of media are questions of power that need to be addressed as such. Of course, addressing questions of power in a field as sensitive as this—the "consciousness" industry—would require the expansion of EU jurisdiction into nation-state policy territories, the redefinition of the raison d'être of the EU, and the repositioning of the polity in relation to its national citizens (Sarikakis 2004). All this would also require an accompanying *normative shift* (away from the strictly economistic remit of the EU) and appropriate *institutional* reform in order to alleviate the legitimation crisis of the polity. These are predominantly addressed through the development of the EP's legislative powers and the establishment of a new legal entity,[10] that of EU citizenship. The latter comes to foster a pan-European identity, based on cultural diversity and the human rights values expressed in the Social Charter for Rights and Fundamental Freedoms (Sarikakis 2007). At the same time, global international affairs present projects such as the EU with new challenges: transnational corporations (TNCs) increasingly occupy a "sovereign" status in world politics through their position at the negotiating tables of summitry, such as the World Summit on the Information Society (Chakravartty and Sarikakis 2006). Transnational capital in TNC form, processes of neo-colonialism through the relocation of wage labor, which is at its weakest in terms of mobility, and outsourcing are accompanied by a form of "embedded neoliberalism," the ideology of legitimation, the adaptation of Europe to global trading, which supports de-regulation and flexibilization (Rhodes and van Apeldoorn 1997, 22). A form of "embedded neoliberalism" places the free market between free trade and social consensus, a form of neoliberalism that Rhodes and van Apeldoorn point to as the possible ideological base of European capitalism, which is "softened" by the existence of political insti-tutions at the national and supranational level. The socioeconomic order emerging from the current transformation of world and also European economies through globalization is still to be defined. Van Kersbergen argues that with the diminishing role of the state and the strengthened role of the market, "consensus" or "allegiance" in both nation-states and the European suprastructure is in danger (1997). Uncertainty and doubt about the signifi-cance of the state and other social institutions as advocated by neoliberalism is often expressed in state analysis: the lack of social policy to guarantee so-cial rights is increasing Euroskepticism among the peoples of Europe (Nugent 1999) and jeopardizing efforts to maintain social cohesion through a cultural and structural set of policies. Aglietta ([1979] 2000) points to the lack of ad-equate political response to the problems caused by the new stage of capital-ist accumulation, not in terms of creating "responsive" institutions able to deal with these problems at an international or global level, but rather in the ability of these modes of regulation to foster social cohesion.

The governing philosophy of the nation-state in Western liberal democra-cies is one associated with the notion of "law and order" or lawful polity, le-gitimacy, and sovereignty. Largely based on the Enlightenment traditions of Rousseau's "Social Contract" and Lafayette's "Declaration of the Rights of Man," this philosophy also,[11] perhaps paradoxically, associates the state with the ideological foundations of the liberty of individuals, equality of individu-als before the law, and popular sovereignty. These ideals have offered the ide-ological glue to the design of the modern European state with the authority (legitimacy) of rule over the public life of individuals and the establishment of common values, based on the separation of powers, equality of opportu-nity, and accountability. However, the state is also based on the assumption of a homogenized "people." Indeed, "'the people' is posed as the original basis of the nation; the modern conception of the people is in fact a product of the nation-state, and survives only within its specific ideological context" (Hardt and Negri 2000, 102). As an inevitable consequence, the modern state ex-cludes the "multitude," as an "irreducible multiplicity,"[12] within the spectrum of a certain territorial realm under the common umbrella of nationhood that consists of common language, cultural traditions, religious orientation, and common history. Obvious cultural policies at national levels aiming at the "homogenization" of populations throughout history have been policies of maintaining one official language, while also providing education in the languages of minorities in Germany, Greece, France, the UK, and so on; untold but widely understood norms of "proper" representation of images of nationhood through, for example, the particular tone and accent of news presenters on the BBC; resurfaced discourses about the "failure" of multiculturalism and the return to discourses of "integration" (Georgiou and Siapera 2006); the new processes of "naturalization" whereby "new" citizens (but not those born to British citizens) in the UK have to swear allegiance to the queen; the renewed agenda of anti-immigration policies, where undocumented people are detained in prisons: and the most recent instructions by the UK Home Office to university faculty to monitor Muslim students' opinions expressed in class and coursework, as well as monitoring international students' (but not UK students') class attendance. This attempt to securitize heterogeneity aims at the promotion of a mythical homogeneity. Of course, the materiality of "homogeneity" does not reflect any distributive equality in wealth and resources, but rather the exposure of citizens to messages and ideas that bear the common thread of "nationhood" and exclusivity.

Again, it would be simplistic and inaccurate to assume that this is the only policy direction. In the EU, homogeneity *and* heterogeneity are negotiated anew, based on three interlocking factors: First, the European nation-states are bringing their "homogenous people" into a new terrain of heterogeneity, the European Union. Second, the construction of a new form of homogeneity (or common identity) at a supranational and transnational level in the EU is necessary for the legitimacy of the EU project and cultural cohesion. Third, assuming some existing homogeneity within national space,[13] the waves of forced or even voluntary migration in and out of nations create new questions about the borders of assigned citizenship, inclusive cultural identity, and assumed universal values.

Internal symbolic cohesion in the EU is pursued through a system of communication symbols, such as the European flag and anthem, and the listing of official languages, but the development of oral histories and mythology enjoyed by cultural and national communities has some way to go. At a constant level, any identity formation depends on the help of contemporary storytellers such as broadcasting programs and the creative industries, as well as on individual experience. The construction of an "imagined community" is founded partly on the common material experience of individuals but also on the fictitious—and imagined—interpretations of these experiences. An EU "identity" spans two levels whereby citizens would experience some of its imagined or other elements. A first level is the ways in which the EU is lived through interactions of citizens and its institutions. Dominant elements here are the "purpose-built" language of Eurospeak and public discourses about the role of the EU as a new and extended home for Europeans (Christiansen,

Jørgensen, and Wiener 1999). Institutional integration and political action are located in the processes of law-making, which serve as a particular form of integration (e.g., Dehousse 1998; Nentwich and Weale 1998; Christiansen and Jørgensen 1999).

The relationship between practices of citizenship and the emerging European polity is still an understudied area. However, the values of protection of human rights, such as the right to personal dignity, equity, protection and respect of family life and private life, freedom of opinion, and the right to efficient law protection, are some of the basic areas of European law, where the foundations of what it might mean to be "European" rest (Ihnen 1997). Sharing respect for these *European values,* expressed in institutional and other official agreements (Human Rights Convention of the Council of Europe [1950], European Social Charter [1961], Declaration of Fundamental Rights and Freedoms of the European Parliament [1989]; see Ihnen 1995, 23), becomes the intersection of institutional and lived identity.

Culture is the level where EU identity can best be demonstrated, an identity that is only possible through a process of cultural integration. As early as 1961, Sombart in his essay *Internationale Kulturpolitik statt Außenpolitik?* addressed culture policy as a question of international relations[14] and of the tertiary level of governance. He argued that cultural relations are a significant influential factor in the process of a silent transformation of foreign affairs through the acquisition of a new, postnational identity and the coexistence of identities and cultures (Sombart 1961). The question of European culture is approached in terms of its *construction,* as an ever-evolving vision, but also in terms of *Realpolitik,* as an integral question in world politics (Weidenfeld 1990).[15] A precondition, but not the only one, for social cohesion is the maintenance of equality of citizens before the law irrespective of their origins in the united Europe. Therefore, with the abolition of barriers European citizens should not be disadvantaged if they move beyond their national territory, as far as at least fundamental rights are concerned. The poles of culture and political action would involve, according to Maihofer (1990), the creation of a "new continent" that overcomes the political catastrophes of the past (totalitarianism and war). The protection of human rights, the right to education, and political participation are seen as the foundation and solution to promoting cultural integration of "immigrants" within the EU (Weidenfeld 1990).

Through cultural policy initiatives, the EU approaches the question of social cohesion from a cultural angle and with the aim to extend perceptions of an "imagined community" to include the abstract (or real) territory of Europe (Sassatelli 2002). These policies aim at the construction and re-narration of Europeanness through projects such as the European City of Culture; the MEDIA program, which finances and trains European AV producers and directors; and the Culture 2000 program and its extension, which have provided for the protection and publicization of European cultural heritage. Moreover educational policies of the harmonization of educational qualifications across Europe and initiatives that promote the exchange of pupils, students, and educators between European countries, such as Erasmus or Socrates, aim to foster a European identity based on Europeans' experiences of their neighbors. These policies aim at creating common spaces of experience of what it may mean to be European, through the understanding of diversity among and within nations, the fostering of arts and the media, and the cultivation of a common sense of purpose.

The difficulty is of course that the pace of economic integration is faster than the pace of constructing and living in an "imagined community." "Unity in Diversity" is the EU's multicultural response to the partial recognition of heterogeneous populations, becoming the ideological framing of European identity. This framing would not be far from the truth, as European geography has contributed to the emergence and development of different cultures that, however, share common, collective memories of the closely interrelated histories of their nations/peoples/countries, histories that are expanding to include those cultures that have enriched Europe through migration and mobility (Weidenfeld 1990). The recent and imminent EU enlargement has not been accompanied by other forms of integration, other than the necessary administrative ones. The "subjective bases of a superstate in one European nation, to which the individual feels essentially connected, are nowhere to be seen" (Bogdandy 1993, 27). The process of enlargement also carries a series of adjustment policies that Eastern European states have to follow, where long-held rights are being overthrown to make room for the complete liberalization of services. Such rights include gender equality in the economic and political domains, which is being eroded by a combination of the withdrawal of the welfare state, which offered women the material conditions to participate more fully in public life, through for example providing affordable childcare; and the rise of masculinist and fundamentalist cultures, including ones based on religion, with the effect that the public life is increasingly excluding women (P. Watson 2000). In the same way, some "visible" minorities, such as the Turkish in Germany or the Indian and Pakistani communities in Britain, are more readily recognizable by the nation-state than others whose numbers may not make them as visible (Greeks in Germany, Nigerians in Greece, Chinese in Britain, etc.). What this also means is that the languages of such minorities are not officially recognized by the EU or the nation-state. Similarly, when one thinks of linguistic minorities, such as speakers of Gaelic in Britain, Plattdeutsch in Germany, or Catalan in Spain, these are more easily "understood" and legitimated as minority languages to be actively protected than those languages spoken by immigrant communities or even the large community of Romas across Central Europe.

The limitations of cultural policy become evident in attempts to encourage linguistic diversity, when policy focuses on official languages, and thereby on parts of "official" cultures (Sarikakis 2005). At the same time, certain supra-national policies, such as the European Convention on Human Rights and Fundamental Freedoms, bring about the possibility of more liberal frame works than those found in the national status quo. Yet, despite the suprana-tional demands upon nations, it is the nation-state that legitimizes the processes of integration and globalization. States police the implementation of laws and new administrative and bureaucratic systems; states also maintain the activity of local communities through labor and consumption in the proj-ect of accumulation. The EU creates largely legal frameworks and guidelines in the form of directives, but it is up to the states to implement these. At this level we find everyday sustenance and resistance, and this is where culture comes to play its most important role of all: to school subjects to adapt to their changing circumstances or, by accommodating the expression of resistance, to legitimize or marginalize beliefs as well as ways of life. This is the domain of consciousness shaping, assisted by conventional media but also by com-municative action among citizens.

THE STATE IN SMALL PLACES: POLICING CULTURAL BOUNDARIES

Bound with territoriality (Axtmann 2004), the modern nation-state holds the power of rule over its subjects, even those without a legal status, within its national space, as the act of a sovereign, an authority and hierarchy (Hardt and Negri 2005, 105). It also holds power, though of a different kind, over its subjects in distant (other national) territories.[16] Some states are more "able" than others to claim sovereignty in their rule over states that may or may not be deemed sovereign, as the Iraq and Afghanistan wars may tell us about the position of not only "imperial" America (the United States) but also EU mem-ber-states such as Great Britain. Again, this fiction of sovereignty is only valid for states at the high end of the ladder of control of resources through economic and military power. The dominance of British, French, and German politics, although not manifested through the formal procedures of the EU, is reflected in the ideological and administrative constellations in the EU. The linguistic privilege of French, only currently being surpassed by English as the unofficially "official" *lingua Europa,* or the administrative separation of institutions that resembles the French system of directorates and dirigisme; the location of the European Central Bank in Germany; and the ideological dominance of the British development policy paradigm (Lock 2006) point to-ward inner European—cultural as well as economic—hierarchies.

The role of the state in citizens' lives, the "small places" of lived experi-ence, and in particular in the communicative action and process becomes the nexus of global economic integration and local sociocultural and political af-firmation. Such "small places" are located in the construction of identity (national or European), where the media as well as general cultural policies play an important role; the quality of communicative action within national boundaries, such as freedom of expression or press freedom, but also across boundaries in the form of communication and information (or content) flow; and human mobility, as in the case of tourism or Internet traffic. The fields of communicative expression, whether through data exchange or mass media consumption, or whether in the form of political protest or media use, are paramount in the state agenda of sovereignty and role transformation. In the current climate of broadening the EU and exercising policing control as a post-9/11 effect, communicative processes become more urgent as they obtain two characteristics, according to which they are classified: first, as an added value through commodification and their position in existing or potential markets; and second, for their political value that may or may not be a source for profit, clash unswervingly with the agenda of securitization and militarization. Technology lies at the core of new profit sources in the field both of the leisure industry (including culture as a commodity and the media) and of the military-government nexus, through the increased interest in biometrics, the privatization of the correction system, contracts with the private sector active in defense and military research, or the collation and monitoring of personal data. The technological possibilities that run through the "small places" of everyday life, whether through ordinary Internet or television consumption or in forms that raise the antennas of civil rights organizations, such as the case of identity cards in the UK, are there, bringing with them an active and sophisticated populace that asserts own strategies to deal with them. Nevertheless,

> as has always been the case in the history of capitalism, this technological revolution is not self-regulating. The policies, mentalities and institutions which interfere with the determinant factors of capital accumulation do not develop at the same rate as techniques, working methods and markets. (Aglietta [1979] 2000, 414)

The development of techniques and markets through the uses of technology concerns not only "mainstream" industries but also those occupying a controversial position in the market. The pornography industry is such a typical case. This "sector" has taken almost pioneering advantage of new technologies, as we know from the study of its history, and in the early twenty-first century it seems to be driving technological adoption. Although this is not the only case that has caused headaches for national governments, it has attracted the attention of the nation-state in cases of transnational content flow. In the EU, one of the early visible consequences of the technological factor undermining the existing authority of the state was direct-to-home (DTH) satellite technology in the 1980s, which allowed the direct reception of satellite programs from countries with different media regulatory frameworks. Although the reception of outside content was not necessarily seen as problematic—mainly due to the fact that programs are transmitted in national, therefore "foreign," languages—in one case (pornographic content) this was deemed too serious by the UK state to be left unaddressed (see for example UK Government 2003). Where national content-related laws clash with each other in the EU, supranational legislation, in this case through the TVWF Directive, has developed clauses that concentrate on the protection of minors and the potential of content to be harmful. Previous such legal, and cultural, clashes with broadcasting materials originating in countries such as Denmark posed the question of sovereign national law over market borderlessness. More recently (February 2005), the UK government issued a proscription order against the Italian satellite adult broadcaster Extasi TV for the transmission of violent pornography, making it illegal to obtain decryption cards for this broadcaster and prohibiting advertising for it in the UK media (UK Government 2005). Similar questions are currently under consideration across the EU on the grounds of Internet access and content.

Cases such as this indicate that despite the added administrative layers and supranational constitutional commitments to issues such as human rights, the nation-state remains intensely felt in everyday life: for one, Hardt and Negri argue that the very construction of national identity has marked a shift in the concept of sovereignty because it focuses on the "nation-subject and its imagined community" (2000, 105). Decisions made by national executives, especially in matters of culture (or "consciousness"), must reflect ideas of national and cultural identity as they become translated into morals, codes of conduct, and common values. Despite the fact that the "commonality" of common values is not necessarily shared across different parts of society, the idea is an assumed consensus about core questions. Therefore, in the European case, the TVWF Directive makes a strong reference to the protection of minors, a value reflected across a number of legislative initiatives, including those concerning the Internet and the information society. In the case of the UK's response to the broadcasting of violent pornography, the national executive bases its decision on accepted norms about explicit material, as defined by long-standing national legislation (Obscenity Act [1957] and subsequent amendments) *as well as* the value of protecting minors *and* human dignity, as being "European" ones.[17] This is one part of the changing role of the state, whereby attention to the national communication landscape can be witnessed through the development of a set of policies that aim to maintain this sovereignty.

On another level, the privatization process is rather complete in the EU and the European national media markets. Commodification of security, through the privatization of prisons and the collaboration of R&D companies with the state, and securitization involve the extension of a "state of emergency" across a broader range of issues. Normatively this is achieved under the rubric of antiterrorism. The recent assault against the normative justification of the protection of human rights by UK government in December 2005,[18] on the grounds of antiterrorism in a speech given to the European Parliament, resulted in the approval of the retention of telecommunication data on an EU level. Here one of the most powerful groups, the Creative and Media Business Alliance (CMBA), which includes EMI, SonyBMG, and TimeWarner, has lobbied the EU to extend data retention to investigate all crimes, not just crimes such as terrorism (Wearden and Gomm 2005). The concern of these TNCs is closer to perceived lost profits and their need to control the telecommunications market, but the alliance between state and TNCs leaves citizens' small places open to intrusion, control, and surveillance. The same energy or concern is not demonstrated in the safeguarding of a free press or in the protection of liberty as an antidote to fundamentalism and unaccountable authority.[19] While the state is withdrawing from the game court of TNCs by regularizing their expansive claims over individual data and by allowing and even promoting ownership of private and public information and spaces, it assumes a more aggressive role in everyday life, subsuming the space of action for citizenship (Sarikakis 2006).

The increasingly visible heterogeneous societies of Europe shed light on the problematic assumptions behind the nation-state, but also on the ideas of the kind of justice and social cohesion achievable and desired. In an attempt to regain its questioned status, the nation-state is making its presence increasingly felt in the small places of border control and urban spaces as well as in sanctioning increased powers of the police,[20] in extraditing political refugees, in developing policies that criminalize behavior,[21] and in preparing the agenda for a new assault against women's earned rights. The most meaningful way in which the state becomes visible and from which it also derives its sovereignty is through laws, regulation, and policy. The process of sovereignty and legitimacy involves three distinct factors: the normative justification of action, a process based on accepted codes, and legality. However, sovereignty remains at the same time with the state as a regularizer (or normalizing agent) not only of stability but also of crisis and transformation, whether concerning economics, as in the case of regional and transnational capital, or military and conflict crises, as witnessed in the extensive process of "securitization" of communications and criminalization of consuming behavior. The domain where the state exercises its regularizing role is in current-day phenomena, such as the privatization process coupled with extensive commodification of security, fragmentation of society, and privatization of public spaces (Lock 2006, 3). In the era of the withdrawal of welfare policies, the state is present in reducing educational resources and funds and childcare support and in privatizing public services. In other words, the redistributive element of the European state, despite considerable differences among European states, as a role that aims to restore to some degree market injustices and cultural discriminating systems, is being overhauled by a revival of a Mc-Carthyite state. The post-9/11 legacy has provided, although not convincingly, the normative justification for a revived assault against civil liberties that aims predominantly at the individual. Here, the individual should not be understood as the deconnected atom of a pancapitalist virtual market but rather as the member of collectivities whose existence and work bring the authority or even sovereignty of the post-9/11 state into question.

As this chapter has sought to demonstrate, the complex system of balancing questions of legitimacy with those of a changing world market system is involved at its very core with questions around the shaping of "soft" policy in constructing a common consciousness in Europe. Since the EU political system is itself complex in its day-to-day workings, procedures, and institutional arrangement, more spaces have been opened up to deal with issues of common concern at a global and certainly European scale, such as questions of multiculturalism, social cohesion, recognition of cultures, and the legitimacy of communicative spaces. All these important questions are not uncontested: in particular, the forcefully economistic normative framework of both European integration and, as a consequence, its legislative approach to social questions creates but does not resolve tensions at a political but also sociocultural level. As the changing role of the state and statelike formations such as the EU polity are under increasing pressure to respond to global challenges, so it appears that the seeming withdrawal of the nation-state from the global pressure of "death to the nation-state" through its participation in supranational formations is diametrically opposite to its presence in the local. Indeed, this reinforced presence, mostly "felt" in the cultural domain, raises questions about the role of citizens before the state—whether nationally bound or globally active.

NOTES

1. The term "consciousness industry" was first coined by Hans Magnus Enzensberger in his 1962 essay "Einzelheiten I. Bewusstseins-Industrie" (Enzensberger 1962). According to Enzensberger, it is not enough to talk about the culture industry and its social(izing) role any more, as the processes of induction and mediation of consciousness in the era of mass communication technologies expand beyond the media, journalism, or even art. Enzensberger includes religion, fashion, and the proclamation of governing ideas as elements worthy of exploration.

2. Here airwaves should be understood to include the whole spectrum of transmission of broadcasting signals, whether facilitated by analog or digital technologies. What is important beyond the details of each technological development is the overall policy patterns and their impact for national and global communication landscapes.

3. In the UK alone in the decade leading to 2002, 3.9 million people entered the country as migrants and 2.8 million left (UK Government 2005a). Across OECD countries for example, "foreign"-born citizens constitute an average of 8 percent of the population while "noncitizens" constitute around 5 percent (Statistical and UN Economic Commission for Europe [UNECE]

2005). Contrary to populist discourses about an "influx" of migrants into industrialized countries, patterns of migration are extremely complex and involve as much inward as outward mobility.

4. Deterministic approaches to the origins of European integration can be found in studies that focus on the role of federalist movements in Europe. Movements such as United Europe Committee, Conseil Français pour l'Europe Unie, Ligue Indépendante de Coopération Européenne, and Pan-Europa Group; and federalist national affiliations such as Ligue pour les Etats-Unis d'Europe, Europa-Union, Europese Aktie, Federal Union, with "aspirations with widely different approaches to the purposes and forms of a European state," are mentioned by Haas (1948, 530). Pressure groups are also listed as influential by Lipgens at a time when the European project was taking shape, but Dedman (1996) finds that the only successful example deriving from such groups was Article 38 of the European Defence Community Treaty, a project that was short-lived.

5. For example, from nationalistic ideas of the supremacy of the (any) "nation" in a member-state and "purity" of nations (or culture) to the hostility derived from the EU being seen as a capitalist, industrialist project that undermines workers' rights (this does not imply hostility to all kinds of integration for the European peoples) or as what Hardt and Negri (2000) call "subaltern nationalism" against the politics of dominance (by more powerful, often imperial, states).

6. This does not mean that the debate is over: the United States has moved towards bilateral agreements with various countries around the world to pursue the liberalization of digital content. The impact of these agreements is yet to be evaluated; however, it has to be significant. Given the drive toward digitalization, once, for example, a film is digitized, then it cannot enjoy the provisions of protection of national culture.

7. According to Milward, it was the role of the nation-state to prove itself as the guarantor of domestic prosperity while at the same time, it was in the international arena where the main source for the reconstruction of new economies, trade, was to be found. Moreover, Germany's markets (and coal and steel sources) were crucial for the reconstruction of Europe. Encouraged by the United States, the process of post–World War II European integration began (Dedman 1996).

8. With the unification of the cities of northern Italy. Later on, in the Renaissance, England became the best-known case of centralizing power and economic expansion; France proceeded to a new phase of integration in 1789 for the abolishment of domestic tariffs. The operation of the Zollverein in Germany and economic and political unification fostered growth after 1848. Domestic or "national" prosperity was conceived as necessary for political and social cohesion, therefore legitimizing state policies that subsequently encouraged the further growth of capital. The latter was Bismarck's state policy, through the creation of the welfare state (see also Sarikakis 2004).

9. An obvious such case is in the dichotomized island of Cyprus.

10. The European Parliament now has co-legislative powers equal to the Council of Ministers in the majority of cases, although interestingly not in areas such as security, privacy, and so on.

11. Literally so. The Declaration of the Rights of Women and of the Citizen (1791) (Déclaration des Droits de la Femme et de la Citoyenne), as a declaration equal to the Declaration of the Rights of Man and of the Citizen (1789) (La Déclaration des droits de l'Homme et du citoyen), drafted by Olympe de Gouges, resulted in the execution of de Gouges on the accusation of treason in 1793. Feminist scholarship (e.g., Iris Young, Ruth Lister, etc.) today points to the ways in which the definition of citizen, although legally expanded to include women, in its conception still takes as its norm the male subject.

12. See Hardt and Negri 2005 in their exploration of the concept of "multitude" as "singularities acting in common" (105). The concept opposes the homogenizing efforts toward the forced construction and maintenance of "national" or other identities—instead it points to the recognition of difference and the erosion of previously "agreed-upon" homogenous identities, as this becomes accentuated through migration, forced mobility, changes in work and family

patterns, and so on. Multitude refers to the common demands for social justice springing out of non-homogenous global communities. Along the same lines Nancy Fraser (2004) projects the claims for redistribution alongside recognition in the politics of social justice, as does Haraway (1995) from an epistemological point of view, when she argues that recognition of situated knowledges does not exclude synergies for social change.

13. Although not necessarily within the boundaries of the nation-state, since some of the fictions about the function of the nation-state (Walby 2003) are contested, as states may contain more than one nation, or be federal, members of a supranational polity, or members in integration projects. Some nations are stateless or have negotiated with central states on conditions for their (relative) autonomy.

14. "Culture Policy *instead of* Foreign Policy?" (italics added)

15. *Weltgesellschaft*—world society—is the term used by Weidenfeld to connote the processes of globalization and the role of Europe in the world.

16. Such as diasporic people who are subject to double state control as in the case of obligatory military service, or regulations that expect citizens to report to embassies in cases of prolonged stay in other countries, for example.

17. To understand the cultural context of this policy, it may be worth considering the difference in understanding fundamental values in the context of free speech and child pornography in the United States. Child pornography in the EU is prohibited by law regardless of method or medium or ways of depiction. In the United States cartoons are excluded from such prohibition on the basis of noninvolvement of real people in the construction of the material. In the EU, free speech in this case is not deemed worth protection as it may result in the victimization of real—and in particular vulnerable—people.

18. For a detailed discussion of the objections to the European Union Data Retention Directive, see Privacy International and European Digital Rights 2005.

19. See the recent protest of the International Federation of Journalists that claims that no serious efforts have been made to uncover the deaths of journalists (IFJ 2006). To that one can add policies that allow cross-ownership and media ownership concentration, also an area of state-TNC synergy (see IFJ 2002).

20. The frantic militarization of the UK's urban spaces and in particular of London after the 7/7 bombings led to the fatal shooting of a non-UK citizen, Jean Charles De Meneze, by the Metropolitan Police. It is rather ironic that according to the organization Liberty, "The UK is the world leader in video surveillance. Britain is monitored by 4 million CCTV cameras, making us the most watched nation in the world" (see www.liberty-human-rights.org.uk/privacy/cctv.shtml).

21. In the UK a series of proposed and existing acts of legislation polices individual behavior through ASBO (Anti-Social Behavior Order) notices issued in cases from annoying neighbors to violent youths, totaling approximately 6500 orders between 1999 and 2005, a figure that results in an average of over 1000 a year (see Crime Reduction at www.crimereduction .gov.uk/asbos2.htm). Although the policy is seen as a way to give back to people who have been intimidated by groups or generally antisocial behavior, it further criminalizes mostly youth without tackling the underlying sources of the problem, such as lack of youth centers and an inadequate youth policy. Moreover, the increasing pressure on single mothers to "return" to work assumes that child rearing is not laborious and therefore not work, constructs single mothers and especially young ones as a social problem, and withdraws the little state support from the mostly deprived. These policies should be seen in the light of the neoliberal state and the withdrawal of funds from social long-term projects. Similar attacks on the idea of the welfare state and its importance as a safety net for social cohesion can be found in Germany with the much-contested Hartz IV social benefits policy that includes unemployment and student grants among other benefits. The commission responsible for this is the Kommission für moderne Dienstleistungen am Arbeitsmarkt, led by the Volkswagen personnel director Peter Hartz.

6

Media, Democracy, and the State in Venezuela's "Bolivarian Revolution"

Robert Duffy and Robert Everton

In the first decade of the twenty-first century, Venezuelan President Hugo Chávez became one of the most polarizing figures of international politics. Critics on the right, including many in the global English-language media, portray Chávez as the demagogic head of an authoritarian government. For the international left, Venezuela's "Bolivarian Revolution" has became an important focus of debates between those who propose "changing the world without taking power" and others who argue for the continued significance of state power in facilitating emancipatory social and political alternatives to neoliberal globalization (see Ali 2004; Holloway 2004; Lebowitz 2006). While debates have often centered on the nature and trajectory of the Venezuelan government's political and economic reforms, the relationship between state, capital, media, and democracy has been an important but in many ways underanalyzed dimension of Venezuela's social and political struggles. These issues have most dramatically crystallized in the Venezuelan commercial media's well-documented complicity in an elite-led coup attempt against the Chávez government in April 2002, but less well known are the government's subsequent efforts to facilitate challenges to the commercial media's previous near monopoly over the country's primary means of mass communication. With these issues in mind, this chapter will attempt to contextualize the commercial media's appropriation as an instrument of Venezuela's right-wing opposition movement, while simultaneously highlighting the communicative capacities and resources that have facilitated subaltern resistance to the political right's dominance of the mainstream media system. Moreover, we will argue that the Venezuelan government's support for efforts to develop and consolidate a pluralistic and democratic post-neoliberal political economy of the media, including a burgeoning independent community media sector, innovative public media projects, and re-regulation of the commercial media, challenges observers on the international left to rethink the dichotomy of "statist" versus "autonomous" strategies of resistance and social transformation.

NEOLIBERALISM IN VENEZUELA:
FROM SOCIAL CRISIS TO HEGEMONIC CRISIS

Before developing our analysis of the media, democracy and the state, it is important to first contextualize, outline, and provide a brief interpretation of Venezuela's anti-neoliberal "Bolivarian Revolution."

Since the mid-twentieth century, Venezuelan politics and society have been shaped largely by contradictions rooted in the nation's status as a major global oil producer. Though Venezuela has the largest proven oil reserves in the Western Hemisphere and generates billions of dollars in oil revenue annually, the domestic economic benefits of Venezuela's oil production have accrued primarily to a relatively narrow elite of wealthy capitalists, state managers, and middle-class professional strata, leaving the bulk of the population economically and politically marginalized. In an almost textbook example of neocolonial economic dependency, investment in domestic economic development has been sporadic, uneven, and limited, with elite and middle-class consumption and investment patterns annexed to the U.S. economy (Buxton 2001). As oil prices fell and the government gutted social programs and other subsidies during the 1980s and 1990s, the majority of Venezuelans slipped below the poverty line, with an increasing percentage subsisting precariously in the informal economy as day laborers, street traders, domestic workers, and sometimes as petty criminals (Leary 2006). By 1997, at least 60 percent of Venezuela's 22.5 million citizens lived below the official poverty line (Weisbrot, Sandoval, and Rosnick 2006). As in many other postcolonial societies of the Americas, Venezuela's class divide is also often a racial divide. Though the majority of Venezuelans are of indigenous, African, or mestizo (mixed) descent, the political and economic elites and even much of the middle class tends to be disproportionately drawn from the country's "white" European-descended population (Fletcher 2004).

After the overthrow of a military dictatorship in 1959, Venezuela was for several decades one of Latin America's more stable electoral democracies. In class terms, the country's post-1959 political system was long dominated by a hegemonic bloc led by big business interests, allied with high-level state officials (especially managers in the state-owned oil sector) and buttressed by a support base in the middle classes and relatively privileged strata of the skilled working class. While entrenched economic disparities and widespread corruption provoked episodic social and political conflict, the ruling bloc generally succeeded in securing an adequate level of consent (or at least acquiescence) from subaltern groups through limited redistribution of oil sector revenues, most often through sporadic state-funded development projects, limited social spending, and patronage networks associated with the dominant political parties and affiliated trade unions (Gott 2005; Buxton 2001). Until the 1990s, Venezuela's corrupt and clientelist electoral politics were dominated by the nominally social democratic Accion Democratica (AD), occasionally alternating in power with the Christian Democratic Comite de Organizacion Politica Electoral Independiente (COPEI).

The specific wave of political and social struggles shaping contemporary Venezuela can be traced to the country's implementation of socially and economically polarizing neoliberal policies during the 1980s and 1990s, and the subsequent collapse in the legitimacy of the political institutions and discourses that had previously organised consent for the hegemonic bloc. In material terms, the foundations of elite legitimacy were undermined as global oil prices declined during the 1980s and early 1990s, reducing state revenue and undermining the state's capacity to buy social peace through economic redistribution. This was compounded by the country's massive debt load and the growing hegemony of the neoliberal "Washington Consensus" within international lending institutions and among Venezuelan elites themselves, which further accelerated the state's unpopular program of spending cuts, privatizations and trade liberalization that had begun early in the 1980s (Buxton 2001).

Although Carlos Andrés Pérez of AD was elected as president in 1989 on a nationalist platform explicitly opposing further neoliberal reforms, one of the first actions of his administration was to eliminate consumer petroleum subsidies, leading to massive increases in domestic fuel prices and public transportation fares. Enraged by Pérez's "great u-turn," and already squeezed by a 50 percent decline in real incomes between 1979 and 1989 (Kelly and Palma 2004, 208), tens of thousands of impoverished protesters took to the streets in Venezuela's four major cities. The government responded to this urban revolt, remembered today as the "Caracazo," with the full coercive force of the state, and anywhere between three hundred and three thousand people died in three days of clashes with the military and police (Burgess 2004, 132). While the Caracazo was surely the most dramatic episode, urban unrest become endemic after 1989, with at least 851 incidents of protest recorded over the following five years (Canache 2004, 36). Clearly, "years of inadequate representation and escalating economic despair pushed the urban poor to the breaking point, and this frustration manifested itself in a prolonged wave of socio-political turmoil" (Canache 2004, 36).

Paralleling this unrest was a rise in electoral abstentionism and collapse in support for traditional political parties. Both AD and COPEI experienced roughly 50 percent declines in their respective shares of the presidential vote between 1988 and 1993 (Molina 2004, 157–58). At the same time, support rose significantly for parties able to position themselves as "outside" the traditional consensus and/or opposed to neoliberal reforms. The social crisis brought on by neoliberalism and decades of systemic corruption had radically undermined the legitimating institutions and political discourses of the Venezuelan state, opening the door to systemic challenges to the hegemonic order.

HUGO CHÁVEZ, BOLIVARIANISM, AND THE ARTICULATION OF AN ANTINEOLIBERAL COUNTERHEGEMONIC BLOC IN THE 1990s

Such a project would eventually coalesce around an electoral alliance supporting the 1998 presidential candidacy of dissident army colonel Hugo Chávez Frias. With a large support base among the urban poor, the embryonic organizational infrastructure of what proponents would come to call the "Bolivarian" movement (in homage to Simon Bolívar, the founder of the Venezuelan state and hero of nineteenth-century Latin American independence struggles) was constituted from heterodox leftist political parties, a variety of subaltern social movements, and semicovert nationalist formations of disaffected personnel from the lower ranks of the Venezuelan military (Gott 2005; Podur 2004; Zelik 2003; Gable 2004).[1]

As a political ideology, Bolivarianism articulates opposition to neoliberalism and makes demands for political, social, and economic reform within an eclectic left-nationalist discourse that references Venezuelan and Latin American historical figures rather than the terminology of the traditional left. Though critics on both the left and right have sometimes criticized Bolivarianism as "populist" (Parenti 2005; Weyland 2001), we argue that the movement cannot simply be dismissed as incoherent, demagogic, or opportunist. Instead, we see Bolivarianism as populist in the sense of Ernesto Laclau's definition of populism as "*the presentation of popular-democratic interpellations as a synthetic-antagonistic complex with respect to the dominant ideology*" (Laclau 1977, 172–73). While Venezuela's plurality of social antagonisms are often directly related to the consequences of neoliberal capitalism, only a minority of the country's subaltern population can be described as "working class" in the traditional Marxist sense. In this context, a politics that articulates heterogeneous subaltern demands through the discursive figure of "the people" or "the nation" in struggle with a collective enemy constructed as the "oligarchy," "elites," "neoliberalism," or "imperialism" seemingly provides a more viable basis for a counterhegemonic—even anticapitalist— collective political subjectivity than would a "traditional" socialist discourse that interpellates the more limited subject position of an "industrial proletariat" in conflict with its "bourgeois" antagonist.[2] As one long-time Venezuelan social activist has commented, "[t]he use of [Simon] Bolívar as a symbol, and other symbols from Venezuelan history, was . . . something new. Before, the reference points for the left were ideologies like communism, marxism, things that didn't speak as clearly to the people" (Podur 2004). Though such "populism" by no means guarantees the progressive political content of the movement, and there is no ironclad guarantee that Bolivarianism will maintain a progressive trajectory, we argue that "populist" characteristics do not in themselves nullify the radically democratic or even potentially socialist trajectory of the Bolivarian Revolution.[3]

The rise of Chávez as a national symbol of subaltern popular resistance and Bolivarianism as a counterhegemonic discourse can be traced to the 1992 coup attempt led by Movimiento Bolivariano Revolucionario-200 (MBR-200), a left-nationalist group launched by Chávez and other junior military officers during the early 1980s. For MBR-200 and others in the lower ranks of the military, long-standing disaffection with corruption and national economic decline was compounded by anger at having been ordered to turn their weapons on civilians during the 1989 Caracazo (Gott 2005, 43–47). While MBR-200's February 1992 coup attempt was countered by forces loyal to then president Carlos Andrés Pérez , a short televised address negotiated as a condition of Chávez's surrender captured the imagination of many politically marginalized and disaffected Venezuelans. In the broadcast, Chávez proclaimed that MBR-200's project of moving the country "definitively towards a better future" was not defeated, but only on hold "for the moment" (Gott 2005, 68–69). According to Venezuelan social activists, this broadcast established Chávez as a potential symbol for articulating widespread but politically fragmented disenchantment with Venezuela's social and political status quo. Chávez and his left-nationalist Bolivarian discourse became "empty signifiers" (see Laclau 2005) capable of providing the discursive "glue" required to link together a plurality of previously uncoordinated subaltern grievances into a more unified counterhegemonic political project. As one social movement activist later recalled,

> People believed in our work and the basic fights for dignity. But Chávez managed to accomplish in two minutes on television what we weren't able to accomplish in years. . . . The uprising put forward the idea that there could be an alternative political project for the country.

> I saw the effect in the barrio. My house was filled all the time with people saying: "Can you believe this?" "Can you believe what Chavez said?" And it wasn't just what he said. It was that he was someone who looked like them: with his black, indigenous looks. People felt represented for the first time. (Podur 2004)

THE "BOLIVARIAN REVOLUTION": TOWARD A "SOCIALISM OF THE TWENTY-FIRST CENTURY"?

By the time of his pardon and release from prison in 1994, Hugo Chávez had become an important symbol of popular opposition to the Venezuelan status quo. Buoyed by nationwide political discontent and the disarray of traditional political elites, Chávez's newly formed civilian-military Movimiento V República (MVR, or "Fifth Republic Movement") and various smaller left-wing parties coalesced in an alliance supporting the 1998 presidential election campaign that would propel Chávez to the presidency.

A detailed treatment of the subsequent "Bolivarian Revolution" is outside the scope of this chapter and has been done well elsewhere (see especially Gott 2005). Nonetheless, it is important to highlight aspects of the process in order to contextualize the backlash from Venezuela's traditional elites, and also to counter simplistic narratives about Venezuelan politics circulated in many mainstream Northern , and particularly North American, media discourses.

Participatory and Protagonist Democracy

While implications that Chávez is an "authoritarian" figure prominently in North American media discourse, and even some progressives are understandably troubled by the "politics of personality" associated with Chávez's presidency, very little mainstream media attention has been given to the radically democratic dimensions of Venezuela's post-1998 political and economic reforms. Beyond the Chávez government's clear legitimacy in representative democratic terms (a fact often ignored in North American media discourse),[4] the Bolivarian revolution has also facilitated the initial stages of a reform process that we argue constitutes a potential expansion of substantive democratic participation.

This process began in 1999, when a Constituent Assembly was elected and drafted a new constitution that passed by popular referendum later that year. Though not in itself socialist, the 1999 Constitution is nonetheless a direct challenge to globally hegemonic "market liberal" notions of democracy, prioritizing social objectives, national economic development and democratic participation over private economic interests (Lebowitz 2006). Perhaps most promising is the Constitution's emphasis on building what proponents call "participatory and protagonist democracy." This "protagonist democracy" calls for the creation of social conditions and institutional structures that transcend the limited representational framework of liberal democracy and allow for the extension of substantive popular participation and collective decision making across the entire spectrum of social life (Lebowitz 2006). Perhaps the most innovative dimension of protagonist democracy is a concept of a state that rejects not only the market-oriented laissez-faire of neoliberalism but also the authoritarian or paternalist control that has all to often characterized past governments of the left. Instead, protagonist democracy proposes a state oriented toward producing structural and subjective conditions that are conducive to collective social development and relatively autonomous popular initiative, or what former Venezuelan communication and information minister Jesse Chacon has described as "a state that has stopped imposing things, to become a collective instrument for social transformation and development" (Iacobelli and Gironi 2004).

While this is an ambitious goal and at the time of our writing clearly only in its initial stages, concrete manifestations can be located in the government's support for economic cooperatives, for worker self-management, and, as will be explored in this paper, for the expansion of the independent community media sector. Potentially the most dramatic step toward "protagonist democracy" to date has been the January 2007 announcement that the central government would be transferring US$5 billion to thousands of federated neighborhood "communal councils" for direct democratic control over "education, construction, transport, health, agriculture and housing related projects" (Mather 2007). While the "politics of personality" and Chávez's constitutionally limited use of temporary "enabling laws" to push through reforms have understandably worried some progressives, it is important to note that these potentially contradictory tendencies within Bolivarianism have so far been embedded in a wider process that has emphasized the radical expansion of democratic participation and decision making (Lebowitz 2007).

Economic and Social Policy Reforms

While the Bolivarian government proceeded cautiously on economic and social reforms during its first years in power, it had shifted in a more radical direction by 2002, with moves to rechannel revenue from the state oil company, Petróleos de Venezuela S.A. (PDVSA), toward economic development initiatives and social programs (Ellsworth 2004; *Economist* 2005). Buoyed by increased oil revenues, the government launched what it calls "Missiones," a series of social development initiatives including literacy programs, free medical care, and discount food markets for low-income Venezuelans. The social impact of these programs has been significant, with 1.4 million Venezuelans becoming literate, 14.5 million accessing free medical care, and an approximately 40 percent drop in the overall poverty rate between 1997 and 2005 (Weisbrot, Sandoval, and Rosnick 2006, 5–6).

Beyond these social welfare initiatives, the government has implemented new regulatory frameworks and subsidy programs to facilitate worker comanagement and the expansion of the collective and cooperative enterprise

sector, including legislation facilitating the seizure of abandoned private factories and underutilized farmland for these purposes (Bowman and Stone
2006). At the international level, the government initiated a new trade alliance
aimed at Latin American integration and has also provided cut-rate petroleum
to countries in Latin America, the Carribean, and even to low-income communities in the United States. In January of 2007, Chávez announced plans to
rescind the autonomy of the central bank, and to renationalize electricity generation, and a telecom company owned by a subsidiary of U.S. multinational
Verizon (Romero 2007a).

Though it is too early to assess the ultimate trajectory of what Chávez has
started to call a "socialism of the twenty-first century," it can safely be as-
serted that these measures constitute the most radical state-led challenge to
the "market fundamentalism" of the neoliberal "Washington Consensus" in
decades. Not surprisingly, this prioritization of collective needs over private
profit, especially the social reappropriation of privately owned productive capacity and oil sector revenue, has been greeted with overt hostility by
Venezuelan capitalist elites and the country's commercial media outlets.

VENEZUELA'S COMMERCIAL MEDIA: FROM RELATIVE
AUTONOMY TO BLUNT INSTRUMENTALISM

Before moving on to discuss the commercial media sector's role in mobilizing opposition to the Bolivarianism, most dramatically as demonstrated in the
complicity of commercial media outlets in a short-lived April 2002 coup
against the Chávez government, we will need to provide a brief overview and
analysis of Venezuela's mass media system.

Media Structure and Ownership in Venezuela

Historically, Venezuela's media system has been dominated by a powerful
private sector, overshadowing a relatively limited and underfunded state sector and a few legally precarious community-run media outlets.[5] Commercial
media outlets have long exercised a virtual monopoly in the country, controlling an estimated 95 percent of the airwaves and a "near monopoly" over
newsprint by 2002 (Lemoine 2002).

Broadcasting, especially, has been dominated by a few large private enterprises owned and managed by families firmly rooted in the economic and political oligarchy. Although by the time of the 2002 coup attempt there were
more than twenty television stations in Venezuela, more than 70 percent of
the total audience regularly viewed the four main commercial broadcasters,
Venevisión, Globovisión, RCTV, and Televen (Lugo and Romero 2003, 13).
While two twenty-four-hour news networks, Globovisión on television and

Union Radio on radio, have been qualitatively important as agenda setters, neither reaches more than 10 percent of the total audience of their respective medium (Lugo and Romero 2003, 13).

Venevisión TV, probably the largest broadcaster in terms of audience share, is owned by Gustavo Cisneros Rendiles, Venezuela's richest man and an heir to considerable wealth from breweries, bottling, and broadcasting. (Romero 2002; Forbes 2001, 2002, 2003, 2006). With assets of US$5 billion in 2006, Cisneros is Latin America's second wealthiest man and maintains extremely close connections to U.S. monopoly capital, holding the licensing rights for Coca-Cola, Pizza Hut, and *Playboy* in a number of Latin American countries (Romero 2002; Forbes 2006). His Cisneros Group of Companies has annual revenue of over US$3.5 billion (Global Information Infrastructure Commission [GIIC] 2004) and is also a major shareholder in U.S.-based Univisión Communications, making it "one of the largest privately held broadcast, media, technology, consumer products and telecommunications organizations in the world" (Golinger-Moncada 2003b). Univisión was authorized in 2003 by the U.S. broadcasting authority, the Federal Communications Commission (FCC), to merge with the Hispanic Broadcasting Corporation, giving Cisneros a significant influence over Hispanic broadcasting in the United States, which may have considerable future consequences for Latin American markets (Golinger-Moncada 2003b). Even prior to this merger, the Cisneros Group was responsible each year for 19,000 hours of Spanish- and Portuguese-language programming in forty million households across twenty-one countries (Romero 2002). The Cisneros Group is also the majority owner of AOL–Latin America, DirecTV Latin America (broadcasting over three hundred channels to Latin America), IARC Chile, and Venevisión Continental (Golinger-Moncada 2003b). With a media empire spanning seventy outlets in thirty-nine countries (Lemoine 2002).Cisneros has been justifiably been described as a "gatekeeper to the Latin American market" (Klein 2003) and "the Rupert Murdoch of Latin America" (Eimer 2004).

Of Venezuela's ten major daily newspapers, only *El Nacional* and *El Universal* had distribution at a truly national level by 2002 (Lugo and Romero 2003, 13–14). Major players in Venezuelan newspaper publishing include Miguel Henrique Otero, owner and publisher of one of the country's most established newspapers, *El Nacional,* as well as the daily *Así es La Noticia* and various magazines (*Economist* 2002a); and Rafael Poleo, owner of *El Nuevo Pais* (Lemoine 2002); the Mata and Nuñez families, owners of *El Universal;* Cuban expatriate Miguel Angel Capriles, owner of more than a dozen publications, including the dailies *El Mundo* and *Últimas Noticias;* and another Cuban expatriate, Armando de Armas, who owns *Meridiano, Diario 2001,* and *Abril* and represents the Hearst Group in Venezuela (Lugo and Romero 2003, 7– 8).

As stalwarts of the country's economic oligarchy, Venezuelan's commercial media owners have generally been vocal proponents of neoliberalism and supporters of the country's pre-Chávez political status quo. Gustavo Cisneros, for example, has publicly expressed a commitment to the consolidation of the neoliberal program in the Americas, arguing in 1999 that "Latin America is now fully committed to free trade and fully committed to globalisation. . . . As a continent it has made a choice" (Klein 2003). The executive editor of the *El Universal* newspaper similarly expressed a commitment to the neoliberal agenda, equating "media freedom" with "market freedom" in arguing that the Chávez government's policies are "contrary to the very vision of a medium that depends . . . on a good private sector . . . which is what feeds the private media from the market of the buying and selling of advertising" (Rojas in Barahona 2005).

Instrumentalization of the Commercial Media and the Coup of April 2002

While long under the economic control of large-scale capitalist interests, Venezuela's commercial media system, it must be emphasized, appears to have paralleled similarly structured North American and European commercial media sectors and operated in line with recognizable liberal democratic notions of a "free and independent press." Indeed, the *Columbia Journalism Review* has described the Venezuelan press as having had a "tradition of high quality" and "a media community that is among the most prosperous, best trained and equipped and—until recently—most respected in Latin America" with "[l]ively talk shows on television and radio [that] explore every shift in the political landscape" (Dinges 2005). Opinion polling from the early and mid-1990s suggest that this positive perception was shared by many Venezuelans themselves, with the media and journalists ranked consistently at or near the top in terms of the credibility and performance of social institutions and professions, which was especially significant at a time when voting patterns, opinion polls, and civil unrest indicated low trust in political parties and the government (Buxton 2001, 73–75). Though the media's pro–status quo orientation was evident in ongoing marginalization of political parties outside the AD-COPEI axis, alleged journalistic negligence in coverage of police and military abuses during the Caracazo (Buxton 2004; Podur 2004), and in media mogul Gustavo Cisneros putting the country's largest television station at "[President] Pérez's disposal" during the 1992 military revolt (Gott 2006, 153), everyday journalistic practice in the Venezuelan commercial media did not appear to be determined through any sort of direct, mechanical control by other centers of political and economic power. This was not a crude "propaganda" system, but a recognizable variant of a liberal democratic "free and independent media."

This is significant to note, as it suggests that the eventual blunt instrumentalization of the commercial media in attempts to oust the Chávez government should not be viewed as a pathological characteristic intrinsic to a "backward" Venezuelan political order or media system, but instead understood in relation to the hegemonic crisis of a ruling bloc threatened with a serious challenge to its political, economic, and coercive power. Direct instrumentalization of the media in the service of capitalist political and economic elites is thus not necessarily an atavistic feature of preliberal democratic social orders that we can safely relegate to the "dustbin of history," nor, as some might argue, is it the everyday preferred and standard mode of ideological operation in capitalist societies. Instead, in the context of the collapse of the traditional political parties, a politically unreliable military, and threats to elite control over the oil industry, the instrumentalization of the media must be understood as an attempt to mobilize the most important political and ideological assets still under elite control. As a *Guardian* columnist has suggested, the private media in Venezuela took on the role of "replacing the old parties of the pre-revolutionary era that had lost their voters" (Gott 2007).

Mobilizing Opposition

Venezuela's commercial media outlets were for the most part not overtly hostile in coverage of Chávez's initial presidential campaign. A few commercial outlets were even supportive of Chávez at the time, perhaps seeing him as simply another demagogue who could be co-opted by traditional elites upon assuming power (Gott 2005, 245). However, commercial media coverage became increasingly hostile after the Chávez government took power and began to make clear that promises of political, constitutional, and economic reform were more than campaign rhetoric. Media hostility escalated dramatically at the end of 2001 when the government announced moves to restructure and reform the oil industry (Ellner 2003b). Control over the state oil company, PDVSA, had long been an economic foundation of elite power in Venezuela, and the Chávez government's efforts to root out corruption and harness oil revenues for social development initiatives represented a direct challenge to the power and wealth of the country's rentier oil oligarchy and their middle-class allies.

Throughout early 2002, Venezuela's private television stations allocated increasingly large blocks of airtime to antigovernment programming, including free broadcasts of oil industry–funded anti-Chávez agitprop clips (*The Revolution Will Not be Televised* 2003). According to a number of journalists and former employees, station owners and management began to interfere frequently in editorial content and reporting in order to ensure negative coverage of the Chávez government and its supporters. One of the early voices from inside the media to speak out was Andrés Izarra, a respected journalist and longtime employee of CNN en espanol, who had taken a job as director of RCTV's flagship news program, *Observador.* Izarra claims that in the weeks leading up to the April 2002 coup there were clear instructions not to run any "information on Chávez, his followers, his ministers, and all others that could in any way be related to him," as well as to provide positive blanket coverage of opposition marches and minimize coverage of progovernment demonstrations (Klein 2003). According to another prominent journalist, many colleagues consciously identified with the political status quo and readily "bought the argument that you have to put journalistic standards aside, that if we don't get rid of Chávez we will have communism" (Moleiro in Dinges 2005). For many working within the commercial press, it apparently became common sentiment that "we can leave aside ethics and rules of journalism" in relation to reporting on Venezuela's social and political turmoil (Dinges 2005).

From Agitprop to Coup Plot

By April of 2002, the commercial media's political intervention had moved beyond simply promoting opposition protests and into direct complicity in the planning and execution of the coup attempt helmed by former PDVSA CEO Pedro Carmona. The media barons most active in the coup seem to have been Gustavo Cisneros, *El Nacional*'s Miguel Henrique Otero, Globovision's Alberto Federico Ravell, RCTV's Marcel Granier (*Economist* 2002a) and *El Nuevo Pais*'s owner, Rafael Poleo (Lemoine 2002).

When violence broke out during an April 10 opposition demonstration in Caracas, several private television stations replaced all regular programming with continuous antigovernment broadcasts, including doctored and selectively edited footage that inaccurately portrayed the government and its supporters as the sole instigators, when in fact both government supporters and opposition demonstrators had been victims of unidentified snipers (Klein 2003 and *The Revolution Will Not be Televised* 2003). Soon after, Venevisión's Caracas studios reportedly hosted a closed-door meeting of the coup's leadership, and similar "meetings held to plan the removal of the president from power were held at [*El Nacional* publisher] Mr. Otero's house" (*Economist* 2002a).

The coup was launched on April 11, after television stations helped mobilize thousands of opposition protesters to march on the presidential palace and opposition-led military units arrested the president and other government officials. On the day of the coup, Venezuelan broadcasters spread false reports that Hugo Chávez had voluntarily resigned as president, when he had in fact been taken prisoner by hostile elements of the armed forces, while the president of the Venezuelan broadcasting chamber went so far as to join coup leaders in signing a decree dissolving Venezuela's elected national assembly (Klein 2003). Commercial media outlets at this point also helped initiate a campaign of terror directed at deposed Chávez government officials and other coup opponents, most notably when "RCTV triggered a manhunt by publishing a list of the most wanted individuals and broadcast violent searches live" (Lemoine 2002). Overconfident in the coup's success, Cisneros' Venevisión televised programming in which prominent members of the oligarchy openly bragged about their roles in organizing the putsch (*The Revolution Will Not be Televised,* 2003), with coup organizer Vice Admiral Victor Ramírez Pérez going so far as to publicly acknowledge that "[w]e had a deadly weapon: the media," (quoted in Lemoine 2002). As a veteran presidential reporter for Venezuela's largest radio chain told the London *Times,* "it was a media coup" (Adams 2002).

During this same period, Venezuela's dominant media outlets were also complicit in repressing criticism or even coverage of opposition to the coup. For example, the Union Radio chain imposed an internal policy forbidding negative reporting about the newly installed Carmona government, while journalists elsewhere were "told by their bosses to "forget being journalists for the next week, we're all working for the [new] government now" (Adams 2002). As the coup unravelled in the face of militant popular opposition, the private media resorted to a self-imposed blackout on coverage of massive street demonstrations by Chávez supporters (with the exceptions of some CNN rebroadcasts on Globovisión), and abruptly stopped all news coverage after the legitimate government regained control of the presidential palace on April 14, choosing instead to broadcast movies and animated cartoons as replacement programming (Klein 2003).

Compounding these abuses, supporters of the coup engaged in efforts to silence potentially pro-Chávez media outlets. The Caracas community stations Catia TVe, TV Caricuao, Radio Perola, Radio Alternativa de Caracas, and Radio Catia Libre were subjected to violent raids, equipment seizures, and detentions of personnel (Lemoine 2002; International Federation of Journalists [IFJ] 2002, 12), and the state channel 8 was shut down for twenty hours until eventually brought back on the air by community media activists under the protection of pro-Chávez soldiers (Lemoine 2002). In at least one case, opposition-controlled Caracas police units moved to seize a community broadcasting station with the apparent foreknowledge of the Venevisión television crew who recorded the entire proceedings (McCaughan 2004, 102).

Confronted with the counter-hegemonic challenge represented by the Bolivarian movement, Venezuela's commercial media sector abandoned any pretence of professional "autonomy" or journalistic "objectivity" and worked openly as an organ of the elite-dominated opposition movement. Simultaneously, the commercial media were demonstrably complicit in efforts to systematically impede, and even undermine, the communicative rights and capacities of Venezuela's subaltern classes, yet ironically tried to defend these actions through liberal discourses of "press freedom." In doing so, Venezuela's commercial media revealed the inherent contradiction in market liberal notions of communication rights. By reducing communication rights to simply the right of media owners to employ their property however they see fit, the market liberal conceptualization of "freedom of the press" in effect constitutes the rationale for an always potentially authoritarian enclosure of the primary channels of mediated public communication and structural blockage of substantively democratic public communication. As Raymond Williams noted in 1962, though probably with less dramatic circumstances in mind, "the control claimed as a matter of power by authoritarians, and as a matter of principle by paternalists, is often achieved as a matter of practice in the operation of the commercial system" (1962, 92).

THE LIMITS OF INSTRUMENTALISM: COUNTERHEGEMONIC COMMUNICATION AND THE COLLAPSE OF THE COUP

Despite fears that the events of April 2002 would end in a tragic echo of the successful 1973 coup against Chile's democratic socialist government,[6] as many as one million people, mostly from Caracas's impoverished barrios, surrounded the presidential palace between April 12 and 14 to demand the restoration of the legitimate government. Emboldened by this popular mobilization, Chávez supporters in the military expelled the coup government from the presidential palace and freed the president from captivity. By April 14, barely forty-eight hours after the coup plotters had seemingly taken power, Chávez had been restored as president, and he has subsequently defeated several further opposition attempts to unseat his government.

Although the traditional elites' instrumentalization of commercial broadcasting allowed them to construct and widely circulate a narrative so divergent from actual events that one commentator called it "an alternate reality" (Wilpert 2002), this was not in the end enough to guarantee even the acquiescence of subaltern groups, much less win consent for the coup regime. In this sense, the Venezuelan experience is a reminder that control over the structurally dominant channels of mass communication is not necessarily determinate of popular political consciousness, especially in a context of intense social polarization and political conflict.

While it is safe to claim that the mass mobilization of the urban poor in Caracas and the actions of loyalist military personnel were the direct cause of the coup's collapse, it is more difficult to arrive at any definitive interpretation of the social and communicative processes that facilitated this popular mobilization and subaltern resistance to the commercial media's ideological onslaught. Nonetheless, available accounts suggest two broad entry points for an analysis. On the one hand, we can understand one "axis of resistance" as centered around the constitution and organization of subaltern subjects as potential "mass active audiences" inclined toward "oppositional readings" of dominant ideologies encoded in media texts. The second axis revolves around the social networks, organizational infrastructure, and technical resources that facilitated the mobilization and coordination of active subaltern resistance to the coup.

Resistant Subjects and Active Audiences

A major factor in the failure of the coup appears to have been widespread identification with the expressed aims of the Bolivarian government, and the associated popular appropriation of Chávez as a symbol of the political aspirations of Venezuela's poor and oppressed (Zelik 2003). Such sentiment was surely a factor in widespread skepticism directed at media accounts of Chávez's supposed "resignation," and also in the refusal to accept the legitimacy of any restoration to power of discredited traditional elites. While media attacks on Chávez and government supporters in the buildup to the coup clearly succeeded in catalyzing a fairly unified elite and middle-class mobilization, it seems probable that these virulent and sometimes racist attacks simultaneously alienated many from the country's working classes and poor (Fletcher 2004). In addition, brazenly counterfactual news narratives in the run-up to the coup would have contradicted the lived experience of tens of thousands of Chávez supporters who had been in the streets at the time, further discrediting the commercial media in the eyes of many. Thus, rather than winning subaltern consent for a neoliberal restoration, commercial media discourses clashed so forcefully with existing subaltern "common sense" as to actually heighten anti-elite sentiment and undermine the commercial media's legitimacy. Reports of attacks on commercial stations as the coup unravelled, and subsequent violence directed at mainstream journalists entering barrios that had once been "media-friendly," suggest that many poor and working-class Venezuelans had indeed come to view the commercial media as discredited instruments of elite power (Dinges 2005).

While some of this resistance could be characterized as contextual and spontaneous, it is worth noting Michael Denning's caveat that "subaltern experience does not necessarily generate social criticism and cultural resistance; the possibility of popular political readings of cultural commodities depends on the cultivation, organisation, and mobilization of audiences by oppositional subcultures and social movements" (Denning 1996, 64). As mentioned earlier, various social movements, leftist parties, community media, and popular education projects had long been active among Venezuelan subaltern strata and had in many cases stepped up their activities after 1998 (Zelik 2003). They were joined in these efforts by "Bolivarian Circles," networks of education and mobilization groups formed to defend the new constitution and advance the wider objectives of the Bolivarian revolution (Gable 2004). More generally, accounts suggest that the mobilization to elect Chávez, combined with mass participation in the subsequent constitutional process, had increased the confidence and assertiveness of many marginalized Venezuelans, perhaps marking initial steps in the "revolution in subjectivity" implied by the 1998 constitution's call for "protagonist democracy" (Zelik 2003; Gable 2004). Whatever the case, structured educational, cultural, and political activities have surely been important constitutive elements of the resistant subjectivities and counterhegemonic discursive frameworks mobilized in subaltern classes' "collective oppositional readings" of commercial media texts.

Technology and Resistance

While the mobilization against the coup suggests that access to mass media technology is not inconsequential, the collective capacity to resist is not an effect of any particular "advanced" technology. Instead, this capacity is immanent to human communicative networks, which can be organized in a multitude of ways and can creatively appropriate a wide array of technologies. For example, the activists of Caracas's Aporrea media collective, which eventually evolved into a kind of Internet-based, nationwide community newswire, locate the genesis of their project not in its present technological form but in "Popular Revolutionary Assemblies" and ad hoc mobilization and pamphleteering groups initiated by activists anticipating the imminent coup attempt (Aporrea.org Collective in Gómez 2005a). Likewise, numerous commentators point to the significance of word-of-mouth communication, or "Radio Bemba," as the rumor mill is colloquially known in some Latin American countries, as an important factor in circulating the information that Chávez had not really resigned and in mobilizing the Caracas barrios to topple the coup (Wilpert 2003).

This is not to claim that technological resources do not matter. While the interpersonal networks that constitute Radio Bemba are in some senses a timeless phenomenon of subaltern communication, this was a Radio Bemba accelerated and enhanced by the wide diffusion of cellular telephones and text messaging and the presence of community media outlets. Also important was access to information from foreign and transnational media sources that contradicted the "alternate reality" constructed by the domestic commercial media (Fernandes 2005). The Radio Bemba of April 2003 was also augmented by activist use of the Internet, despite relatively low overall usage in the country at the time (Aporrea.org Collective in Gómez 2005a).

Although the forces involved in the coup succeeded in temporarily shutting down many independent and community media outlets, alternative media activism nonetheless appears to have played a role in facilitating resistance. (Catia TVe Collective 2006; Fernandes 2005). Caracas's Catia TVe, for example, claims to have played a role in circumventing the commercial media's efforts to prevent news coverage of the anticoup mobilizations in Caracas, while a community radio station initially shut down by coup supporters eventually returned to the air and promoted street demonstrations (Catia TVe Collective 2006; Fernandes 2005). In more spontaneous appropriations of media technology, workers at the Caracas Municipal Press reportedly produced 100,000 copies of a bulletin advocating resistance to the coup, and community media activists, supported by Chavista soldiers, reactivated the main state television channel, reportedly a crucial event in the restoration of the legitimate government (Catia TVe Collective 2006).

MEDIA, STATE, AND SOCIETY AFTER THE COUP: TOWARD A POSTNEOLIBERAL MEDIA SYSTEM?

Despite the success of the anticoup mobilizations, elite domination of major channels of communication had proven to be a powerful political weapon, and the relatively diffuse and often ad hoc structures and channels of communication available to the social protagonists of the Bolivarian revolution were clearly in need of strengthening.

While some in Venezuela and abroad predicted an authoritarian crackdown on the coup's aftermath, at the time of writing the Bolivarian government has avoided coercive measures and media censorship, and even private media outlets that were openly complicit in the coup escaped without immediate formal sanction.[7] Indeed, rather than contracting and restricting opportunities for mediated expression, the government has responded with a set of policies that suggest an expanded realization of democratic communication rights.

Broadly speaking, these moves toward a postneoliberal, participatory democratic communication order have progressed along three main paths: regulatory and infrastructural support for the community media sector; investment in an expanded, reconceptualized, and restructured public media sector; and re-regulation of the broadcast sector to stimulate the growth, deconcentration, and diversification of domestic audiovisual cultural production. The overarching goal of these policies is to strengthen the domestic media's role in cultural self-representation and in other processes of social, political, and economic development.

Venezuela's Community Media Sector

Historical precursors to Venezuela's contemporary community media movement date back to at least the 1960s, ranging from leftist newspapers and "megaphone radio" broadcast from cars and vans to community cultural and popular education projects and "CineClubs," which were community film screenings that originated as "client networks and patronage of the major political parties" but were eventually appropriated as "instruments of the organized communities" as popular discontent with neoliberalism and corruption grew during the 1980s and 1990s (Podur 2004). As of 2007, Venezuela's community media sector encompassed outlets ranging from low-power neighborhood radio stations to relatively sophisticated, semiprofessional UHF TV stations broadcasting across large urban areas (Leary 2004, 19). While such outlets formerly operated outside the law and had historically been subject to state repression, the Chávez government quickly moved to end this harassment after taking power (Wilpert 2004), though reports of persecution by opposition-controlled municipal governments continued until as late as 2003. In 2000, the government passed an "Organic Telecommunications Law," which established legal recognition and regulatory parameters for the community media sector (Wilpert 2004, 35). Though the legalization process at first proceeded sluggishly, only about thirty stations having received permits by late 2003, the Venezuelan communication minister promised to dramatically accelerate the process in 2004 (Iacobelli and Gironi 2004). In this climate, the total number of community broadcasters in Venezuela (licensed and unlicensed) soared from fifty in 2001 to about three hundred by 2004 (Forero 2004), with at least thirty community-run independent television stations on the air by 2006 (Catia TVe Collective 2006).

Structurally, this burgeoning community media sector embodies many characteristics of the speculative "democratic system of communication" Raymond Williams posited as a contrast to existing commercial, paternalist, or authoritarian communication systems (Williams 1962). Unlike commercial media, Venezuelan community broadcasters attempt to be both politically representative of, and materially accessible to, a majority population previously marginalized in the country's dominant political and cultural spheres. In principle, and evidence suggests in practice as well, the community media sector is guided and driven by the initiative of organized subaltern communities and independent media producers rather than by commercial imperatives, state paternalism, or the strategic requirements of particular politicians or parties.

Available accounts provide a sense of the general character of the community broadcast sector, ranging from Radio Perola, where local volunteers broadcast music and leftist political programming from a converted storage room in an impoverished housing project (Forero 2004), to Catia TVe, an ambitious Caracas independent television station that is developing innovative forms of participatory community journalism as part of a "cultural transformation" in line with the new constitution's concept of "protagonist democracy" (Leary 2004).

Catia TVe, to date the best-documented of Venezuela's community broadcasters, has an organizational lineage that can be traced back to the Cineclub movement and other politicized cultural projects of the 1980s and 1990s (Catia TVe Collective 2006). Supported by a sympathetic LCR municipal administration, Catia began to facilitate the production and screening of community-produced televisual projects (Podur 2004). Attendance at Catia-sponsored cultural nights reportedly "exploded" in response to this opportunity to participate in community self-representation; close to 2000 people attended inaugural screenings of local productions in 1995 (Catia TVe collective 2006; Podur 2004). Over time, a "network of barrio news was created, based on creating and passing these films," with strong organic connections to contemporaneous subaltern social struggles, such as the 1990s movement against water privatization (Podur 2004). The project thus "started to become the cables of a network to connect the community" well before the move to broadcast transmission (Podur 2004).

With technical assistance from sympathetic university personnel, Catia TVe became operational as a television broadcaster in 2000 and used the launch of the station as a platform to demand the implementation of government promises to establish a regulatory framework for the community media (Podur 2004, Catia TVe Collective 2006). Though communication was recognized as a social right in the 1999 constitution, media activists found that the state regulatory body, Comisión Nacional de Telecomunicaciones (CONATEL), was still predicated on a "neoliberal idea of the state" and oriented primarily toward the commercial media (Podur 2004). Efforts to formally legalize Catia, and community media more broadly, thus typified a "major task of the movements: to force compliance with the constitution" and institutionalize its promise of participatory democracy through transformation of the Venezuelan state (Podur 2004).

Operating under the slogan "Don't watch television, make television," Catia TVe's five-hour daily programming blocs are 70 percent volunteer produced, with the remaining 30 percent a mix of material produced by paid staff and programming from other community and independent producers (Catia Tve Collective 2006). The station's small roster of paid staff focuses on providing training, technical assistance, and organizational support for groups of volunteers organized into collective production teams called Community Teams of Independent Audiovisual Production ("ECPAIs" in the Spanish acronym) (Catia TVe Collective 2006; Leary 2004, 18). Programming ranges from "Cayapa [collective work] in the Community," which compiles on-location interviews about pertinent community issues, to documentaries on topics ranging from local history to garbage collection, and even short fictional films (Leary 2004, 18). Catia TVe's participatory governance process includes weekly open meetings, where community members can provide input and even develop new programming ideas (Leary 2004, 20).

Similarly oriented community broadcasters deal with everything from national political debates to "mundane matters like trash pickups or road conditions" and "are staffed by volunteers, from teenagers eager for the chance to play Venezuelan hip-hop or salsa to homemakers who want to tell listeners how to stretch earnings in tough times" (Forero 2004). A statement from a Catia TVe engineer perhaps encapsulates the operational philosophy of the wider community media sector: "the idea is that the communities make television and they communicate with themselves this way, through the neighborhood broadcaster. It's not one person speaking to everyone else, like in the commercial news, or the product of one leader who turns out a single line for every issue" (Leary 2004, 18). In contrast to the disempowering and spectatorial logic of commercial or paternalist/authoritarian state media, this model suggests the reappropriation of media technology in a process of a self-representation and self-recognition that help facilitate the constitution of subaltern groups as political, social, and cultural subjects. Media production and consumption thus become components of social agency and collective political action, part of the constituent power of subaltern groups to realize new social-political relationships and forms of subjectivity.

Community Media and the Bolivarian State

While the Bolivarian Constitution and subsequent legislation laid legal foundations for the growth of community media, government initiatives to consolidate the sector accelerated in the wake of the April 2002 coup. Indeed, the government seems to have initially been caught off guard by the vitality of the community media, with then communication minister Jesse Chacon commenting in 2004 that the government was "astonished" by the growth and dynamism of the sector since its legalization (Iacobelli and Gironi 2004). Expressing enthusiasm for the community media's democratic potential, Chacon argued in 2004 that

> if communication is a social and an individual right, people must be able to practice it. We are absolutely convinced that this right is limited and denied in many countries. People cannot be represented by private interests as is the case in the North American model. To be able to have access to media you have to have great economic resources. Now, if a community wants access, it should have the same possibility.
>
> We must privilege the right of communities over private interest. The private media are exerting their right to make a profit, while the organized communities use it as a mechanism for social development. And, because our Constitution privileges social development over individual interest, far more than simply accepting them, this government sponsors communitarian and alternative media by many means. (Chacon in Iacobelli and Gironi 2004)

Drawing on this conception of communication rights, a regulatory framework has been developed to define the community media sector, designed not only to determine eligibility requirements for subsidy programs and tax breaks but also to enshrine the sector's participatory democratic character and institutional autonomy. Criteria for legal recognition include stipulations that stations be nonprofit, that at least 70 percent of the programming be produced within the community, and that 85 percent of content should be volunteer produced, with ongoing training of new volunteers (Wilpert 2004, 35).

The communication minister implementing this framework publicly emphasized the goal of maintaining the sector's independence, stating "the Venezuelan state does not interfere with the conception of these media. It is a risk, but we assumed it" (Iacobelli and Gironi 2004). Station directors cannot be political party officials, military personnel, or employees of the commercial media (Wilpert 2004, 35). For its part, the community media sector, while often in sympathy with the general trajectory of government reforms, has been protective of its autonomy. The Catia TVe collective, for example, sees the relationship between community media and the Chávez government as a contingent alliance, arguing that

> community television . . . is a space where all the exploited sectors in Venezuela can participate. And so long as the Venezuelan Government supports these struggles, these community media sectors identify with the Bolivarian Revolution. . . . At the same time, Venezuelans will also struggle against any elements of the bureaucracy that tries to usurp power for personal gain. For that reason, we say that community television stations engage in the revolution inside the revolution. (Catia TVe Collective 2006)

Indeed, community media outlets have already provided platforms for progressive criticism of government policy, opposition to government plans to increase environmentally damaging coal extraction being a notable example of the community media's "willingness to criticize the government when community interests are at stake" (Fernandes 2005).

In conjunction with regulatory support, material commitments from the state announced since 2003 have paved the way for technical improvements and expansion of the community media sector, most notably a $3.1 million investment in infrastructure which will include the creation of "a news agency exclusively dedicated to the alternative media" and "the installation of a technological platform for satellite distribution which will be at the service of any community media outlet" (Rivero 2003). This capacity of community media to network and cooperate at the national level will be an important step forward, with Chávez noting that these satellite linkages even open up the possibility of "an international neighbourhood newscast," for people in the neighborhoods of Latin America and the Caribbean (Rivero 2003). Support for the sector further expanded in 2004, with the government taking steps to "not only legalize and enable approximately 200 more communitarian radios and televisions with equipment, but . . . also promote them; making a reality of the communication rights guaranteed in our constitution"

(Chacon in Iacobelli and Gironi 2004). The government has also encouraged the development of the sector by funding consultative and networking conferences that have brought together community media activists from across Latin America (Wilpert 2004, 35). While community and public access broadcasting elsewhere has often been limited by technological and regulatory factors to a type of localism that "cannot address the problem of scale that modern nation states present to any democratic system" (Stein 2001, 322), state infrastructural and regulatory support for community broadcasting opens up the possibility of an accessible and participatory democratic community media sector capable of eventually playing a central role in public communication.

Reinvigorating State and Public Media

The growth and consolidation of the community media sector is hopeful and important, but it is important not to lose sight of its limitations or represent its development in naive, utopian terms. On its own, Venezuela's community media are as yet insufficient in scale, resources, and technical capacity to facilitate a comprehensive alternative to the commercial sector, much less constitute an autonomous and self-contained media system. Without belittling the achievements of the community media, it is worth keeping in mind Nestor Garcia Canclini's reflections regarding the problematic nature of research, and by extension political strategies, that naively

> imagine[s] that the multiplication of microgroup actions will someday bring about transformations in society as a whole, without considering that the big components of popular forms of thought and sensibility—the culture industry, the state—are spaces in which popular interests must be made present or must struggle for hegemony. (1995, 196)

Given these limitations and the open hostility of the corporate media, it is not surprising that the Chávez government has also moved toward reinvigorating the state and public media sectors, even joining with several other Latin American countries in 2004 to launch Telesur, a transnational public satellite television station (which space and scope unfortunately prevent us from exploring in this chapter).

Faced with continued low ratings for underfunded state broadcasters, the government announced in 2004 that it would invest $56 million in state-run television (Kozloff 2005). While Venezolana de Television has been strengthened to play a more effective role as a direct instrument of government communication, the station continues to broadcast a more or less typical South American state television roster of news, public affairs, educational, and cultural programming. Its most popular program is *Alo Presidente,* Hugo

Chávez's eclectic weekly hybrid of "features of a mass rally with . . . a late night talk-show" (Fletcher 2004) that has been described by the Venezuela correspondent of the *Economist* as perhaps "the iconic institution of the Bolivarian revolution" (*Economist* 2005). Though clearly fraught with the danger of reinforcing an overdependence on Chávez as a unifying political symbol, or even reducing politics to pop-culture spectacle, *Alo Presidente* broadcasts have in the short term nonetheless proven valuable in the consolidation of a political project that has lacked many of the conventional organizational and technological structures of political communication.

A more promising and innovative media model can be found in ViVe, a state-funded public television station launched in late 2003 that attempts to fuse community media practices with a national public broadcasting mission, and that is at the time of writing available to about 60–70 percent of Venezuela's population (Podur 2004). The station's founding director, Blanca Eekhout, a former activist with the Catia TVe collective, describes ViVe as a project of national self-representation and integration that is intended to challenge the racial, colonial, and class hierarchies embedded in the existing domestic media system. According to Eekhout,

> [*ViVe's*] intention is to make visible the population that has been excluded to date—the majority—afro-descendent, campesino, indigenous, who were erased from the possibility of appearing in the media until now. Or rather, these communities have appeared in the media, but in a stigmatized way: They are shown as marginal people, criminals. They are not shown building, constructing, part of the struggle for the development of the country. (Eekhout in Podur 2004)

As an antidote to the ubiquity of North American media content in Latin America, ViVe dedicates prime airtime to Latin American documentaries, cinema, and coverage of regional social and political movements on the premise that

> empires have built barriers between the peoples of this continent, and in this process the media have played an important role. For us it's much easier to turn on the television and see any neighbourhood of Chicago than it is to see Honduras, Guatemala, El Salvador, Nicaragua, Colombia, even Venezuela. (Podur 2004)

In keeping with these objectives, 60 percent of ViVe's content must be produced within Venezuela, with 60 percent of that total coming from independent domestic producers. Content ranges beyond the overtly political to include children's shows and cultural programming highlighting local artists and musicians long excluded from the dominant commercial broadcasters (Podur 2004). As with the community media, ViVe is not simply a government instrument and includes voices critical of government policy, though generally from the perspective of the left and subaltern social movements (Kozloff 2005).

Though public broadcasting aimed at national representation and integration is obviously not in itself a new phenomenon, ViVe's appropriation of participatory practices developed in the community media sector suggest a trajectory that goes beyond the "benevolent paternalism" of conventional public broadcasting and instead aims for "media democratization, diversity, plurality" (Podur 2004). According to Eekhout, consultations that preceded the launch of ViVe "made it obvious that people didn't just want to see new programming, they wanted to make it." Drawing from community media models, ViVe has offered community media production workshops and regularly broadcasts programming produced by members of Venezuelan social movements.

Viewed together, ViVe and the community sector suggest the potentially most promising and radical trajectory implicit in the Bolivarian process: a rethinking of the relationship between state power and democratic participation, with the state acting as facilitator, rather than paternalist or authoritarian dictator, of popular initiative. Longtime social movement activist and one-time Venezuelan vice minister of planning and development Roland Denis has proposed that such a radical restructuring of the state is an emergent and innovative, though by no means yet dominant or guaranteed, feature of the Bolivarian process, stating in a 2003 interview that

> in some areas here it has been possible to reconcile grassroots movements inspired by anarchism with a conception of a different state. In this way an answer to the historical conflict between local power and society is being designed. There are projects in Venezuela that demonstrate that it is possible to transcend the contradiction between self-governance and the state. (Zelik 2003)

Re-regulating the Commercial Media Sector

More controversial has been the introduction in 2003 of the "Law of Social Responsibility in Radio and Television" (*Resorte* in its Spanish acronym), a broad package of regulatory legislation purportedly intended to

> uphold freedom of expression and information, support parents by limiting daytime media content deemed inappropriate for children and adolescents, encourage more educational programming on TV and radio, guarantee citizen participation in the communications sector, and promote growth within the country's communications industry. (Venezuela Information Office [VIO] 2005)

Though domestic opponents of the government and some international commentators portray *Resorte* as opening the door to a crackdown on freedom of expression, the government and its supporters point out that much of the legislation is similar to (and in fact directly draws upon) regulatory frameworks found in Europe, North America, and elsewhere. Audiovisual broadcasts in Venezuela had long been governed under outdated telecommunications laws dating from the 1940s, and the government argues that *Resorte* is simply an effort to modernize media regulations (VIO 2005).

Much of *Resorte* is taken up with implementing a classificatory system designed to protect children and adolescents from excessively violent and sexualized television content, and is in principle not a dramatic departure from the FCC or CRTC (Canadian Radio-television and Telecommunications Commission) regulation in North America. More radical in the context of contemporary international pressures to "deregulate" are clauses that prioritize social and cultural objectives above the commercial imperatives of owners, including regulations requiring deconcentration and diversification of domestic media production and minimum quotas for domestic content and children's educational programming. *Resorte* also restricts television advertising to fifteen minutes per hour and bans advertisements for alcohol, weapons, and tobacco. *Resorte* further challenges private prerogative by establishing representative institutional structures to concretize the legal rights of civil society groups to oversee, intervene, and participate in broadcasting. A Social Responsibility Fund drawn from a tax on commercial broadcasting will finance these structures and will also be used to promote domestic media production, train domestic producers, fund research, and develop critical media education programs (VIO 2005).

The most contentious aspects of the *Resorte* laws have revolved around two interrelated issues: clauses that place legal parameters on critical speech directed at politicians and government bodies, and clauses that guarantee the government limited access to commercial media airtime. In conjunction with limitations on airtime for "propaganda" and campaigning, such clauses are clearly an attempt to check further instrumentalization of the dominant media by the right-wing opposition. The government, for its part, portrays these clauses as expansion of information rights, in that the laws guarantee Venezuelans access to information from government and state agencies and protect citizens from campaigns of disinformation and manipulation—not entirely unreasonable concerns when even the Venezuelan chapter of the Institute for Press and Society admitted that the media's political role in 2002 was a convergence of "grave journalistic errors—to the extreme of silencing information on the most important news events and taking political positions to the extreme of advocating a nondemocratic, insurrectional path" (Dinges 2005).

While few would argue against legal restrictions meant to counter violent sedition and protect the public from conscious disinformation campaigns, even some Chávez supporters have expressed worries that open-ended language in these clauses could open the door to authoritarian abuses in the future. Most troubling for many international and domestic observers have been changes to sections of the criminal code dealing with libel and defamation. Though commercial media broadcasts have taken oppositional speech to extremes in directing racist insults and violent incitement against government supporters (Fletcher 2004), laws that increase fines and prison sentences for violations such as insults to an individual's "honour," "offending by word or in writing, or in any other manner, showing disrespect for the president" (Dinges 2005), and "expos[ing] another person to contempt or public hatred" (Reporters Without Borders 2005) could potentially be used to stifle legitimate expressions of dissent. Similarly problematic are sections of the code that penalize the use of media and communications technology to spread "false information" with the aim of "causing panic" (Reporters Without Borders 2005), and in 2005 even the Venezuelan communications minister expressed opposition to clauses proposing special protections for high government officials (Dinges 2005).

The need to prevent a repeat of April 2002 is a legitimate concern, but legislation prohibiting hate speech and violent incitement perhaps carries less danger of authoritarian slippage. Commentators have also pointed out that the social delegitimization of commercial media and mainstream journalism in the wake of the coup attempt, and the Chávez government's subsequent decisive electoral victories, seem to have already encouraged most commercial media outlets to curb their worst excesses (Dinges 2005). Moreover, given the failure of coercive strategies and censorship to guarantee even the political stability of past revolutionary regimes, much less their integrity as emancipatory projects, "positive" strategies such as support for community and public media, which place an emphasis on the expansion of substantive democratic communication rights and capacities, may well prove to constitute a more durable and effective long-term challenge to the entrenched power of capitalist oligarchies.

Despite the concerns expressed above, it is important to point out that a *New York Times* report from late 2006 found that "no journalists were in jail for criticizing the government," and the Venezuelan media "remains exceptionally freewheeling and boisterous," with "Mr. Chávez and his policies . . . still pilloried daily on television, radio and in established daily newspapers" (Romero 2006). Even the government's controversial announcement that it was planning to reallocate the frequency occupied by RCTV after its license expiry in May 2007 is hardly draconian, given that the station will retain its content production capacity and be eligible to broadcast via cable (Reporters Without Borders 2007; Wilpert 2007).[8] Thus at the time of writing, claims that the Bolivarian government is threatening free expression may figure prominently in the rhetoric of the revolution's domestic and international opponents, but these seem to have little substantive basis.

CONCLUSION

Venezuela's Bolivarian revolution raises many provocative issues, both for the international left and for critical communication scholars. On one level, the commercial media's transformation into a blunt propaganda instrument in the face of a serious challenge to elite hegemony suggests a reconceptualization of both "relative autonomy" and "instrumentalization" as historically contingent articulations between media and capitalist elites, rather than as distinct evolutionary stages or mutually exclusive explanations of the "normal" functioning of commercial media systems. At the same time, the commercial media's failure to demobilize the social base of Bolivarianism during the coup attempt of April 2002 also points to the limits of media instrumentalism as a strategy of social control and undermines pessimistic notions of an all-powerful corporate media. Most promising, from the perspective of a postneoliberal emancipatory politics, are the Bolivarian state's infrastructural and regulatory support for the expansion of the independent community media sector and for innovative public media projects such as ViVe TV. These measures suggest both an innovative model of the state as facilitator of relatively autonomous participatory democratic initiative and also the possibility of a post-neoliberal communicative order based on a radical reconceptualization of democratic communication rights. While history unfortunately offers no guarantees, and Venezuela's Bolivarian revolution is a complex political phenomenon with its own potential internal contradictions, it is nonetheless possible that this trajectory of structural media reform could indeed play an important role in the construction of a democratic "socialism for the twenty-first century."

NOTES

An earlier draft of this chapter was prepared by Robert Everton in 2004, focusing primarily on the Venezuelan commercial media's role in the April 2002 coup attempt and international media coverage of those same events. Sadly, Robert Everton passed away in December of 2004 and was unable to complete this project. However, significant elements of his initial draft have been incorporated into this chapter, especially his thorough research on the structure of Venezuela's commercial media sector and on the coup.

1. While Chavez's articulation of "Bolivarianism" ultimately provided a discursive framework that linked together Venezuela's plurality of subaltern strata into a left-populist political project, it is important to emphasize that the energies and even organizational models underlying this process are not simply a top-down product of Hugo Chavez's charismatic leadership. Instead, Bolivarianism is better understood as the coordination and magnification of tendencies rooted in earlier defensive responses to neocolonial dependency, economic exploitation, systemic corruption, and neoliberal "reforms." Though some commentators suggest that Venezuela's subaltern "civil society" had slipped into an organizational slump prior to the emergence of Bolivarianism, interviews with Venezuelan activists allude to fragmented but

qualitatively important social movement activity during the 1980s and early 1990s, especially in Caracas (Podur 2004; Zelik 2003). Similarly, leftist urban guerrilla groups established durable, semi-clandestine organizational structures in a few urban areas during the 1980s and 1990s, including even social programs and paramilitary policing (Gable 2004). A better-documented precursor is "La Causa Radical" (LCR, or "The Radical Cause" in English), a heterodox split from the Venezuelan Communist Party that anticipated the participatory democratic, anti-neoliberal and left-patriotic discourses of later Bolivarianism (Gott 2005; Buxton 2001; Chávez and Harnecker 2005). LCR rode a post-Caracazo wave of popular anger into a second-place result in the 1993 presidential election, but later split into pro- and anti-Chávez factions, with the pro-Chávez Patria Para Todos (PPT, or "Homeland for All") providing important figures in the Bolivarian government (Buxton 2001, 155).

2. As Hugo Chávez himself has noted, though Venezuela is highly urbanized and rife with class oppression and poverty, the country's quantitatively predominant social contradictions do not revolve around the "bourgeoisie versus proletariat" binary posited in traditional Marxist discourse. Historically, only a small percentage of Venezuela's population could be described as "working class" in terms of structural location within relations of production (Chávez and Harnecker 2004, 24). Instead, the social base of Bolivarianism is drawn from a heterogeneous array of subaltern classes and class fractions, many situated materially within the "informal economy," whose grievances against the country's oligarchical social order are rooted in a variety of potentially intersecting antagonisms, including opposition to corruption, economic underdevelopment, poverty, economic marginalization, various forms of economic exploitation, and racial and gender oppression.

3. As theorised by Laclau, populism is neither inherently regressive nor progressive in character, but rather

[p]opulism starts at the point where popular-democratic elements are presented as an antagonistic option against the ideology of the dominant bloc. Note that this does not mean that populism is *always* revolutionary. It is sufficient for a class or class fraction to need a substantial transformation in order to assert its hegemony, for a populist experience to be possible. We can indicate in this sense a populism of the dominated classes and a populism of the dominant classes. (Laclau 1977, 173)

4. It is important to emphasize that the political alliance around Chavez has decisively won four elections and also easily defeated an opposition-initiated presidential recall referendum in 2004, and that all of these votes have been recognized as legitimate by independent observers such as the Organization for American States and the Carter Center.

5. We deliberately use the term "state" broadcasting rather than "public," as state broadcasting in Venezuela has traditionally operated not according to the "arm's-length" paradigm of public broadcasting as it has come to be understood in Western Europe and North America but instead as a direct instrument of the particular government in power.

6. This had special resonance for this chapter's coauthor Robert Everton, who was imprisoned by Pinochet's military in the aftermath of the 1973 coup in Chilé.

7. In January 2007, the government announced that it will not be renewing the frequency allocation held by RCTV, but there will be no restrictions preventing the station from continuing to produce television content or from broadcasting via cable (Reporters Without Borders 2007).

8. In December 2006 and January 2007, Communication Minister William Lara outlined a number of possibilities for reallocation of the frequency occupied by RCTV, including turning it over to the community media sector, a new joint public/private broadcaster, launching a state-owned entertainment channel, or even re-licensing the station to a workers' cooperative composed of former RCTV employees (Reporters Without Borders 2007; Wilpert 2007).

II

EMBEDDED MARKETS
AND CULTURAL TRANSFORMATIONS

Cultures of Empire: Transnational Media Flows and Cultural (Dis)Connections in East Asia

Koichi Iwabuchi

GLOBALIZATION AND THE RISE OF MEDIA CONNECTIONS IN EAST ASIA

A series of events since September 11, 2001, has re-highlighted American economic and military supremacy, so much so that one is apt to conclude that globalization is after all Americanization. However, in analyzing cultural globalization, there are still nonetheless good grounds for maintaining the necessity to complicate the straightforward view of a cultural imperialism thesis that stresses the homogenization and domination of the world by American mass culture (e.g., H. Schiller 1976). American cultural imaginaries are undoubtedly still by far the most influential, and power does matter in the uneven process of globalization. Yet power relations operate in cultural globalization processes in a rather dispersed and decentered manner. Put bluntly, the conception of rigidly demarcated national and cultural boundaries has become implausible and tenuous, and it has become untenable to single out the absolute symbolic center that belongs to a particular country or region. In the era of empire (Hardt and Negri 2000), theoretical reformulation is imperative in order to grasp the gist of the decentering power operation of globalization that makes the configuration of transnational media and cultural power much more non-isomorphic and complex than can be understood in terms of a center-periphery paradigm that is commonly assumed in a cultural imperialism thesis (Appadurai 1996; Hannerz 1996).

The examination of the rise of non-Western media culture and its regional flows and connections would be a useful way to analyze these cultural dynamics. In recent years, the analyses of transnational media and cultural flows in non-Western contexts have gradually departed from an exclusive interest in the examination of how the non-West is dominated by, resists, or appropriates the global impact of American culture. Instead of such a bipolar assumption about the West and the non-West, what has been increasingly attracting academic concern in the study of global-local complexity is a dynamic interaction among non-Western media cultures. The activation of regional cultural connections, especially among the youth, has attracted much academic interest, not simply because it shows the recent decentering of America-dominated global media circulations, but more importantly because it is a site of the conjunction of global standardizing forces and local diversifying practices. It also testifies to the emerging cultural resonance within the non-West, and at the same time as it newly highlights uneven power relations in the region under the system of global capitalism. The analysis of non-Western regional media connections is thus significant since it would illuminate these complicated issues about the cultures of empire, in which transgressive cultural connections are variously and contradictorily engendered in a highly decentered transnational power structure.

This chapter aims to elucidate such cultural complexities in the context of East Asia, with a particular focus on Japan. I will discuss the development of the media and cultural flows in East Asia, especially among Japan, Korea, Hong Kong, Taiwan, and to a lesser extent China, since the early 1990s when the media globalization process has been drastically intensifying the intraregional flows and connections. By analyzing production of media texts, industry marketing strategies, and audience reception, I will explore global-local dynamics of cultural formatting of media texts, transnational industry collaboration and market integration, and audience consumption of cultural neighbors. While the regional media connections have significantly brought about new kinds of self-reflexive understanding of self and others to many populaces in East Asia, it also (re)produces various kinds of unevenness. I will conclude the paper with skepticism toward the thesis that the unevenness of East Asian media connections is closely related to the global trend in which decentralization of an America-dominated structure is accompanied by media-corporate-driven re-centralization with a dispersed transnational power.

LOCALIZATION AND FORMATTING
DIFFERENCES IN ASIAN MARKETS

In the 1990s the intensification of regional media flows was widely observed in areas such as Latin America, the Middle East, the Indian subcontinent, and East Asia (e.g., Sinclair, Jacka, and Cunningham 1996). Most notably shown by the increase in the regional circulation of TV media texts, such a development can be seen as a sign of decentralization of American cultural hegemony. The circulation of American media culture in the world has not wiped out local products. On the contrary, it actually does not compete well with most local and regional products in terms of popularity (see Tomlinson 1991). This does not mean, however, the end of the era where the "media are American" (Tunstall 1977). To what extent and in what sense media cultures that are produced in many parts of the world are fundamentally different from their American counterparts is highly arguable. While American media culture has not straightforwardly homogenized the world, it has nevertheless globally diffused a series of cultural "formats," based on which various differences can be expressed and elucidated in many parts of the world. As Hall (1991, 28) points out, this is a "peculiar form of homogenization" that does not destroy but rather "recognize[s] and absorb[s] those differences within the larger, overarching framework of what is essentially an American conception of the world." It can be seen even as the furthering of Americanization at a deeper level in terms of the spread of production conventions such as genre, format, and marketing strategies (Morley and Robins 1995).

Formatting differences have been thoroughly incorporated into the media industry's transnational strategies through the common practice of imitating popular TV programs and the prevalence of the TV format business (see Iwabuchi 2004a). It also involves various forms of localizing practices that aim to produce media texts tailored for a particular market as media corporations are increasingly more sensitive to the diversity and tastes of local markets. Euro-American transnational media industries have been perhaps the most aggressive in entering non-Western markets; however, localization strategy has also been well-developed in East Asian media flows, and "American" media formats are actively disseminated in a local disguise by media industries in East Asia.

This is clearly shown by the Japanese media industries' strategies to enter the booming Asian audiovisual markets since the early 1990s. Although the export of Japanese TV programs and popular music to other parts of Asia has drastically increased during the 1990s, the Japanese TV and music industries were more interested in localization strategy than in exporting their cultural products to Asian audiovisual markets in the early to mid-1990s. There are several reasons for this. One is the existence of a profitable and wealthy domestic market in Japan and the difficulty of making profits in Asian markets where TV programs are traded for low prices. The reluctance of the Japanese TV industry to enter Asian markets was also due to the obstacle posed by the historical legacy of Japanese imperialism. No less important is that the localization strategies of Japanese media industries in Asian markets are much informed by their reflections on Japan's own experience of indigenization of American popular cultural influence.

Since World War II, Japanese popular culture has been deeply influenced by American counterparts. But Japan quickly indigenized these influences for the development of local production rather than letting its media industries be dominated by American products. If we look at the beginning of the Japanese TV history in 1953, for example, programming relied enormously upon imports from Hollywood. This imbalance drastically diminished starting in the mid-1960s without any kind of quota policy limiting imports. By 1980, Japan was importing only 5 percent of all its television programming, a trend that continues to this day (Hara 2004). Japanese media industries assumed from this experience of the quick indigenization of American popular cultural influence that other Asian countries would take a similar path. Japanese media industries seemed to believe that the hyperactive indigenization of "America" in Japan, which led to the creation of its own media culture, could be marketed in other Asian markets.

While the Japanese TV industry tried to practice localization strategies by selling its TV program format as well as coproducing local programs, it was the music industry that most actively developed localization strategies in the early 1990s. Although some Japanese pop idols have been popular across Asia, the Japanese music industries aimed to produce "local" pop stars in China, Indonesia, and so on, who could then be marketed to other Asian markets with the Japanese know-how of the cultural appropriation of American pop culture. It was commonly believed that Japanese media industries held a comparative advantage in their fifty years of experience and accumulated know-how drawn from their "American education." As the director of Sony Music explained in an interview in 1994, "the Japaneseness of Japanese popular music production can be found in its capacity for cultural mixing which makes the original source irrelevant. . . . In the same vein, if we produce something stunning, trendy and newly stylish in local languages by local singers, I am sure that it can sell in Asian markets. But the base [of the stunning style] is American popular culture."[1]

In this project of finding Asian pop singers through cross-fertilization with Japanese initiatives, music producers deployed the same strategy that they had developed in Japan in the 1970s. They held auditions in the booming East and Southeast Asian markets—China in particular—where there so far had been no established system of providing an opportunity for young people who dream of becoming pop singers. The growing economic power in East and Southeast Asia throughout the 1990s and the rapid growth of commercialized TV markets in the region were a reminder to Japanese music producers of the height of the Japanese idol boom in the late 1970s and early 1980s. This convinced industry insiders that the same path should be taken across other parts of the region.

It can be argued that the Japanese music industries did not try to export anything authentically "Japanese." Likewise, Asian pop stars (including Japanese pop stars) did not represent a local "traditional" culture per se, but relied instead on new kinds of "Asian localness," which intensely indigenized and hybridized foreign, most importantly American, influences. Japanese localization strategies attempt to create local zones by gauging the local practices of dynamic indigenization processes. These are strategies that incorporate the experience of those who have long learned to negotiate the flow of American culture in shaping the production and consumption of media products. "What was marked as foreign and exotic yesterday can become familiar today and traditionally Japanese tomorrow" (Tobin 1992, 26). This dynamic is exactly what Japanese media corporations such as Sony have tried to produce across Asian markets and what they believe is the commonality between other Asian nations and Japan, firmly convinced that the media formats they employ are primarily American (see Iwabuchi 2002, chap. 3).

Yet, we can nevertheless see here how Japanese localization practices in Asian markets are imbued with a condescending posture toward other Asian nations. It is an unambiguous presupposition held by Japanese media producers that Japan's successful indigenization of foreign (American) cultural influence presents a developmental model for other Asian countries to follow. A newly articulated conception of "Asia" as the site of dynamic cultural indigenization embedded in the localizing strategies of the Japanese music industry thus illuminates a historically constituted perception of Japan's position in Asia in the course of Japanese imperialism and colonialism over other Asian countries.

Some scholars underscore the Japanese experience of indigenization as an exemplar to be followed by other non-Western countries. Arguing for the relative decline of American media power in the world, Tunstall (1995) suggests that the Japanese mode of indigenization of American-originated media products can be seen as a pattern for the development of non-Western TV industries that, he predicts, other non-Western countries such as China or India will follow. The Japanese capacity for indigenizing the foreign has also been positively re-evaluated in globalization theories; Sony's strategy of global localization has come to signify a new meaning of "Japanization," which is seen as "a global strategy which does not seek to impose a standard product or image, but instead is tailored to the demands of the local market" (Featherstone 1995, 9).

This uncritical association of "glocalism" with "Japanization" is not just tenuous and essentialist (Iwabuchi 1998) but also analytically too narrow. The localizing strategies of Japanese media industries in Asian markets in the 1990s, I would argue, are symptomatic of a widely discerned shift in the strategies of transnational media industries from "global standardization" to "global localization" or "glocalization," from the distribution of the same products all over the world to marketing localness, the strategy that aims to combine the global dynamics of cultural economy and locally specified practices of media production and consumption (see Robins 1997; Robertson 1995). The objective here is to simultaneously muster local negotiations and global structural control. Profits are to be made less through the symbolic and ideological domination by the media industries of powerful nation-states than through local camouflaging that smooths the economic expansion of transnational corporations. Indeed, it is a subtle realization by transnational media industries that cultural imperialism does not make a profit (Sinclair 1997).

Glocalization strategies testify to the reconfiguration of transnational cultural power in the context in which uneven distribution and circulation of such cultural products are becoming more difficult to trace, and the origins of images and commodities are becoming increasingly insignificant and irrelevant. With the proliferation and accelerated transmission speed of globally circulated images and commodities, the local transculturation process has come to be a quotidian site. As images and commodities of "foreign" origin are appropriated, hybridized, indigenized, and consumed in multiple unforeseeable ways, even American culture is conceived as being "ours" in many places (see J. Watson 1997). This does not suggest the eradication of (still Western/American-dominated) transnational cultural power. Transnational cultural power does not operate as the absolute symbolic center but is deeply intermingled with local indigenizing processes in a way in which cultural diversity is organized through globally shared formats rather than through the replication of uniform cultural models (Hannerz 1996; Wilk 1995). The world is standardized through diversification and diversified through standardization. The development of the TV format business is a good testimony to this. The operation of global cultural power can only be found in local practice, while cultural reworking and appropriation at the local level necessarily takes place within the matrix of global homogenizing forces. By developing the localization strategies in Asian markets, the Japanese media industries actually promote this global trend as strategically located intermediators.

INTENSIFICATION OF TRANSNATIONAL INDUSTRY ALLIANCES

While Japanese ventures of glocalization continue in various forms, what has become even more notable since the 1990s is the wide circulation of Japanese TV programs and popular music in East Asian markets. Apart from the textual appeal for these audiences, which I will discuss shortly, cross-national industry cooperation in promoting a mutual media culture in East Asian markets is a significant factor behind this novel development. Here again, the rise of Japanese cultural exports can be read as a symptom of the shifting nature of transnational cultural power, where the main actors are not particular (Western) nation-states but the collaborative activities of transnational media and media industries across strategic parts of the world.

The imperatives for transnational corporations to enter new markets are based on the establishment of business tie-ups with other firms across the local, national, and transnational levels—whether in the form of buyouts or joint ventures. The structure of transnational cultural power has become simultaneously dispersed and more ubiquitous through increasing transnational integration, networking, and cooperation among worldwide media industries, including non-Western players. As Hall (1991, 28) argues, transnational capital attempts to "rule through other local capitals, rule alongside and in partnership with other economic and political elites."

The collaborative role that Japanese media industries play in cultural globalization articulates a new phase of transnational cultural flows dominated by a limited number of firms (Aksoy and Robins 1992). It is important, for example, to place the significance of Sony's inroads into Hollywood in the 1980s as well as the international popularity of Japanese animation and computer games in the last decade within a wider picture of the increasing interconnectedness of transnational media industries. This development exemplifies the trend of global media mergers, which aim to offer a "total cultural package" of various media products under a single media conglomerate (Schiller 1991). In this process, it can be argued, Japanese companies try not to replace but to strengthen American cultural hegemony by investing in the production of Hollywood films and by facilitating their distribution all over the globe (see Miller et al. 2005).

Conversely, finding a local partner is much more imperative for non-Western media industries targeting global (i.e., including Western) markets. The Japanese case shows that media industries and media products cannot successfully become global without Western partners. The advent of Japanese animation and characters such as Pokémon clearly show that global cultural appeal and success are dependent on partnerships with Nintendo of America and Time-Warner in terms of the promotion, distribution, and even localization of the content for global marketing (see Iwabuchi 2004b).

The same trend can be discerned in the spread of Japanese popular culture in East Asian markets. Cultural flows and connections among East Asian countries, particularly between Japan, Korea, Taiwan, Hong Kong, and China, are certainly becoming the norm rather than the irregularity. Needless to say, Japan as the colonial power has long been exerting cultural influence and exporting cultural products overseas to East and Southeast Asia. But it was only in the early to mid-1990s that Japanese cultural presence became more conspicuous and systematic in the region. Local marketing promotion through transnational corporate alliances is an important aspect of this development. While the export of the Japanese idol system was at best partially successful, the circulation of Japanese television programs and popular music in Asia has become widespread thanks to the local industries' marketing efforts. Here arises another meaning of localization than the export of Japanese know-how about local indigenization: the local promotion of Japanese cultural products, which synchronizes with trends in the Japanese domestic market. And the increasing affiliation and integration between Japanese and other East Asian media industries and markets have further highlighted the transnational appeal of Japanese popular culture.

In a feature article in the Japanese popular magazine *Bart* (March 10, 1997), the "real-time" popularity of Japanese pop songs in Taiwan, Hong Kong, and Singapore is described as an "unassuming stance" (*shizentai*). Referring to the increasing cooperation and coproduction among Asian cultural producers and musicians, the article implies not only that the emerging trend toward regional synchronization of popular culture in Asia is enabled by the development of communication technologies, but that it is also seen by the trade press as somehow an organic development among East Asian nations. However, what is less apparent are the massive promotional efforts and investment by local media industries in East Asia. "Real time" and similar expressions like "simultaneity" or "no time lag" are the terms that I frequently heard in my interviews with Japanese as well as Taiwanese and Hong Kong music producers in the mid-1990s. These terms are not simply the expression of increasing confidence in the Hong Kong and Taiwanese industries in terms of cultural production capacity, but are also uttered as a key marketing strategy for promoting Japanese popular music in East Asia.

The same holds true with the spread of Japanese TV dramas in the 1990s. The nearly synchronous circulation of Japanese TV dramas in Taiwan and Hong Kong is not a result of successful promotion by Japanese media industries. Rather it is the local cable channels, STAR TV, and local industries, including pirate VCD (video CD) manufacturers, outside Japan that recognized the commercial value of selling Japanese TV dramas in the local market. In Taiwan, for example, along with political and economic liberalization and the legalization of cable TV operations, the expansion of the entertainment market has been important in facilitating the influx of Japanese popular culture since the late 1980s. This has exposed the audience in Taiwan to more information about Japanese pop icons, through newspapers, magazines, and television, and given the local media industries an incentive for exploiting the commercial value of Japanese popular music, encouraging them to invest a large amount of money in promoting it in Taiwan. An especially important factor to consider in the popularization of Japanese television programs in Taiwan is the rapid development of cable television. Cable TV emerged as an illegal business in the 1980s. After a long battle between the government and the cable operators, the government changed its policy from prohibition to regulation. The 1993 Cable TV Law legalized cable television, but even before this law came into force about 50 percent of households were watching cable (known as "the fourth channel"). Under the Cable TV Law, levels of viewing have continued to rise; as early as 1998 nearly 80 percent of households were enjoying cable television. In Taiwan, with its rapid expansion of media markets, Taiwanese cable television companies saw a great business opportunity in broadcasting Japanese TV programs in Taiwan and rushed to buy them, immediately after Japanese-language TV programs were officially allowed to be broadcast at the end of 1993. At that time, there were at least five Japanese cable channels in Taiwan, in addition to other channels that also broadcast Japanese TV programs. These media environments have made Japanese TV dramas that depict youths' lives in urban settings hot topics of everyday conversation among many young people in Taiwan who identify themselves with the stories and characters.

In addition, the comprehensive picture of the transnational alliance in the promotion of Japanese TV dramas in Asian markets cannot be captured solely by the examination of the formal business and distributional routes. The underground market routes of pirated software have played an even more significant role in transnationally popularizing Japanese TV dramas. Particularly vital in this process is the spread of the "Asian" consumer technology, VCD. Hu (2004) gives us great insights into the underground political economy of this Asian cultural technology, the new way of consuming TV dramas engendered by it, and the process in which Japanese media industries are completely left out in the transnationalization of Japanese TV dramas. While Japanese TV drama producers are exclusively concerned with the Japanese domestic market, not having Asian markets in sight, the East Asian (illegitimate) VCD repackaging has gained for Japan TV dramas new transnational cultural meanings and connections outside Japan.

The disappearance of time lag thus operates in a double sense, as the vanishing developmental lag in popular music production capacity and market expansion, and as the transnationalization of fame facilitated by the instantaneous circulation of imagery and information. Both factors have been responsible for the local promotion of Japanese popular culture in Taiwan and Hong Kong. In turn, this local initiative has given Japanese TV industries more confidence in the exportability of Japanese TV programs and an incentive for forging business tie-ups with Taiwanese media industries for its promotion.

ASIAWOOD AND THE KOREAN WAVE

In the new millennium, East Asian media firms are becoming even more collaborative and the media flows more multi-vectored. An interesting trend in this respect is the hybridization of TV drama production. For example, *101 Proposal,* a highly successful Japanese drama series in 1993, which was also well received in East Asian markets, was remade by Korean TV Production Company. This local company purchased the rights to remake the drama from the Japanese company but its main market is China as opposed to Korea. The drama features both Korean and Chinese actors and is bilingual.

As the term, "Asiawood" suggests (Beales 2001), multinational moviemaking is increasingly targeting pan-Asian audiences. A recent good example is the film *Initial D The Movie* (2005), which was based on a popular Japanese comic series, was coproduced by Hong Kong and Japanese firms, and was directed by a Hong Kong staff from a popular film series, *Internal Affairs*. It features a multinational cast and Mandarin-, Cantonese-, and Japanese-subtitled versions targeting East and Southeast Asian markets.

Many Japanese TV dramas are also based on Japanese comic series, a practice that has become common in Taiwan as well. This demonstrates the creative localization of Japanese cultural influence in Taiwan. For example, the TV drama *Liuxing Huayuan* (Meteor Garden) is based on a Japanese comic series about high school students' lives, *Hana yori dango*. There is no original Japanese TV program based on this comic series, but Taiwanese producers skillfully adapted the comic series to a TV drama based on their own initiative. While the TV program features characters with Japanese names, the story is told in Taiwanese high school settings, featuring the Taiwanese pop idol group F4, which plays the original theme songs. The program has been phenomenally well received by younger people not just in Taiwan but also in Hong Kong, Singapore, Thailand, Malaysia, Indonesia, and China. In China, the authorities banned the broadcast of the program on the grounds that the love affairs and violence shown in a high school setting would have a negative influence on the behavior and attitude of Chinese youth, but younger people continued to watch it through the pirated VCDs or illegal Internet sites (*Asahi Shinbun,* July 12, 2002). In this case we see that a hybrid composition of Japanese and Taiwanese cultural imaginations has led to a new East Asian youth culture that resists rigid norms of state censorship.

Collaboration between Japanese and Korean media industries has also intensified since 2000. BoA, a popular Korean singer, who is quite successful in Korea, Japan, and Taiwan, is a case in point. In addition to her talents of dancing, singing, and mastering Korean and Japanese, the music companies SME of Korea and AVEX of Japan worked together from the outset to market BoA in various East Asian countries simultaneously. She received an MTV Asia award in 2003, representing both Korea and Japan. BoA is truly a transnational artist in East Asia, one whose origins cannot be attributed to a single nation.

Another conspicuous development in East Asian media flows since the early beginning of the new millennium is the rise of Korean popular culture. Korean popular culture products, including films, TV dramas, and popular music, have become popular across much of East Asia in the 1990s, often surpassing the appeal of their Japanese counterparts. In the case of TV dramas, it is often suggested that Korean producers have significantly been influenced by and subtly reworked Japanese TV programs, especially youth-oriented dramas (D. Lee 2004). Although Korean audiences still can view Japanese TV dramas only on the cable channels, not on the free-to-air channels, due to import restrictions, Korean TV producers have been deeply influenced by watching these programs, and they have adapted the format, stories, and settings for their own productions. In the first half of the 1990s, critics chastised the Korean TV industry for disgracefully imitating the culture of the former colonizer. However, Korean TV producers have not just imitated but also creatively appropriated and transformed Japanese TV dramas, so much so that Korean youth drama has now become popular throughout East Asian markets, including Japan, a well-known phenomenon called *Hanliu* (the Korean Wave) (D. Lee 2004).

In terms of content, Korean popular dramas depict the lives of youth in urban settings, but in contrast to the "small universe" depicted in Japanese programs where young people are seen as cut off from the complexity of the real world (Ito 2004), family relationships are an integral part of Korean programs. This factor allows for wider appeal across generations and a sense that Korean dramas are more "realistic" than their Japanese counterparts. According to my interviews in Taipei in March 2002, young viewers greatly sympathized with Korean dramas because the lives of young people were intertwined within family relationships. This was seen as much closer to the Taiwanese context, and thus Korean dramas were seen as more realistically depicting life than the closed universe of the youth associated with Japanese dramas.

The Korean Wave has also come to Japan, though belatedly. Since the phenomenal hit *Shiri* in 1999, Korean films have established their status in the Japanese film market. Furthermore, in 2003, a Korean TV series, *Winter Sonata,* for the first time became a phenomenally popular East Asian TV drama series. While Asian films and popular music have been occasionally successful in Japan since the 1970s, such as movies featuring stars like Bruce Lee, Jackie Chan, Wong Kar-Wai, and Dick Lee, Asian television programs have not been well received there. *Winter Sonata* was first broadcast on NHK Satellite channel in 2003 as opposed to the more widely watched terrestrial television channels, showing that the national network was uncertain how the program would perform in Japan.[2] However, *Winter Sonata* attracted good responses from audiences, who are mostly women in their forties, fifties and sixties, much more than the NHK producer expected, and was gradually attracting wider audiences week by week. Following this trend, NHK decided to broadcast it on its terrestrial channel from April 2004 and its popularity surpassed that of most Japanese TV dramas. Though it was programmed at 11 p.m. Saturday, its average rating was about 15 percent, which is higher than most Japanese TV drama series that are broadcast in the prime time slot.

MEDIA CONSUMPTION AND
SPATIOTEMPORAL POWER GEOMETRY

While these developments of regional media flows and connections can be seen as a form of market integration within East Asia, we cannot dismiss this trend as merely the replication of global mass cultural production. It is also important to consider the ways in which these new flows have the potential to promote cultural dialogue among citizens and audiences in East Asia. We therefore move from our discussion of production and distribution to audience reception.

Many scholars have argued that the recent rise of regional media flows in several parts of the world can be explained by the notion of cultural proximity. There is indeed the empirical validity of the existence of geo-linguistic and geo-cultural TV markets (Sinclair, Cunningham, and Jacka 1996). The notion of cultural proximity is useful in explaining the general tendency of audience preference for local programs and programs imported from countries of similar cultural makeup, and the significance of cultural-linguistic regional centers such as Brazil, Mexico, Hong Kong, India, and Egypt in terms of regional film/television export. However, precisely because of its seeming empirical validity, we need to probe the notion of cultural proximity a bit more cautiously. Explanations based on the notion of cultural proximity become unproductive when there is an assumption about the essence of a culture/civilization as ahistorical and static. Such analysis would risk presupposing the existence of some essential cultural similarities that automatically urge the audience to be attracted to media texts of culturally proximate regions without considering socio-historical contexts and the contradictory dynamics of audience reception. Arguments that assume this kind of primordial cultural similarities fail to account for what sort of pleasure, if any, audiences find in identifying cultural proximity in a particular program. Here, if we look at the circulation of cultural goods in a more rigorous manner, we can see that this explanation is far too simple.

The increasing mutual consumption of East Asian popular cultures suggests that audiences find resonance in other Asian popular cultures in terms of the ways of being modern in East Asian contexts, something that is not simply a response to or imitation of Western modernity. In the long history of Western imperial expansion, uneven power relations unequivocally mark the global experience of modernization in a West-dominated history. However, this historical process has not simply produced the Westernization of the world; its impact on the constitution of the world has been much more heterogeneous and contradictory. The unambiguously dominant Western cultural political, economic, and military power has constructed a modern world-system covering the whole globe (Wallerstein 1991), but at the same time the experience of "the forced appropriation of modernity" in the non-West has produced polymorphic indigenized modernities in the world (Ang and Stratton 1996).

It is important to stress here that what has substantiated the cultural geography of "Asia" in the 1990s is less some essential and distinct set of "Asian values" than the advent of global capitalism and modernity (Dirlik 1994). The latter have shed light on (dis)similar experiences in which cultural specificities are brought into relief in the East Asian contexts, such as the development of urban consumerism, the expansion of the middle class, the changes in gender/sexuality relationships, and the ordinariness of (simultaneous) transnational media consumption. Under these contexts, economic growth in Asia has not just given birth to affluent youth cultural markets in the region to be penetrated by American popular culture but also offered a context in which new patterns of regional media flows and collaboration among local media industries have been developed.

Unlike conservative Asian value discourses, the emerging resonance felt among young people in East Asia is not based upon exclusive views of primordial cultural traditions. The image of Asian youth, at least in marketing terms, might be defined as one of a consuming hybrid: youths who have material power and passion for consuming fashionable cultural products and who do not care about the origin of those consumer items or media products. Nevertheless, preferred cultural products are not without East Asian flavor, as those are reworked in Asian context by hybridizing various latest fads all over the world; affluent Asian youths are keen to consume things that are inescapably global and (East) Asian at the same time.

Non-Western countries have long faced toward the West to interpret their position and understand their distance from modernity. The encounter has always been based upon the expectation of difference and time lag. However, now some non-Western modern countries are facing each other to find neighbors experiencing and feeling similar things and the similar temporality of East Asian vernacular modernities. If Japanese popular culture tastes and smells like *dim sum* (Chinese snacks) and *kimchi* (Korean spicy pickles) to media producers and consumers in Hong Kong, Taiwan, and Korea, it might be because it lucidly represents the intertwined composition of global homogenization and heterogenization in the East Asian context. This kind of expression should not be automatically interpreted as evidence that the popularity of Japanese TV dramas is driven by the perception of "cultural proximity" in a primordial sense (cf. Straubhaar 1991).

Elsewhere I argued that the perception of cultural proximity as such needs to be understood less as the manifestation of given cultural attributes and values than the dynamic process of "becoming" (Iwabuchi 2001). Japan and other nations might share certain cultural values, and Asian viewers often refer to this cultural affinity as a reason for their preference for Japanese TV dramas. However, the perception of cultural proximity is a matter of time as well as of space. The emerging sense of cultural similarity between Japan and other Asian nations that these viewers experience seems to be based upon a consciousness that they all live in the same modern temporality and spatiality.

For example, to the audience of Taiwan, where modernity is no longer just dreams, images, and yearnings of affluence, but reality—that is, the social and material conditions in which people live—Japanese popular culture offers an "operational realism"; American dreams are concretized into something ready for use. It should be noted here that even for those who delight in Japanese TV dramas, "Japan" does not enjoy the status as an object of yearning that "America" once did. Although the recent influx of Japanese popular culture in Taiwan might be reminiscent of the legacy of Japanese colonial rule, the popularity of Japanese television dramas in Taiwan does not suggest that the relationship between Japan and Taiwan is a straightforwardly conceived one of center-periphery. It is not the pleasure of "identifying with the powerful," but rather a sense of living in the same temporality and sociality, a sense of being equal that sustains Japanese cultural presence as the practical, not abstract, reference of becoming in Taiwan.

Here, it is crucial to remember that the other side of intimate similarity is pleasant distance. As a corollary of ongoing asymmetrical cultural encounters in the course of the spread of Western modernity, as Ang and Stratton (1996, 22–24) argue, we have come to live in "a world where all cultures are both (like) 'us' and (not like) 'us,'" one where familiar difference and bizarre sameness are simultaneously articulated in multiple ways through the unpredictable dynamic of uneven global cultural encounters. The sense of cultural similarity is closely interconnected with the sense of difference. The dynamic context of the 1990s has promoted the intraregional cultural resonance among the youth in East and Southeast Asia, who meet cultural neighbors vis-à-vis a common but different experience of indigenizing modernity. The entangled perception of cultural distance/closeness is constantly reformulated under globalization and differently articulated in each locality. Similar and dissimilar, different and same, close and distant, fantasizing and realistic, all of these intertwined perceptions subtly intersect so as to arouse a sense of cultural identification, relatedness, and empowerment in the eyes of young people in East and Southeast Asia.

Seen this way, cultural proximity should not be conceived in terms of a static attribute of "being" but as a dynamic process of "becoming." The comfortable distance and cultural proximity between Japan and Taiwan seem to be based upon a sense that Taiwan and Japan live in the same time and a (dis)similar social situation. Cultural proximity in the consumption of media texts is thus being articulated and brought to consciousness under homogenizing forces of "modernization" and "globalization." Convergence between Japan and Taiwan is occurring in terms of material conditions, emerging urban consumerism with a large middle class, the changing role of women in the society, and the development of the simultaneous circulation of information and media culture. Those elements complicatedly interact to articulate the cultural resonance of Japanese TV dramas for viewers in Taiwan who synchronously and contemporaneously experience and feel "Asian modernity," which American popular culture could never have presented.

UNEVENNESS EMBEDDED IN INTRAREGIONAL
CULTURAL FLOWS IN EAST ASIA

The intensification of media and popular culture flows in East Asia suggests a possibility that the diminishing temporal lag, thanks to the shared experience of industrialization, global spread of consumerist lifestyles, and the (simultaneous) transnational circulation of media images and information, (re)activates the sense of spatial affiliation in the region. It is important, however, to note that the analysis of intraregional cultural flows and consumption highlights the newly articulated asymmetrical power relations in the region.

Mark Liechty (1995, 194), for example, elucidated the Nepali experience of modernity as "the ever growing gap between imagination and reality, becoming and being." The disappearance of a time lag in the distribution of cultural products in many parts of the world has left wide political, economic, and cultural gaps intact, so much so that they have facilitated the feeling in non-Western countries that "'catching up' is never really possible" (Morley and Robins 1995, 226–27). The cultural immediacy and resonance that Asian audiences feel in other Asian media texts does not necessarily lead to cultural dialogue on equal terms. The asymmetry is evident not just in terms of quantity but also in terms of the perception of temporality manifest in the consumption of media products of cultural neighbors. This point becomes manifest when we look at the other trajectory of intra-regional cultural flow: the consumption of East Asian popular cultural forms in Japan.

The activated intra-regional cultural flows have brought about an unprecedented influx of Asian pop culture into Japan since the mid-1990s, but Japanese consumption of East Asian media cultures is contradictory. On the one hand, Japanese media consumption of East Asian popular culture is sharply marked by a nostalgic longing for a loss. It shows that many Japanese are attempting to recuperate something they believe Japan allegedly is losing or has lost. For the case of Hong Kong, it is mostly social energy and vigor that audiences nostalgically appreciate. And it is pure love that connotes innocent sentiment and caring human relationships in the case of the Korean TV drama *Winter Sonata*. As Japan has struggled with an economic slump after the so-called bubble economy and there has been an increase in gloomy incidents such as brutal murders by youths, a sense of social and economic crisis and a pessimistic atmosphere about the future have prevailed in Japan. It is not simply Japan's economic development in the past but society's energy and caring relationships in the present and the hope for the future that Japan nostalgically projects onto Hong Kong or Korea.

Whether Japan ever had such social vigor or caring human relations is highly debatable—and ultimately irrelevant. As many have pointed out, the object of nostalgia is not necessarily some "real" past—the things that used to be (see Davis 1979; Stewart [1984] 1993). The important point here is that nostalgia arises out of a sense of insecurity and anguish in the present. The nostalgia for a modern Asia is fed by a desire to make life in actual, modern Japan more promising and humane, and this sense of urgency explains, if partly, why the object of nostalgia is directed to East Asia's present. Japan's newly imagined "Asia" functions as a contraposition to its own society—one that is widely regarded as suffocating, closed, and rigidly structured with no promising future. Here, "Asia" is not simply idealized as the way things were in Japan. Some people in Japan also appreciate it, for the purpose of reflexive self-reformation, as representing an alternative, more uplifting cultural modernity. This attitude is accompanied by the self-critical examination of oneself and one's own society. This tendency is particularly prominent in the case of Korean drama audiences. They do not just watch dramas to get inspired but also are quite passionately engaged in post-text activities. Many of them start learning the Korean language and visit Korea by joining a tour to the shooting site of *Winter Sonata*. No small number of them come to realize how their images of Korea as a "backward" society are biased and condescending, and some even begin studying Japanese colonial history to consider the relationship between the two countries (see Iwabuchi, forthcoming). This shows a great possibility for East Asian media cultural connection to promote transnational dialogue. Personal sentiments are indeed sources of political agency.

Yet, it can also be argued that while Hong Kong or Korea is not conceived as "premodern" here, what some Japanese audiences endeavor to see is not a neighbor inhabiting exactly the same temporality. Rather, they still tend to show "the kind of sympathy that identifies with the Other and yet denies him 'coevalness,' which is constitutive of 'the Orientalizing of the Other'" (Dirlik 1991, 406). Here, the consumption of popular culture from other parts of Asia in Japan is marked by the conception of temporal distance between Japan and other Asian nations. Good old Japan is to be found in the landscape of East Asia, which is marked out by an immutable, though narrowing, temporal and economic lag. Compared to the audiences for Hong Kong media culture, Japanese audience consumption of Korean media culture does not seem to show this kind of conception, as shown by their vigorous post-text activities. Yet, Japanese (male-dominated) media still tend to stress the temporal difference between Korea and Japan by pointing out that the pure love plots of Korean dramas are quite similar to those produced in the 1970s in Japan. This posture displays Japanese failure and refusal to see other Asians as modern equals who share the same temporality, a conception that is overdetermined by Japan's historically constituted condescending perception of other Asian societies.

Furthermore, the intensification of intra-regional cultural consumptions newly produces a "backward" Asia. Being critical of the Japanese mode of negotiation with the West nonetheless affirms capitalist modernity. As Morris-Suzuki (1998, 20) argues, the new Asianism in Japan "no longer implies rejection of material wealth and economic success, but rather represents a yearning for a wealth and success which will be somehow *different*" (emphasis in original). Audiences' media engagement with "Hong Kong" and "Korean" modernity depends crucially on their capitalist sophistication as opposed to the lack thereof in "Asia." The imagining of a modern, intimate Asian fellow is still based upon the reconstruction of an oriental Orientalism. A certain degree of economic development is a minimum condition for other Asian cultures to enter "our" realm of modernity. In the case of Hong Kong, China is regarded as the den of backwardness that would corrupt Hong Kong's cosmopolitan appeal. In the case of Korea, as the abduction of Japanese nationals is officially acknowledged by North Korea, it has been severely demonized as an authoritarian terrorist country whose people live in a wretched condition. This "premodern" Asia conceived as such never occupies a coeval space with capitalist Asia but represents a place and a time that some Japanese fans of Hong Kong or Korean popular culture have no desire to consume.

POWER GEOMETRY AND
TRANSNATIONAL MEDIA CONNECTIONS

The above consideration of media consumption poses a highly arguable question as to whether and how the emerging connections forged through commercialized popular cultures lead to nurturing transnational dialogue. In Japan, there has been a strong expectation for the spread of Japanese popular culture to promote national interest as a vehicle of soft power, particularly in terms of the improvement of Japan's images and the overcoming of the historically constituted problematic relations with other East and Southeast Asian countries. It might be true that the dissemination of enjoyable Japanese contemporary culture has introduced the sociocultural issues and concerns that many young people in the regions share. Most notably, media connections have dramatically improved the relationship between Japan and Korea as their people have come to hold much better images of their neighbors. As the popular cultural flows are becoming more multilateral and regular, they might have also significantly furthered cultural exchange and mutual understanding among youths in East Asia on a large scale that has never been observed.

However, this opportunistic view proves to be tenuous, as clearly shown by the recent anti-Japanese movements in China, Korea, and Hong Kong. Popular culture can enhance mutual understanding, but it can never erase the history and memory of colonialism. The dialogic potentiality of popular cultural connections should not be uncritically embraced in exchange for inattention to the fact that increasing intra-Asian cultural flows newly highlight structural asymmetry and uneven power relations in the region. There is much imbalanced difference not just in the quantity and the vector of the flows but also in terms of the perception and appreciation of spatiotemporal distance/proximity, as discussed above. It is also necessary to direct our attention to how we can make an effective critique of globally diffused consumerism and market determinism, on which uneven intraregional cultural flows are founded and through which inequalities and discriminations in terms of race, ethnicity, gender, sexuality, class, and immigration are institutionalized nationally *and* transnationally. We should remember that emerging transnational connections through popular culture are predominantly ones among relatively affluent youth (and mostly women in the case of TV dramas) and among media and media industries in urban areas of developed countries. So many people and regions are excluded from this connection. This imbalance is ubiquitously structured by a general increase in transnational cultural connections and links under the decentering forces of cultural globalization. While the circulation and mutual consumption of made-in-Asia texts are becoming more common in many parts of urban space in East Asia, what we are now witnessing is the exchange among the dominant cultures and the loose network among East Asian media industries that produce, distribute, and market "Asian mass culture," the kind of texts that are mostly restricted to commercially and ideologically hegemonic ones in each nation. Such an international framework tends to suppress attention to the marginalized within each society.[3]

While the main corporate actors of cultural globalization are located in urban cities and disregard the rigid boundaries of nation-states, their national origins are limited to a small number of powerful nations, and transnational corporations still operate most of their transnational business from their home country—hence their profits are enjoyed largely within national boundaries (Hirst and Thompson 1997). Cultural commodities and images are predominantly produced by a small number of wealthy countries, and many parts of the world still cannot even afford to enjoy global cultural consumption. The framework of the nation-state, both as a spatially controlled entity and as a discursively articulated geography, does not lose its prominence in the analysis of uneven global cultural flows (Sreberny-Mohammadi 1991). This point has become more imperative as most governments are now keen to promote their own national cultural exports in developing the policy of cultural economy or creative industry.

It needs to be reiterated that the decentering process of globalization makes it untenable to single out the absolute symbolic center that belongs to a particular country or region, but this never means that global cultural power has disappeared: it has been dispersed but made even more solid as well. However, such a view is misleading in analyzing the cultural dimensions of globalization, not simply because the exercise of American cultural power is deeply intermingled with local practices of appropriation and consumption of foreign cultural products and meanings. More importantly, it also conceals the fact that the unevenness in transnational cultural flows is intensified not solely by American cultural power but by the various kinds of alliances among transnational media industries in developed countries. While popular cultural flows and connections will become more active and multivectored in East Asia and more actors will join from China or Thailand, the importance of attending to how East Asian media industries and products are collusive in producing cultural asymmetry and indifference nationally and transnationally will not be diminishing. The development of transnational media studies, which critically examines globally diffused uneven power relations at the site of cultural production, circulation, and consumption in the East Asian context, will remain rather imperative in the age of the cultures of empire.

NOTES

1. Interview conducted in Tokyo in October 1994.

2. The failure of *All About Eve*, another Korean drama series that was broadcast on a terrestrial commercial channel in 2002, also might have made the producer cautious.

3. For example, see Iwabuchi (forthcoming) for how the "Korean Wave" in Japan, which has been celebrated as it improved the international relationship between Japan and South Korea, had contradictory impacts on the social recognition of the resident Koreans in Japan.

8

Local and Global Sites of Power in the Circulation of Ghanaian Adinkra

Boatema Boateng

Adinkra cloth is produced mainly in the Asante region of Ghana and is used primarily as funeral attire (the word *adinkra* means to part or take one's leave). It is made by stenciling motifs onto cloth using black dye. Motifs have symbolic meanings, many of which reflect the beliefs and values of the Asante people. Others may be named for historical events or events in the life of the person who designs the motif. In the years since the incorporation of the Asante and other ethnic groups into the nation-state of Ghana in 1957, adinkra and other cultural forms have been thought of as both ethnic — in this case Asante — and Ghanaian.

A significant recent development in the history of adinkra has been its inclusion in global networks of commodified culture. These circuits are somewhat different from those along which adinkra traveled internationally in the past. "Authentic" hand-stenciled adinkra cloth has been a collector's item for several decades and is found in African art museums and galleries in Europe and North America. With its emphasis on the singular (and preferably antique) original, rather than mass-produced pieces, the international market for African art constrained the circulation of adinkra cloth and other artifacts and left local production systems mostly intact.[1] An additional route along which adinkra traveled was the tourist market that, again, supported local production. In the current phase of the global economy, the circulation of "exotic" and "ethnic" culture has expanded and is no longer the exclusive preserve of the well-heeled or well-traveled. In this context the art world's strict regimes of taste and value are almost irrelevant, and the criterion of authenticity is applied far more loosely or dispensed with altogether.[2]

While this development may be celebrated as the democratization of culture, its consequences for producers are not always positive. Where it is no longer important that a piece of adinkra cloth be hand stenciled in Asokwa, Asante, or even in the Republic of Ghana; where it no longer matters that it follow the aesthetic conventions of adinkra design, then it might as well be mass produced in Korea and its motifs combined with other markers of "Africa," such as the color schemes and designs of Malian bogolan cloth. This is precisely what has happened with adinkra and countless other examples of indigenous cultural products ranging from textiles to music (Feld 2000). Their production has shifted from local communities to sites that can optimize labor and markets. Along with the loss of revenue to the original producers there are changes in symbolic power and cultural expression. A symbol that means "unity" in Asante becomes, simply, "Africa" in its new context.

The local is understood here as a site within the nation-state but distinct from it. That distinction is important because even though nations generally have more prominence than local communities in the international sphere, it cannot be assumed that they always fully represent the interests of those communities. Additionally, local sites are distinct from global ones but not necessarily separate from them. As noted above, adinkra cloth production in local communities in Ghana is connected to global art and tourist markets. The physical nature of the cloth itself has also been shaped by contact with the global economy (this is discussed further in the next section of the chapter).

Given this interaction of local and global sites, the concern here is not with the "purity" of the local in contrast with a contaminating global economy. Such binary oppositions are often deployed in the art market's policing of authenticity, but they obscure the fact that few local communities are hermetically sealed off from the global economy.[3] They further undervalue the dynamism of local cultural production as well as the new local cultural forms that emerge in the exchanges that occur around globalization. Rather than reinforcing such binaries, the interaction between local and global is evaluated here on the basis of its consequences for the exercise of power by actors in the two sites rather than the erosion of cultural purity.

The commodification of culture, such that its control shifts from small local and indigenous producers to those with superior capital and mobility within markets, can be understood as a classic case of the tendency of capitalism to consume everything in its path. This is both facilitated and accelerated by the technological advances of the last three decades that have made it possible to transmit any content (including cultural and economic information) around the globe instantaneously. In this context, the symbols of adinkra, the mourning cloth of the Asante people of Ghana, West Africa, find their way into the Hallmark company's "Mahogany" line of greeting cards aimed at the African American market, and into the "ethnic" sections of fabric stores in the United States where it is sold alongside fabric featuring designs appropriated from other "exotic" locations.[4]

In response to these developments Third World nations and indigenous peoples have increasingly turned to intellectual property law, over the last two decades, in an effort to exert greater control over their cultural production. Thus Ghana revised its copyright laws in 1985 to include "folklore" among protected works.[5] This application of intellectual property law is interesting because it challenges the conventional wisdom that places such cultural production in the public domain. It is also interesting because it challenges an international intellectual property regulatory sphere that has seen major institutional changes in favor of industrialized nations since the mid-1990s.

MEDIATING MULTIPLE SITES OF POWER THROUGH REGULATORY AND THEORETICAL FRAMEWORKS

A major shift in international intellectual property regulation occurred in 1994 with the establishment of the Agreement on Trade Related Aspects of Intellectual Property Rights (TRIPS) in 1994. TRIPS was drawn up within the context of the erstwhile General Agreement on Tariffs and Trade (GATT) that has now been replaced by the World Trade Organization (WTO). Prior to 1994 most international intellectual property conventions were administered by the World Intellectual Property Organization (WIPO), which became a specialized agency of the United Nations in 1974.[6] In the 1970s and 1980s, as information-based industries became increasingly important to the economies of major industrialized nations, the latter pressed for intellectual property to be regulated as part of international trade. These efforts culminated in the establishment of TRIPS, which upheld the major conventions administered by WIPO but with some significant exceptions.[7] Another significant feature of TRIPS has to do with the nature of decision making within the WTO. Unlike the relatively democratic one-nation-one-vote system used in the UN system, decisionmaking in the WTO is tied to economic power in a system of "linkage-bargaining" (Ryan 1998). In this system developing countries are granted certain concessions in international trade in exchange for consenting to agreements (such as TRIPS) proposed by the industrialized nations.

This shift has not gone unchallenged, however, and even as major industrialized nations sought an international intellectual property regime that would protect their economic interests, Third World nations and indigenous peoples were pressing for the expansion of intellectual property law to protect their cultural production. This process found support in the United Nations Education, Scientific and Cultural Organization (UNESCO) and WIPO, and in 1982 the two agencies developed the Model Provisions for National Laws on Protection of Expressions of Folklore against Illicit Exploitation and Other Prejudicial Actions, which Ghana used as a guideline for its copyright protection of folklore. More recently, the 2004 General Assembly of WIPO adopted a Development Agenda in response to a proposal put forward by Brazil and Argentina. Some of the proposals of this agenda are the creation of a standing committee on intellectual property and technology transfer, and increased civil society participation in the activities of WIPO (*Intellectual Property Watch* [*IP Watch*] 2004). Despite resistance to the agenda from countries like the United States and UK, the Development Agenda represents an important sign that Third World countries are gradually gaining ground in introducing their priorities into an international regulatory framework that has worked to the advantage of industrialized nations in the WTO/TRIPS era.

The case of adinkra in global circuits shows that relations of power around cultural production in the global economy need to be understood in more complex terms than Third World versus industrialized nations or global hegemony versus local victimization. Rather, one can identify multiple sites of power that are gendered and derived simultaneously from cultural, political, and economic sources. In the case discussed here, royal privilege, ethnic, cultural, and gender identity shape economic factors in transforming the negotiation of power.

Against this background, this chapter uses the issues raised by Ghana's copyright protection of folklore, particularly adinkra designs, to examine some of these sites of power in the production and global circulation of cultural goods. The chapter further considers how these sites are mediated by the global economy, and what this suggests for understanding power in relation to the global circulation of local cultural production,[8] and the use of intellectual property law to regulate global cultural flows. In undertaking this examination, the chapter both builds upon and departs from earlier analytical approaches.

Several excellent studies have been undertaken on the recent changes in intellectual property regimes as well as the encounter between intellectual property law and local and indigenous cultural production. These have been undertaken from a range of perspectives and examine a range of issues, including the changing nature of international diplomacy and policymaking (Ryan 1998; Sell 1998, 2003; Drahos and Braithwaite 2002); the implications of expanded intellectual property rights for access to information and creative resources in democratic societies (Boyle 1996; Halbert 1999; Lessig 2002, 2004); the corporate control of culture (Bettig 1996; McLeod 2001); the problems that arise from applying notions of authorship anchored in a Western Enlightenment worldview to cultural production that occurs under different concepts of alienability and ownership (Jaszi and Woodmansee 2003; Coombe 1998); and the competing claims and unequal power relations that come to the fore with the increased appropriation of indigenous and local cultural production (Shiva 1997; Ziff and Rao 1997; Coombe 1998; N. Brown 2003).

Of most importance to this chapter is whether and how these studies account for power in examining these issues. Thus, for example, Lessig's influential work on the implications of the increasing enclosure of the commons of creative and information resources is not very helpful here because his conceptualization of the commons is premised on a liberal democratic public sphere of information use and access (Lessig 2002, 2004). Inequalities between different players with a stake in the commons are deemphasized in this approach. An additional limitation arises from Lessig's focus on the Internet both as an outcome of and catalyst for creative activity. While the development of the Internet was clearly enhanced by its creators' principle of ease of access and sharing, such a principle can be a recipe for exploitation when extended to the cultural production of less powerful groups. Further, Lessig's approach does not hold up very well in the international context where developing nations have consistently sought to use patent laws as a means of technology transfer whereby they gain *legal* access to the technological knowledge of industrialized nations. Taking the democratic principle of access to information to its logical international conclusion would make this a reasonable goal, yet it has been actively resisted by liberal democratic nations like the United States. Indeed, such access has been eroded under the WTO/TRIPS regime and is one of the key demands of the WIPO Development Agenda.

Studies that are considered most helpful here are those that acknowledge and seek to account for differences in power among the players engaged in struggles over cultural production and intellectual property regulation. Many of these share Lessig's concern with the enclosure of the commons but make power differences a more central focus of their analysis. One of the most radical of these studies is Ron Bettig's *Copyrighting Culture* (1996, 34), in which he examines the harnessing of intellectual property law to the motion picture and cable television industries' expanded control over filmed entertainment, from an analytical perspective of "radical political economy of communications." In this perspective, the expansion of control over cultural production is understood as part of the process of capital accumulation. In that process motion pictures, for example, are not valued primarily for their cultural content but for their ability to generate profit through the sale of the films themselves as well as secondary products like games and toys. Expanded intellectual property rights extend the capacity of the owners of such cultural products to profit exclusively from such cultural products. Arguing from quite different perspectives, Deborah Halbert, Peter Drahos, and John Braithwaite arrive at similar conclusions about power imbalances in intellectual property regimes. Political scientist Halbert, applies a discursive analysis to the exercise of power by the United States around copyright protection through the deployment of terms like "pirates" and "hacker." Halbert argues that such terms determine what constitutes legitimate behavior in relation to intellectual property in a way that works internationally to align the rest of the world with the interests of the United States. Drahos and Braithwaite (2002, 15) bring together perspectives from their respective backgrounds of social science and business to evaluate international intellectual property policymaking on the basis of economic theories of democratic bargaining conducted according to three conditions: "representation," "full information," and "nondomination." Their conclusion is that "international intellectual property regimes including TRIPS have not met the three conditions that characterize democratic bargaining."

A different set of analyses of power and intellectual property rights is more ethnographic and focuses on local communities and indigenous people and the appropriation of their cultural production. These include the work of legal scholars Bruce Ziff, Pratima Rao, and Rosemary Coombe, and scientist and environmental activist Vandana Shiva. These scholars raise a number of concerns, including the inadequacy of intellectual property regimes for protecting the cultural production of local communities and indigenous people. They further highlight the power imbalance that arises from applying intellectual property laws that are premised upon Western Enlightenment principles of authorship and private property to forms of knowledge and cultural production that may follow different norms of alienability and ownership.

Ziff and Rao place the direct exercise of power by groups and individuals at the center of questions of cultural appropriation. Depending on how power is exercised in the process of taking a cultural product that is not one's own, the act of taking may be described as assimilation or appropriation. In their framework (1997, 7) assimilation occurs where a dominated group "is encouraged, if not obliged, to adapt or assimilate the cultural forms and practices of the dominant group" while appropriation takes place in the case of a dominant group taking from the culture of a dominated group. Rosemary Coombe (1998, 209) complicates this somewhat in her application of the term appropriation to "cultural agency and subaltern struggle within media-saturated societies." However, as Coombe notes, the term is increasingly being applied not to subaltern agency but in the sense suggested by Ziff and Rao, where a group with superior power takes from the culture of a less powerful group. Coombe also draws attention to the dominance exercised over local and indigenous cultural production by intellectual property regimes based on Western notions of individual authorship. Since local cultural production often does not follow this framework's criteria of authorship, such production is considered to be part of the creative commons and free for the taking by "authors" and "inventors," who can use it, modify it, and claim ownership of the resulting "creations" through the application of intellectual property law.

The appropriation that is facilitated by this uneven recognition of different kinds of cultural production within intellectual property law is central to Vandana Shiva's work (1997) on "biopiracy" where pharmaceutical and agricultural companies in industrialized nations have used intellectual property protection to claim ownership of products they develop based on the plant knowledge of local communities. An additional contribution by Shiva is her attention to the gender dimension of indigenous and local cultural production; she conceptualizes the regenerative nature of agriculture in local communities, as well as much of the labor involved in such production, as female.

This chapter combines the critical political economy perspective exemplified by Bettig with Coombe's "critical legal cultural studies" analysis that conceives of power as being exercised not only through the expansion of capital but also through cultural action such as legal discourse (also exemplified by Halbert's work) and the assertion of identity. Shiva's work is another useful resource in its attention to the gendered nature of cultural production. These approaches shed light on different facets of the case of the global commodification of adinkra. Critical political economy is helpful in understanding why and how that commodification occurs and, in this chapter, how the exercise of power at local and global sites is a function of capital and markets. This perspective is also useful given the current regulatory context that favors transnational corporations, not only in the filmed entertainment industries discussed by Bettig, but also in pharmaceuticals, computing, and biotechnology. However, critical political economy leaves little room for considering the exercise of power by social actors who do not easily fit into a Marxist analytical framework. How, for example, does one account for adinkra craftsmen[9] who may simultaneously occupy different class positions within the nation-state of Ghana and within the ethnic and political space of Asante society?[10] Additionally, how does one account for women and men who move back and forth between industrialized and artisanal production methods? Finally, how does one account, from a perspective of critical political economy, for gender as a source of power and privilege for male adinkra producers? A cultural approach helps to account for these additional questions because it enables consideration of the ways in which power is exercised discursively as well as on the basis of factors like ethnicity and gender.

In examining the gendered nature of cultural production, I depart somewhat from Vandana Shiva's approach. As she correctly points out, certain kinds of cultural production and preservation are specifically assigned to women or men in local communities. While all such knowledge tends to be gendered female in the encounter with the West (due to the perception of such knowledge as "traditional," and therefore feminine, in relation to a masculine, Western "modernity"), female knowledges are more likely to be undervalued and are open to appropriation by both men and capital. In her discussion of female cultural production Shiva tends to focus on such appropriation and the attendant loss of women's agency. Such an approach can obscure the fact that cultural production may in fact shift back and forth between women and men.

Elisha Renne (1997) discusses such shifts in the production of handwoven cloth by Yoruba women and men depending on changes in the larger economic context. An additional problem arises from the association of feminization with weakness and vulnerability. While such vulnerability is certainly evident, feminization can also mean alternative strategies in the negotiation of power relationships — strategies that can be empowering.

Further, the case of adinkra cloth shows that even where the gendering of production is fairly stable, it may be more accurate to characterize female and male production as interdependent rather than hierarchical. An additional problem with Shiva's approach is that it does not take into account the fact that, as the adinkra case shows, women may derive power from factors other than gender, such as ethnicity and class. Finally, the adinkra case provides a basis for extending feminist analyses that conceive of the law as a masculinized space.[11] In the case of cloth production in Ghana, women cloth traders have operated skillfully within this space for years while male adinkra producers are virtually absent from it.

The local and global appropriation of adinkra raise important issues of local, national, and international power relations, and therefore provide a useful basis for examining the relationship between the local and global in the current context of globalization. In using the above analytical perspectives to illuminate the exercise and negotiation of power around the global commodification of adinkra, this chapter focuses on two sites. The first of these is the site of adinkra production in Asante, Ghana. Adinkra cloth and designs have been appropriated in Ghana for decades, and in the recent past, women have emerged as important actors in the local appropriation of adinkra. At the local site I discuss the power that adinkra craftsmen exercise as producers of a prestigious cultural product for the Asante ethnic group, and for Asante royalty, as well as for the Ghanaian nation-state. I also discuss the ways in which the prestige of the cloth translates into a source of male privilege for cloth producers, as well as the undermining of that privilege by Ghanaian women engaged in the cloth trade. Data on this site come primarily from interviews and ethnographic research conducted in Ghana in 1999, 2000, and 2004.

The second site is that of the African diaspora in the United States, which is important as a market for African and African-inspired cultural products, and therefore is a key site of consumption of mass-produced adinkra designs. While local Ghanaian markets are also important sites of consumption, a focus on this external market makes it possible to examine the global dimensions of the appropriation of adinkra. For many African Americans, their consumption choices concerning those products are bound up with struggles over politics and identity, in which they look to Africa as a source. This is very different from the consumption of groups and individuals in mainstream U.S. society for whom such products have a less politically charged cultural significance. Consideration of the African American market therefore has the value of making possible an examination of the racial politics of consumption in global markets. In examining the African American community as a site of consumption, I focus not only on purchasing power in and of itself but also on the ways in which that power is harnessed to cultural and political ends. Data on this site are derived mainly from secondary sources, including scholarship on the Pan-African movement of the mid-twentieth century and on the use of African cultural production in the assertion of African American identity in the 1960s and 1990s.[12]

Mediating these two sites are global circuits and actors who try either to control those circuits (such as nation-states and international regulatory organizations) or to exploit them. This second group of actors includes local and transnational corporate entities that are skilled at navigating the global economy to their advantage and, in this case, appropriating adinkra cloth for the African American market. In considering these actors who mediate the local and the global, this chapter draws attention to the continued importance of the nation-state. Contemporary theories of globalization tend to prescribe a diminished role for the nation-state as a mediator in global governance. Communications infrastructures such as the Internet hold the promise of instant connection between local sites on opposite sides of the globe. Along with increased physical mobility through migration and its attendant dislocation, advanced communications technologies offer the possibility of translocal mobilization around identities and ideologies that are not necessarily based within national boundaries (Appadurai 1996). While acknowledging the importance of these developments for giving voice to local aspirations that may be suppressed by national state actors, the approach taken here draws attention to the continuing importance of the nation-state as the primary actor in the global arena (Morris and Waisbord 2001). It also underscores the fact that while national interests do not always coincide with local ones, nations have privileged access to the international policymaking spheres that determine many of the channels through which globalization flows.

In looking at the different state actors concerned in this case, the chapter also seeks to expand upon the standard North-South approach, which tends to homogenize the parties involved and their power relative to each other. This framework is useful in understanding the power struggles in the context of international intellectual property regulation where there is a clear divide between the interests of nations in the two groups. However, it can obscure the fact that there may be other poles of interaction—South-South, for example. The emphasis on *both* the local *and* the national, in relation to the global, undermines the polarized approach in showing how relationships between major national players may be moderated or intensified by local relationships of power.

In the next two sections I discuss, in turn, the site of local adinkra production and that of African American consumption. In doing so I consider the ways in which power is exercised at each site and the mediation of the two sites by global circuits. In the concluding section, I reexamine intellectual property regimes as a means of regulating global flows of cultural production in the light of this examination of different sites of power. I also consider how the analysis undertaken in this chapter might inform further scholarship, activism, and regulatory change.

GENDER, PRODUCTION, AND LOCAL SITES OF POWER

The commodification of the cultural production of indigenous peoples and local communities is not a new phenomenon but rather the intensification of an old one.[13] Adinkra cloth is no exception to this trend. Originally introduced to the Asante through conquest in the early nineteenth century, the cloth was initially produced for the exclusive use of the Asante ruler, the *Asantehene*. That restriction was gradually relaxed as minor rulers sought and obtained permission to procure and wear the cloth, and by the early twentieth century the use of the adinkra had spread to nonroyals.[14] Today, while certain families and individuals in cloth-producing communities are designated as the Asantehene's cloth producers and observe a number of restrictions in making his cloth, they operate as autonomous entrepreneurs and make cloth for anyone who wishes to purchase it. Adinkra cloth has therefore been widely available as a commodity for a long time.

As mentioned in the previous section, adinkra cloth circulates internationally through art and tourist markets. Links with the global economy are also evident in changes in the physical nature of adinkra cloth. Initially, the background cloth was locally produced handwoven cotton. With the establishment of a mechanized textile manufacturing industry in Ghana following independence in 1957, cotton from local textile mills replaced handwoven cloth. In the 1990s, with the liberalization of the country's trade policies in line with IMF requirements, local factories found themselves unable to compete with cloth imported from China, and most adinkra producers now use this imported cloth.[15] An additional link with globalization is adinkra producers' incorporation of elements from other parts of the world into their design pool. Their use of the Mercedes Benz logo is often cited as an example of this and of the fact that they are not above appropriation in their own creative practices.

Adinkra cloth production has also been the target of several attempts at "modernization," mainly by faculty and students of the Kwame Nkrumah University of Science and Technology, located in the Asante capital, Kumasi. These attempts have centered around the improvement of the dye used in stenciling the designs but have been largely unsuccessful and have not had a major impact on the production of, or market for, adinkra cloth. The most important recent innovation has come from an adinkra producer who has combined commercial dyes with silk-screen printing on handwoven cloth to produce a distinctive version of adinkra cloth. An important feature of these changes in the nature of adinkra, as mass-produced cotton and new methods and dyes have been incorporated into its production, is that they represent successful responses of adinkra producers to changing materials and technologies arising from the encounter of local and global economies, such that cloth production has remained in local control.

The gender division of labor is evident in the different kinds of funeral cloth made in adinkra-producing communities. Apart from adinkra there are also black *kuntunkuni,* indigo *brisi,* and red *kobene.* The last two of these have been largely replaced by mass-produced substitutes and are therefore not discussed here. While adinkra is produced almost exclusively by men, kuntunkuni is made by women who also produce the dyes used in adinkra stenciling. Kuntunkuni is used not only for funeral wear but also for conducting business at the Asantehene's palace. It is produced and worn plain or stencilled with adinkra symbols. It is also a means of recycling old adinkra cloth which is often dyed into kuntunkuni for reuse. The production of the latter involves repeated immersion of cloth in dye baths alternated with mud treatment, a process that is said to help fix the dye, and while a piece of adinkra cloth can be stenciled in a few hours or at most a couple of days, kuntunkuni requires a month for its production. Although kuntunkuni serves functions that are at least as important as those of adinkra, it is clearly more tedious to make. Its symbolism is also less elaborate and it therefore lacks the same prestige and attracts far less interest outside Asante than adinkra does.

In the case of adinkra producers who make the Asantehene's cloth, the royal connection is an additional source of male prestige and power. The Asantehene functions as both a political and spiritual ruler and his spiritual duties require the observance of certain codes of purity. In Asante, as in several other societies, menstruation is associated with impurity. While the resulting restrictions on women in the wider society have virtually disappeared, they continue to be upheld in matters concerning the Asantehene. Thus one way in which the Asantehene's purity is maintained is through the exclusion of women from duties, like food preparation, that they would normally be expected to perform in an ordinary household. Women are also excluded from all aspects of production of the Asantehene's cloth.[16] As explained by a kuntunkuni maker in the community of Asokwa, the official source of Asantehene's adinkra cloth,

It may be that . . . as you are stenciling it you may be in your menses, so if you are in that state you cannot prepare the dye (for stenciling). If that happened, in the olden days, it would mean that you had soiled the chief's cloth so, as for that, they do not allow the women to make it. (Life history narration, Asokwa, Asante, 1999)

Women may make kuntunkuni for other members of the royal household, but not for the Asantehene. While the material rewards for making the king's cloth may be minimal, cloth makers greatly value the recognition and status that they derive from being associated with the palace. Although it accounts for a small fraction of adinkra production, cloth making for the Asantehene carries with it a high degree of social recognition that women cannot attain— at least not through cloth production.[17] It is also a source of class privilege that cannot be accounted for in terms of economic status. Rather it is based on association with indigenous systems of authority that remain within the space of the contemporary nation-state and are recognized by that state.

In addition to their responsibility for kuntunkuni and dye production, women in adinkra-producing communities are also often responsible for the sale of both their own cloth and adinkra. It is common for the two kinds of cloth to be produced by a husband and wife and for the former to rely on the latter for the sale of his cloth in cases where he has sufficient capital to maintain his own inventory of cloth (in addition to cloth commissioned by clients). Apart from individual clients who order cloth for their own use, adinkra is also commissioned by women cloth traders who do not produce cloth themselves and do not necessarily reside in the community. Under this set of arrangements, men and women produce different kinds of cloth while women are additionally responsible for the sale of cloth.

It is clear from this division of labor around cloth production that adinkra production is gendered male. Even though the roles of women and men in cloth-producing communities are often interdependent, adinkra production is a source of male privilege and power. This is particularly so because of the status of adinkra as a royal cloth whose production was introduced into Asante on the orders of the Asantehene, an indigenous ruler who continues to command great respect within the nation-state of Ghana. For adinkra craftsmen who are designated as the Asantehene's cloth producers, the association with the king is a source of tremendous prestige and pride that are purely male. For cloth producers who are outside this circle of prestige, the historical link of adinkra with the Asantehene is nevertheless an important one, because it reinforces their claims about the exemplary status of the cloth and of themselves as craftsmen—claims that they assert to their advantage in tourist markets.

This is particularly evident in the case of the adinkra-producing community of Ntonso, Asante. Although the official producers of the Asantehene's adinkra cloth are located at Asokwa, a suburb of the Asante capital, Kumasi, it is the town of Ntonso that appears in Ghanaian tourist brochures as a site of adinkra production, thus giving male adinkra producers within that community privileged access to the lucrative tourist market. While the household-based production of adinkra means that women may share the benefits of that access, the most important actors here are male. The claims that adinkra makers can make about the royal status of their craft, and parlay into monetary gains, are claims that no woman can make except by association with a male producer or as an independent seller of adinkra cloth procured from men. However, the power and privilege that craftsmen enjoy on the basis of gender and association with royalty diminish considerably in the wider Ghanaian cloth market.

This loss of power is due to the proliferation in Ghana of mass-produced imitation adinkra cloth since the late 1980s. Although disdained by some adinkra makers as inauthentic, these imitations have gained wide acceptance by the Ghanaian public as a cheaper and more practical (i.e., washable) substitute for the handmade version. This cloth is not the only appropriation of adinkra designs, which have been imitated in a range of media. Ghanaian goldsmiths frequently reproduce the symbols as earrings and pendants while religious, educational, and business institutions use them in their corporate insignia. The University of Ghana, for example, has an adinkra symbol in its crest, and the *gye Nyame* symbol, which refers to the power of God, is often appropriated by Ghanaian Christians as an emblem of their faith. While Ghana's copyright law does not distinguish between different media in its protection of adinkra designs, for adinkra producers it is the imitation of their cloth in textile form that causes the most concern—especially where the imitation can be substituted for the original. The fact that such substitution occurs with the factory-printed imitations makes these the most serious instance of appropriation.[18] Another significant feature of this cloth is that the role of women in its production and sale changes the gendered division of labor and prestige in the production of adinkra.

Women's activity in the cloth trade extends beyond cloth produced by local communities. In Ghana and a number of other West African countries, women control much of the retail trade in food and other consumer products. A few of these women operate as wholesalers who procure goods and sell them to retailers. The sale of cloth produced in local and foreign factories for "traditional" Ghanaian attire has long been an important commercial and symbolic sphere of activity for such market women (Domowitz 1992; Yankah 1995).[19] There is evidence that factory-printed imitations of adinkra have been produced for over two decades (Polakoff 1980). However, the procurement and sale of such cloth by women as well as its widespread acceptance by Ghanaians appears to have begun in the late 1980s. These imitations are produced by factories as in-house designs, in which case they belong to the factory. They are also produced for women cloth traders who commission factories to produce cloth to their own designs. In the latter case, the designs are owned by the women commissioning the cloth.[20] In either case, the sale of the cloth is controlled predominantly by women.

The ability of women to produce this fabric despite the existence of the law copyrighting the designs is due to a number of factors. First, the folklore section of the copyright law is virtually unknown, minimally enforced, and therefore easily flouted. A second factor is a clause in the textile designs registration decree governing the protection of such designs that was in effect until 2003. Under that law, any persons registering a cloth design using symbols from kente or adinkra cloth were merely required to include a disclaimer in their applications stating that they did not claim ownership of those symbols. This clause operated as a loophole enabling the production of close imitations of adinkra cloth. In becoming serious competitors to male adinkra producers, therefore, women were aided not only by public acceptance of the imitations but also by intellectual property law. The loophole was removed by the replacement of the textile designs registration decree with an industrial designs law in 2003. It remains to be seen whether this new law will be effective in preventing the local appropriation of adinkra cloth.

Unlike the innovations discussed earlier, factory-produced adinkra is totally outside the control of male adinkra producers. It can be argued that the proliferation of these imitations expands the market for adinkra cloth by opening it up to clients who might not otherwise purchase adinkra. In that case imitation adinkra could be said to constitute a case of successful mark t segmentation rather than competition with handmade adinkra. However, the sense of threat expressed by some adinkra producers suggests that they perceive the imitations as appropriations that infringe upon a sphere that is properly theirs. Other adinkra producers who do not feel directly threatened by the imitations consider, nonetheless, that they demean a distinguished and royal craft.

However benignly one regards imitation adinkra, the fact remains that the section of the market that is served by imitations is a market that is lost to adinkra producers. The wide acceptance of mass-produced adinkra as a substitute for handmade adinkra also means that the different spheres within which the two are produced have become even more closely interrelated than before. Women have effectively challenged male control of adinkra, not by directly taking over production of the handmade cloth, but by their control of the production and sale of the substitute. They have, in effect, shifted a considerable portion of adinkra production from a sphere in which they have little influence to one that they control. In doing so they challenge not only the relations of gender power around the production of adinkra cloth but also the equally gendered tradition-modernity divide between different kinds of cultural production.

This divide is considered here, not because it is necessarily legitimate, but because of its pervasiveness. As noted in the previous section, forms of cultural production other than those routinely protected by intellectual property law are increasingly being referred to as "traditional knowledge." Because the modern is commonly conceptualized as superior to the traditional, this designation implies an inferior status for these kinds of cultural production. The situation is no different in relation to gender, where modernity is typically gendered male and tradition female; the former is conceived of as active and public and the latter as passive and domestic. Given these connotations of the terms "modern" and "traditional," the ways in which they are undermined in the Ghanaian case are significant.

Despite the convergence of "modern" textiles and "traditional" adinkra production well before the advent of mass-produced imitations, handmade adinkra cloth production is regarded as traditional and is marketed as such both by cloth makers and by the Ghanaian state. Women's trading activities are also regarded as traditional because they belong in the "informal sector" of the economy that escapes the accounting systems of the "formal sector" of "modern" financial and commercial institutions (Lyon 2003). Thus despite the key roles they play in the distribution of food and other goods, the market women of Ghana are often regarded as a quaint traditional phenomenon, and the open-air markets in which they operate are popular tourist destinations.

The reality, however, is a lot less romantic and simplistic. Market women routinely cross back and forth between modern and traditional financial sectors. They may raise funds from traditional sources that include kinship and mutual help associations (such as the fabled *susu* groups)[21] and save excess capital in modern banking institutions (in cases where they operate at levels that permit the generation of such capital). Furthermore, in cloth production, they deal in the end products of modern manufacturing processes and sometimes engage the services of those manufacturers to obtain products that suit their commercial ends. Imitation adinkra cloth may mimic traditional cloth and be used for traditional attire, but its mechanized production makes it quite a different product from handmade adinkra.

The traditional-modern divide is evident not only in the mass production of imitation adinkra in the modern sphere of textile mills as opposed to the production of the "traditional" hand-stenciled cloth. It is also evident in the relationship between producers in the two spheres and Ghana's copyright law. While the textile registration decree lasted, women cloth traders operated skillfully within the space of the law—a space of modernity—and turned its limitations to their advantage. Male producers, on the other hand, operate almost entirely outside the sphere of intellectual property law. Ghana's copyright protection of folklore vests the rights to such folklore in the president of the republic on behalf of the people and not in the producers of folklore. Many craftsmen were unaware of the existence of this copyright protection of folklore when I spoke with them in 1999 and 2000, and it is unlikely that that situation has changed. In December 2004 a public forum was held in Ghana to discuss a draft copyright bill that was being considered by the parliament in a legal reform program intended to bring the country's intellectual property laws into compliance with TRIPS. Most participants were from the music industry, with a few representatives of theater groups, writers, publishers, and software programmers. There were no representatives of adinkra or other

cloth producers, and while musicians included concerns about the legal provision on folklore among their proposals, these did not specifically refer to
material forms of folklore.[22]

One of the principal features by which Ghana identifies itself as a "modern" nation-state is through the use of formal laws in national governance.
While the state has brought local cultural production into that sphere of governance through its copyright protection of folklore, those who produce an
important part of that folklore remain outside this sphere. Thus the gendered
labor arrangements around adinkra production are not only inverted by female control of the mass-produced appropriation of adinkra. They are also inverted by women cloth traders' presence in, and skilled navigation of, the
spheres of modernity in the nation-state, such as mechanized mass production
and national laws, and by male adinkra producers' absence from those
spheres.

At the site of local production, then, one finds male control over handmade
adinkra cloth, and male privilege that is derived from the royal status of the
cloth. However, as one moves away from the local communities in Asante
where these men operate and into the wider economy, that male power dis-
appears. Through their successful appropriation of adinkra cloth and control
of the sale of the appropriations, women occupy a position of dominance in
the production of imitation adinkra cloth and use it to invert the power relations around cloth production. In this they are assisted by a cloth-buying public that is willing to use imitation cloth for purposes originally associated with
the handmade version. Craftsmen and purists might disparage the lack of authenticity of mass-produced imitations of adinkra, but the consumption
choices of Ghanaians mean that imitation adinkra has been incorporated into
the other kinds of cloth that that are commonly used in daily life and in the
observation of important events such as birth and death. Accordingly, at the
local level, male privilege derived from royal association and the gendered division of labor in cloth production is replaced in the wider national sphere by
superior female access to capital, markets, and mass-production technologies,
thereby inverting the gender of cultural production. In yet another inversion,
when it comes to cloth production, women, and not men, are the privileged
actors in the male-gendered space of the law.

To characterize cloth traders as sabotaging and contaminating a pure and
royal tradition would be to repeat Ghana's unfortunate history of demonizing
market women in times of economic crisis. Rather, it is useful to consider
women's actions in the same light as those of male adinkra producers when
the latter make changes to their craft in relation to changing local and global
contexts. Those male producers who are not dependent on royal patronage
and have been successful in repositioning themselves as suppliers for local
tourist markets and the continuing local demand for funeral attire seem to be
less concerned about women as competitors. Like many Ghanaians, they rank

the different kinds of cloth available on the market in a hierarchy where the hand-made version continues to be preeminent. Thus, in the Ghanaian case, gendered cloth production translates into power not simply on the basis of the gender of the producers but as a result of positioning within markets, responsiveness to changing technology and tastes, and access to capital. This gives pause to any claims of female and feminized local cultural production being under assault from masculinized sources of appropriation.

When one moves to the global sphere, the challenges to craftsmen's power over cloth production extend to the rights claimed by the Ghanaian state over "national" cultural production. Despite the state's assertion of ownership rights over cultural production at home, it has not been very successful at insisting on those rights internationally. In order to examine this further I turn, in the following section, to one of the most important spheres of consumption outside Ghana—the African American community in the United States.

DIASPORA AND CONSUMPTION

Africans in the diaspora have often looked to the symbolic and material culture of continental African peoples in creating a distinct image for themselves. During the height of the Black nationalist struggle in the United States in the 1960s, many African Americans strongly rejected expectations that they conform to mainstream norms in their clothing and drew from Africa in their clothing and hairstyles. One of the most famous icons of such Black identity was the image of Angela Davis wearing her hair in a large "Afro." While political Black nationalism was effectively suppressed by the state, its cultural version remains—most notably in the festival of Kwanzaa, which has gained mainstream acceptance. African and African-inspired clothing and hairstyles also continue to be popular as a means of asserting a distinct identity.

The 1960s were also "the decade of Africa," during which many former colonies on the continent gained political independence and became sovereign nations.[23] Ghana was prominent among these, having gained its independence in the late 1950s under the leadership of Kwame Nkrumah. Ghana's cultural nationalism included the promotion of indigenous textiles and clothing. Nkrumah and other Ghanaian dignitaries appeared at major national and international events wearing such clothing. Additionally the period from the 1940s to the 1960s also saw the peak of the pan-African movement, which was led by figures from both continental and diasporic Africa. This movement was aimed not only at uniting Africans on the continent but also at linking their political goals with those of Africans in the diaspora (Esedebe 1994; Ofuatey-Kodjoe 1986; Geiss 1974).[24] Nkrumah's additional status as a pan-African leader helped to bring Ghanaian material culture to a wider African American audience (D. Ross 1998).

An additional and important factor in this awareness can be found in the journeys made by African Americans to Africa as they seek to reconnect with their origins. One prominent African American who was drawn to adinkra symbols through such a trip was Audre Lorde. In a visit to Ghana in 1974, the feminist poet and activist is reported to have been

> particularly fascinated with the adinkra cloths of the Asante: traditionally hand-stenciled symbolic designs were individually named and were proverbs encoding historical, allegorical, or magical information. Many of the stamped messages were variations of phrases she remembered hearing from her mother and other Grenadian kin. (De Veaux 2004, 144–45)

De Veaux further reports that this fascination led to Lorde's incorporation of an adinkra symbol, *funtumfunafu denkyem,* and a *sankofa* symbol from a linguist's staff in the cover design of her collection of poems *Between Ourselves.*[25]

Due to the connections forged by Black political and cultural nationalism, pan-Africanism, and journeys to the continent, the African American community is an important market for continental African material culture. Adinkra, though not as well known in this market as Asante kente and Malian bogolanfini, is valued for its symbolic system, and its motifs appear in greeting card and jewelry designs. Where adinkra is reproduced in textile form for this market, it is usually different from the reproductions that are made for the Ghanaian market. Adinkra motifs appear in "ethnic" fabrics for the North American market, usually in combination with other designs and in color schemes that are quite different from those of handmade adinkra cloth. In this regard they vary from imitations of kente and bogolanfini fabric, which are often found in versions that closely mimic the originals as well as versions that mix their motifs with other designs.[26]

In the United States these fabrics are used for a variety of purposes, including clothing, accessories, toys, and soft furnishings that are targeted mainly at the African American community, An important section of the market is made up of African American quilters, who spent $40.3 million on fabric in 2001 (Hicks 2003). Such quilters reported that the fabrics they most frequently purchase are "African prints, batiks, and hand-dyed cloths" (Hicks 2003, 184). This level of demand for African prints, which include the imitations and adaptations described above, suggests that the overall African American market is quite large.

While some African American fashion designers and vendors of African prints use and stock handmade cloth from the continent, the high overheads involved mean that such entrepreneurs are the exception rather than the norm (Boateng 2004). As a result most of the "African" textiles purchased by African Americans are imitations rather than handmade originals. This predominance of imitation African textiles in the African American market is alternatively disparaged, defended, or celebrated by different commentators. In his study of African street vendors in New York City, Paul Stoller (2002) notes these entrepreneurs' success in exploiting African American customers' ignorance about African textiles. Stoller reports and seems to echo the vendors' disdain for African Americans who are so easily duped into buying imitations in their search for "authentic" African cultural goods. A wider range of responses can be found in Doran Ross's landmark volume, *Wrapped in Pride* (1998), about the use of another important Ghanaian fabric, kente, in the creation of African American identity. Different contributors to the book in turn defend African Americans' use of inauthentic cloth, noting Ghanaians' own acceptance and use of imitation cloth; point to the limited opportunities for African Americans to learn about African culture and thereby become more discriminating in their purchase and use of African cloth; challenge the ownership claims of local craftsmen who appropriate each other's designs; and celebrate the globalization of culture that makes authenticity claims irrelevant.

The historical and political links between African Americans and continental Africans, as well as the location of the two groups in relation to the centers of global corporate power, suggest an alternative way of understanding the relationship of the two groups to each other around African material culture. A useful model for this is the conceptualization of the Third World by some scholars as including not only geographical locations but also locations of class. In this framework, one can identify connections between groups within *both* the Third World *and* the industrialized world. Where such groups are similarly dispossessed in the global economy, they can be considered as belonging together conceptually and politically.[27] While neither all African Americans nor the whole of Ghanaian society can be placed uniformly in the Third World, the global economy has similar consequences for both groups. The ascendancy of neoliberal economic policies in the United States and internationally has meant that state support of social services like education has shrunk in both locations. In the case of African American communities, the adverse effects of these policies are exacerbated by the historically disadvantaged position of African Americans in U.S. society.

Given these links between the two groups, one cannot simply dismiss and ridicule African Americans' ignorance of African culture or celebrate their use of imitation African cloth as evidence of the cultural mixing that globalization facilitates. Rather, both the African American market and local producers need to be considered in terms of a changing political, economic, and cultural context. The links between African Americans and continental Africans have changed from their highly political nature in the mid-twentieth century to being increasingly cultural. In African American discourse, Africa is often "the Motherland" and tends to be portrayed as such in popular

culture. This view of Africa is informed by the cultural nationalism represented by Kwanzaa and by theories of Afrocentrism that deliberately focus on
Africa as a whole rather than on its ethnic and political components, and on
the glory of ancient African civilizations rather than the realities of contemporary Africa (Asante 1996). While African American lobbies have inter-
vened politically in African affairs—for example, by leading the call for the
imposition of U.S. sanctions against the apartheid government in South
Africa in the 1980s—such political action is intermittent.

The depoliticized relationship between continental and diasporic Africans
has important implications for the global commodification of African cultural
production. In this absence of political engagement around culture, the "voice
of America" in the international regulatory sphere is one that expresses the
concerns of major information-based industries in the United States rather than
those of racial and other minorities. The result is that the considerable economic power of the African American market ultimately wins out over cultural
and political affinity with Africa and sustains the production of imitation
adinkra. In this context, the most important feature of the relationship between
the African American market and cloth producers in Asante and other African
locations is a gap between production and consumption knowledge that is mediated most effectively by producers of imitations (Appadurai 1986).

In this case those producers are not the women entrepreneurs who dominate the trade in imitation adinkra in Ghana but factories located predominantly in Asia—particularly East Asia. The role of China is especially interesting in this regard because its dominance in global textile markets, which
has long been evident in Ghana, is beginning to be felt in the United States
and Europe. This has forced the issue onto the international agenda in a way
that countries like Ghana have not been able to do. At the same time, until
very recently, China has been regarded more as part of the global South than
the North—as much for its political (communist) as its economic status. The
mediation of the sites of adinkra production in Ghana and consumption in the
African American community by the Chinese textile industry is therefore significant not only because China dominates that industry but also because this
mediation confounds the North-South character of much of the appropriation
of local and indigenous culture, and the framing of the debate around such appropriation in North-South terms.

Globally, then, while consumption choices in the African American market
may translate into cultural and political self-assertion within the context of
mainstream U.S. society, the cultural affinity with Africa that those choices
express does not go so far as to constitute consumer activism in support of
African producers. Neither does it support Third World aspirations in the international regulatory sphere and challenge the goals pursued by the United
States in this sphere. Additionally, in a parallel with the Ghanaian situation,
demand at this site of consumption is met by producers with superior access

to capital and markets rather than by those who make legal or identity-based claims to ownership.[28]

The African American site of consumption and the producers that supply it also reveal the strong contrast between the Ghanaian state's assertion of power at the national level in including adinkra designs in protected folklore and its near powerlessness in controlling the global appropriation of such folklore. While the state seems to be taking stronger measures to enforce the protection of folklore at the national level, its ability to do so globally is dependent on the international regulatory framework, and at present, the protection of local and indigenous cultural production is not a priority in the most powerful international institution for the enforcement of intellectual property protection—the WTO. In the following section, I conclude this discussion by reviewing the multiple ways in which power is exercised in the two sites and how the analysis undertaken here is linked to wider debates on intellectual property regulation in the transnational context.

LOCAL AND GLOBAL SITES OF POWER

Ghana's copyright protection of folklore was partly intended to counteract the production of imitations of kente and adinkra cloth in global markets. This suggested a simple case of external exploitation of local cultural production—a case intensified by the lack of recognition of folklore as a legitimate candidate for protection in major international intellectual property agreements. That lack of recognition means that Ghana and countries with similar laws are indeed pitted against a global intellectual property regime that is hardly receptive to the interests of Third World nations. However, as the preceding discussion shows, the situation is rendered far more complex by the ways in which power is exercised by different actors at different sites of production and consumption.

At the local and national levels in Ghana the gendered nature of adinkra production challenges the common characterization of local cultural production as female. Rather it is a sphere of male power and privilege that some male producers are able to use to their advantage not only in local markets but also in the global tourist markets that provide part of their clientele. At this site, women exercise power primarily by association with men. However, the mass production of imitation adinkra for local markets is a female sphere that challenges male power in the sphere of handmade cloth. Women's success in this sphere undermines the characterization of appropriation as male. Such a characterization only applies where one conceives of the gendering of adinkra production not in terms of the subjectivity of its producers but in terms of its status as traditional—a feminized status in contrast to a masculinized modernity. It also applies in the context of feminist scholarship that conceives of the law as a male sphere. Even so the analogy ends when one considers that in this case it is women who are the privileged actors in the masculinized spheres of modern textile manufacturing processes and the law.

These challenges to male power and common assumptions about gender are not an outcome of gender-based struggle but rather of the peculiar ways in which gender and capital combine to empower women in Ghana and several other parts of West Africa. Male producers are only able to hold their own in this context where they position themselves as the suppliers of a niche market in handmade cloth targeted at discriminating consumers who include both Ghanaians and foreign tourists. Both sets of actors exist in relation to the law in ways that undermine it—women cloth traders through their ability to skillfully maneuver within national intellectual property laws and male producers through their lack of a stake in those laws. These gendered power dynamics around local cultural production and appropriation also undermine the legitimacy of the state's project of gaining international recognition for the protection of "national" folklore, since ultimately the laws enacted by the state operate more in the interests of the state itself and of women than of male cloth producers. Against this background it can be argued that international recognition of adinkra and kente designs as protected Ghanaian folklore amounts to recognition of the priority of the state over cultural producers.

At the global level, the African American market for adinkra and other African fabrics complicates the common view of an industrialized world appropriating the cultural production of the global South. This is because the corporations that appropriate these fabric designs for the U.S. market are Asian and have tended to be regarded as part of the South. Additionally, the consumption choices that constitute African Americans into a market for African and African-inspired cultural products have cultural and political origins that suggest the potential for consumer activism in solidarity with African producers in relation both to African states and to international regulatory organizations. The depoliticization of the links between continental and diasporic Africans since the 1960s, however, means that this potential is not realized either at the national level within the United States or in international regulatory debates.

The examination of local and global sites of power in this chapter reveals resources for activism in the national and international regulatory spheres that as yet remain untapped. Those resources include the African American market for African cultural production and local communities whose cultural production is the subject of national intellectual property laws. In examining power based not only on capital and markets but also on gender, ethnic, and racial identities, this analysis also suggests ways of conceptualizing the issue of cultural appropriation that are more nuanced than approaches that focus exclusively on the operations of capital or identity. It further reveals the limitations of conceiving of gender only in terms of subjectivity and female victimization by showing how, in the Ghanaian context, gender works in combination with capital and class to empower women.

Yet another contradiction revealed by this analysis is the relationship between Chinese and Ghanaian producers. Clearly, like market women at the local level in Ghana, the Chinese textile industry has maximized its access to markets and capital at the global level. Should Asian-African relations around the commodification of culture be understood in the same terms as the appropriation of Asian or African cultural production by North American or European pharmaceutical and agricultural companies? The response offered here is that those relations open up both the possibility of appropriation and opportunities for new South-South alliances around cultural production—alliances that challenge the hegemonic tendencies inherent in the harnessing of intellectual property regulation to an international trade regime that has not historically concerned itself with the interests of either Ghana or China. However, while China may be regarded among Western industrialized nations as part of the global South, it stands in relation to countries like Ghana as a superior economic power (evident in its provision of development assistance to Ghana and other African nations). Furthermore, China has had this power much longer than it has enjoyed its recent status as a major force in the global economy. The Ghana-China case therefore suggests that the possibilities for South-South exploitation around global cultural commodification are as real as those for coalitions that challenge the biases inherent in the prevailing regulatory framework. WIPO's adoption of the Development Agenda offers an opportunity for the pursuit of such South-South partnership.

This examination of some of the different sites around the global commodification of Ghanaian adinkra cloth points us to shifts in power that challenge our understanding of the global commodification of culture. Those shifts also point to the possibility of new opportunities for aligning players who could all too easily be cast as antagonistic: Ghanaian women traders and male adinkra producers; diasporic and continental Africans; Ghanaian adinkra producers and Chinese textile factories. Finally, the analysis undertaken in this chapter shows how the insights provided by analytical approaches rooted in political economy or cultural studies can be extended when one combines these approaches. Such an approach, applied to specific examples of local cultural production that travel along local and global circuits, and to the different kinds of power that are exercised in those circuits, makes it possible to avoid the danger of excessively romanticizing local cultural production and producers and casting the latter exclusively as victims. It also offers an essential complement to more macrolevel studies of power struggles around cultural production within the international regulatory framework.

NOTES

1. Some new production systems have emerged in response to this market. For example, there is a thriving industry in several parts of Africa producing "instant antiques" (see, for example, Steiner 1994 and Appiah 1992). Also, old production systems have expanded to meet the demand from tourists and those collectors who buy contemporary pieces.

2. Arjun Appadurai (1986) partly attributes this diminished emphasis on authenticity to the distance between "production knowledge" and "consumption knowledge." The greater the distance between the two, the less likely consumers are to follow the norms of use at the site of production—a gap that works to the advantage of middlemen who intervene between producers and consumers. In markets where a low premium is placed on authenticity the knowledge gap is especially wide and is successfully exploited by entrepreneurs who mass-produce "ethnic" cultural items like imitation adinkra.

3. Kwame Anthony Appiah (1992) offers an excellent discussion of this policing and its pitfalls.

4. Personal observation in fabric and greeting card stores in Illinois and California between 2001 and 2006.

5. A primary reason given for this protection was the appropriation of Ghanaian adinkra and kente cloth by factories outside Ghana for sale to foreign markets. While mass production of imitation adinkra cloth also occurs in Ghana, the focus of the state was on imitations produced and sold outside the country. For Ghana, this represented not only an assault on its cultural sovereignty but also a loss in potential foreign exchange earnings. Folklore was therefore defined in the revised law to include not only the oral cultural forms commonly associated with the term but also material culture—particularly adinkra and kente cloth designs.

6. WIPO had its origins in the merger in 1893 of the offices administering the Paris Convention for the Protection of Industrial Property and the Berne Convention for the Protection of Literary and Artistic Works. The result of this merger was the United International Bureau for the Protection of Intellectual Property, which became WIPO in 1970 (see www.wipo.int/about-wipo/en/gib.htm#P29_4637, accessed December 27, 2005). An exception to the agreements administered by WIPO was UNESCO's Universal Copyright Convention.

7. For example, TRIPS does not uphold the provision in the Berne Convention that protects the moral rights of authors (the right of an author to have a say in how a work is used even after the economic rights to it have been transferred).

8. Local cultural production is more commonly referred to in the literature as "indigenous knowledge," "folklore," "traditional knowledge," or "traditional cultural expressions." The last two are favored by WIPO and the use of the term "traditional knowledge" is becoming quite widespread as shorthand for all forms of cultural production by indigenous peoples and local communities that were previously thought of as folkloric and therefore a part of the public domain. All these terms are problematic—the more politically correct "traditional knowledge" still sets up an opposition between this kind of knowledge and (presumably) "modern" knowledge. Given the common ranking of the modern as superior as to the traditional, this alternative raises as many problems as it solves. This chapter therefore refers to these works and forms of knowledge as indigenous and/or local cultural production.

9. As will be seen in the following section, adinkra production is a predominantly male activity.

10. The contemporary nation-state of Ghana provides limited authority to indigenous political groupings such as the Asante state. Asante is therefore both a political and an ethnic identity, a fact that helps to explain the importance of Asante royalty as a source of the prestige of adinkra cloth.

11. Feminist scholars conceive of the law as male for a number of reasons, including the premise of a male legal subject that persisted well into the twentieth century; and the perception of authorship and invention—the activities covered by intellectual property laws—as spheres of male activity. See, for example, Halbert (1999).

12. My discussion of these two sites draws upon arguments that I have made elsewhere. I discuss the gendered nature of cultural production and appropriation in relation to adinkra at greater length in "Walking the Tradition-Modernity Tightrope: Gender Contradictions in Textile Production and Intellectual Property Law in Ghana," *American University Journal of Gender, Social Policy and the Law* 15(2), 2007. My discussion of the African-American market for adinkra draws partly on my chapter "African Textiles and the Politics of Diasporic Identity-Making" in Jean Allman, ed., *Fashioning Africa: Power and the Politics of Dress* (Bloomington: Indiana University Press, 2004).

13. Indigenous peoples are groups of people who have endured settler colonialism, have resisted integration into the dominant culture, and are not organized into nation-states that represent their interests internationally. Some scholars therefore distinguish between them and local communities in Third World countries that are perceived to be more integrated into the global economy and that may not have experienced colonization at all or have gained independence—at least nominally.

14. A cautious estimate based on the length of time the craft had been practiced by older respondents and the deceased relatives who taught them the craft; use by nonroyals may have begun as early as the late nineteenth century.

15. Life history narration, Asokwa Asante, 1999; interview with marketing manager of Printex textile factory, Accra, 2000.

16. Apart from the restrictions banning women's participation in production, the cloth is produced away from the public eye. In the past certain motifs were reserved exclusively for the Asantehene's cloth, but this restriction no longer holds at the point of production, although wearing cloth identical to that of the Asanthene in his presence is forbidden and subject to sanction.

17. The taboos around menstruation do not translate into an unreservedly inferior status for women in Asante. On the contrary, they have considerable autonomy in marriage, access to property through their maternal lineage—even after marriage—and in royal households important decisions of state cannot be made without consulting the senior woman in the household, who is designated as the queen. In line with the matrilineal practice of the Asante, that woman is not the Asantehene's wife but his sister, mother, or maternal aunt.

18. Adinkra symbols are widely used in the local batik industry, but the end product is usually quite different from adinkra cloth and cannot be used for the same purposes. Factory-produced imitation cloth, on the other hand, uses the aesthetic conventions of adinkra cloth production (such as color schemes and the arrangement of motifs on the cloth) and has become accepted wear at funerals, especially outside the Asante area, and among other ethnic groups, such as the Ga.

19. It is an important symbolic sphere of activity because women in Ghana and other West African countries name the cloth that they sell partly as a marketing strategy and also as a means of expressing opinions that they might not be able to express in other spheres of discourse.

20. In an interview in 2004, an official of the Registrar-General's Department, which administers industrial property law in Ghana, stated that most individuals registering cloth designs under the textile registration decree were women.

21. Susu (also known in some societies as esusu) groups are associations whose members contribute money to a fund that rotates among them. In Ghana they are a common means of raising funds not only among market women but also among junior-level female clerical workers who contribute a portion of their monthly salary to the fund.

22. Participant observation, Accra, Ghana, 2004. Musicians have dominated the national debate on copyright law for over two decades. This dominance is evident not only in their presence at the forum but in the responses of craftsmen when I asked them if they knew anything about copyright in 1999 and 2000. Several responded that that was what the musicians did. With one exception, they did not associate this or any other aspect of intellectual property law with their own work as producers of "folklore."

23. It is important to distinguish between political and economic independence here. The latter has proved far more elusive than what some refer to as "flag independence," and this is at the heart of efforts by nations like Ghana to maximize all foreign exchange–earning opportunities—including international demand for their cultural production.

24. The pan-African movement that resulted from resistance to slavery in the United States and colonization on the African continent ranges from the back-to-Africa movements, beginning in the eighteenth century, to the twentieth-century movement in which Africans from the Caribbean, the United States, and the African continent acted politically on the basis of their vision of a common destiny. The movement began to decline in the 1960s.

25. Funtumfunafu denkyem is a motif showing two crocodiles joined in the middle, symbolizing the futility of strife between those who share a common stomach—or destiny. Linguists in Akan society mediate the communication between rulers and their audiences. They carry a staff of office carved out of wood with a figure at the top that has a symbolic meaning. The sankofa figure is a bird with its neck and head turned toward its back. It signifies the possibility of returning to the past to recover what has been forgotten or to make amends for mistakes. It is also found in stylized form in the adinkra motif pool.

26. Observation in fabric stores in Illinois and California, between 2001 and 2006.

27. Transnational feminist scholar Chandra Mohanty (2003), for example, offers this understanding of Third World women as a conceptual category.

28. That is, claims based on a tradition of production that makes adinkra producers the "source" of the craft and its symbols and gives them the "right" to benefit from its appropriation. Such claims are similar to the principle in intellectual property law of moral rights where creative work is bound up with the person of whoever produces it, giving that producer a say in how the work is used even after the economic rights to it have been transferred.

9

Critical Transculturalism and Arab Reality Television: A Preliminary Theoretical Exploration

Marwan Kraidy

The contemporary Arab satellite television industry presents an auspicious opportunity to further explore theoretical issues related to the dynamic links between the political-economic structure of mass media and their cultural dimensions. In this chapter, I explore these theoretical issues through the prism of entertainment programs on transnational Arab satellite television, focusing on one genre: reality television. With its reliance on Saudi capital, Lebanese talent, and Western formats, the Arab reality television industry is a laboratory of transcultural media industry practices. Destined to be commercially successful while remaining within the boundaries of prevailing social and cultural values, reality television has been very popular with Arab viewers but very controversial with socially influential groups in the Arab world. Drawing on an ongoing book project focusing on the social and political impact of Arab reality television, this chapter is a preliminary theoretical exploration whose objective is to suggest an initial application of *critical transculturalism* to the study of Arab television.

At a basic level, the framework of *critical transculturalism* that I recently proposed (Kraidy 2005) reflects a commitment to understanding the complexity of culture and communication processes. This entails, first, focusing simultaneously on both political economic and cultural aspects of Arab television. For example, this chapter contains both an analysis of Arab media ownership and textual analysis of some television content. This approach is informed by extensive fieldwork, in which I became cognizant of the complexity of the active links between "structure" and "culture" in the Arab media industry.[1] In addition, critical transculturalism provides a flexible mechanism for analyzing the multiple interactions of material, structural, and discursive forces, focused on social practice. An example of social practice to be discussed further in this chapter is the way in which creative talent working within the Arab media structure both reproduces and subverts that structure. Critical transculturalism is also concerned with the scale and scope of power in global media and communication. This means that a discussion of Arab entertainment television ought to include a discussion of the extent to which the Arab television industry is integrated in the global media market in addition to the national and international factors that affect that transnational industry. Analyzing the economic, political, and social underpinnings of Arab reality television provides a map of the tensions inherent in transcultural practices that connect Arab societies to global trends. This chapter addresses questions such as the following: What transcultural practices are used when Western television formats are "translated" to Arab viewers? How do ownership structures and creative control shape television programs? How do differences between Arab countries emerge in the cultural reproduction of Arab reality television? Before proceeding to these issues, two reminders are in order about the usefulness of the critical transculturalism framework to understanding Arab reality television.

First, critical transculturalism's dual focus on both structure and culture i based on a specific conception of culture. Critical transculturalism views each culture as *synthetic,* marked by internal differences and fusions, unlike the *holistic* view of culture implicitly espoused in much of the cultural imperialism literature (Kraidy 2005). Critics of cultural imperialism, however, often lapse into noncritical views about media globalization and audience resistance. In contrast, critical transculturalism recognizes that symptoms of cultural hybridity do not mean an ebbing of power from transcultural processes (see Kraidy 2004 for an elaboration of this argument). For the purposes of this chapter, this means that hybrid Arab cultural forms reflect fusions within each Arab "national" culture and between these different entities to an extent that at least equals fusions between Arab cultural forms and "global," that is, Western forms.

Second, critical transculturalism calls for rethinking "the local," advocating a focus on *translocal* and *intercontextual* practices. This decouples cultural analysis from the often unproductive opposition between local and global, paving the way for a more nuanced understanding of how a variety of "local" forces compete for power through practices that are described as intercontextual in the sense that they shape the context in which they operate often to the same extent that they themselves are shaped by that context. This is important in that it enables an examination of the *regional* scope of the Arab media structure and its primacy over the global and national levels. Intercontextuality, a term coined by Arjun Appadurai (1996), thus enables a productive consideration of scale in the analysis without predetermining the outcome of transcultural practices.

TRANSNATIONAL (SATELLITE) TELEVISION
IN THE ARAB WORLD: A BRIEF HISTORY

The Arab satellite television industry began in the early 1990s in the wake of the Gulf War. After Arab viewers turned en masse to CNN to watch U.S.-led coalition troops ousting Iraqi armed forces from Kuwait, Arab entrepreneurs and Arab governments became interested in launching regional Arabic-language satellite channels, the former in pursuit of financial gain, the latter in search of some influence over editorial lines, programs, and pan-Arab public opinion. The early channels launched in the early 1990s, such as the government-owned Egypt Satellite Channel (ESC) and the privately owned (but close to the Saudi royal family) Middle East Broadcasting Center (MBC), focused on news, but it was not until the 1996 launch of Al-Jazeera that Arabic speakers got their first twenty-four-hour Arabic-language satellite channel. That same year, however, the Lebanese channels Lebanese Broadcasting Corporation (LBC) and Future Television (FTV) initiated satellite broadcasting with a full slate of entertainment programs focused on game shows, variety programs, and sports.

The rise of the Lebanese networks contributed to MBC's shift in focus to primarily entertainment. Reality television became the dominant genre in which LBC, FTV, and MBC fought their battle for Arab viewers (Sakr 2002; Kraidy 2006b; Kraidy and Khalil 2006a; Khalil 2006). There are several reasons why reality television came to dominate over other fiction genres such as soap operas. First is the difference in cost, with reality television's talent consisting mainly of unpaid volunteers while drama's success often depends on highly paid screen actors. This could change, as competition and the search for novelty have pushed Arab reality television production costs upwards. Second is the coincidence between increasing reliance in the Arab television sector on television formats, and the fact that the most popular formats in the first half of the 2000s were reality shows. For a "young" industry with relatively limited pan-Arab production experience, formats of shows that had previously been globally popular provided a safer production strategy. Finally, drama production was led by Egypt and Syria, both with state-supported, well-established television drama traditions. New satellite channels figured that competing in that sector would be costly and risky; hence the focus on format-tested reality television shows.

These developments indicate the growing integration of Arab television into the structure of the global media industry. Arab transnational broadcasting platforms have existed since the first Arabsat satellites were launched in the 1980s; now many Arab satellite channels use other European and North American geostationary satellites to have a truly global reach. In addition to technology, war and post-Fordist media practices have animated the growth of the transnational satellite industry in the Arab world. It is not precise to speak of deregulation per se, since the Arab satellite television industry was never regulated to begin with. Using "liberalization" is closer to reality, since that term describes the partial relinquishing of control over broadcasting by Arab regimes and the breaking of state monopolies over television through-out the region. Nonetheless, the extent of government broadcasting owner-ship and control are still uneven in the Arab world. In the United Arab Emirates, individual emirates (Abu Dhabi, Dubai, etc.) have a great deal of autonomy in media matters. The Dubai government, for instance, operates Dubai TV for citizens and One TV for expatriates, in addition to sports and promotional channels, all with the graphic look of private channels but all in fact government owned. In Qatar, Al-Jazeera is supported by state grants but independently operated, while Qatar Television is a classic news-of-the-court state channel. With a historically weak state having minimal control over satellite broadcasts from the country, Lebanon is the base for several private terrestrial and satellite broadcasters, and has arguably the most liberalized Arab television industry. The Moroccan state is poised to award several tele-vision licenses to private interests in spring 2006. In contrast, the Egyptian government retains near-total control over satellite broadcasting from Egypt, but has allowed very limited private ownership of terrestrial channels. Most Saudi satellite broadcasting is privately owned, but the owners have business or family ties to the royal family. In countries under authoritarian regimes like Syria, the state retains full control over television, although some privately owned channels are poised to be launched in the near future, and the first pri-vately owned channel is conducting test broadcasts in Jordan at the time of this writing. The regional momentum is clearly toward increased privatization of satellite television.

The second decade of the Arab satellite television industry is also marked by a transformation from single channels to television networks, not in the (U.S.) American sense of major broadcasters with nationwide affiliates, but in the sense of multiple channels grouped under one name and providing complementary services that range from general "family" stations to niche channels. While this appears to be similar to the European public service model or the commercialized Indian public channels (i.e., BBC 1, BBC 2, Rai 1, Rai 2, Doordarshan, etc.), the content is vastly different, since secondary channels in Arab network lineups are often exclusively devoted to Western entertainment programs (i.e., sitcoms, comedy shows, Hollywood movies). This includes both news and entertainment. In addition to its flagship Arabic-language news channel, Al-Jazeera now explicitly refers to itself as a *shabaka* (network) and not simply a *qanat* (channel) in the wake of the launch of Al-Jazeera Sports, Al-Jazeera Children, Al-Jazeera Live, and the much-discussed launch of Al-Jazeera English in late 2006. Al-Jazeera English now broadcasts in English and has major offices in Doha, Washington, DC, London, and

Kuala Lumpur. Another example is the Saudi-owned Middle East Broadcasting Center (MBC). Since its 2003 move from London to Dubai, MBC has expanded to include MBC1, a family-oriented channel with a large entertainment schedule punctuated by newscasts and current affairs programs; MBC2, which features Western, mostly American movies; MBC3, focusing on children and youth; MBC 4, which plays mostly American sitcoms, drama series, and comedy shows; and Al-Arabiya, launched in 2003 to counteract Al-Jazeera's editorial line critical of the Saudi regime. A more specialized Saudi-owned and Lebanon-based network, Rotana, carries several niche channels, including Rotana Clip (pop music videos), Rotana Tarab (classical Arabic song), Rotana Films (Arabic movies), and Rotana Khaleejiyah, focusing on the wealthy Gulf markets of Saudi Arabia, Kuwait, United Arab Emirates, and to a lesser extent Qatar, Bahrain, and Oman. Owned by Saudi prince and international investor Al-Waleed Bin Talal, Rotana is now the undisputed leader in music production and distribution in the Arab world (Kraidy and Khalil 2006b).

In addition to liberalization and the emergence of networks, post-Fordist practices now pervade the transnational Arab satellite industry. Joint ventures, multidivisional competition, subcontracting, and outsourcing are now commonplace. Take for example the practices of the Lebanese Broadcasting Corporation: The newsgathering joint venture between LBC and the pan-Arab daily *Al-Hayat* is perhaps the best example of a multiple media venture. At the same time, there are several event management and production companies in LBC's orbit. The network outsourced the production of its four-month-long reality show based on the Miss Lebanon 2004 pageant to Starwave, an event-management company that organizes concerts and other show business activities. Many LBC productions are technically subcontracted to PAC Ltd., an LBC-affiliated production house.[2] LBC itself includes several corporations, such as LBCI, the terrestrial station; and Al-Fada'iyya al-Lubnaniah (the Lebanese Space Channel or LBC-Satellite), which is registered in the Cayman Islands to circumvent Lebanese laws and is partially owned by Al-Waleed Bin Talal.

The most significant venture undertaken by LBC that can be described as post-Fordist is its purchasing of reality television formats from Western companies, most notably in the case of *Star Academy,* a format LBC acquired from the Dutch format house Endemol. *Star Academy,* more than any other program, illustrates the active but nonnecessary links between ownership structure, content design, and audience participation. For example, while a Saudi Prince (Bin Talal) owns a large stake in LBC-Sat, the company still produces programs that run against the sensibilities of the Saudi religious establishment and one segment of the royal family, while some Saudi telecommunications companies cash in on viewers voting via mobile phones for contestants in the show. The remainder of this chapter explores these multiple articulations through an exploration of *Star Academy* as an archetype of hybrid media texts that fill program grids in the contemporary Arab television industry.

HYBRID TEXTS ON ARAB TELEVISION

Cultural industries worldwide have a history of borrowing from each other. This is especially the case for the television industry, where endemic transnational appropriation led the Australian scholar Albert Moran (1998) to give it the moniker "Copycat TV." While regional media centers were beginning to produce what the British researcher Jeremy Tunstall (1977) termed "hybrid genres" in the 1970s, recent post-Fordist practices occur in a regulatory environment marked by intellectual property laws that permit creators to sell basic "formats" to television channels around the world. A format, as Moran defined it, "is that set of invariable elements out of which the variable elements of an individual episode are produced" (1998, 13). When purchased, formats are accompanied by a production "bible" that standardizes production style. In the Arab world, format acquisition and adaptation have been hallmarks of entertainment television for the past decade, with reality television leading the way.

While there have been several programs since the 1970s that can be described as "reality" shows, three programs define the "boundaries" of Arab reality television. The first, *Man Sa Yarbah Al-Malyoun?* ("Who Will Win the Million?"), was first broadcast in 2000 by MBC, which purchased the format from Britain's Fremantle Media. In January 2003 Future TV launched *Superstar,* the Arabic version of the Fremantle-owned format *Pop Idol* (UK) or *American Idol* (U.S.). In December 2003, LBC launched *Star Academy,* which was to become the most popular show in Arab satellite television history. Another show, MBC's *Al-Ra'is,* the Arabic version of *Big Brother,* was cancelled seven days after it went on air in early 2004, setting the stage for MBC's focus on less controversial, nonlive, easily controllable "reality" shows.[3] "Who Will Win the Million?" *Superstar,* and *Star Academy* have been the three most popular programs in Arab television history, raising advertising rates on Arab television to more than US$12,000 per thirty-second spot, three times higher than rates for other popular programs. The three shows mentioned above were watershed media events that elicited widespread audience excitement, press commentary, and public discourse. However, while controversy elided *Superstar* and led to the cancellation of *Al-Ra'is, Star Academy* was highly managed to survive controversy and is now in its third season. Why is *Star Academy* so controversial? Why and how did it survive controversy? Answers to these questions are found in the transcultural dynamics of Arab satellite television.

Star Academy had received a relatively high level of promotion prior to its broadcast through a wide-ranging pan-Arab recruitment and promotion campaign launched in the summer of 2003. A multinational Arab pool of three thousand Arab applicants was whittled down to sixteen contestants, referred to by the show as "students." These students were then sequestered for four months in "the Academy," the place where they were set to live, train, and compete. Their only forays out of the Academy were program-sponsored field trips and the Friday prime, a two-hour weekly show with a live amphitheater audience. For the four months of its duration, *Star Academy* was a daily presence on LBC's program schedule with a half-hour "access" show that aired every evening except Saturday. Two students were nominated by a jury on Monday for possible termination by votes from viewers by Friday. More importantly, LBC dedicated a satellite channel that broadcast live from the Academy twenty-four hours a day, seven days a week, from December 2003 to April 2004, an unprecedented undertaking that probably required more manpower and financing than any previous Arab television show. *Star Academy* aired on both LBCI and its satellite counterpart the Lebanese Space Channel, and different sponsors underwrote the terrestrial and satellite broadcasts. In addition, there was an active and frequently updated official *Star Academy* website, along with several promotional print publications that included magazine inserts, booklets, and even some specially produced magazines. Finally, LBC promoted the program heavily on its airwaves and took out advertisements in Lebanon's leading daily newspapers and weekly magazines.[4]

This intensive multimedia marketing and promotional campaign, which continued when the program aired, contributed to making *Star Academy* a phenomenal success by Arab television standards. Viewers from all over the Arab world followed the program and it attracted record audiences in several countries. Its viewers came from all demographic groups, but it held a special hold on the fifteen-to-thirty-five age bracket. According to one LBC official I spoke with, this was "the perfect program, with a seven-to-seventy-seven demographic." Regional market researchers I interviewed, though unable to share statistics they said were proprietary, agreed that *Star Academy*'s first installment in 2003 and 2004 was the most popular television program in Arab satellite television history.[5] But with popularity came controversy, as clerics in the Gulf countries issued several *fatwas* (unenforceable religious opinions) against it, parliamentarians debated legislation limiting or banning broadcasts, op-ed columnists argued its merits and drawbacks in heated tones and with strong words, and talk shows on Al-Jazeera and other networks brought various talking heads to argue over *Star Academy*'s impact on Arab societies.

The case of *Star Academy* provides a map for understanding the interplay of structural and cultural forces in Arab satellite television. In pan-Arab public discourse, *Star Academy* came to represent the wave of Arab "reality television" programs and the ways in which these programs articulated the concerns and agendas of various social and political groups in Arab societies. These debates placed satellite television at the heart of the contemporary Arab crisis in its political, economic, and and cultural dimensions. Is Arab satellite television a neocolonial instrument perpetuating Western dominance over Arab affairs, or is it a tool allowing Arabs to weave a view of the world that is an alternative to Western perspectives? Is satellite television manipulated by Arab regimes and the business elite for their own purposes, or does it serve the Arab public by addressing its concerns and questioning its leaders? More to the point, does reality television perpetuate Western cultural hegemony and distract Arab viewers from more pressing political and social concerns? Or does it, as some observers have argued, contribute to broadening avenues of political participation in Arab systems that are all but closed to ordinary people? (MacKenzie 2004; Kraidy 2006a). The following analysis will tackle several axes of tension, including language, gender norms, and political participation.

As a hybrid text, *Star Academy* is both "Western" and "Arab." Some Arabs were familiar with the French version of the show broadcast on TF1 and available in countries with significant Francophone (postcolonial) populations like Algeria, Lebanon, Morocco, Tunisia, and even in Egypt, where French was for a long time the language of the upper bourgeoisie. On the program itself, contestants from these countries often mixed French with Arabic. While a number of structuralist, poststructuralist, and postcolonial theorists (e.g., Saussure, Bakhtin, Kristeva, Bhabha, among others) have emphasized the cultural and political importance of language, the sacred status of Arabic as the language of divine revelation in Islam compounds the complexity of this issue in the Arab context. The Moroccan contestant Sophia could barely express herself in Arabic, and a Lebanese contestant would translate her sentences to non-Francophone participants hailing primarily from the Gulf countries of Saudi Arabia, Kuwait, and the United Arab Emirates. Also, the director in the first two seasons was French, and the dance instructor was a Frenchman of African origin who instructed students in French peppered with English. Occasionally, students performed French songs, and French music stars made guest appearances during Friday primes. The Lebanese contestant who was voted out early in the show made a guest appearance on the French *Star Academy,* while members of the production team of the French version made guest appearances on the Arab show. Finally, French words were used, such as "nominé" in reference to nominees.[6]

Beginning with the program's name, English is also heavily present. The English word "nominee" was used as often as its French synonym. One could argue that the concept of "star" itself is inextricably attached to the Hollywood studio system and United States popular culture. The program's hostess speaks English to any non-Arabic-speaking guest (apparently she is not Francophone), and several English-language colloquialisms ("cool," "great," "nice") are occasionally uttered by the contestants. English-language songs are performed during primes every once in a while. Words like "access" and "prime," used to denote respectively the daily and weekly shows, make the English language a constantly visible aspect of the show. This is also accentuated in the dedicated satellite channel, usually a music-video channel called Nagham ("tune" or "melody"), renamed "LBC Reality" (in English) during the fourth month of the year when *Star Academy* is on air. Finally, it is worth recalling that when it was launched in 1985, LBC was the first Arab television channel to have an American-style three-letter acronym name (in addition to being the first privately owned Arab television channel in modern history), beginning a trend that became a hallmark of the Arab satellite television industry.

Beyond these linguistic markers of foreignness, the behaviors in which the program compels contestants to engage are seen as foreign by a small but vocal group who claim to speak in the name of Islam. The central issue in this respect was gender relations and identities. The strictest interpretations of Islam, which are influential in countries like Kuwait and Saudi Arabia, hold that unmarried men and women cannot interact without the presence of a supervisor. Clerics who subscribed to this interpretation of Islamic texts issued fatwas, notably in Saudi Arabia and Kuwait, that opposed *Star Academy*'s portrayal of gender relations. While the program features no nudity or obscenity, and both male and female contestants on *Star Academy* are dressed more conservatively than actors in Arab music videos, there are numerous close interactions between men and women: hand holding, hugging, and dancing occur on a regular basis. While this is inevitable when sixteen people are confined to one building for four months, it led to criticism of the show, ranging from muffled criticism in Morocco and Lebanon, to more heated arguments in Egypt and Jordan, to accusations of being a "whorehouse" and "another kind of terrorism" in Saudi Arabia, where fatwas called on Muslims to not watch it, not participate in it, not vote for contestants, and not contribute to financing it (Kraidy 2006a).

Despite these vocal objections, *Star Academy* was not banned.[7] Governments, telecommunications companies, clerics, intellectuals, columnists, and writers of "letters to the editor" felt compelled to comment on the *Star Academy* phenomenon, and the tenor of public discourse surrounding the program grew more intense as *Star Academy* gained in popularity, becoming a pan-Arab household name by March 2004. Why wasn't *Star Academy* banned? Obviously, the fact that it is broadcast via satellite makes it difficult to ban it. Another evident reason would be that the show is highly profitable, which is only part of the explanation. Had the Saudi government really wanted to ban it, it could have ordered an interruption of LBC-Sat's uplink on the Arabsat satellites, which it controls. All the talk of government losing control over the media notwithstanding, powerful and wealthy regimes like that of Saudi Arabia can still influence media content and access: at least one other show,

Al-Ra'is, which attracted a large following from the first hours of its broadcast on MBC, was canceled for "moral" reasons. The myriad connections between the ruling class, the business elite, and the religious establishment(s) in
the Arab world bring out indirect methods of influence, control, and deal
making. The overlapping economic, political, social, and religious forces an-
imating Arab satellite entertainment television can be understood in the relationship between the Saudi and Lebanese political-business-media elite.

Indeed, at the heart of the transcultural political economy of Arab reality
television stands the combination of Saudi capital and Lebanese talent
(Kraidy 2007). The fact that Prince Al-Waleed Bin Talal, Saudi royal and
global businessman, owns 49 percent of LBC's satellite operation undoubtedly gave *Star Academy* some "protection" in Saudi Arabia. When a young
Saudi man was imprisoned in Saudi Arabia after being kissed by girls in a
Saudi mall in the wake of his winning *Star Academy* 2, Bin Talal invited the
young man to his offices and made sure the visit was covered by the news media. In some ways, the "liberal wing" of the Saudi royal family uses opportunities like this in its battle with the religious radical conservatives to win the
sympathy of Saudi society.

More importantly, the Saudi-Lebanese link may appear very unlikely:
Saudi Arabia is the cradle of Islam, the Arab world's wealthiest country with
abundant natural resources, its most conservative society, and arguably the
most powerful Arab nation-state in global geopolitics (Kraidy 2007). In contrast, Lebanon has a large and influential Christian population, has no natural
resources, is the Arab world's most liberal society, and is one of its smallest
and weakest states. Since the Saudis own most Arab media institutions and
the Lebanese populate their ranks, a politico-economic perspective that pays
less than full attention to the complex interplay of structure and culture would
be tempted to conclude that Saudi social, cultural, and religious sensibilities
permeate the Arab satellite industry. From a critical transculturalist perspective, however, the Saudi-Lebanese link explains the disjunctures that characterize how the Arab business class, states, public, and media institutions re-
late to each other. In this vein, *Star Academy* is an excellent example of a
hybrid media text that expresses the indirect, multifaceted, and fluid intercultural power relations in the Arab world having to do with language, gender,
and the role of religion in public life (Kraidy 2007). The case of *Star Academy* suggests the following points for the elaboration of a transcultural political economy of Arab television.

CONCLUSION

The first contribution of the analysis presented in this chapter is to provide
an empirical case study of the complex interplay between national, regional,

and global factors in studies of media and cultural flows. With several scholars who have questioned the formulaic use of the local-global dyad, we can conclude that whether set up in structural opposition or understood in terms of dialogical interaction, the global and the local are perhaps necessary but not sufficient categories for understanding contemporary communication dynamics. The question "Is *Star Academy* a local production or a global text?" cannot be answered easily. The global spread of post-Fordist cultural production practices and influences makes it increasingly difficult to distinguish the "domestic" from the "foreign." Indeed, it is difficult to classify *Star Academy* and give it a distinct identity grounded in a specific context. It is both an Arab, hence regional (i.e., the Arab region, as different from national or global), and a non-Arab (national and/or global) show. In some ways, with its mixture of Arabic and English, with its slightly eroticized, slightly exoticized aesthetic, it is very Lebanese. In participation, however, it is definitely Arab, even pan-Arab, with contestants hailing from a number of the twenty-two Arab states. A variety of Arab accents can be heard on the show, and a variety of looks can be seen, from blonde and white-skinned to dark-haired and dark-skinned contestants, displaying a wide diversity within the Arab world. Contestants sing songs from several repertoires, including the Gulf, Egyptian, and Lebanese genres, mixing Arabic pop with *tarab* classics, also showing diversity across the history of Arab popular culture. Also, the pan-Arab success of the show suggests that regionwide productions for an audience estimated at more than 200 million are likely to succeed. This will surely intensify the trend toward regionalization that characterizes the Arab media industry.

Another implication of the *Star Academy* case is that specific case studies can provide a heuristic framework for scholarship that can be described as "transcultural political economy." In addition to cultural diversity and hybridity, such a perspective would do well to incorporate production and financing structures in its analysis. In terms of production, post-Fordist practices have turned the Arab television industry into an amalgam of mutually overlapping small and large companies, as outsourcing, joint ventures, and subcontracting have become increasingly standard practices. In this context, *Star Academy* demonstrates the success of format adaptation, not only in attracting viewers and as a result large advertising expenditures, but also in attracting new partners in profit making to the television industry. Along with other reality television programs, *Star Academy* indicates that television channels can make enormous profits when they integrate "value added services" such as text messaging, ringtones, and so on, in partnership with telecommunications, music, and other interested companies. A transcultural political economy of media has therefore no choice but to include the Internet, mobile telephony, and the myriad "small media" accessories in its analysis.

NOTES

1. I have been doing research for this project since the mid-1990s. The latest and most intensive round of fieldwork took place in March–August 2004, May–August 2005, November–December 2005, and the summer of 2006, and included visits to Beirut, Cairo, Dubai, Kuwait, London, and Paris, in addition to interviews with Arab journalists in New York and Washington, DC. A research grant from the United States Institute of Peace funded a significant portion of my fieldwork, and sustained traveling, reading, and writing was enabled by a 2005–2006 Fellowship at the Woodrow Wilson International Center for Scholars.

2. PAC Ltd. was set up by LBC CEO and Lebanese advertising mogul Antoine Choueiry in the late 1990s, when LBC was in danger of being shut down and under constant harassment from Lebanese authorities under Syrian control. Making most LBC productions legally owned by a separate entity (PAC, Ltd.) gave a measure of protection and preserved the productions in case of a shutdown.

3. Whether a show that is under such a degree of production and transmission control (such as *Thadda Al-Khawf,* the Arabic version of *Fear Factor,* where women performing underwater stunts, to accommodate conservative social norms in the Gulf countries, had to wear full-body suits, which, as many viewers noted to me, were more revealing than swimsuits) can still qualify as "reality" television is a question that falls beyond the scope of this chapter. It is useful to remember that the boundaries of the reality genre have never been rigorously defined.

4. Based on personal interviews that I conducted with LBC officials in the summers of 2004 and 2005 (including LBC's CEO, director of programming, and director of promotion and marketing).

5. I interviewed researchers and research managers at companies such as IPSOS-STAT (in Beirut and Dubai), the Gallup-affiliated PARC (Pan-Arab Research Center, in Dubai), and OMD (Dubai).

6. Unless otherwise indicated, the analysis refers to the first season in 2003–2004.

7. There was one exception. In January 2006, Algerian president Boutelfiqa ordered that broadcasts of *Star Academy 3* be suspended for violating social and religious values in Algeria.

10

Rethinking the U.S. Spanish-Language Media Market in an Era of Deregulation

Mari Castañeda

Since the late-1990s the Spanish-language media market has experienced enormous growth and transformation, especially in the United States. Today, there are more radio stations, television networks, magazines, newspapers, and Internet portals geared toward Latino audiences than toward any other ethnic minority group on the North American continent. In the United States alone, the number of outlets grew 125 percent between 2000 and 2004, and this percentage is expected to grow exponentially in the next two decades (Eric Herman 2004). Currently, there are over 1700 regional and community-based newspapers, 900 radio stations, 150 television stations, and 6 television networks that constitute Spanish-language media in the United States (Project for Excellence in Journalism 2004). Jorge Ramos, a highly respected Latino journalist, argues that the current growth of Spanish-language media in the United States is indeed historically unprecedented and "must not be underestimated" (2005, 110).

Yet, within the scholarship of Latina/o media studies and political economy of communication, very little has been written that explains the recent industrial growth of Spanish-language media and how these changes across the broader sector are transforming the presence of Latinos in U.S. society. While there is a large body of literature that examines U.S. Latina/o popular culture, and Latin American, Caribbean, and Mexican popular culture in all their various forms and practices, not many studies examine the intersection of Latina/o cultural studies and political economy as it relates to U.S. Spanish-language media, and Latino mass media more generally. Similarly, within the area of political economy of communication, recent studies that examine the public policy and industrial changes of the U.S. media landscape have not specifically examined how political and economic shifts have impacted Spanish-language media, and consequently, the participation of Latina/o communities in the creation of a democratic public sphere. Previously, scholars in this area such as Herbert Schiller (1976) examined the ways in which the U.S. military-industrial-entertainment complex restricted the political and economic empowerment of countries located in the global South and how the consumption of "American media" in non-U.S. communities worked as a form of cultural imperialism. Although this position has been vigorously debated since the late 1960s, it is still important to acknowledge that scholars such as Schiller, and others like Smythe (1981) and Mosco (1982), were concerned with the democratic access of communication resources despite a media system that emphasized a capitalist logic.

More recently, scholars in the political economy of communication have explored these questions in an increasingly globalized and digitized media environment. For instance, McChesney (2000a) examines the "deterioration of journalism" in an era of hypercommercialism and dubious media policy-making. Schiller (1999) investigates the extension of capitalist accumulation and neoliberal policies to digital media and telecommunication networks. Blevins (2002) maps the ways in which corporate ownership, especially after the passage of the Telecommunications Act of 1996, is affecting content diversity in traditional media outlets as well as those in cyberspace. Meehan and Riordan (2002a) argue that the "patriarchal institution" at the core of capitalism needs to be scrutinized in order to better understand structural as well as everyday communicative forms and practices and thus create a more democratic society. Although these issues are also critical within the Spanish-language and Latino media context, they do not address the specific ways in which the broad trends of media globalization and deregulation have reconfigured this particular market and created new patterns of inclusion and exclusion in popular expression and democratic participation by the U.S. Latino/a population. This essay is an attempt to begin filling the gap.

In the following sections of this essay I will examine how critiques of deregulation have left out the complicated story of Latino media, the positive ways in which Spanish-language media have evolved since 1996, how regulatory and economic changes have limited the potential of Spanish-language media, and whether the increased visibility of Spanish-language media will actually lead to empowerment for Latina/o communities. It is important to note that while the number of Spanish-language media outlets in the United States has grown steadily since the advent of Latino-oriented television in the 1960s, the present expansion of the industry is momentous because it points to two significant issues: the expansion of the Latino diaspora in the United States and the broadened exploitation of Latina cultural production in the wake of digital capitalism. By analyzing the transformation of Latino media in light of these two issues, this essay will explore how the imperfect growth of Spanish-language media demonstrates the contradictions that "point to the complex dynamics affecting both [Latinos'] public recognition and continued invisibility in society" (A. Dávila 2001, 3).

THE IMPACT OF PROMARKET POLICY ON MEDIA AND DEMOCRACY

As Herbert Schiller argued, "democratic communication has rarely, if ever, existed in its ideal state in any political formation. Yet the long march toward humanization has been in the direction of new voices constantly being added to the dialogue, locally, nationally, and internationally" (1989, 56). The passage of the North American Free Trade Agreement and the Free Trade Agreement of the Americas in the mid-1990s were, in some ways, methods for including more voices, labor, capital, and products in the expansion of a transnational "American" market. Not only were mass-produced commodities gaining a commercial voice but also cultural products such as the MOMA-sponsored Mexican art show *Splendors of Thirty Centuries,* which traveled between museums in the United States, Canada, and Latin America (Fox 1999; Castañeda Paredes 2003b). Spanish-language cultural industries in the free trade agreements of the last decade have been become an "antidote to the dislocations [and continuities] brought about by global economic restructuration," deterritorialization, and hybridity (Fox 1999, 17). Predictably, it's been the private market sector that has promoted the potential gains "associated with a hemispheric economic integration" (Fox 1999, 17).

One reason has to do with the anticipated population growth in Mexico and Latin America, which transnational corporations hope will translate into increased consumer spending. Another reason, as Du Boff (2001) notes, is the assumption that free trade can easily move capital, labor, and products in an even fashion. Since this is not the case, such agreements can also become methods for pressuring countries like Mexico to open their communication sectors to international corporate media (Paxman and Saragoza 2001). In the mass media sector, the post-NAFTA environment has led content providers to develop fare with a cross-cultural, transnational appeal. Increasingly, television casts include actors from various Latin American countries, including Latino cities in the United States, and stories are often told in ways that are not culturally or nationally specific or even "Latin American" for that matter. One programming executive noted that media content must be neutral in order to participate in free trade and attract a large, global audience as well as represent the cross-border experience of immigrants coming to the United States from Latin America and the Caribbean (Morales 2004).

Although communication scholars using a political economy approach have examined the impact of free trade policy on media institutions and practices in North America (see Mosco and Schiller 2001), the impact on Spanish-language media in the United States more specifically has not been as closely examined. One particular measure whose consequences need more thorough examination in relation to Spanish-language media is the Telecommunications Act of 1996. In the mid-1990s, the U.S. Congress passed a historic piece of legislation that essentially replaced the sixty-year-old Communications Act of 1934. The Telecommunications Act of 1996 was expected to create an environment of broad deregulation and competition within media and telecommunications in the United States (Aufderheide 1999). Since its passage, the Telecom Act has significantly altered the media terrain in the United States.

For instance, before 1996, national radio ownership was capped at twelve FM and twelve AM stations per company; therefore corporate outfits could not own more than twenty-four radio stations nationally. The Telecommunications Act, however, eliminated the national ownership capacity rules for broadcast radio, and companies, if antitrust laws were not being violated, could now own an unlimited amount of FM and AM radio stations across the country. Media corporations like Clear Channel Communications have exploited the new broadcast rules by acquiring an unprecedented amount of broadcast radio outlets. Clear Channel went from being one of the smaller, midsized radio station owners in the United States to one of the largest with more than two thousand outlets across a variety of media markets (Boucher 2005). Clear Channel was now the largest radio station owner and was increasingly moving into the Spanish-language media market as well, and smaller television and newspaper outfits were being integrated into the fold of larger conglomerates. By the late 1990s, various studies showed that the diversity and local control of programming were being deeply affected by the wave of mergers and acquisitions.

According to McChesney, "the relaxation of restrictions on ownership in the Telecommunications Act—ostensibly to encourage competition—has led instead to a massive wave of corporate consolidation throughout the communication industries" 2000b, 74–75). As a result, the goal of more democratic communication is being impeded by communication and information policies that favor corporate interests (Mosco and Rideout 1997). In addition, scholars such as McChesney (2000), Mark Crispin Miller (2002), and Crandall (2005) have criticized the recent regulatory and industrial changes since such concentration of capital and media power seriously threatens the application of democratic practices in civil society. Lastly, the negative impact of market-oriented regulatory policies is also affecting other media outlets such as public broadcasting, low-power stations, and ethnic sectors like Spanish-language media (see Kelliher 2003).

However, such broad assumptions overlook the specificity and complexity of media production, distribution, and consumption in different markets and tend to generalize the effects of deregulation across the U.S. media landscape in ways that are not easily applicable to Spanish-language media (see McChesney 2000; Aufderheide 1999; Blevins 2002). Although there are some similarities in how the Telecommunications Act has affected the Spanish-language and English-language media sectors, there are also some critical differences that require paying attention to the specificity of each sector when examining the impact of deregulation on ethnic media markets. Most importantly, the argument that media deregulation is detrimental to communities and democratic processes fails to acknowledge the opportunities, albeit limited, that such political and economic action can provide for disenfranchised sectors of the population. Media deregulation has certainly had negative outcomes in terms of Spanish-language media (Castañeda Paredes 2003c), but it is important to acknowledge how it has also created new spaces for political and cultural empowerment.

LOCATING LATINOS IN THE MEDIA LANDSCAPE

The expansion of the Latino diaspora is often cited as the primary reason why Spanish-language media and Latino popular culture are experiencing tremendous growth. The 1980 U.S. Census, for instance, predicted that Latinos would become the largest ethnic minority and that by 2000, one in four births would be of Latino origin. With most Latinos, especially in the coveted eighteen-to-twenty-four demographic, consuming more Spanish-language media than English-language offerings, the Latino demographic is increasingly recognized as a valuable consumer segment, and Spanish-language media are often regarded as the central marketing tool by which Latino consumers can be reached (Grover 2004). Interestingly, media marketers assumed that Spanish-speaking consumers would eventually integrate themselves into the English-language media fold, and that hence Spanish-language broadcasting would no longer be necessary for closing the linguistic gap in the United States. Yet despite political efforts to suppress Spanish in the public sphere, especially in educational institutions, the continuous circular migration of people from Mexico, Latin America, and the Caribbean, and Latino people's deep linguistic, religious, and cultural connections to their countries of origin, have threatened the expectation that Latina/o immigrants will completely assimilate into mainstream American culture (see Hutchinson and Smith 1996; Torres 2003).

Arlene Dávila (2001) notes that although business is interested in the political economic status of Latino markets, only a particular type of Latino consumer, with lucrative economic and cultural capital, is worth targeting. The experience for most Spanish-speaking Latinos is one in which the dynamics of political and economic power are unbalanced and "replete with stories of racial discrimination, lack of respect, and humiliation" (W. Flores 1997, 262).

Ilan Stavans notes that "since Spanish was for many decades a domestic tongue forbidden in schools and public places in the Southwest, Florida, and parts of New England, the community saw it as a form of resistance. . . . *Yo hablo español* meant I will not surrender to Anglo values and ways of life" even though storefront signs in the 1960s declared that "Dogs and Mexicans are not allowed!" (2001, 191).

Latino scholars such as Rudy Acuña (1988) and Duany (2003) question whether the expansion of the Spanish-language media market will be influential enough to help shift the dynamics of power for a certain segment of the population that continues to be colonized in the broadest of terms. As Latino populations are changing the demographics of each state, an increasingly visible English Only movement, demonstrated by the passage of Proposition 227 in California, Proposition 203 in Arizona, and Question 2 in Massachusetts, works as a method of denying equal rights and empowerment for Latino communities, and is exacerbating the economic and social marginalization of many Latina/os, especially those who are poor. According to Anzaldúa, "repeated attacks on our native tongue diminish our sense of self" (2004, 270), which may help explain why cities like Holyoke, Massachusetts, with one of the largest populations of Puerto Ricans, has the highest rates of high school dropouts, teen pregnancies, and drug addiction in all the state (Third Tier Cities Project 2002).

Given the many challenges to Latino cultural expression and ways of life in the United States, there is hope that the increased coverage of Latino issues in the media and the spread of Latina popular culture will help empower ethnic communities "under siege" (Godfrey 2004). For Latino audiences and cultural workers at the front lines of Latino cultural production, the growth of Spanish-language media is viewed as a positive shift (Melendez 2005). According to Flores and Yúdice, "Latinos . . . do not aspire to enter an already given America, but to participate in the construction of a new hegemony dependent upon their cultural practices and discourses" (1993, 216). Thus, we need to better understand how their glocal interactions with media as expressed through production and consumption practices are helping in the transcreation of a new America in spite of the exclusionist pressures from state apparatuses. We need to rethink Spanish-language media in order to account for how "the market [is] not only a place for the exchange of commodities, but is part of more complex sociocultural interactions" (García-Canclini 2001, 46).

Yet despite the potential of the market, it is also important to critically examine whether the rise of Spanish-language media will ultimately translate into political or cultural empowerment for Latino communities in the United States. This is perhaps the crux of the debate between those scholars who critique the deregulation and the liberalization of media as the reinforcement of undemocratic practices, and those who view such processes as openings to rethink culture, politics, and markets through more nuanced understandings of audience reception, subversive labor, and hybrid cultural forms (Yúdice 2003). With Spanish-language media, these issues are much more complicated, as we will see below.

POSITIVE CHANGES IN THE WAKE OF DEREGULATION

The relaxation of ownership restrictions in local markets, while problematic in the broader media landscape because it has created considerable consolidation, has also permitted a range of positive changes in Spanish-language media markets, especially in communities that historically have not had such outlets. Spanish-language radio is perhaps the best example of the tensions and contradictions of media deregulation and market relations. Since the passage of the Telecommunications Act of 1996, the number of Spanish-language radio stations has grown nearly 40 percent. The growth in the emerging Latino media markets is perhaps one of the most impressive results of Congress's overhaul of broadcast ownership rules (Ward 2001).

Cities such as Charleston, South Carolina; Atlanta, Georgia; and Walla Walla, Washington are witnessing a Latino population boom as well as a sudden rise of Spanish-language media outlets. According to Ramos, "the really interesting thing is that Latinos are starting to settle in large numbers in places that have never before been thought of as being very attractive to Hispanics or even tolerant of immigrants" (2005, 78). In Atlanta, for instance, the number of Latinos between 1980 and 2000 grew nearly 1000 percent. The population boom, coupled with the loosening of media ownership rules, has fostered an environment in which corporate owners are able to provide an assortment of media outlets in order to attract the wide array of (profitable) audiences in specific markets.

The increasing reach and power of the various forms of Latino media, especially those in Spanish, have changed the meanings of cultural diversity, citizenship, and community in contemporary America. This is especially significant as "Latinos negotiate the transition from political and cultural minority to political and cultural majority" not only in metropolitan cities like Los Angeles, Miami, New York, and Chicago but also Walla Walla, Charleston, Holyoke, Hartford, and Atlanta (Davis 2000, 385). There are growing opportunities for increased cultural influence offered by enhanced public participation and the construction of new of Latina/o political identities. Davis notes that "in Los Angeles [for instance], the work of reconceptualization becomes especially urgent as Latino political leadership increases its policymaking role in the transition to an economy based upon cultural production. . . . [Consequently], increased Latino representation will mean greater access to the levers of government and, as a result, a larger niche in the state's ecology of representation" (2000, 385). In Miami, for instance, the Spanish-language press has played a critical role in the Latinization of the city and, more recently, has become the forum in which to debate race within the Latino diaspora and race relations between Latinos, African Americans, and Anglos (L. Chavez 2001). Davis (2000) affirms that the growth of Spanish-language media in cities across the United States has opened the opportunity for Latinos "to acquire the institutional standing to open up what has been a closed dialogue on the matter of race and class" (20–21).

Such dialogues are often spurred by Latino journalists who feel a deeper sense of social responsibility to the communities they reach and thus often assume an advocacy role on behalf of their audience. Maria Elena Salinas, a very popular and important newscaster on Spanish-language television, is known for her active involvement in community events and promotion of diversity within news media. She has consistently challenged the idea that Spanish-language media and Latinos will eventually meld into U.S. culture. She argues that since Latinos increasingly have their own voice, . . . Spanish-language television is not minority television [but a source of] quality and vital information that is helping bind together the Hispanic population" (Thuermer 2003, 21).

The increased flexibility in the development and expansion of Spanish-language media outlets across the United States in familiar as well as emerging Latino markets is seemingly, for the present time, benefiting both owners and audiences. One particular trend that is emerging is the reconfiguration of low-performing English-language broadcast stations into Spanish-language outlets. This is an especially lucrative practice in areas where Spanish-language outlets have not previously existed but where Latinos are quickly becoming a facet of the larger population. These new scalar configurations of market power are thus changing the regional and translocal geographies in profound ways that are intimately intertwined with urban policy, educational opportunities, economic stability, and media consumption. According to Diaz (2005, 137), the changing economic and social landscape is also drawing on a new generation of Latina/os who are broadening (non)traditional sectors of the economy as well as critically addressing racism and negative stereotypes of Latina/os in the marketplace.

Advancements in digital technologies have also greatly influenced the expansion of crossover and cross-border programming. As more homes in Mexico and Latin America are fitted with digital cable and satellite television, audiences are having greater access to a diversity of media outlets, including U.S.-based Spanish-language and English-language media outlets. These outlets are increasing the shelf life of programs produced in the United States, extending the value of advertisements inserted within those programs, and providing, as one woman commented to me in Teochitlan, Mexico, a glimpse of what life is like for Latino immigrants to the United States, including many of their family members and acquaintances. New cable and satellite television networks such as SiTV and Voy are being rolled out not only in the United States but also in Mexico and the Caribbean. In doing so, Spanish-language media companies are able to target the biggest Latino immigrant groups, such as Mexicans, Puerto Ricans, and Dominicans, before they reach the United States.

Programs aired on Spanish-language television outlets are being exchanged more frequently between U.S. and Latin American media systems. Increasingly, U.S. Spanish-language newscasters and telenovela stars are guests on programs that air in Latin American, especially Mexican, media outlets. They also appear in English-language outlets in the United States. Additionally, the latest trend in telenovelas is the inclusion of characters and storylines that have ties to both sides of the border. This cross-cultural flow has historically been part of the nightly national news programming that appears on Univisión and Telemundo known as *Noticieros,* which includes news from the United States as well as from Latin America. The crossover development and reverse flow of cross-border programming are obvious attempts to capitalize on the ever-expanding U.S. Latino and Latin American market.

In addition to the changes in media policy in the United States, Mexico, Puerto Rico, and the Dominican Republic have also experienced media reform. Mexico, for instance, amended its federal telecommunications law soon after the United States passed the Telecommunications Act of 1996, and as a result, it has created more opportunities for foreign companies to enter its national markets. One area in particular that has become highly competitive is the digital cable sector. Not only does the system grant consumers access to over three hundred television channels, but digital cable is also one of Latin America's gateways to the Internet. The synergy between traditional and new media, as demonstrated by digital cable, is stimulating openings in the Spanish-language audiovisual market that otherwise would not be occurring if deregulatory actions had not been taken. These changes have also benefited audiences because they are gaining access to news and entertainment programming that historically was not available. In addition, consumers, like those I interviewed in Teochitlan, Mexico, were making use of new communication technologies in order to maintain connections with family and friends within and outside their home country.

The media and telecommunications deregulation that has occurred in the United States and Latin America has indeed opened new sectors of media development and new forms of communicative engagement. The uniqueness of Spanish-language media is that they bring to the forefront the complexity of diaspora and how "the intensifying scale and speed of transnational flows of people, capital, and media has disregarded, though not entirely, the efficacy of clearly demarcated national boundaries and identities, from below as well as from above" (Iwabuchi 2002, 52). Most recently, the phenomenal crossover appeal of reggaetón has transformed Latin music into an even bigger genre. As a result, one development that has ensued is the rise of reggaeton/hip-hop radio stations, which in some ways are recreating the linguistic and cultural experience of Latinidad in North America (Flores and Yúdice 1993).

According to Frere-Jones, not only is reggaetón popular with Latinos, but it is increasingly broadcast over mainstream pop radio stations, especially those that have "adopted the Hispanic urban format [known as] 'hurban'—a mix of reggaetón and hip hop. Hollywood has also discovered reggaetón; several films about the music are currently in development" (2005, 96). Although there is a capitalist strategy in which companies are "lured by the potential of the booming [Spanish-language] audiovisual markets," the continuous circulation of Latino popular culture also challenges the hegemonic narrative of the Latino/Latin American geography and its future on the American continent (Iwabuchi 2002, 85). As a result, the media and their ties to the market have become important locations for cultural affirmation. Negron-Muntaner (2004) insists that "with neither nation-state nor a privileged economic position in American society to underscore [their] value, many [Latinos] have relied on consumption and self-commodification as two of several means to attenuate shame, negotiate colonial subjection, and acquire self-worth" (26).

However, this does not mean that debates over cultural politics, economic power, and racial and gender discrimination have ceased to exist. Although there are more media outlets in which to address these critical issues, they are not necessarily being consistently discussed. There is also the danger that the growth of media outlets will give the false impression that Latinos have reached broad political, cultural, and economic empowerment in the United States and abroad. The strides that have been made have not overturned the subjugated position of the Latina diaspora. In fact, the struggle for Latino empowerment is ongoing, and it is the media and cultural landscape where the struggle is most contentious.

MERGERS, ACQUISITIONS, AND THE CONSOLIDATION OF POWER

It is important to acknowledge that the evolution of Spanish-language media has not been a simple process and, in fact, has been wrought with contradictions, opportunities, and difficulties. The relaxation of broadcast and newspaper ownership restrictions, for instance, has made it easier for companies to invest in ethnic media, especially Spanish-language media. Yet such policies have also encouraged consolidation and the reduction of local content. The majority of programming is not locally produced but nationally syndicated, such as variety shows, talk shows, telenovelas, reality TV shows, entertainment news, and sports. Spanish-language radio is perhaps the best example of the tensions and contradictions of media deregulation and market relations. While there has been tremendous growth, we have also seen the consolidation of corporate power. Like their English-language counterparts, Spanish-language media have experienced hyperconcentration, conglomeration, and commercialism. This is evident by the surge of mergers within the sector and the intensification of marketing campaigns targeting Latino consumers.

In 2003, seven years after Congress passed the Telecommunications Act of 1996, the Federal Communications Commission and the Department of Justice approved the merger between Univisión and Hispanic Broadcasting Company. This merger combined two of the largest Spanish-language media companies in the United States, Univisión in television and Hispanic Broadcasting Company in radio (Balve 2004). With each company towering over its particular sector—reaching nearly 90 percent of their respective audiences—the combined market power of Univisión/HBC created a transnational media conglomerate that could now dominate Spanish-language radio, television, and print media in the United States and propel its presence into media markets in areas like Mexico, Latin America, and the Caribbean as well as the Iberian peninsula (Castañeda Paredes 2003a). The Univisión/HBC merger also solidified Univisión's commercial and cultural access to Latino communities in the United States and granted the seemingly politically conservative conglomerate the economic muscle to compete with mainstream media (James and Leeds 2002). Moreover, the merger will also negatively impact the production of local, innovative, and diverse entertainment and news programming (Castañeda Paredes 2003b).

Media activists and scholars opposed the merger because the Spanish-language media market, although growing, is still much smaller than the English-language sector (Guadalupe 2003). Consequently, the newly reformulated Univisión/HBC corporation would control the lion's share of Spanish-language media in the United States. Media producers and independent owners protested that the merger would only exacerbate the rapid shrinkage of the world of Spanish-language media ownership while expanding the production of homogenous nationally oriented programming (Gregor 2003). In the end, the Federal Communications Commission and the Federal Trade Commission approved the merger on the grounds that the combined conglomerate would be able to better compete in the mainstream media market than if both corporations remained as single business enterprises.

As the fifth largest media conglomerate in North America (Copps 2003) in terms of advertising revenue and successful media properties, Univisión is quickly leaving behind one of Mexico's largest media companies, Televisa, which also owns 25 percent of Univisión. This rapid growth has created enormous tension between Univisión's primary owner, the famed California investor and Italian-American Jerrold Perenchio, and Televisa's Azcarraga family (Malkin 2005). Televisa, which once owned Univisión's former self, the Spanish International Network, wants to increase its market share of the U.S. Spanish-language media market and take control of Univisión. This battle over the Spanish-language and broader Latino market will only intensify as the population, along with its purchasing power, continues to grow.

This emerging battle was in part inspired by another merger that occurred in 2002 when General Electric's NBC acquired Telemundo, the second-largest Spanish-language television network in the United States (M. Torres 2003). With the newly revamped ownership rules expanding the number of broadcast, radio, and newspaper outlets that companies could own in local markets, conglomerates like NBC began entering additional "niche" markets in order to complement their primary properties. Other companies, like Border Media Partners (BMP), which acquired twenty-six of its thirty-two Spanish-language radio stations in 2004, have also followed suit (Campo-Flores 2004). In the Spanish-language media market, such acquisitions are even more problematic because the sector is already undersized compared to its English-language counterpart. In addition, these mergers and acquisitions are part of a strategy of global capital accumulation, rather than a real commitment to serving the media and information needs of Latino communities.

The torrent of media mergers and buyouts in the wake of media deregulation has affected not only the Spanish-language broadcast industry but also the newspaper sector. In January 2004, for instance, two of the largest Latino-oriented newspapers in the United States, La Opinión and El Diario–La Prensa (EDLP), joined forces in order to create the first nationwide Spanish-language chain in the United States: Impremedia (Vincent 2004). This new alliance was created soon after the Canadian media company CPK Media Holdings acquired EDLP. The company had been quietly acquiring respected but languishing Spanish-language newspapers in North America in an effort to break into the Latino market. According to executives, the formation of Impremedia was the first step toward creating a nationwide print network of weekly and daily newspapers across the country that would compete with Spanish-language versions of mainstream media products that are targeting Latino readers (Kaufer 2004).

In recent years, English-language media outlets have begun producing Spanish-language versions of their products in an effort to secure a share in local media markets. Both the *Dallas Morning News* and the *Fort Worth Star-Telegram,* for example, launched Spanish-language newspapers, *Al Dia* and *La Estrella,* in their respective markets, thus maximizing their content by creating synergistic links between their media holdings (Porter 2003). Yet this sort of synergy has also created serious problems. When CPK Media Holdings acquired *El Diario–La Prensa* in 2004, it cancelled a column that was going to be written by Fidel Castro. The new Canadian owners said the impending column was bad for business, although the oldest Spanish-language newspaper in New York City is highly respected and trusted for the content it provides its readers. In the wake of the column's termination, the highly lauded editor in chief of EDLP, Gerson Borrero, resigned from the newspaper and Latino community groups in New York City were outraged with the newspaper's owners. Borrero observed that "many of these companies that are purchasing [Spanish-language media outlets] are seeing us as dollar signs, [but] I live in the community I cover; I see my readers every day. This is not a market for us, this is 'mi casa'" (Llorente 2003, 16). In short, capitalist imperatives are shutting out progressive Latino media producers and stifling meaningful empowerment of Latino communities.

Lastly, despite the corporate interest in Spanish-language media, the advertising revenue in the sector remains below mainstream market values. Currently there exists a discrepancy of 40 percent in advertising revenues between Spanish-language and English-language media outlets (Anderson and Rose 2004). Although the sector is growing, the Spanish-language media's $9 billion in advertising profits is still quite undersized compared to the $100 billion in profits that U.S. English-language media produce. Deregulation may have spurred market development, but it has not transformed what some Latino creatives perceive as the racist and stereotypical assumptions that American corporations continue to hold about Latino consumers (A. Dávila 2001). The business sector maintains that most Latinos are poor, uneducated, and unsophisticated, and thus unsuitable as consumers. The racial bias against Latina/o media also affects the status of labor in the Spanish-language media industry, where workers continue to be undervalued and exploited. Not surprisingly, given its ownership structure, Univisión is notorious for its low wages, grueling working conditions, and nominal support of local content production (*New York Times* 2000).

Consequently, one major limitation of Spanish-language media in the global market is the exacerbation of the contradictory condition of Latinos in which they are exploited as workers while simultaneously heralded as a critical mass of consumers. Despite the strides that have occurred, media producers and activists such as Maclovio Pérez insist that there is still a long way to go before Latinos and Spanish-language media attain parity with mainstream media and audiences. Pérez (2003, 4A) notes that the number of Hispanic journalists and media producers, for instance, is "painfully low," and this is very problematic if communities of color are going to participate in democratic society. He also contends, "having people with Spanish surnames is not enough. There has to be a commitment to the greater good. It is not about your last name or the color of your skin, [but] about the color of your heart."

CONCLUSION

Although deregulation and market imperatives are imposing structural limits on Spanish-language media, it is worth recognizing the ways in which the sector is permanently changing the political and cultural landscape of North America. How can we examine and understand the multilayered, contradictory, and ongoing development of Spanish-language media and Latino audiences, especially in the United States? Studies on media ownership, programming, and audiences are important initial points of entry for mapping out the global contours of the broader industry, but we also need scholarship that critically examines the role of policy in the transformation of the sector and the role of consumption in the transformation of citizens.

Valle and Torres (2002, 381–82) note, "with increased contact between people and cultures . . . the notion of a transnational or hybrid identity presents an interesting personal and political vision for diaspora communities. It proposes not only that communities be transformed, but that their host and home countries undergo transformation as well." In the Spanish-language media market, the roles of trans(g)local cultural practices and commercial imperatives remain complicated issues that are not easily resolved or defined, especially if we acknowledge the reality that "all of us inhabit a interdependent late-twentieth century world marked by borrowing and lending across porous national and cultural boundaries that are saturated with inequality, power, and domination" (Rosaldo 1997, 59).

The current era of Latino multiculturalism is in fact a push toward the standardization of a commercialized panethnic Latinidad that is globally acceptable. In her study of Latino marketing, Dávila (2001, 158) demonstrates how Univisión, in its quest to create one culture, has been "a primary promoter of Latindad as an 'ethnoscape,' a diasporic community transcending the United States and Latin American nation states," which unfortunately has lead to a kind of reductive homogenization of Latino identity. According to Mato (1998, 601), the production of a homogenous and commercialized Latinidad, an imagined "transnational U.S. Latina/o-'Latin' American identity," has become a way for marketers to "reach the widest possible audiences with their campaigns." Not only has marketing been affected, but in the last three years, companies that have traditionally shied away from the Latino media sector are now capitalizing on the "Latin Boom Craze" by either acquiring or investing in Spanish-language media. As the number of people of color increase and their disposable incomes grow as well, marketers, media industries, and legislators/policymakers are rethinking minority-oriented audiovisual outlets as cultural and commercial spaces capable of attracting consumers who have traditionally been located on the periphery of the marketplace.

Jimenez contends, however, that "Latino academics should acknowledge those moments when the Spanish-language media effectively counter mainstream media's racializing representations of Latinos and criticize the Spanish-language media when they reaffirm 'race' as an objective reality. Latino intellectuals should encourage the Spanish-language media's efforts to construct a pan-Latino political culture based upon a critical analysis of Latino multiethnicity and criticize those media when they commodify mestizaje as a means to mercenary marketing ends" (1998, 405). Consequently, there are some important issues that any future analyses of Spanish-language media must consider. These include asking the following questions: how the limitations of the commercial media market, especially in a deregulated environment, are expanding the role of nonprofit media and inspiring citizens to develop media resources that fit their needs as well as challenge the status quo? how the development and expansion of Spanish-language media are challenging conceptions of Latinidad, cultural citizenship, and processes of assimilation? and how translocal political, economic, and cultural practices are reconceptualizing Spanish-language media in a global context.

In conclusion, it is important to note that while the changing media regulatory landscape has opened the floodgates for new forms of Latino cultural production, there are also limitations that deregulation has produced in this expansion. Consequently, discussions regarding the empowerment of the Latina diaspora must be tempered with the acknowledgment that Latinos continue to face economic, political, and social marginality. Perhaps the next step in resisting and countering the duress imposed by capitalist and nation-state structures of power is to look even closer at the "creative interventions that networks of minoritized cultures produce within and across national boundaries" (Lionnet and Shih 2005). This essay is an attempt to begin such a discussion.

III

CIVIL SOCIETY AND MULTIPLE PUBLICS

11

Gender and Empire:
Veilomentaries and the War on Terror

Sunera Thobani

The much-acclaimed documentary *Return to Kandahar* is introduced with shots from the quasi-fictional film, *Kandahar,* directed by the noted Iranian filmmaker Mohsen Makhmalbaf.[1] Among the first few images is a group of veiled women walking in a desert, followed by a close-up of the Afghan-Canadian journalist and human rights activist Nilufer Pazira. A burqa frames her unveiled face as she stares fully into the camera. In a reversal of the iconic image of the veiled Muslim woman (who is usually shown fully covered and lifting the burqa to signal her emancipation), Pazira's face is unveiled as she stares mutely into the camera. She then lowers the burqa to completely cover her face.

The image of the veiled woman is, as a number of scholars have noted, a staple within the overarching Orientalist frame used to depict "Muslim" women in the Western imagination (Bailey and Tawadros 2003; Hoodfar 1993; Steet 2000). The veil operates as a signifier of the passivity and silence of the women, victims of their culture, religion, and communities. In the Orientalist repertoire, however, the usual practice of the lifting of the burqa to reveal the hidden, mysterious Oriental woman for all the world to gaze upon signals her liberation, as in the opening shots of Sally Armstrong's documentary, *Daughters of Afghanistan,* when one of the four Afghan women featured in the film (Sogra) lifts the veil to reveal her face to the viewer. The reversal of this practice in Pazira's case signals a reverse process, that of an emancipated woman going underground, engaged in a covert operation as it were, to save her friend, which is the central plot of the documentary, as it was of the quasi-fictional predecessor, *Kandahar.*[2] Utilizing the Orientalist trope in reverse, this opening shot signals that this Muslim woman is different. It graphically performs Pazira's authenticity as a native informant, as well as her heroic duplicity as covert agent/journalist. She will lead her audiences on a journey into the "real" lives of Afghan women.[3]

Produced before the 9/11 attacks in the United States, the film *Kandahar* features Pazira's journey as she sets out to locate and rescue her sister Dyana, who was left behind in Afghanistan when the family fled the civil war that followed the withdrawal of the Soviet occupation forces. Pazira plays the role of the protagonist, Nafas, a character based on herself. Nafas receives a letter from Dyana informing her that she is tired of living under the harshness of the Taliban regime and has decided to end her life at the last lunar eclipse of the twentieth century. With time quickly running out, Nafas travels to Afghanistan (via Iran) three days before the looming eclipse. Facing numerous obstacles on her sojourn, at the end of the film Nafas is still on her journey to Kandahar.

Kandahar garnered much international attention and critical acclaim after the 9/11 attacks and was awarded the Prize of the Ecumenical Jury at Cannes (2001), the Federico Fellini Honour of UNESCO (2001), and a four-star rating by the BBC and *Guardian* film guides in the United Kingdom.[4] The *Guardian* praised the film as a "historical document," and the BBC's review found the film's representation to be one of "unrelenting sadness," concluding that it was "impossible not to emerge from the cinema and wonder about the plight of the Afghan people today" ("Release of Kandahar Film in London" 2001).

Return to Kandahar (codirected and coedited by Paul Jay, a white Canadian male, and Nilufer Pazira) documents yet another attempt to locate her friend Dyana in June 2002. The documentary refers explicitly to the earlier film several times, including its use of the introductory shots discussed above. The documentary too has won significant awards,[5] and like the film, it begins with the letter from Dyana and charts Pazira's journey through Afghanistan (Kabul, Kandahar, and ultimately Mazar-i-Sharif) as she continues to search for her friend. In both the film and documentary, the plight of Dyana is presented as the plight of all Afghan women; she is the absent, haunting—and haunted—presence in the film, against which the active presence of Pazira dominates the frame. Ultimately unable to locate or save Dyana, who we eventually learn has taken her own life four years ago, a disheartened Pazira leaves Afghanistan at the end of the documentary. Dyana is the unlucky Afghan woman, driven to desperate suicide by her fanatic Muslim leaders' perverse social order, while Pazira, the lucky one, has found a new life of freedom by escaping to the West: Canada, in this case.

Made in 2002 by the well-known Canadian journalist, filmmaker, and women's/human rights activist Sally Armstrong, *Daughters of Afghanistan* (directed by Robin Benger) documents the experiences of four Afghan women: Dr. Sima Samar, a Hazara woman and a human/women's rights activist, introduced as "the remarkable woman who wanted to lead them

[Afghan women] out of the long night of the Taliban to freedom and equality"; Hamida Omed (or Umed), a teacher and activist at Dr. Samar's high school for women, introduced as "a gutsy school principal"; Sogra, a Hazara woman introduced as "a refugee woman who survived a massacre," and who subsequently sought shelter with her children at one of Dr. Samar's projects; and Lima, introduced "as a young girl in a ruined village," orphaned and left with the responsibility of raising her younger siblings.[6] Although the documentary features four women, it is an unabashed endorsement and promotion of the activism of the well-known Dr. Samar, who served as deputy prime minister and minister of women's affairs for a very brief period at the beginning of the current Karzai regime. The documentary chronicles her activism and the political challenges she faces in post-Taliban Afghanistan.[7] Armstrong has been writing about Afghan women since 1996,[8] and her documentary has been widely screened and recommended for inclusion in the high school curriculum for subjects including "geography, world history, sociology and psychology," as well as "comparative religion and ethics."[9] As she highlights Dr. Samar's activism, Armstrong secures for herself the position of the quintessential Western feminist working in solidarity with "non-Western" women to further their gender equality.

Both documentaries claim to be centrally concerned with the status of Afghan women; they want to help "save" these women by bringing international attention to their plight, albeit in different ways: Pazira wants to rescue her friend, Dyana, and in the process, raise awareness about the general plight of Afghan women; Armstrong wants to raise such awareness too, through her support for Dr. Samar's political activism. Presented as telling *the* truth about the "reality" of Afghan women's lives to the world, both documentaries have been repeatedly broadcast by the Canadian Broadcasting Corporation (CBC, the national public broadcaster). They have also been screened widely at numerous other local and international venues, where they are reputed to move audiences to tears.

In this chapter I argue that rather than telling *the* truth about Afghan women's lives, these two feminist documentaries can be more usefully classified as "veilomentaries," in that they are more about the constitution of the Western woman as an emancipated gendered subject, a constitution that relies on the Othering of Muslim women as gendered hypervictims. "Liberating" Afghan women emerged as a key justification for the War on Terror. The image of "the" Afghan woman that emerges in these documentaries dovetails with, rather than contradicts, the hegemonic representation of the "Muslim" woman in U.S. foreign policy as one who requires Western intervention to liberate her from her culture, community, and coreligionists, a discursive construct indispensable to legitimating the war on Afghanistan. Both documentaries use Afghan women's lives as the resources—raw material, as it were—for constituting the subjectivity of the Western female subject as "liberated," in a manner that corresponds starkly with the Bush administration's attempts to secure and control the material resources—oil and natural gas—of the Middle East and Central Asia. Empire building relies in no small measure on the efficacy of the disciplinary practices that constitute the subjectivities of the subjects/objects who reproduce imperial power relations, and veilomentaries, such as the two that are the subject of this study, have become indispensable to governance in the contemporary remaking of the global order.

These films provoke troubling questions about the role of independent women filmmakers in furthering imperialist objectives. Documentary filmmakers are often accorded greater authenticity, and considered closer to "reality," than those who make fictional, dramatic films. Women filmmakers, and in particular those who are human rights activists, are seen as having greater access to the "truths" of women's lives, given their own lived experiences. My reading of these films finds that they revive and enliven stale Orientalist clichés of the West as harbinger of civilization and gender freedoms, while veiling the predatory violence—economic, political, and epistemic—unleashed against Afghan women, as it was inflicted on Afghan society in general, including on Afghan men.

Beginning with a discussion of the complex relationship between gender, race, and empire building, I interrogate questions of epistemic prerogative, highlighting in particular the pitfalls of the role of the native informant; representations of gender relations in Islamic and Western contexts; and the various subject positions being constituted for general consumption. I also discuss the role of the media, particularly of "veilomentaries," in the organizing of governmentality and processes of subject formation. A brief exposition of feminist involvements in the war concludes the essay.

WOMEN, GENDER, AND EMPIRE

The question of gender, long marginalized by policymakers and analysts of globalization, emerged as a major concern as the Bush administration identified the rooting out of Al-Qaeda and the "liberating" of Afghan women as major objectives in the war on Afghanistan. "Good morning. I'm Laura Bush, and I'm delivering this week's radio address to kick off a world-wide effort to focus on the brutality against women and children by the al-Qaeda terrorist network and the regime it supports in Afghanistan, the Taliban," announced the U.S. president's wife on November 17, 2001. "That regime is in retreat across much of the country, and the people of Afghanistan—especially women—are rejoicing." A war of retaliation driven equally by the United States' ambition of increasing its global reach and power over Central Asia and the Middle East, areas which were of great strategic interest during the Cold War, was here being recast as essentially concerned with the goal of liberating Afghan women. Previously part of the Soviet Republic, the Central Asian republics had come to acquire even greater importance after the collapse of the Soviet Union with the recent discoveries of fossil fuels in the region. International oil companies had been vying to build an oil pipeline through Afghanistan and to acquire oil concessions under the Caspian Sea (Mahajan 2002; Mamdani 2004; Rashid 2001). These considerations were shunted from public view as the mantra of "freeing" Afghan women was embraced as part of the dominant narrative framing the war, with the willing compliance of both mainstream U.S. and Canadian media.

The trope of the non-Western woman as victim of tradition in need of Western rescue was historically constitutive of colonialism and imperialism. The British, for example, deployed the rhetoric of "saving" Indian women from Indian men during the Raj, highlighting the practices of dowry, child marriage, and sati as evidence of widespread misogyny within Indian society (Oldenberg 2002; Mani 1998; Sangari and Vaid 1989). Leila Ahmed has demonstrated how colonial administrators in Egypt used the status of Egyptian women, and in particular the practice of veiling, to legitimize colonial rule, even as they vociferously opposed feminist movements and the extension of women's rights in their own societies: "Even as the Victorian male establishment devised theories to contest the claims of feminism, and derided and rejected the ideas of feminism, and the notion of men's oppressing women with respect to itself, it captured the language of feminism and redirected it, in the service of colonialism, toward Other men and the cultures of Other men" (1992, 151). Ahmed argues that the existence of patriarchal practices within Western societies was displaced as colonial powers focused on the "barbarian" patriarchal practices within non-Western societies to justify their conquest and colonization.

The representation of colonized peoples as hypertraditional, and of Muslim women in particular as uniformly and unrelentingly oppressed, continued in the "postcolonial" era. Chandra Mohanty famously traced how Third World women were constituted as victims in modern liberal development discourse (1991). Discussing the first Gulf War and the "new" imperialism, Spivak noted that the "benevolent self-representation of the imperialist as savior" is a "long-term toxic effect" of imperialism (1992). In her recent examination of the discourse of "forced marriages" in European countries, Razack reveals the prevalence of this "toxic effect" in the "culturalization" of violence against Muslim women, constituting the European subject as "civilized," the Muslim woman as "imperiled," and the Muslim man as "dangerous" (2004). Both point out how these discursive practices give rise to the politics of military intervention and surveillance as Western subjects are mobilized to "save" Muslim women from their own communities and societies.

While white men and women have had access to the subject-position of the "savior," Third World women in the West have had to negotiate such access differently. Third World women in the West have gained access to the politics of "saving" the Third World most commonly through upholding the claims to superiority by Western subjects, and of the concurrent inferiority of their own cultures, religions, and communities. Razack points out how the "flow of ideas, labour, and capital that marks the financialization of the globe . . . scripts" women of color as the "native informant," whose role "is frequently to help the First World engage in a politics of saving the women of the Third World" (2000, 42).

Women in the West, then, have long been heavily invested in "saving" Third World women. As the world's remaining superpower resorted once again to drawing upon gender as a significant marker of its difference from Islam, women in the West were once again called upon to identify with—and legitimize—war and colonial occupation as being in the best interests of women. The propaganda value of emphasizing the plight of Afghan women, and thereby shifting the focus from the imperialist designs of the United States to that of oppressive patriarchal societies to mobilize support, was not lost on the British government, which quickly recruited the services of Cherie Booth, prime minister Tony Blair's wife. In the United States, the president's wife continued to use her husband's weekly radio address to the nation to build support for "saving" Afghan women: "Because of our recent military gains in much of Afghanistan, women are no longer imprisoned in their homes. They can listen to music and teach their daughters without fear of punishment. Yet the terrorists who helped rule that country now plot and plan in many countries. And they must be stopped. The fight against terrorism is also a fight for the rights and dignity of women" (Quoted in Donnell 2003, 126). Cherie Booth hosted a meeting with Afghan women and called on the British nation to play its part in helping save Afghan women: "The women here prove that the women of Afghanistan still have a spirit that belies their unfair, downtrodden image. We need to help them free that spirit and give them their voice back, so they can create the better Afghanistan we all want to see" (BBC News 2001). Both Laura Bush and Cherie Booth made uncharacteristic forays into the front lines of national and global politics in the war effort. In Canada, politicians and media commentators, including human/women's rights activists such as Armstrong and Pazira, were not to be left behind in the clamor to "save" Afghan women.

MEDIA, WAR, AND TERROR

The live broadcasting of the attacks on the twin towers and the vying of spokespeople on all sides of the conflict to shape public understandings of the event highlighted the critical importance of globalized media to global governance. Scholars have noted that the media shape, in very significant ways, the "commonsense" understandings that publics come to acquire about the nature of the social world and about major international events and their consequences. Robert Hackett and Yuezhi Zhao point out that "journalism is arguably the most important form of public knowledge in contemporary society" (1998, 1). At the best of times, publics rely heavily on the media for their understanding of current events, and this is particularly so with regard to international events.

With few other options available for public dissemination of information about such events, the media have, in many ways, become the only public space for such discussion and debate. In moments of global crisis, this reliance becomes even more acute in order to acquire information about rapidly unfolding events, about national and international interests, alliances, and enmities.

In his examination of the politics of representation of the Orient and Islam, Edward Said demonstrated the link between the forms of "cultural" knowledge produced about the Orient and the workings of colonial power. Identifying Orientalism as a discourse that homogenized widely divergent peoples and societies, he argued that the process of "knowing" them became inseparable from the process of dominating them (1978). Said found this discourse to be rife in his study of U.S. media reporting of Islam in the last decades of the twentieth century: "In many instances," he noted, "'Islam' has licensed not only patent inaccuracy, but also expressions of unrestrained ethnocentrism, cultural and even racial hatred, deep yet paradoxically free-floating hostility" (1981, xi). As a consequence of the grossly simplistic and overgeneralized reporting, as well as of misrepresentations and omissions, he concluded that "a great deal of covering up" of Islam was taking place (1981, xi).

Ironically, at the very moment that media reporting became absolutely indispensable in the global crisis that the 9/11 attacks precipitated, the utter collapse of even the flimsiest of claims to "objectivity" was revealed in North American mainstream media reporting. Expressions of support for the prowar rhetoric emanating from the Bush administration became not only a measure of the patriotism of journalists, but also proof of their opposition to terrorism.[10] Critics of the war were attacked as being "un-American": those who did not march in step with the drumbeat of war were publicly reviled as apologists for terrorists, their perspectives quickly marginalized when not entirely silenced.[11] With journalists solemnly donning stars and stripes lapel pins and brooches, the death of irony was literally proclaimed.

The Canadian media responded to the 9/11 attacks by presenting Canada as a likely target for terrorist attacks because it too was a part of the West, committed to democracy and freedom (Thobani, forthcoming). In their study of print media, T. Y. Ismael and J. Measor found this reporting "sensational," "emotional," and "repetitive."[12] Identifying "the lack of context" and "racist notions" as particularly problematic, their study echoed the earlier findings of Karim H. Karim, who traced the resilience of "centuries-old primary stereotypes," particularly that of the "Islamic peril" and "the violent Muslim," in the media prior to 9/11. Karim noted that media discourses "accord an implicit primacy to nation-states, particularly to elite nations such as the American superpower," making "invisible" the "wholesale violence" of these nations while "highlighting" the violence of "sub-national groups" (2003, 175).

Moreover, in a blatant act of kowtowing to the Bush administration, the CBC, along with CanWest's Global National network, announced their voluntary adoption of guidelines developed by the administration for the most popular American news networks. Alarmed about the potential impact on American audiences of these networks' repetition of news broadcasts from Al-Jazeera, the Qatar-based Middle Eastern news network, of statements made by Osama bin Laden, then secretary of state Condoleezza Rice asked the heads of these networks to refrain from such broadcasts.[13] The CBC and CanWest followed suit, although no formal request was made of them (MacLeod 2004). It would not be unfair, therefore, to say that when not actually cheerleading for the Bush administration, the Canadian media played a pivotal role in legitimizing the war on Afghanistan outside the borders of the United States, thereby granting it international legitimacy.

It is in the context of such heightened anxieties and fears regarding national and global (in)security, and a long-standing media hostility toward Islam, that the two documentaries discussed below were produced and broadcast. Women journalists and filmmakers, including Muslim women, who have historically been marginalized and have had far less access to the resources necessary to address gender issues and the inequalities experienced by women, were suddenly in great demand in the mainstream media (Meehan and Riordan 2002b). They acquired previously unequalled access to producing and circulating knowledge about Afghanistan, Muslim men and women, and Islam. In turn, these women have contributed to the discourse of imperialism, relating to "non-Western" women and men differently as a result of their different locations within the terrain of the West.

EPISTEMIC PREROGATIVE AND PRESENTING THE OTHER

Among the very first differences that strike the viewer upon watching *Return to Kandahar* and *Daughters of Afghanistan* are their very different aesthetic sensibilities, and the very different roles assumed by the two journalists in their respective documentaries. These aesthetic sensibilities are directly linked to the manner in which the two journalists position themselves and are positioned by others. Visually, *Return to Kandahar* reproduces a luxurious, colorful, and mysterious Orientalist sensibility, seductive and sumptuous to watch. Like the film *Kandahar*, the documentary presents numerous images

of Pazira in pensive, exoticized, and romanticized images, the camera linger-
ing on her face in the many close-up shots, highlighting her beauty, showcas-
ing her flowing dresses, repeatedly drawing attention to her jewelry. Numerous shots of the journalist-as-heroine are interspersed throughout the
documentary, showing her sitting alone and forlorn in stark desertlike landscapes, looking off silently toward the setting sun. She is shown laying a
chadar on a tomb and praying at the shrine in Kandahar. (A chadar is a long
shawl or sheet, and it is considered to be an especially propitious act to lay
one on the shrine of a Muslim *pir* [saint].) The documentary, like the film
Kandahar, rides very much on Pazira's personal beauty.[14]

The casting of Pazira in this highly feminized frame, with the heavy emphasis on her personal beauty, on her face, and on her dramatic lowering of
the burqa, underscores the ambiguity of the position she can occupy: she can
represent Afghan women to white audiences, and Canadians to the Afghans
she interacts with (as all the Afghan men who interact with her in the documentary demonstrate).[15] Wielding her Afghan identity as central to the narrative plot of the documentary and to gaining access to Afghan refugees, Pazira
claims the role of the native informant with great aplomb. She explains in her
comments on the making of the film *Kandahar:* "On first meeting the leaders of the refugee community I didn't exist for them. But then I spoke to them
in their own language Pashtu. They poured their hearts out to me, telling me
of their suffering and their pain" (Bright 2001).

This strategy of auto-Orientalizing highlights her translatable Oriental
beauty as a "globally recognized signifier" (Mazzarella 2003, 138). This
beauty is now Canadian; it can be imagined as a beauty that belongs to the
nation that can be possessed by it. Her Canadian-ness is also repeatedly emphasized; she is the grateful immigrant who is mindful—and constantly re-
minds her audiences that she is—of the freedoms she has acquired as a
woman by becoming Canadian. In her very many assertions of her "Canadian-ness," she reassures the viewing public that she might look like one of
"them," she might even talk like one of "them," but she thinks (reasons?) like
one of "us." This then is a domesticated Oriental, and the shock of her fair
face and blue eyes, particularly when dramatically framed by the burqa,
stresses her similarity, not her difference, with a Western viewing public.

The protagonist of the other documentary, Sally Armstrong, on the other
hand, secure in her national/racial location as a white woman, positions
herself as the sympathetic Western feminist, engaged in the politics of international solidarity with her downtrodden Muslim sisters. Although the Orientalist visual frame is certainly present in *Daughters of Afghanistan*—
unidentified burqa-clad women traversing unnamed city streets are regularly
interspersed throughout the documentary—it is far less blatant. This journalist is not presented in an as overtly feminized fashion. Instead, in a truly "sis-
terly," sometimes even "maternalist" manner, she is shown holding the hands

of the women she interviews, hugging them, receiving little notes from them. Early in the film she is shown sitting at her desk, working on a computer, talking on a cell phone; that is to say, she is clearly engaged in "work" activities. Therefore, although this film also relies on the iconic image of the burqa-clad Afghan woman as the Other—indeed Armstrong reproduces this image on the cover of her book on Afghan women—the documentary's presentations of the four women, who are all differently attired, visually undercut its iconicity. Armstrong can then position herself as different from these women, but not so different that she cannot claim any commonality with them.

This contrasting presentation and positioning of the two journalists is directly linked to the question of epistemic prerogative, and the very distinct spaces available to them to stake their respective claims to producing "authentic" knowledge. After the attacks of 9/11, the production of knowledge about Afghanistan, and the question of who could claim authenticity as a knowledge producer, assumed heightened importance. The similarities and differences in the two documentaries regarding these questions are intriguing and reveal some of the perils of assuming the role of native informant, as Pazira does.

Armstrong's assumption of the role of expert is unproblematic; it is never contested in the film. Acting as a possessor of authority, she refrains from either explaining her positionality or accounting for her views. Indeed, she can even grant some of this authority to Dr. Samar through her unambiguous support of Dr. Samar's activism. Dr. Samar is treated as a significant political actor, albeit a more "culturally" constrained one, and her agency is underscored through her activism, although this simultaneously homogenizes and silences more radical and complex feminist perspectives in Afghanistan. Presenting Dr. Samar as a political actor enables Armstrong's own presentation as a sister-in-the-struggle, and not an imperialist-feminist who comes from an occupying power.

In contrast, Pazira's role as "expert" is both individualized and, ultimately, undermined. No effort is made to include Afghan feminists in the narrative, or to try and locate the displaced Dyana through the existing network of women's organizations or through other human rights and nongovernmental agencies in the country. This erasure of Afghan women's activism in resisting the Taliban, and the Northern Alliance before them, enables Pazira to appear as a one-woman rescue mission (plus the camera crew). The documentary thus contributes to the erasure of the agency and resistance of the very women who it claims need to be "saved": if these women are presented as having agency, Pazira's role as "savior," and by extension, that of Canadians and other Westerners, could well be called into question.

However, Pazira's role as "expert" is also perilous, as this role generally tends to be for native informants. Even before her arrival in Afghanistan, she is shown in conversation with her codirector. He can be heard throughout the documentary, asking her questions, pushing for answers and explanations, as he establishes his presence as authoritative, even when off camera. In contrast, the director of *Daughters of Afghanistan* is absent from the documentary. Pazira's codirector thus assumes the role of the benevolent white male *in the documentary*. Through his constant interventions, the audience (and Pazira) is reminded that he is in charge of this show. Informant Pazira may aspire to be, but "native" she is made to remain.

Pazira's expertise is recognized by virtue of two factors in the film: first, because she is an Afghan woman by birth, she is therefore assumed to have access to local cultural capital through language and custom; and second, because she is a "Canadian," she possesses the requisite transnational cultural capital to speak in a mode resonant to Westerners. For instance, images of her laying a chadar on a tomb, head covered, praying at the shrine establish that she is native enough for the film to work, but not enough to unsettle the audience. Pazira goes to great lengths to put social and cultural distance between herself and the locals, to demonstrate that although she "knows" "them," she is not like "them." But this stance gives rise to numerous anxieties and tensions. The first occurs as the plane carrying Pazira and the crew is landing in Kabul. She describes to her codirector the location of her family house in relation to the airport, and recounts her witnessing of bombs falling and the burning down of a nearby house. But as soon as they disembark, she tells him that it "feels like a strange place." About the people she sees around her, she bemoans that "none of them I can connect with." The men on the streets look completely different: they used to wear "modern" clothes, but now, she tells him/us, "it looks so strange, like a different planet." The distance between Pazira and resident natives is thus established as soon as she lands.

Pazira thus enters "home" through a disavowal of its evocative familiarity. Yet she clings to her expert status as somebody who deeply and intimately knows this strange "home," who can make it knowable to her codirector and to the viewing publics back in Canada. Searching for her old house, Pazira has difficulty recognizing the street and she tells her codirector she feels "terrible" that she can't remember. When she finally sees/recognizes the house, she says, "Oh my God, it's so rotten." The misrecognition of old homes and neighborhoods is, of course, a fairly common experience for returning migrants: memories tend to ossify while landscapes tend to change. But Pazira is not just any returning migrant; she is returning as an "expert," with a foreign camera crew in tow that relies in no small measure on the efficacy of her remembering "home." Her expert status cannot be allowed to slip in the face of the changing reality on the ground, although, after all, it is only to be expected that much would indeed have changed during the years of her absence. "Nothing I saw would look like anything I'd ever remembered," she laments. In Mazar-i-Sharif, she finds it "incredible" that women are vendors in the

street markets, selling goods. She explains that traditionally, "economic interaction" was a man's job. The specific class-based nature of Pazira's past
experience in Afghanistan (as a member of an urban professional family)
leaves her perplexed in her experience with this other class of women she encounters on the streets. Such differences of class, marital status, and ethnicity
among women, which have (now, as in the past) different consequences for
their economic activities in the public sphere, do not exist in her memory. In
her study of Egyptian television serials, Lila Abu-Lughod argues that the perspectives of the producers of these serials, who are mainly urban professionals, "can be quite different from those of their viewers" (1993, 496). The very
divergent class positions, perspectives, and experiences between Pazira and
the women she "presents" to the world are never discussed.

Yet, despite such initial misrecognitions of home, and of the homeliness of
home, and despite her "surprise" that women are engaged in economic exchange on the streets, Pazira allows no self-doubt to creep into her pronouncements of what life is "really" like for all Afghan women. She is careful to draw on her Afghan identity in order to interpret "their" environment
but carefully maintains her distance from the Other "native" women.

REPRESENTING AFGHANISTAN

The plethora of newly fashionable books and films of Afghanistan tend to be
fairly uniform in their representation of the country. The following comments
are fairly typical of most of these contemporary representations:

> Perhaps Afghanistan is coming out of a long night. A twenty-three-year ordeal
> combining several wars and every possible atrocity—coup d'etat, invasion, war
> of liberations, civil war, vengeance in various forms, barbaric acts, torture, sum-
> mary executions, and holy wars changed into dirty wars, have left a country in
> ruins, a people traumatized, minds in confusion, and a way of life that has been
> lost. . . . But at the heart of this night an even darker region existed, still un-
> known, still ignored, still muzzled, and sometimes murdered. . . . Little girls,
> daughters, wives, mothers, widows, grandmothers—those who hold up half the
> sky, as once was said elsewhere—were kept in submission here, moved under
> surveillance from one residence to another, if not in a household prison under
> the successive or joint control of a father, brother, husband, or son. (Velter 2003)

In similar manner, Afghanistan is presented in both documentaries as a place
of death and destruction, of violence and particularly grave danger for
women. Prison and living death are the most common metaphors used to describe the situation, and for the women, this "prison" and "living death" is
symbolized by the veil. The country becomes nothing more than a land stuck
in time, its women mired in grief and mourning, desperate for the world to

come and rescue them. While there can be little doubt that the situation for women in Afghanistan was grave indeed, it is Afghan men and Islamic culture that are made solely responsible for these conditions in both documentaries. Pazira does mention the past U.S. support for the Taliban, but she does not examine the ongoing role of the United States in the violence, death, and destruction in the country. As I demonstrate below, Afghan men are represented as unidimensionally misogynist and Afghan women as victims of this unrelenting misogyny, and thus as requiring rescue from their own families and communities.

The Taliban regime was brutal indeed in its treatment of women and girls, as well as of sexual "deviance." The question that begs answer, however, is why and how this regime, which initially had significant support from large sections of the population, including women and women's organizations, as a desirable alternative to the Northern Alliance, became so brutal and targeted women so specifically in its governance? It should be remembered that Mullah Omar, the Taliban leader, was reported to emerge as a "Robin Hood figure" after being approached to "save" two young women who had been abducted and raped, and was quoted as saying "How could we remain quiet when we could see crimes being committed against women and the poor?" (Rashid 2001, 25). According to the journalist Ahmed Rashid, the Northern Alliance was notorious for widespread atrocities and for abductions and rapes of women and young boys in the pre-Taliban era, and Mullah Omar is reported to have mobilized his men to rescue some of these women and young boys. He was also apparently committed to providing greater security for the population, including the women and girls.

In *Good Muslim Bad Muslim*, Mahmood Mamdani draws attention to the very modern history of militant Islamic fundamentalism. Rejecting the "clash of civilizations" paradigm, he traces the role of the United States in supporting the rise of the various Mujahiddin factions in Afghanistan against the Soviets, and argues that terror as a counterinsurgency strategy was developed by the United States in its fight against militant nationalist movements in the Third World after the end of the Vietnam War (2004). Although Mamdani does not address the question of gender, he relates an interesting discussion with an Afghan colleague about the Taliban's treatment of women. Mamdani echoes Rashid in noting that the Taliban came to power with a promise to defend women and young people (a defense that initially won them the support of the population) as one of their objectives, and he asks his colleague why the Taliban later turned against them so ferociously. His colleague responded by pointing out the following factors, also discussed by Rashid: the Taliban's actions were partly a reaction to the previous top-down attempts of the communists to impose women's equality; the seclusion of the Taliban in the madrassas and their militarist training had cut them off from daily life in the community of women; the regime's leadership feared that their men might

also rape and abduct women; and they supported the seclusion of women because they were unsure of their ability to control their own men (Mamdani
2004, 162). The Revolutionary Association of the Women of Afghanistan
(RAWA), among the most internationally well known of Afghan feminist organizations, has also claimed that the Northern Alliance, with whom the
United States allied itself in its invasion of Afghanistan, and whom it allowed
to share power with Karzai in the post-Taliban era, perpetrated some of the
gravest human rights violations and acts of violence against women. Yet neither of the two documentaries treats these questions as significant, let alone
attempts to answer them. Instead, Armstrong tells the viewer, "After the hated
Taliban fell, I cheered for the women." She anticipated that the women's liberation would quickly follow, she tells the viewer. She remains unconcerned
about the conditions under which the Taliban fell, how many women might
have been killed in the war that defeated them, how many women have been
displaced as refugees, or how many women and girls make up the ongoing
civilian death toll of the war.

To her credit, Pazira asks Imam Poplalzai, a former member of the Taliban,
why the population supported the Taliban in *Return to Kandahar*. He responds that Mullah Omar wanted peace and security, and that the Mujahiddin
were engaged in widespread abduction of women, killing, and stealing. He
explains that Mullah Omar was used by Arabs and Pakistanis for their own
interests. However, Pazira does not take this discussion any further and does
not attempt to explore what this might mean for the women in the country.
She does not allow such important questions to disrupt the dominant narrative of misogynist Muslim men and victimized Muslim women that shapes
the film.

Return to Kandahar opens with a busy Kabul street scene, an urban setting
that depicts a "modern" environment. However, the scene is immediately followed by one of a bombed-out, rubble-strewn building, evoking a cavelike
environment. A lone female figure, shrouded in white, moves away from the
camera in slow motion. This scene undercuts the existence of the "modern"
urban environment of Kabul, and signals instead that the viewer has entered
a different time, not just a different place. "All are like the walking dead,"
Pazira is heard quoting from the letter said to have been written by Dyana.

For its part, *Daughters of Afghanistan* begins its narrative in this manner:
"Out of the ashes, the women and girls of Afghanistan are stumbling back to
life." Both films focus centrally on violence against women, but they present
the death and destruction prevalent in the country as mainly the outcome of
Afghan men's misogyny, and as perpetrated mainly by Afghan men against
Afghan women. So, for example, Armstrong says of Dr. Samar, "She's had to
fight for everything she's ever had. She fought the suffocating rules in her
own family, she fought the Soviets, the Mujahiddin and the Taliban." Dr.
Samar's struggles against her family's "rules" are here equated with her

"fight" against the Soviet occupation, with her "fight" against the various armed Mujahiddin factions and the Taliban regime. Although Dr. Samar states that she agreed to an arranged marriage so that she could pursue her studies, presumably with the support of her husband, this support from husband and family is not allowed to disrupt the narrative of Afghan men as uniformly oppressive.

Both journalists also present themselves as being in great peril themselves in this dangerous place of death and destruction. Pazira tells Dyana/the viewer, "my sister, only for you I am in prison." Armstrong describes a sleepless night spent in a Kandahar compound when she was held by the Taliban during a previous trip. By presenting themselves as imprisoned and in danger, the two journalists reverse the power relations that actually privilege them as Canadians. They implicitly present the reach of the Taliban as spilling over into the lives of Western women like themselves, giving credence to the Bush administration's propaganda that the regime was a threat to all women everywhere. Neither journalist makes reference to her own power as a Canadian citizen, a power that places them at considerable advantage and gives them access to travel inside the country and to meet with ex-Taliban leaders and with the current Islamist and Mujahiddin leaders, including General Dostum. Films like these clearly cannot be produced in war zones without some level of official support or protection. And after all, it is occupation of the country by Western troops that allows the safe mobility of Westerners in Afghanistan as a war rages. This access to power as Westerners is instead turned into their vulnerability as women by both journalists. Canadian troops were present in the country as part of the occupation forces at the time of the making of both films, yet neither makes reference to this fact.

The Bush "doctrine," infamous for its simplistic binaries of the "good" West and "evil" Islamists, drew easy connections between the attacks of 9/11 (attributed to Al-Qaeda) and the Taliban. Both documentaries accept this attribution of responsibility to the Taliban unquestioningly. A scene at a graveyard in *Return to Kandahar* captures this problematic logic. It features Pazira asking a group of Afghan men she encounters what they think of the (foreign) Arabs in their country. The men are divided in their opinions. One says he would like to find them and kill them; another points out that they were kind to poor people and gave them money. Pazira then asks if they thought the Arabs based in Afghanistan were responsible for the 9/11 attacks. One man replies that he does not know whether it was these Arabs, or others from the United States, or even from another country, who were responsible (most of the perpetrators have been identified by the United States as Saudis). Another man says that "it would be a sin to accuse someone falsely." Yet another states, "people say different things . . . we Kandaharis have to see it with our own eyes to believe it . . . can't accept or deny the story of who did it." As this exchange ends and Pazira walks away from the men, her codirector asks her what she thinks of the men's responses. This is how she responds: "Refusing to take responsibility for September 11 is unfortunately common in this part of the world . . . (inaudible) gets people to rely on a very simplified view of the world. There is very little analysis or self-criticism here."

This is an extraordinary response, as the men were very obviously ambivalent about the identity of the perpetrators. It is also notable that Pazira attributes responsibility for the attacks to "this part of the world," casting a net wider than even the Bush administration, which accused Al-Qaeda and the Taliban. Pazira's confident assertion provides legitimacy for the U.S. bombing of Afghanistan by furthering the claim that "this part of the world" was responsible for the 9/11 attacks. It helps secure her location/identity as that of a Westerner as she reproduces the dominant Western perspective that the devious native avoids responsibility for his actions, and hence has to be forced—by resort to violence, if necessary—to accept it. The assertion also contributes to the erasure of the reality that the Taliban offered to negotiate with the United States to turn over Osama bin Laden to a third (Muslim) country if the Americans provided evidence that he was indeed responsible for the attacks. She thus brings false closure to a debate that has remained ongoing in many parts of the world, including in the United States.[16] This questioning of Pazira by her codirector serves as a test of where Pazira's sympathies might really lie. She rises to the challenge, unambiguously confirming Afghan (and Arab/Afghan) men's culpability, guilt, and (pathological) disavowal of responsibility.

In a powerful scene in *Daughters of Afghanistan,* a group of young Afghan women are shown in Dr. Samar's school. "Within the confines of the school, they can finally dream out loud," Armstrong tells viewers, as the young women talk about their dreams and hopes for the future. "But when Sima's students leave the school, the burqas erase their individuality" intones Armstrong (the young women are shown lowering their burqas and leaving the school), "and a hundred yards down the street, the men start to hiss and jeer." A man is shown sitting on a stool in the street, and he shouts "Just get outta here" at the camera. The initial impression seems to be that he is hissing at the young Afghan women. Yet, as the scene continues, it becomes apparent that he is angry about quite something else. "We have fought you and we will fight you till the end of our days," he shouts to the camera. Armstrong explains in a voice-over, "Seeing the women being filmed by foreigners in public is more than he can bear." "We have religion, you don't," the man continues. "To infidels, we don't talk." "He is sick of foreigners invading his culture," sums up Armstrong. What is interesting about this exchange is that the man makes it clear that he is angry at the foreigners. He confronts and challenges them, not the young women, yet the voice-over in the presentation of this scene makes it appear that he is hostile to the young Afghan women's presence on the street, about which he says nothing in the entire scene. More-over, Armstrong represents his clear antipathy toward her and her crew on the streets of his city, foreigners who represent a country that is involved in the occupation of his country, as hostility toward the invasion of "his culture." Armstrong takes an expression of anger at, and defiance of, foreign occupa-tion, and turns it instead into a cultural matter, depoliticizing his opposition to occupation into opposition to "Western" culture.

Both documentaries remain reluctant to consider how the Karzai regime, defined by many locals as a puppet regime imposed by the United States, came to power. There is no discussion of Hamid Karzai's alleged past work as a consultant for Unocal, the California-based company that was attempting to negotiate the contract from the Taliban to build a pipeline through Afghanistan. No reference is made to the fact that Karzai was being guarded by U.S. security forces, not Afghans, and that he could not travel outside Kabul except under heavy security. The Loya Jirga convened during the war is shown by Armstrong, but as the venue for the pushing out of Dr. Samar by religious "fundamentalists," with no examination of the legitimacy of the "democratic" process whereby Karzai was anointed as president of Afghanistan. The "fundamentalists" are said to be obsessed with plotting against Dr. Samar only because she is a woman. When ousted from her posi-tion in the government, Dr. Samar muses that Karzai did not take the threats against her seriously, and that he is occupied with other important concerns. The U.S. administration is likewise presented as distracted from doing more to support Dr. Samar by the war on Iraq, but as essentially committed to Afghan women's equality. The constraints within which the Karzai govern-ment was allowed to "govern" the country are left unexplored.[17] That neither film discusses these political complexities is interesting, given that Dr. Samar served as a member of this regime as deputy prime minister and minister of women's affairs. Instead, Dr. Samar is shown getting a standing ovation when President Bush addressed the U.S. Congress after the defeat of the Taliban as proof of the liberation of Afghan women. Later, Dr. Samar's meeting with a U.S. delegation in the hopes of getting more financial support is shown, but she is said to have lost their interest when she voices her opposition to the U.S. plan to attack Iraq. What this might reveal about the administration's rhetoric about furthering "democracy" and its opportunistic support for some women's groups is not discussed.

Although both documentaries are self-consciously made for Western audi-ences, and both set out to highlight the status of Afghan women, they are as much about the self-constitution of the two women journalists located in Canada, Pazira and Armstrong. Both present themselves as free, modern sub-jects while Othering the Afghan women they seek to represent. It is in rela-tion to this gendered "Other" that both journalists tangibly define, and experience, their own sense of agency, mobility, and "freedoms," and through themselves, those of the viewing public. The Othering is less explicit for the benevolent Armstrong: her whiteness implicitly inscribes her as "liberated," and this affords her the privilege of being able to (relatively) give more space to the Afghan girls and women to speak.

Pazira, on the other hand, is constantly mindful of her "freedoms" in the West, and she loses no opportunity to point this out. But her presentation of the self as liberated is more tenuous; she has to carefully guard against being reduced to the denigrated status of the Other. After a hostile encounter with some young men at Balkh University, where she has met with a group of young women, she states emotionally, "I get to go back to Canada but these women have to live with this mentality and face these guys for a long time." Later, in reference to Dyana, she says, "I got my chance to live an independent life, but did Dyana?" She quotes the letter from Dyana: "Sometime I think I am going to die from loneliness and grief. I continually think that I have become a useless and helpless thing. . . . Or we are forced to become like that." Pazira is the woman who has been saved by the West, and now she will help it save other Afghan women. Yet the Afghan bodies that are allowed into the frame contest the dominant narrative Pazira (and Jay) are constructing. Although the women vendors on the street who shock her by their participation in economic exchange could potentially disrupt this narrative, they are not allowed to do so. Instead of recognizing their strength and resilience, Pazira remains at a loss to explain how this could be and can only tell viewers this is not how things once were. No attempt is made to ask the women what it means to them to have some measure of economic agency, whether they have always had it, or how they acquired it. Instead she recreates their victim status by asking them only about the conditions under which they were forced to flee their homes.

Armstrong ends her journey with the following thoughts: "The women wait, still trapped by history and prejudice, for their emancipation." Pazira reads out loud from Dyana's letter: "The walls are closing in, life does not have the same meaning any more, music doesn't sound the same—you will have to live for both of us now." Only the West can save these women, both documentaries suggest.

My point is not simply that the two documentaries misrepresent the "realities" of Afghan women's lives, or that they omit to provide other "truths" to their viewers. These they most certainly do. My concern, however, is more with the discursive logic they construct, and its role in the restructuring of imperialist power relations that is being facilitated by the War on Terror. In other words, it is their relationship to the "truths" being realized on the ground as Afghanistan was being pulverized by U.S. bombs, its population living under a U.S.-led Anglo–North American occupation that is so very problematic.

VEILOMENTARIES AND WAR

The Canada's national public broadcaster, the CBC, has been deeply shaped by the Canadian state's nation-building policies. Initially established to help foster a national community, and to articulate the "national" values of democracy, equality, and multiculturalism, the institution continues to feature prominently in the state's attempts at "mediation of social relations by cultural policy" (Beale 1999). While the CBC has received some attention for its role in accomplishing such national objectives, few scholars have attempted to examine with similar rigor the many documentaries produced by (semi)independent journalists and filmmakers, particularly those who are also women's/human rights activists, that the public broadcaster airs.[18] Serving an important function complementing news reports, such documentaries have assumed an important role in providing in-depth "knowledge" and analysis about the War on Terror. Noting that Western audiences "hungered" for images of Afghanistan, Martin Kramer, the editor of the *Middle East Quarterly,* argued that "it is at moments like this, when time is short and the subject is foreign, that documentary and foreign films attain an influence they never enjoy in peacetime" (2002). News networks provided these aplenty as documentaries on Afghanistan were promoted from their previously obscure position into prime time.[19] In the case of the CBC, the focus on programs dealing with Afghan women's (lack of) rights, such as the two documentaries discussed in this essay, not only enabled the broadcaster to increase its programming on women, but also enabled it to implicitly foster nation building by reinforcing the recasting of the nation as once more engaged in a civilizing mission.

Although documentary films are popularly treated as having a great proximity to "reality" and "truth," critical scholars have argued that they too should be examined with great caution, that they too are as ideologically informed as other forms of representation. The blurring of the lines between documentary and fiction films has been particularly pronounced in the case of recent films about Afghanistan. Thus the film *Kandahar,* despite being described as a docudrama, has been repeatedly lauded by reviewers for its presentation of the unvarnished "truth" about Afghanistan and its women to the world.[20] Astonishingly, President Bush was reported to have made a request to see the film in order to "help him understand the situation in Afghanistan" (Bright 2002). With *Return to Kandahar* using the same aesthetic sensibility, plot, and casting of Pazira as Makhmalbaf's quasi-fictional film, the documentary reinforces the "realness" of the semifictional film, even as it rides on the film's widespread acclaim.

It is in the context of geopolitics, war, and empire that this genre of documentaries about women in Afghanistan (and other Muslim societies) can be

usefully referred to as "veilomentaries," for their problematic and uncritical
use of the veil as signifier par excellence of women's oppression, and their
equation of this oppression with a religio-traditional and cultural Islamic misogyny. With their singular and simplistic focus on the veil, and their treatment of gender as the primary social relation, they draw attention away from
the imperialist violence that shapes the lives of the women they purport to
represent, veiling empire building, as it were. Numerous scholars have commented upon this use of the veil as an emblematic representation of Muslim
women, a signifier that invokes their Orientalist construction as universally
oppressed. In contrast, Fanon described how the French defined the unveiling
of Algerian women as key to the "domestication" of Algerian society, and
how women used the veil to move out of the *Kasbah* in the Algerian revolutionary movement and war against the French (1965). Feminists have also
convincingly and repeatedly argued for the complex and nuanced meanings
of this practice. Deconstructing the signifier of the "veil," they have demonstrated that it is lazily used in the West to refer to articles of clothing ranging
from the lightest head covering worn by Muslim women, the headscarf, to the
full chador, which covers the entire body (Bailey and Tawadros 2003). Contesting the notion that the veil signifies a premodern and traditionalist sensibility, Nilufer Gole describes the use of the headscarf by Islamist Turkish
women as signaling a non-Western form of modernity, and as enabling them
to gain greater access to public spaces and political participation (2002).
Young Muslim women who veil themselves in North America and Europe
routinely describe how they have negotiated greater freedoms and mobility in
their personal lives, as well as greater access to education and employment,
by donning "Islamic" attire (Hoodfar 1993; Samad 1998).

Veilomentaries, however, remain unconcerned with the complexities that
surround the use of the veil. In discussing the power of the iconic image of
the veil as a symbol of women's oppression to overwhelm all other readings,
it is important to remember Stuart Hall's caution that images have many different meanings, and that they are not always necessarily read as they are intended by their producers (Jhally 1997). In the case of the veil, however, I
would argue that counterhegemonic readings of the images (and narratives)
being presented in these two documentaries would require much more information about the issues at hand than is popularly available. Indeed, veilomentaries actively contribute to the further marginalization of informed discussions of the practice of veiling. Furthermore, as Hall cautions us,
representations are deeply implicated in the process of making meanings;
they are "constitutive" of the meanings they produce. Veilomentaries invoke
deeply embedded emotive readings of veiled Muslim women as irremediably
"Other," reenacting binary constructs of the self and Other that have been so
crucial to the Western imagining of Islam as its absolute alterity.

These documentaries, along with many others of a similar genre, have been made and screened with the aid and support of institutional actors ranging from women's and human rights organizations to journalists and public and private broadcasters. They are often used to raise funds for projects to provide aid to Afghan women, and the propaganda value of such films has not been lost to the U.S. government. The Department of State has funded, through the Asia Foundation, documentary film projects such as *Afghanistan Unveiled*, as well as other projects to collect oral histories and train Afghan video artists and documentary filmmakers (U.S. Embassy, Islamabad n.d.). With their focus on individual women, these documentaries can be seen as going beyond and under the news, as presenting a picture of what is "really" happening on the ground. Women are seen as having especial insight into the status of other women, as being more sensitive and so more effective in producing this kind of propaganda. As women, they are able to lend greater credence to claims about the "truths" of Afghan women's lives than can male filmmakers. With the "liberation" of Afghan women having become a major ideological plank of the War on Terror, such documentaries have carved out a particularly popular niche for themselves. Their endorsement by women's and human rights organizations, and the powerful circuits of their widespread distribution and promotion, ensure that their discursive practices become hegemonic, pushing to the margins perspectives that might challenge these simplistic representations.

CONCLUSION

Referring to the many books published on Afghan women in the wake of 9/11, Alison Donnell states, "While there is no denying that the situation of Afghan women has become newsworthy since 11 September, it is not always easy to decide whether the coverage has helped to campaign for social justice or has simply reiterated simplistic assumptions, stereotyped representations and political justifications for continued Western military intervention in the Middle East" (2003, 124). I cannot end this essay on such an ambiguous note. Not only have the two documentaries analyzed above reiterated simplistic assumptions, but they are playing a critical role in the deployment of feminism to support the War on Terror, despite the best intentions of their makers. They have helped legitimize a war of aggression that has shunted aside the paradigm of the international rule of law, however inadequate that paradigm was, and they have helped sanction a return to colonial invasions and occupations. Both documentaries attribute gender oppression to culture and religion, disassociating it from imperialist relations, and in this manner contribute to the demonization of Muslims, both men and women, and of Afghan culture. Their refusal to examine the conditions of their own privileges, the forms of inequalities widespread within Western societies, and how these are all related to the First World/Third World divide needs to be challenged.

The domination of Afghan women should not be denied or trivialized, nor should women's oppression be ignored in Canada, the United States, or elsewhere. This should be particularly the case regarding Western societies. Because women are routinely portrayed as liberated and emancipated in the West, it is imperative that the forms their domination assumes receive urgent attention. For their part, these documentaries help direct attention away from gender domination in the West.

It must, of course, be acknowledged that these two filmmakers have more power than do most of the Afghan women, and men, whom they seek to represent. One cannot deny that these filmmakers are "freer" to act and have greater mobility than the Afghans whose lives they enter and leave. However, neither filmmaker examines why this is the case. The underlying condition for this freedom and mobility of the Western subject, including that of the gendered female subject, remains the deeply entrenched inequalities in the global order. Both filmmakers enter Afghanistan, a country under occupation by a coalition that includes Canada. The consequences of this colonial relationship remain unmentioned in the narratives they construct. Instead, gender equality is presented as an intrinsic and essential quality of Canada and other Western societies, available to all women, while gender oppression and inequality is presented as an essential and inherent quality of the Muslim world.

In a revealing scene, Pazira discusses the glamour and fame she acquired by acting in the film *Kandahar*. She stayed at five-star hotels and was treated like a movie star, she tells the viewer. She then asks the question, what would Dyana have thought of her traveling from "one corner of the world to another" when Dyana could not even leave her house? The question of what Dyana might have thought about Pazira showing up at her house with a film crew in tow, and with the numerous prestigious international awards the film has received, apparently does not enter her mind.

NOTES

1. The film was produced in 2000, and features Ms. Pazira in the role of the protagonist.

2. Dyana is identified as a friend in the documentary, *Return to Kandahar*, and not as a sister, as was the case with Kandahar.

3. The voice-over introducing the documentary, *Return to Kandahar*, defines it as "A true story of her second effort to find a lost friend."

4. The film was screened at the most prestigious film festivals, including the Edinburgh Film Festival, and the Cannes, Moscow, Munich, Toronto, Tokyo, Sao Paolo, and Singapore festivals. It also received the following awards: "Public Prize," Festival des Cinemas du Sud (2001); "Best Actress Award," Montreal Neuveau Cinema Neuveau Media Film Festival (2001); UNESCO "Honorary Diploma" for Kandahar Actress (2001); "FIPRESCI Award," Thessaloniki In-

ternational Film Festival (2001); "Freedom of Expression Award," National Board of Review, United States (2001); Best Film, Ajaccio Film Festival (2001); and Best Director, Riga International Film Forum (2002). See www.makhmalbaf.com/movies.asp?m=10 (accessed June 3, 2005).

5. Premiering at the Hot Docs festival in Toronto, the documentary was screened at numerous international film festivals. It received the following awards: the Best International Documentary Feature at Bare Bones International Film festival; Best International Documentary at the Wine Country Film Festival; Best of Festival, The Columbus International Film and Video Awards; and the Donald Brittain Gemini Award. See jfilm.org/rtk/festivals/index.htm.

6. Armstrong's first trip for the documentary was made in April 2002, and she returned a few months later during the same year.

7. Dr. Samar has received much support from feminist movements in North America. She has traveled to North America on speaking tours, and has been honored by feminist publications such as *Ms Magazine.*

8. Sally Armstrong is the recipient of numerous, and prestigious, awards, including the Order of Canada, the Gold Award from the National Magazine Awards foundation, the Amnesty International Media Award (twice, 2000, 2002), the YWCA Women of Distinction Award, Media Watch's Dodi Robb Award, an Honorary Doctor of Law Degree from Royal Roads University, and an Honorary Doctor of Letters from McGill University. She has more recently also actively supported the anti-Sharia campaign in Ontario (Jimenez 2005).

9. See *Library Media Connection,* March 2005. Choices Video, Inc. "highly recommended" the video, as did the Educational Media Reviews Online, for "its relevance to women's studies, sociology, and Middle Eastern Studies"; see cjoicesvideo.net/html/awards/daughtersreviews.html.

10. News anchor Dan Rather, in tears, asked the President where he could sign up on air. The wearing of U.S. flags as lapel pins became de riguer on most mainstream television channels in the United States. A Texas company that owned over one thousand radio stations recommended that disc jockeys refrain from playing the hugely popular pro-peace song by John Lennon, "Imagine," on these stations. See "A Peace of Ono," *Macleans,* November 5, 2001. Angus Reid (2003), the Canadian pollster, described the news reporting by American television as "gung-ho patriotism."

11. Bill Maher, the host of the popular show *Politically Incorrect,* had his show taken off the air for criticizing the claim that suicide bombers were cowards. Critics are reported to have "lambasted" the actor, Tim Robbins, as "a limousine liberal" for his play *Embedded,* which was deemed very critical of the White House (Lepage 2004). In the recent report on an art exhibition examining the impact of the Patriot Act on artists, Caryn James (2005) noted in his review of the exhibition that "the last four years have shown that any departure from gooey sentimentality is likely to provoke uproar."

12. Ismael and Measor argue that the media have "uniformly failed to perform their traditional watchdog function over the Canadian government in analyzing and presenting alternatives to the selection of government policy" (2003, 16).

13. CNN, CBS, ABC, NBC, and Fox News were reported to have agreed to adopt the guidelines emanating from the Bush administration. See Huff 2001 and MacDonald 2001.

14. Pazira's beauty is highlighted in most reviews of the film *Kandahar.* The following comment by one reviewer is typical of other reviews: "Pazira is a striking beauty with a wounded, almost distracted air"; see Andrew O'Hehir, "Kandahar," *Salon.com,* December 14, 2001, web.lexis-nexis.com/universe/document?-m=b697e809cae8436333558619a0a3d4cf&. . . (accessed June 3, 2005).

15. General Dostum refers to her in this way, talking to her about Canada and America; the man who is the leader of the landmine clearing team tells her to tell the world to stop the sending landmines to his country; the army general who owns the hotel that she stays at in Mazar tells her that she can tell the Canadian crew that the hotel swimming pool water is clean.

16. In the United States, "conspiracy theorists" have even argued that the Bush administration was involved in orchestrating the attacks. See BeyondTreason.com; Infowars.com; and 911isalie.com.

17. For one example, the question of who wielded real power in Afghanistan was being discussed in the U.S. media: "'So what are we going to do today?' Afghanistan's president, Hamid Karzai, asked the United States ambassador, Zalmay M. Khalilzad, as they sat in Mr. Karzai's office. Mr. Khalilzad patiently explained that they would attend a ceremony to kick of the 'greening' of Kabul—the planting and seeding of 850,000 trees—in honor of the Afghan New Year. . . . Mr. Karzai said that he would speak off-the-cuff. Mr. Khalilzad, sounding more mentor than diplomat, approved: 'It's good you don't have a text,' he told Mr. Karzai. 'You tend to do better.' The genial M. Karzai may be Afghanistan's president but the affable, ambitious Mr. Khalilzad often seems more like its chief executive. With his command of both details and American largesse, the Afghan-born envoy has created an alternate seat of power since his arrival on Thanksgiving." See Waldman 2004.

18. See P. Norris, M. Kern, and M. Just, eds. (2003), *Framing Terrorism: The News Media, the Government and the Public* (New York and London: Routledge). Also see David Teather, "New York Times Says It Was Duped by Pentagon 'Cunning,'" *Guardian,* May 31, 2004. Mr. Teather reported that the ombudsman for the *New York Times* criticized the war reporting of that newspaper, pointing out that certain news reports "pushed Pentagon assertions so aggressively you could almost sense the epaulets on the shoulders of the editors." It is interesting that the criticism of media reporting has focused mainly on its willing repetition of the Bush administration's claims, particularly regarding Iraq and weapons of mass destruction. The coverage of the war on Afghanistan, however, continues to receive very little attention.

19. Not surprisingly, Kramer also noted that "films that received the most airtime and acclaim effectively served to justify the war" (2002).

20. The film *Kandahar* is repeatedly referred to as "unveiling" Afghanistan, and as drawing international attention to the "realities" of life in Afghanistan. See, for example, the following reviews of the film: Jay Stone, "Unveiling Afghanistan," *Vancouver Sun,* November 12, 2001; Jeff Strickler, "Kandahar" Makes a Bittersweet Journey," *Star Tribune* (Minneapolis, MN), March 1, 2002; Martin Bright, "Heartbroken of Afghanistan," *Observer,* November 4, 2001; Kate Goldberg, "Kandahar: The Movie," BBC News Online, November 19, 2001, news.bbc.co.uk/2/hi/entertainment/1664617.stm.

12

Neoliberalism, Nongovernmental Organizations, and Communication in Sub-Saharan Africa

Arthur-Martins Aginam

The last two decades have witnessed an exponential growth in the number of nongovernmental organizations (NGOs), particularly in the developing world. So ubiquitous is their presence and ever growing global influence that they are now commonly theorized in transnational terms (Keane 2003; Colas 2002).[1] For Ann Florini (2000), NGOs have since emerged as the "third force"—ostensibly only after the nation-state and supranational bodies on the one hand and transnational capital on the other. Yet, opinions remain divided as to their relevance both within the nation-state and internationally. While David Korten (cited in MacDonald 1997, 8) celebrates the humanistic role of NGOs as responding to "shared values" in contrast to, for instance, the exploitative tendencies of the market and the state's monopoly of constitutional threat and coercion, Michael Hardt and Antonio Negri (2000) see NGOs primarily as the "moral instruments" of "Empire," even if they are also quick to concede that such organizations are too heterogeneous in structure, objectives, and mode of operation to be rigidly categorized. What follows from this caveat is that the nature and role of NGOs vary in different contexts and situations and can at best be described as somewhat dialectical rather than decidedly hegemonic.

This chapter discusses the structure, ideology, key programs, and sources of funding for these advocacy groups in sub-Saharan Africa, where they have emerged as some of the fastest-growing institutions spawned by globalization. The primary focus is on advocacy media NGOs working broadly in such overlapping areas as democratization, freedom of expression, civic education, and human rights. Since Africa has long been the poster continent of "failed states" theorists (Zartman 1995; Jackson 1990), such organizations often come into being primarily in response to the failures, or if you will, the excesses of the African state. The perennial abuse of state power in postcolonial Africa, coupled with the unidirectional flow of development funds from North to South, have left such NGOs with a more decidedly antistatist mindset and something of an ambivalent attitude toward neoliberalism. While not endorsing "free trade," they tend to view it as a lesser threat than the authoritarian tendencies of the African state. I have limited my focus to key media NGOs in two of the continent's most influential nations—Nigeria and South Africa. Besides the widely acknowledged clout of both countries, this choice is also predicated on the markedly contrasting nature of their political transitions; South Africa is emblematic of substantive social democratic efforts and Nigeria has a model of minimal democracy that is reduced to the periodic conduct of often fundamentally flawed plebiscites. As expected, the nature and stage of neoliberal democratization in each country largely determine the strategy and key concerns of its NGOs. For instance, while the Nigerian groups are still mostly concerned with establishing basic democratic media legislations following nearly thirty years of military rule, their South African counterparts have moved beyond issues of state abuse to also address threats from an increasingly market-driven media environment.

This chapter grew out of fieldwork conducted in Nigeria in 2004. The materials on South(ern) Africa, however, derive largely from web resources, e-mail exchanges, and phone interviews with principal officials of the NGOs. I focus on the Media Institute of Southern Africa (MISA), the Freedom of Expression Institute (FXI) of South Africa; and the following Nigeria-based organizations: Media Rights Agenda (MRA), Center for Free Speech (CFS), Journalists for Democratic Rights (JODER), and the Institute for Media and Society (IMS). Although these groups manifest in varying degrees some measure of progressivism, none, with the relative exception of MISA and, even less so, the Freedom of Expression Institute, comes close to being a self-sustaining membership collective with something of an egalitarian governance philosophy and an unwavering commitment to populist developmental goals. This, in part, raises questions about the location of NGOs both in the broader civil society and in social movement discourses as well as in critical postcolonial development theory.

NGOS, STATES, DONORS, AND THE DISCOURSE OF DEVELOPMENT IN AFRICA: AN OVERVIEW

Contemporary discourses of NGOs are most commonly framed around the rather idealistic notion of civil society and associational life as the driving force of popular, non-state-driven development (Ferguson 2006, 96). Yet such an overly flattering vision of NGOs fails to take into account the global political economy in which they operate and the intensely ambiguous nature of the concept of civil society, which at best has been described as a "polysemic signifier" (Keane 1998, 36) and at worst as a "promiscuous" idea (Jenkins 2001, 251) appropriated by every conceivable contemporary political ideology. By way of definition, civil society refers loosely to a variety of organizations of different ideological persuasions that are not formally a part of governmental structures or the profit-driven private sector, although they can collaborate with or try to influence them on whatever issues such organizations deem important. And while civil society groups adopt a broad variety of strategies (lobbying, advocacy, public campaigns, litigation, civil disobedience and more) to realize their goals, some notable exceptions include violent agitations in the pursuit of such efforts and systematic attempts to directly take over state power (Scholte 2000, 174–78).[2] However, in developing and largely authoritarian societies like many in Africa where political ethnicism and ethnoreligious conflicts are endemic, civil society is often not just cast in opposition to the state but recognizes the extrademocratic struggles of aggrieved groups against the state and or other dominant interests (Monga 1996; Chabal 1992; Bayart 1986). Although Western theorists and international donor agencies often exclude Africa's traditional social sphere from their conception of civil society, even if mostly at the policy level (Mamdani 1995, 3–4; Ottaway 2000), ethnic movements and in some cases militias fighting for resource control and cultural identity have become either concurrent developments with or the consequences of neoliberal democratization in the continent (Obi 2001; Mbembe 2001, 78; Chua 2004; Adekson 2004).

Without doubt, the dominant institutional discourse of civil society is largely shaped by neoliberalism. Since the 1990s, international donor assistance to civil society in the South has been invariably geared toward three mutually reinforcing outcomes: transitions to multiparty politics, the strengthening of fledgling democracies, and the adoption of market-oriented policies that would lead to a economic boom (Jenkins 2001, 253–55). In development circles, these processes are more commonly referred to as the New Policy Agenda (NPA). While the policy varies slightly from one funding agency to the other, its core assumptions are twofold. First is the preeminence of the market and private initiatives as the most efficient and cost-effective way for both economic growth and service delivery. Under this framework, governments should merely facilitate the private provision of services as well as assist NGOs in providing welfare support—but only for the few who cannot afford market options. Second, the New Policy Agenda sees NGOs and grassroots groups both as veritable tools for democratization and more importantly as a "counterweight to state power." The inherent logic here is that the weaker the state, the more likely the market will operate without interference (Hulme and Edwards 1997, 5–6). In either case, the nation-state remains the prime target of this donor assistance policy, with transnational capital threatening from above and local NGOs backed by foreign money nibbling from below.

Given the underlying objective of the New Policy Agenda, which is "government-by-NGOs" (Ferguson 2006, 40), or what some have called the privatization of the state (Hibou 2004), it is hardly surprising that many indigenous NGOs in Africa have had a rather frosty relationship with their home governments, which sometimes accuse them of colluding with imperialists. Since the late 1980s, a number of African governments have introduced some form of legislation aimed at keeping NGOs in check. Two of the better-known examples are the Kenyan NGO Coordination Act of 1990, which sought to closely monitor and control NGO activities, and the 1989 legislation in Uganda that placed NGOs under the government's internal security department (Ndegwa 1996, 21–24). In Zimbabwe, the Robert Mugabe government not only banned foreign NGOs from operating in the country but also enacted laws aimed at tightening the noose on their indigenous collaborators. Although the "adversarial" state-NGO relationship is still evident in Africa, the political liberalization of the last two decades has fostered a more genial climate for partnership between NGOs and the state on issues both sides can agree on (Clarke 1997, 52–53). This has created new opportunities for local NGO advocacy as well as substantial international (mostly Western) funding of their work; the latter sometimes results in the mushrooming of "self-interested and potentially rent seeking" (Jenkins 2001, 263) organizations derogatorily labeled "brief-case NGOs" (Dicklitch 1998, 6–8),[3] which primarily set up shop to play "the aid game" (Jenkins 2001, 253) or what Marina Ottaway (2000, 98) calls "grantmanship."

Four categories of such donors abound in sub-Saharan Africa. First, and often the most substantial, is direct or indirect government support where the link between the foreign government and the funding agency is sometimes obvious. Two key players in this category within the last decade are the United States Agency for International Development (USAID) and Britain's Department for International Development (DFID). Virtually all the Nigerian groups under study have substantially benefited from USAID funds, either directly through its Office of Transition Initiatives or indirectly through fronts like the International Human Rights Law Group. Similarly, the U.S. National Endowment for Democracy (NED)[4] provides substantial support to numerous African NGOs, sometimes through proxies. DFID dispenses its funds either directly or through the local British Council offices. There are also the "democracy and good governance grants" doled out by virtually every Western embassy in Africa. In the second category are multilateral donors, of which the European Union (EU) and the European Commission (EC) are the major players. The EC's "media for democracy program," established in virtually all regions of Africa, has the twin objectives of reforming draconian media laws and professionalizing journalism.[5] The third category of international donors comprises quasi-professional organizations like the Commonwealth Broadcasting Association (CBA), the International Federation of Journalists (IFJ), the International Press Institute (IPI), the World Association of Community Radio Broadcasters (AMARC), and many more. Finally, there are private (predominantly Western) foundations with no formal affiliations with their home governments, as well as international advocacy NGOs. Notable names under this category in Africa include PEN American Center, Freedom House (Washington, DC), Freedom Forum, the Global Opportunities Fund, the Joseph Rowntree Charitable Trust, the Rosa Luxemburg Foundation, the Panos Institute and the Open Society Initiative (both founded by George Soros), the Ford Foundation, and the Friedrich Ebert Stiftung (Germany). The donors, as it were, represent the entire range of the ideological spectrum—neo-Marxist (Rosa Luxemburg Foundation), mainstream liberal (the Panos Institute), and neoliberal (USAID).[6]

As earlier observed, the proliferation and pervasive abuse of the NGO institution in Africa have led some to question its credibility and relevance. Such criticisms are in part fueled by the donors' largely ethnocentric notion of civil society, which privileges advocacy "intermediary" networks of mostly middle-class, educated professionals (Pearce 1997, 259–60) over the strong, voluntary, often ethnically based but highly problematic social pluralism of African societies. In articulating and promoting the interests of constituencies who do not speak for themselves, such "trustee organizations" (Ottaway 2000, 78–79, 83) stand in contrast to the membership-based, authentic, bottom-up, internally democratic, and largely self-organizing grassroots social movements long idolized by radical development theorists. The "elitism" of "professional NGOs" made up of just the founder(s) and staff, coupled with their extensive affiliations with and near-total dependence on Western donors, have caused critical theorists to label them "the Trojan horses of neoliberalism" (T. Wallace cited in Harvey 2005, 177), which at best merely try to alleviate the worst excesses of the global capitalist system without challenging its exploitative ethos (Ali 2006). But such rigid binaries between altruistic and fiercely independent social movements with no foreign linkages on the one hand and self-serving, pliant, and utterly dependent NGOs on the other have been faulted for being stuck in the traditional "vertical topography of power" paradigm in which progressive grassroots movements are locked in largely localized trench warfare with the nation-state and other hegemonic forces within it. With the emergence of forms of governmentality that increasingly bypass states altogether, some of the most successful grassroots movements, such as the Zapatistas and South Africa's anti-apartheid groups, have had to adapt by combining a fundamentally strong community base with extensive international alliances without compromising their core ideals (Ferguson 2006, 103–6). While none of the six

NGOs who are the focus of this study comes even remotely close to a grass-roots social movement, it will be presumptuous to question their credibility solely on their reliance on international donors, since such relationships are too complex for observers to assume "an all-or-nothing loss of independence" (Nelson 1995, 50). As will become evident, many African NGOs have not only been in the vanguard of the struggles against state authoritarianism but have continued to champion the cause of freedom of expression and more substantive democratization in the continent.

MEDIA NGOS AND COMMUNICATION IN SUB-SAHARAN AFRICA: AN OVERVIEW AND TYPOLOGY OF PROGRAMS

The emergence of media NGOs is part of the broader rethinking of development and the increasingly pivotal role the mass media play in the process. As concerned stakeholders, various African social groups have since the late 1980s sought to play a more active role in shaping the direction of the continent. Arguably the first and most prominent of such interventions was the 1990 African Charter for Popular Participation in Development and Transformation, initiated by a mix of grassroots groups, local development NGOs, and progressive academics. The charter identified "human-centered development" built on "economic and social justice" as the key condition for Africa's growth policies with political liberalization, popular participation, and freedom of expression and association providing the enabling environment for its actualization. It also pointedly rejected the neoliberal programs of such multilateral institutions as the World Bank and the International Monetary Fund (IMF) in favor of home-grown policies geared toward what it called "the democratization of development."[7]

If the mass media got only scant mention in the charter on popular participation in development, they would, a decade later, become the centerpiece of another continental NGO initiative. Troubled by the stranglehold of successive African governments on the mass media, particularly broadcasting,[8] NGOs working broadly in the areas of democratization and freedom of expression adopted in May 2001, in Windhoek, Namibia, the African Charter on Broadcasting. Sponsored by UNESCO in partnership with the MISA, the charter demands among other things the establishment of a three-tier system of broadcasting: public service, commercial, and community; guaranteed independence for all public authorities involved in broadcasting and telecommunication regulation; a transparent and participatory spectrum allocation and licensing process; the transformation of all government-controlled broadcasting outlets into public service stations; and adequate funding of such stations that is not subject to the whims of some government bureaucrats or politicians. With respect to telecommunications, it made universal service and access the key conditions for the privatization and/or liberalization of the sector while also urging member-states of UNESCO to prevail on the World Trade Organization (WTO) to recognize broadcasting productions as cultural goods and bestow on them a special status accordingly (African Charter on Broadcasting 2001). The charter has not only become the benchmark for national and regional broadcasting reform advocacy in the continent but was also the centerpiece of Africa's media NGO contribution at the World Summit on the Information Society (WSIS) held in Geneva (2003) and Tunisia (2005).[9] Provisions of the charter were also in October 2002 incorporated into the African Commission of Human and Peoples Rights' (ACHPR) "Declaration on Freedom of Expression in Africa."[10]

The broadcasting charter was an effort to fill the void left by an earlier 1991 UNESCO-sponsored declaration (again in Windhoek) that an "independent, pluralistic and free press" is essential to Africa's economic and political development. Although the 1991 declaration focused exclusively on the print media, it recognized the immense popularity of broadcasting in Africa and recommended the reconvening of another conference with the goal of applying the same ideals to the broadcast media (UNESCO 1996). True to UNESCO's time-honored commitment to the ideals of public service and cultural diversity, both documents were as critical of the prevalent state control of the media in Africa along with the emerging shift toward the privatization and commercialization of telecommunications and broadcasting.

The Media Institute of Southern Africa (MISA), arguably the preeminent media NGO in Africa and the indigenous driving force behind the African Charter on Broadcasting, was formed in September 1992 primarily to actualize the objectives of the first Windhoek declaration. Conceived originally as a regional network of activists with a commitment to the ideals of media pluralism and independence, in 1996 MISA transformed itself into a membership-based organization with representation in at least eleven members of the fourteen-nation Southern African Development Community (SADC). Each national chapter consists of both individual (media professionals) and institutional (media organizations and enterprises) members; the regional secretariat is located in Windhoek, Namibia. MISA operates as a regional "trust" with elected regional and national councils and nonelected regional and chapter secretariats. It strives "to create an environment in which civil society is empowered to claim information and access to it as inalienable rights and in which the resultant freer information flow strengthens democracy by enabling more informed citizen participation."[11] A prominent regional partner of MISA is the Braamfontein-based Freedom of Expression Institute (FXI), which was formed in 1994 to protect the rights to freedom of expression and access to information in post-apartheid South Africa. FXI is managed by an executive committee that is elected every two years by secret balloting of members and boasts of a constitution with strong mechanisms to hold the leadership accountable.[12] The Media Rights Agenda (MRA), arguably the most prominent media NGO in Nigeria, was established in August 1993 in response to the sustained clampdown on the press by successive military governments. Precisely the same reason led to the 1995 formation of both the Center for Free Speech (CFS) and Journalists for Democratic Rights (JODER). The fourth Nigeria group—the Institute for Media and Society (IMS)—was formed in 2000 as a post–military era initiative aimed at facilitating popular participation in governance and development by improving the communicative capacity of all stakeholders in the development process, particularly Nigeria's marginalized rural majority.

A key structural difference between the South African and Nigerian groups is that the former have some semblance of formal membership with mechanisms to hold the leadership accountable. This relatively collectivist approach is arguably a carryover from the epic struggles against apartheid in which mass movements played a crucial role. In contrast, the Nigerian groups lack wide membership and are mostly composed of the founder(s), staff (full- and part-time), and an appointed nonexecutive board of distinguished professionals with name recognition.[13] Under this model, which is prevalent among African NGOs, power and responsibilities are often personalized, and the organizations tend to operate with minimal constitutional checks and balances.

South Africa and Nigeria also offer slightly contrasting experiences in terms of the role of these NGOs, reflecting differences in their political culture. For instance, while South Africa's Freedom of Expression Institute is primarily concerned with nurturing and consolidating the "post-social democratic"[14] media framework brought about by the end of apartheid, its Nigerian counterparts are still battling to put in place basic liberal democratic media policies following three decades of military despotism. Nigerian media NGO activism can be divided into two periods: the military and post-military eras, with 1999 as the watershed. While the former period was largely marked by antagonism and confrontation with the state, the latter saw a change in both strategy and programs in which the NGOs, although still wary of the state, tried to work with it to effect desired policy changes (Adeoye 2004; Ojo 2004; Arogundade 2004a). Richard Akinola (2004) of the Center for Free Speech (CFS) calls this post-military approach "constructive engagement." Key features of the adversarial military-era approach included documenting the rampant violations of press freedom and other human rights abuses and digitally alerting the world about them through such organizations like Amnesty International and the International Freedom of Expression Exchange (IFEX); litigating on broad issues of freedom of expression, especially with respect to journalists whose rights had been violated; and joining the broader Nigerian prodemocracy community in lobbying for international sanctions on Nigeria as a way of breaking the junta's resolve. The post-military era marked by the May 29, 1999, "multiparty" elections saw the

NGOs move beyond the narrow focus on media infractions to also address broader issues critical to the role of the media in a fledgling democratic process.

Regardless of national experiences, media NGO advocacy in Africa can be reduced to the following five core overlapping areas:

- Freedom of expression advocacy, including legal defense for litigants
- Civic and human rights education of the citizenry
- Legislative advocacy toward reform of draconian and obsolete media laws and a policy framework that guarantees the independence and transparency of the regulatory process
- Training of journalists and the "professionalization" of journalism
- Media pluralism and access, particularly with respect to such marginalized demographics as ethnic minorities, women, and the continent's vast rural populations

Given that the media NGOs are often founded by journalists and human rights lawyers primarily in response to the authoritarian tendencies of the African state, it is not surprising that freedom of expression, even if sometimes narrowly viewed as freedom of the press, is easily their number one issue. Covert infractions of freedom of the press in Africa take various forms, such as the licensing of journalists by way of government-controlled press councils, economic sanctions through the denial of government patronage such as paid advertisements, and obnoxious taxes, among others. The more overt means of repression include extrajudicial acts like the arrest, detention, imprisonment, and torture of journalists; disruption of distribution and sometimes seizure of media products by state security operatives; and the outright closure of critical media organizations. Media NGO activism in this area usually involves documenting such abuses and bringing them to the attention of the international community as well as challenging the most egregious cases in the courts of law. While all the groups under study are, in some form, involved in freedom of expression litigation, sometimes on a pro bono arrangement, the FXI particularly has a strong track record in that regard as its Legal Unit (formerly known as the Freedom of Expression Defense Fund) is committed to funding precedent-setting cases that will foster a freer environment for freedom of expression and access to information .[15] One of the most litigated of such cases in the SADC countries is "criminal defamation," which makes publishing anything that embarrasses or insults the head of state an offense punishable by jail time.[16] Similar initiatives like MISA's SADC Journalists under Fire Campaign launched in 2003 also offer moral and practical support to victims of media repression.[17]

Perhaps the realization that freedom of expression violations are rampant in Africa due in part to the widespread "culture of ignorance" about rights among citizens has led virtually all the media NGOs to address the problem through media education. This usually takes a variety of forms—campaigns in the print and electronic media, posters, stickers, community forums, and town hall meetings aimed at sensitizing citizens about a broad range of rights and how to guard against their infractions.

Even more crucial to safeguarding freedom of expression is the urgent need to reform Africa's largely draconian media laws and to adopt a policy framework that guarantees the independence of regulatory agencies in the communications sector as demanded by the Charter on Broadcasting. In South Africa, the legislative reform programs of the FXI point to a more substantive effort at the democratization of communication. For instance, having helped secure the February 2000 enactment of the Promotion of Access to Information Act (PAIA), a law it now fears "risks becoming an elite instrument," the FXI has since proposed changes aimed at its "social appropriation." This requires dramatically expanding its focus to include the quality of delivery of basic services such as water, waste management, electricity, health, and transport, which the South African constitution has recognized as basic rights.[18] Similarly, MISA is also exploring how access to information laws in the southern Africa region can be used to better the socioeconomic conditions of ordinary citizens. This follows its 2003 annual conference, where poverty became a streamlined thematic issue in its program activities.[19] Such shift is also evident in FXI's other policy reform programs in areas like community media, where in conjunction with the National Community Media Forum (NCRF) it has led efforts to develop a faster and less cumbersome licensing process, greater independence of the regulatory agencies, and a more participatory grassroots communication.

In Nigeria, the advocacy for the reform of media laws came largely by way of the 1999 EC-sponsored Media for Democracy Program, aimed at facilitating the transition of the Nigerian media from military authoritarianism to civil rule. Much of the work in this regard centers around two key bills—the Nigerian Media Bill and the Access to Information Bill—both of which were initiated in 1999 by the Media Rights Agenda on behalf of the "media for democracy" coalition. The media bill has two primary goals—to harmonize media laws that are scattered under several statutes into a single and easily accessible document; and to reform the draconian components of such laws, some of which date back to the colonial period, by bringing them up to international standards.[20] The bill also includes laws that have implications for but are not directly related to the media. On the deregulation of broadcasting, the bill found the existing act inadequate because it places the regulatory commission under the direct control of the minister of information. Instead, it proposes a truly independent regulatory body and a three-tier system of public service, commercial, and community broadcasting in line with the Charter on Broadcasting (Ojo 2004). For its part, the Access to Information Bill aims to make public records and information more freely available in the public interest while at the same time protecting both personal privacy and national security issues. The overriding objective, as with all access laws, is to facilitate transparency in public life (Freedom of Information Bill 1999), but to counter the perception in government circles that such a law would only give inordinate powers to the press, proponents of the bill couched it primarily as a citizens' law that would empower every member of society to play a more active role in the political process, because access to information about government policies and activities would lead to greater participation in policy formulation and implementation (Ojo 2004; Aginam 2005b). After six tortuous years in both houses of parliament, the Access to Information Bill, renamed the Freedom of Information Bill, finally passed in November 2006, with the "media bill" all but abandoned, having failed to get even a first reading.[21]

Besides legislative reforms, another component of the EC's Media for Democracy Program in Nigeria is the "professionalization" of journalism. To this end, it established the International Press Center (IPC) in 1999 to help transform the Nigerian press from a combative opponent of military dictatorship into an ethically sound and socially responsible vector of democratic politics. With a strong focus on the training and retraining of journalists, the center conducts seminars and workshops on a wide range of topical media issues and serves as an information, Internet, and technological resource base for media workers and other civil society groups. It also periodically reviews local media coverage of major events and issues to determine if they meet the tests of balance and social responsibility.[22] The reviews have so far scrutinized local media coverage of the transition program and national elections, the conduct of democratic politics, access to justice by lower cadres of society, local terrorism issues following the 9/11 attacks in the United States, ethnoreligious conflicts, and more. The results of such studies are distributed to media organizations with a view to offering them some empirical data about their performance and the hope that they can take voluntary measures to improve their coverage of such issues (Arogundade 2004a; Ojo 2004).

While MISA is also concerned with media "professionalization," ethical standards, and improving the skills levels of media practitioners in the southern African region,[23] the primary focus in South Africa, particularly with respect to the FXI, appears to be hard-nosed research and policy advocacy aimed at a plural, more democratic media environment. Both MISA and the FXI place as much of a premium on the ideals of media access, diversity, and pluralism as on a firmly entrenched policy framework to ensure their actualization. For instance, the FXI's Media and ICT Program continually canvasses new policy options to increase diversity, foster social pluralism, and facilitate popular access across the entire communications sector of South Africa.[24] Such progressive advocacy underscores South Africa's relatively more advanced social democratic experience in comparison with most other countries of Africa.

Two modest efforts at empowerment of marginalized groups deserve some mention in the Nigerian context. One is the "unheard voices" project, a monthly forum organized by Journalists for Democratic Rights in which representatives of religious and ethnic minorities usually shut out by the media get to meet mainstream journalists and directly tell their stories of disempowerment. The goal is to help the media better understand their perspectives to ensure more responsive reporting (Adeoye 2004). Another is the community media coalition led by the Institute of Media and Society. Inspired by the vision of community radio enunciated in the Charter on Broadcasting, the coalition, through sustained policy advocacy, has managed to convince the Nigerian government on the need to license community radio stations to help provide a voice to the country's often marginalized rural majority (Akingbolu 2004). Nigeria is one of the few countries in Africa without some form of community radio, even if in most of these countries they are either donor-funded or localized state broadcasting outlets.[25]

Interestingly, the media NGOs have been very active on the issue of gender. While some groups focus more exclusively on women journalists by trying to increase their numbers and enhance their profiles, others adopt a broader approach that is geared toward a more equitable, gender-balanced public sphere. A good example of the former is the Dakar, Senegal–based African Women's Media Center (AWMC), which was established in 1997 by the International Women's Media Foundation (IWMF). Through a network of NGOs, media companies, and professional organizations across the continent, the center strives to arm African female media practitioners with the training and tools they need to compete effectively with their male colleagues (African Women's Media Center 1999). The IPC in Nigeria, in association with the International Federation of Journalists (Brussels) and the National Association of Women Journalists (Nigeria), went even further by attempting to articulate a charter of rights for female journalists in Nigeria. However, after a series of workshops between 2000 and 2003 that explored universal conventions and declarations relating to the rights of women, international and local labor laws, and the unique on-the-job experiences of Nigeria's female journalists, it deferred action on the matter to allow for more extensive consultations and debates on the issue (Arogundade 2004b, ii–iii).

When it comes to a comprehensive gender advocacy that is not limited to female media professionals, MISA appears to be well ahead of the pack. This is amply illustrated by the Gender and Media Baseline Study, which it released in March 2003 in conjunction with Gender Links, another southern African NGO. The study reviewed gender representation in the editorial content of the media in twelve southern African countries and found it blatantly lopsided in favor of men. According to the study, female journalists wrote less than 20 percent of the stories reviewed while women constituted only 17 percent of news sources—1 percent lower than the global average of 18 percent.

For MISA, giving voice to all segments of society is intrinsic to participation, citizenship, and democracy, and this requires working with regulatory authorities, media training institutions, and media companies on measures to ensure that gender and all forms of diversity are reflected in media policy and practice. It consequently made effective "mainstreaming" of gender one of the key indicators for measuring its overall success as an organization (Media Institute of Southern Africa [MISA] Annual Report 2004–2005).

In contrast, the reluctance of donor agencies to embrace the often messy ethnoreligious pluralism of African societies means that such problematic categories do not feature prominently in the programs of the media NGOs. When they do, as in JODER's "unheard voices" project, they are broached more or less in the context of a nation-state bound by a common imaginary, which may preclude more radical options like self-determination.

AFRICAN MEDIA NGOS AND
THE CHALLENGE OF NEOLIBERALISM

From the foregoing, it is obvious that the media NGOs continue to play a pivotal role in Africa's political transition by championing the cause of freedom of expression among other related issues. Yet close scrutiny of their programs shows, with a few important exceptions like gender equity, an almost overwhelming focus on nation-state accountability. This is not unusual given the perennial abuse of state power in Africa, particularly its stranglehold on the mass media. But the danger with this approach is that it may blind the NGOs from equally recognizing the limits to citizenship participation imposed by the neoliberal reforms gradually taking root in Africa. This speaks somewhat to the classic liberal watchdog theory of the media in which a deregulated media environment is romanticized as everything a state-involved system is not—open, accessible, plural, and above all protective of freedom of expression. Yet, abundant empirical evidence has shown that private media are not only an integral part of the system of power in all societies but that they are as complicit as the state in using the media for their own interests rather than the needs of citizens (Curran 2002, 217–18; Hallin 2000, 100–2). The relative exception in this regard is South Africa, where NGOs like the FXI with a social democratic rights-based philosophy of media advocacy are beginning to broaden critiques of freedom of expression infractions to include the shortcomings of the market model.

The emerging regime of media deregulation in Africa poses a number of challenges to NGO advocacy in the continent. These include the threat of a market-driven system to public broadcasting; the question of pluralism and access in a deregulated system, particularly among commercial operators; and the vexed issue of universal service and access in telecommunications.

A key demand of the Charter on Broadcasting discussed earlier is the transformation of all state broadcasters into truly independent public service outlets and adequate funding of such stations that is not subject to political influence. Such a transformation, even at the most rudimentary level, is yet to be made in most African countries, including Nigeria, and getting the state to let go has remained a hot-button issue for media NGOs. However, in South Africa, the FXI and its partners have waged a two-pronged campaign to safeguard the relative editorial and institutional independence of the South African Broadcasting Corporation (SABC)—arguably the best example of a public service broadcaster in the continent—as well as ensure its survival in an increasingly market-driven broadcast industry. Starved of funds by the state and with only a paltry 15 percent of its revenues coming from the ever unpopular television license fees, the SABC has had to rely on commercial sources for the bulk of its revenue, of which advertising alone accounts for over 70 percent. Fearing that the SABC's continuing reliance on commercial revenue would compromise its public service mandate, the FXI along with like-minded organizations has formed a "social movement" around public broadcasting with the hope of securing adequate public funding for the corporation and safeguarding its overall institutional independence.[26]

Media pluralism and diversity are two ideals that feature prominently in the mission statements of most African media NGOs. What those precisely mean is often not quite clear. The 1991 Windhoek declaration that inspired the Charter on Broadcasting defined a "pluralistic press" as a monopoly free media system where the greatest possible number of publications reflects "the widest possible range of opinion within the community" (UNESCO 1996). Implicit in this definition is the belief that diversity in ownership and access will lead to a plurality of viewpoints. Given the great urban-rural divide in Africa, most media NGOs see the establishment of community media, particularly radio stations, as key to fostering pluralism. Such community media, which have become popular in various parts of rural Africa, derive their relevance by dealing with content specific to their communities that commercial or public radio stations would have ignored. A major concern of MISA is the continuing development and sustainability of community radio stations in the southern African region, which at present are mostly either donor funded or state supported (Kangwa-Wilkie 2006).[27] It is debatable to what extent such initiatives normatively qualify as community media. But given the debilitating levels of poverty in rural Africa, it is hard to imagine how else such projects can survive for any length of time (Aginam 2005a). The establishment of the Media Development and Diversity Agency (MDDA) by the South African government in 2002 marks yet another NGO-led initiative aimed at fostering pluralism and diversity in the media. Basically the brainchild of the FXI and other rights groups that relentlessly canvassed for it, the agency addresses the exclusion and marginalization of disadvantaged communities and persons from access to the media by helping them establish mostly community or small commercial print or electronic media outlets. MDDA is substantially funded by the state with voluntary contributions from willing commercial media operators.[28] Since 2003, the agency has supported more than ninety-seven different media projects, with the assistance ranging from seed money to skills training, technical support, and resource development.[29]

Curiously, commercial broadcasters, the second tier of the Charter on Broadcasting, seem to be largely missing in the NGO discourse on media pluralism and access in Africa. For instance, what their specific responsibilities should be in fostering both core ideals is often never clearly articulated beyond the vague platitudes of a media system not beholden to political or commercial interests. However, conventional thinking within the media NGO ranks suggests that the very existence of commercial broadcasters embodies some pluralism to the extent that they offer an alternative of sorts to the propagandist monologue of the government broadcaster. This may well be true, but the prevalent cronyism in the issuance of broadcast licenses in Africa, of which the NGOs have been very critical, raises serious questions about the nature of the pluralism such a system fosters. While a few commercial broadcasters have defied the odds by making substantive contributions to critical public policy discourses, the overwhelming majority are content to follow the government line, partly for fear of retribution if they oppose the government. Ultimately, all commercial operators are driven by the bottom line, offering mostly music and other entertainment programming aimed at maximizing audiences (Ojo 2004; Kangwa-Wilkie 2006). Ownership restrictions and quota programming are two policy areas MISA feels can help contribute to plurality and diversity in commercial broadcasting (Kangwa-Wilkie 2006). Even with those measures in place, market pluralism based largely on social and economic status is antithetical to genuine diversity anchored on universal access and citizenship rights.

More than anything else the ongoing massive deregulation of the telecommunications sector in Africa underscores the limits of Africa's media NGO advocacy. Despite the Charter on Broadcasting identifying universal service and access as two key conditions for the liberalization of the sector, media NGO advocacy in this area is solely lacking with the possible exception of South Africa, where the FXI combines robust lobbying of the regulator with direct action against the major operators.[30] The June 2000 merger of the South African Telecommunications Regulatory Authority (SATRA) and the Independent Broadcasting Authority (IBA) gave rise to the megaregulator—the Independent Communications Authority of South Africa (ICASA) charged with a mandate to facilitate "effective and seamless regulation of telecommunications and broadcasting and to accommodate the convergence of technologies."[31] This set the stage for the introduction of such megapolicies as the August 2005 "Convergence Bill," which the FXI stridently opposes for the lack of objective conditions for its implementation except for the wealthiest users. In a submission to parliament, the FXI argued that any objective convergence policy must first meet the following basic conditions—the provision of affordable fixed telephone lines, which have yet to reach whole townships and villages; the drastic reduction of the excessively high prepaid cell phone charges that well over half of the population cannot afford; and the development of affordable protocols for accessing data through cell phones. In the apparent absence of such basic conditions, it argued, fixed line rollout remains key to addressing the digital divide, as taking the convergence route risks further "dividing the country into information haves and information have-nots" by "replacing the analogue divide with the digital divide."[32] Frustrated by the regulator's reluctance to compel operators like Telkom to meet their universal service and affordable access obligations, the FXI, along with groups like Communication Rights Agenda, has since 2004 resorted to direct action (mostly picketing) to force the issue.[33] Although similar problems, like the absence of universal service and excessive charges, abound in Nigeria,[34] none of the country's major media NGOs consider them central to their programs. Instead, advocacy on such issues is usually undertaken by some "consumers'" rights groups, one of which in 2002 spearheaded a one-day national boycott of GSM mobile phone operators in protest over exorbitant charges for sloppy services. Consequently, the regulator, the Nigerian Communications Commission (NCC), instituted a monthly "consumers' parliament" where aggrieved customers can confront the operators over such sundry matters like disputed billings and other minor contractual issues.

Despite the great efforts of groups like the FXI, the odds seem heavily stacked against them, for as William Hueva, Keyan Tomaselli, and Ruth Tomaselli (2004, 116) observed, "the transformation and restructuring of communication systems in the (Southern African) region is driven by economic imperatives, despite the rhetoric of universal access that have accompanied these processes. Moreover, partnerships between state and capital have increased, while media rights groups and other actors in civil society continue to be locked out of major restructuring decisions." This is even worse in other parts of the continent where the governments and NGOs are less ideologically progressive.

All too often, democratization in Africa is portrayed in very romantic terms—freedom of expression, multiparty elections, good governance, rule of law, poverty alleviation, and many more benefits. What is usually not made obvious is that the rolled-back state will be replaced by strong markets; such basic services like healthcare and education, hitherto subsidized by the state, will now be the preserve of profiteering private providers. The grave implications of this in a continent with debilitating levels of poverty can only be imagined. The Nigerian experience further underscores the dangers of the minimalist model of neoliberal democratization prevalent in Africa where the transition from authoritarianism is never followed by the consolidatory phase of substantive legislative reforms required of a truly free and democratic society.

Perhaps African media NGOs will benefit from a more critical questioning of the impact of the emerging regime of media deregulation on their respective countries and citizens even as they continue to scrutinize the state—neoliberalism's quintessential bogeyman. A good starting point should be the adoption of communication as a basic right, which the Charter on Broadcasting came very close to doing. But that will also require a broader reconceptualization of media to include new information and communication technologies (ICTs) and how their regulation and possible commercial appropriation can impact the dignity of the human person, particularly the marginalized. Groups like the FXI in South Africa have taken the lead; it is about time the rest followed.

NOTES

1. A 1995 UN report on global governance estimated there were about twenty-nine thousand international NGOs globally. The growth is even more rapid domestically with about two million existing in the United States alone and about 240 formed every year in Kenya (*Economist*, 2000).

2. For a similar definition of civil society, see Keane (1998, 6). While Habermas (1996), and Ray (2001, 225) rule out civil society's recourse to extrademocratic means in the pursuit of its goals Baker (2002) and Hill and Montag (2000, 7) recognize that possibility. White (1995) on his part argues that recourse to political, economic, or military confrontation negates the essence of social movements and turns the effort into a coercive campaign.

3. For Marina Ottaway (2000, 97) "brief-case NGOs" are organizations made up of just the founder(s) and skeletal staff.

4. Although the National Endowment for Democracy (NED) usually projects itself as a nongovernmental entity, its close relationship with the U.S. government, particularly the CIA, makes such a claim questionable.

5. For instance, the EC program in Nigeria was largely a partnership between the London-based Article 19, the International Federation of Journalists (IFJ) in Brussels and three local NGOs—the Media Rights Agenda (MRA), Journalists for Democratic Rights (JODER), and the Independent Journalism Center (IJC). Another key player among multilateral organizations is the World Bank Institute, which is in partnership with the Commonwealth Parliamentary Association (CPA), which canvasses for better access laws as a condition for good governance in Africa.

6. For example, in a 1996 policy change, USAID decided to fund only market-friendly "Civic Advocacy Organizations" (CAOs) as distinct from the more inclusive "Civil Society Organizations" (CSOs); see Rob Jenkins (2001, 253–55).

7. While the African Union and the United Nations embraced the charter, the vehement opposition of the World Bank and the International Monetary Fund (IMF) effectively killed it—see Bade Onimode et al. (2004). Since 2001, the New Partnership for African Development (NEPAD), a neoliberal framework endorsed by G-7 nations and donor agencies, has become the

blueprint for development in the continent. It aims "to halt the marginalization of Africa in the globalization process and enhance its full and beneficial integration into the global economy" (NEPAD 2005).

8. For accounts of governments" control of the media (particularly broadcasting) in Africa, see Aginam (2005a), Van der Veur (2002), Bourgault (1995), and Katz and Wedell (1977).

9. See www.misa.org/broadcasting/resource-acb/introduction%20to%20charter.pdf.

10. See www.misa.org/aboutmisa.html.

11. See www.misa.org/programmes.html.

12. See www.fxi.org.za/PDFs/Governance/FXI%20Constitution%202006.pdf.

13. The public profiles of the board members help enhance the legitimacy and stature of the organization, particularly with funding agencies.

14. Robert Horwitz (2001, 45) used the term "post-social democratic" to explain the relatively progressive civil society–driven media policy and legislative framework that South Africa adopted following the end of apartheid. It must also be stressed that South Africa is a unique case in that its democratization did not follow the traditional two-step approach of "transition" and "consolidation," because a detailed constitutional framework was adopted prior to its first multiracial elections.

15. See www.fxi.org.za/Main%20Pages/legalunit.html.

16. See www.misa.org/legalsupport.html.

17. See www.misa.org/mediamonitoring.html.

18. See www.fxi.org.za/Main%20Pages/accesstoinfo.html.

19. See www.misa.org/freedomofexpression.html. The big challenge for MISA is that respect for freedom of expression and access to information vary substantially among the countries of the SADC region.

20. The current Nigerian laws on sedition and the Official Secrets Act are actually carry-overs from the colonial period. Also, many of the prevailing laws, like the deregulation of Broadcasting Decree 38 of 1992 as amended by Act 55 of 1999, amount to no more than a rechristening of the military decree of 1992 setting up the National Broadcasting Commission. To date, the act places the commission under the minister of information and by extension the president. The same makeover applies to the military-constituted Nigerian Press Council established under Decree 85 of 1992 as amended by Decree 60 of 1999.

21. For details of the sometimes bizarre politics of access law in Nigeria, see MRA 2003.

22. Although a section of the nongovernment press in Nigeria stood up to decades of military despotism, the ethical code for Nigerian journalists is substantially based on the mainstream Western model of objectivity, fairness, and balance, derived from the country's heritage as a former British colony. For a critical discussion of this model, see Hackett and Zhao (1998).

23. See www.misa.org/aboutmisa.html.

24. See www.fxi.org.za/Main%20Pages/media_ict.html.

25. The National Broadcasting Commission (NBC) announced in February 2005 that it was finally ready to license community broadcasters who must be nonprofit, community owned, and committed to serving the communal and developmental objectives of their communities. This is substantially in line with the ideals of community radio as enunciated in the African Charter on Broadcasting.

26. See www.fxi.org.za/pages/Media%20%26%20ICT/Campaigns%20M%26I/Public%20Broadcasting/public%20broadcasting%20new.html.

27. For a range of discussions on community radio experiments in Africa, see Fardon and Furniss (2000).

28. Concerned about its sustainability, the FXI would rather have the commercial media operators be required to fund the agency.

29. See www.mdda.org.za/docs/misc/stratplan2006-9.pdf.

30. MISA is concerned about universal access in telecommunication and ICTs and is currently studying the issue in the southern African region (Kangwa-Wilkie 2006).

31. See www.icasa.org.za/Content.aspx?Page=17.

32. See www.fxi.org.za/pages/Media%20%26%20ICT/Press/Press%20Statements/PR_11%20August%2005.html.

33. See www.fxi.org.za/pages/Media%20%26%20ICT/Press/Press%20Statements/PR_14%20Sept%2005.html.

34. Late in 2006, the Nigerian government signaled its intention to create a megaregulator that will eventually see the Broadcasting Commission taken over by the Nigerian Communications Commission.

13

Move Over Bangalore, Here Comes . . . Palestine? Western Funding and "Internet Development" in the Shrinking Palestinian State

Helga Tawil Souri

Standing behind a one-way mirror looking over the "data-entry floor"—sixty computers to be used by a still-imaginary workforce—the chief technical officer of the Palestinian Information and Communications Technology Incubator (PICTI) in Ramallah suggested that "one day we will compete with India. We will become the high-tech center for the region, outsourcing to Dubai, Israel, Saudi, Ghana, and eventually into Asia."

The CTO expressed a latent desire that exists across a number of information technology (IT) projects across the Gaza Strip and West Bank. In a small rural village south of Jenin, an Internet center established in 2003 was meant to get the youth off the streets, enhance their future work skills, and bridge the digital divide. But the IT4Youth project is also centered around the belief that building Internet and computer access is an integral part of Palestinian state building and development, a way to integrate "Palestine" into the global economy.

Ramallah's Incubator and the IT4Youth project are certainly not unique, but representative of development trends in the Palestinian Territories that posit information technologies (IT) and the Internet specifically as being at the center of progress, modernization, and growth. Since the Second Intifada erupted in September 2000, "Internet development" (not the development of the Internet itself, but development through the Internet) projects have proliferated at astounding rates across the territories. Beneath this growth is the dreamlike promise of Palestine one day becoming a new Bangalore—the Bangalore of a capitalist's dreams, where everyone is happily employed behind a computer screen, and cultural, religious, gender, socioeconomic inequalities are nonexistent. Despite the increase in violence, political instability, and economic poverty since 1994, telecommunications (Internet and cellular telephony) has become the only area of growth in the Palestinian Territories. Like many Palestinian state-building and development endeavors, the push to join the digital age and create a cheap labor pool of IT workers that will ideally compete with the likes of India exposes contradictions on multiple levels.

Based on materials gathered from fieldwork, in-depth interviews with Palestinian Internet and telecommunications practitioners and regulators, and participatory observation with NGOs involved in Internet development in the Palestinian Territories, this chapter contextualizes and analyzes "Internet development" in the Palestinian Territories since 2000 by examining three different kinds of IT foreign aid programs: Internet centers targeted at children and youth, IT training and vocational programs targeted at the employable population, and the creation of technology incubators as foundations for an IT industry. In particular, this analysis highlights the dilemmas of integrating Palestinians into the global economy in a territorially shrinking and fragmented space and the contradiction of creating free-trade zones in a society that has no control over its own borders and economy. Finally, this chapter questions whether civil society is a necessary component that can facilitate the painful processes of economic and political change in the face of global capitalism or whether it remains impotent in their face.

IT EXPANSION AMID SHRINKING BORDERS AND A GROWING FOREIGN DEBT

The promise of a Palestinian state after the 1993 Oslo Agreements and establishment of the Palestinian Authority (PA) in 1994 have done little to promote political or economic stability (Robinson 1997; N. Brown 2003; Hass 2000, 2002; Roy 1993, 1994a, 1994b, 1996, 1999, 2001). The hegemonic system imposed by Israel during the twenty-six years of direct rule did not disappear with the implementation of the peace process, but became largely mediated by the PA. While the PA pursued many corrupt controls over Palestinian internal affairs, the Israeli government remained the final arbiter of Palestinian life. Throughout the 1990s, Palestinian society was weakened, its grassroots groups marginalized, its economy on the brink of collapse, as the promise of a peaceful future receded. It was against this background that the violence of the Second Intifada erupted. The abysmal realities of the "peace years" can be best understood through two examples: shrinking territorial control and a flailing economy, both of which became pretexts for the need for Internet development.

The Oslo Agreements institutionalized territorial division and segmentation by stipulating what Palestinians call the "10–40–50 plan": Israel annexed 10 percent of the West Bank, 50 percent was to be under Palestinian sovereignty, and 40 percent was to be fully controlled by Israel—areas in which Palestinians are not allowed to build, settle, farm, or even pass through. Two million Palestinians in the West Bank were crowded into four isolated enclaves (without connection to each other) that together consisted of half of the West Bank's land, the other half blocked by the defense array of Israeli settlers. With Oslo II, signed in 1995, the final stage of Palestinian territorial segmentation was achieved with the division of the West Bank into a confusing mosaic of territories with differing status: Area A was to have "full" (in fact limited) Palestinian security and civil control, Area B had Israeli security and Palestinian civil control, and Area C (the great mass of the land) was under full Israeli control. By the eve of the Second Intifada, area A enclaves totaled 18 percent, whereas area C covered a full 60 percent. With most of the Palestinian population living in the scattered islands of A and B, separated from each other by vast areas of C lands, hundreds of villages and towns were totally paralyzed, devastating their economy and disrupting social life.

Territorial segmentation was further reinforced by the policy of closures. On March 30, 1993 (six months prior to Agreements), the Israeli government sealed off the West Bank and the Gaza Strip. Since then closures have varied in intensity but have *never* been lifted.[1] Closure is meant to deprive Palestinians of their right to free movement. What legalized closures was the 1994 Paris Economic Protocol, which also institutionalized Israel's de facto rule over Palestinian trade, economy, and sovereignty. The "security" concerns, of which closures were argued to be an integral part, dovetailed nicely with developments in the Israeli labor market and concerns about reducing dependence on Palestinian labor, damaging the already weak Palestinian economy.

The economic reality of the West Bank and Gaza has been summed up as one of de-development, defined as a structural relationship between a stronger and weaker economy, which has not only distorted the development process but has undermined it entirely (Roy 1999; 2000). While the economy had been subservient to Israel's for decades, the peace process did not brighten the conditions. In the ten years since the establishment of the protostate, poverty rates, unemployment and reliance on foreign aid have steadily risen.[2]

Foreign aid has prevented Palestinians from free-falling into abject poverty. Given the dire economic and social conditions, the majority of Palestinians look to aid institutions for their basic needs. The World Bank estimates that without assistance programs the 16 percent of the population unable to afford basic subsistence would climb to 35 percent (World Bank Group 2004b). It has thus been up to Palestinian and foreign nongovernmental organizations (NGOs) to provide many of the services that the lack of a state, followed by the defunct protostate, could not provide.

The Oslo Agreements opened the flood gates for foreign investors and aid, following the familiar rhetoric of mainstream development in the developing world: promises of modernization, democratization, strengthening civil society, integrating into the global economy, and sustaining "peace." In 1994 yearly foreign aid amounted to $130 million; in 2004 it reached almost $800 million (PASSIA 2004; PCBS 2005). So while Palestinian economic productivity has dropped, aid has become a growing percentage of domestic income, from 12 percent in 1994 to 44 percent in 2004 (PCBS 2005). As a result, the PA, which began in 1994 as a debt-free government, ten years later has become a government riddled with over $1.5 billion of debt (PCBS 2005; World Bank Group 2004b). The Palestinian experience has become a case of foreign aid as a means to control and govern economic and political growth (Brynen 2000; Roy 1996, 1999, 2001; Jamal 2004).

It is important to recognize that the majority of Western funding, and particularly American funding (through USAID), since 1993 has been defined by the broader dynamics of the peace process (Brynen 1996a, 1996b; Tawil Souri 2006). Peace, as delineated in the Oslo Accords and the Paris Economic Protocol, ignored issues of Palestinian economic, political, or territorial sovereignty, and left Palestinians unable to control their own economic future or direct a development strategy.

NGOs have historically been the backbone of Palestinian development, with the indigenous groups often symbolizing a major part of the political struggle as the civil society denied to Palestinians (Barghouti 1994; Frisch 1998; N. Brown 2003). The Palestinian case is not necessarily identical to the Middle Eastern one. For example, Peter Mansfield (1991) and Elia Zureik (in Schwedler 1995) argue that the lack of civil society in Arab nations results from the failure of the state to create such institutions; the failure of societies to organize in a way that would allow them to challenge state authority; or the failure of organizations to resist being co-opted by the state. Bernard Lewis (1994) blames the lack of civil society on the region's Islamic tradition. But these studies are problematic: for one, many civil society groups in the Palestinian Territories stem from Islamic groups that one cannot lump together as the same—they range from the charitable to the political, from ones promoting fundamentalism to ones supporting workers' rights. Moreover, it is illusory to think that civil society and progress toward democracy can be made without including Islamists. Rather, I agree with Norton (1996) that the region is replete with voluntary organizations, trade organizations, human rights groups, women's associations, and many other groups that qualify as making up civil society. And, in the Palestinian case, these groups have played an important role in the absence of a state, as is demonstrated by the advent of Hamas (Barghouti 1994; Schwedler 1995; Muslih 1995; Robinson 1997; Brown 2003). However, with the onset of the peace years, the 1990s also offered attractive opportunities for choice and investment for Western NGOs and multinational institutions such as the World Bank.

What "peace funding" resulted in is the marginalization of indigenous institutions and grassroots organizations due to favoring of aid projects that bolster Western and American corporate, strategic, and ideological presence in the territories. "Peace funding" overlooked organizations that had been helping Palestinians sustain themselves, such as the General Union of Palestinian Charitable Societies (GUPCS) (Jamal 2004). The Palestinian civic institutions that would survive the 1990s were those that could court international rather than domestic constituencies, so the professionalized and increasingly Westernized ones obtained most of the funding.

"Peace funding" also required donors to create projects that were short-term and highly visible and that would quickly make "peace dividends" tangible to the population. Therefore, in part as a response to the limitations of constructing aid under the umbrella of peace, and in part as a response to shrinking territorial and economic freedom experienced by Palestinians, IT became a viable sector for donors. Investment in IT, often framed in the language of "bridging the digital divide" and "strengthening civil society" was also at the forefront of global development trends in the 1990s, which dovetailed with USAID's restructuring, and the growing dominance and expansion of the United States in the IT industry (Howell and Pearce 2001; Warkentin 2001).

THE GROWTH OF IT

Though Israel maintains strict limits on the speed, types, and quantity of technology imports into the territories, the Internet has been a booming business since the mid-1990s. The growth has been led primarily by Western diasporic Palestinians (with Western NGO funding) wishing to invest in the "homeland," who stress the importance of IT in the new world order—a view shared by official development organizations. The Internet is deemed necessary not just for development, but because today's world makes it so: "A modern and competitive Palestinian economy must be information-based—or risk being neither modern nor competitive. . . . We Palestinians must be part of the global 'new economy' or we're nowhere" ("UNDP Focus" 2001, 6).

Between 1994 and 2004, IT funding in the territories amounted to over $150 million, not including the over $100 million that went directly into upgrading the communications infrastructure (PASSIA 2004). The Second Intifada, while devastating politically, economically, and territorially to the territories, propelled phenomenal growth in the Internet and IT sector. Closures, curfews, and checkpoints forced Palestinians to find alternative solutions to overcome problems of physical separation. Cellular phone calls, text messaging, e-mails, and Internet chat sessions became the most affordable way of staying in contact with friends and relatives. The Internet also became a means for people to share experiences of the incursions with web surfers all around the world, to continue their education through outreach programs, and to sustain a social life (Hass 2002; Mitnick 2004; El-Haddad 2003; Federman 2003). Essentially, the Second Intifada opened the way for providing Internet access and connected businesses to "become one of the few growth industries in the Palestinian economy" (Mitnick 2004). A virtual economy seemed like a plausible solution to a population increasingly fragmented by Israeli policies and with little opportunity for employment. More importantly, the vision was compatible with the growing presence of Western/Westernized NGOs in the territories speaking the language of "modernization" and "integration into the global economy" and their tacit goal of engineering the economy according to neoliberal values.

Before Oslo, the Palestinian telecommunications and technology infrastructure had been essentially unchanged since the 1940s primarily because of Israel's unwillingness to upgrade the connection to the increasingly sophisticated Israeli backbone. Personal computers and Internet use before 1995 were practically nonexistent; international telephone connections were forbidden prior to Oslo. In the wake of the peace talks, Palestinians found themselves with international phone and Internet access. In 2001, there were 60,000 Internet users, a number that rose to 105,000 in 2002 (World Bank Group 2002, 2004a), and to over 225,000 in 2003, about a tenth of the population (Internet World Stats 2004), and reaching over one-third of the population by the end of 2005 (PCBS 2005). Internet centers and cafés sprouted up around the territories, with access programs launched in schools, refugee camps, urban centers, and rural areas.

By September 2000, a dozen ISPs were operating in the Territories (PCBS 2003). An IT-based Ramallah advocacy group claimed to represent more than 70 IT companies in 2002, and more than 120 in 2004, from various subsectors, including hardware distributors, software development firms, office automation vendors, ISPs, and IT consulting, IT training, and related businesses (*MENA Business Reports* 2003; PITA 2005). Palestinian software houses were launched, having economic advantages over competitors in the Arab world because of lower wages, and because many programmers were deemed more "sophisticated than their peers elsewhere in the region because of their exposure to Israel's technology" (Mitnick 2004). By the end of 2003, the number of high-tech firms operating in the territories had increased by 88 percent since 2000; more than one hundred high-tech firms were doing business in the territories (*MENA Business Reports* 2003). Although the figures for Palestinian Internet growth put other Arab nations to shame, most of the growth was coming in the form of foreign aid.

THE THREE FLAVORS OF "INTERNET DEVELOPMENT"

Internet development in the Palestinian Territories has generally come in three forms, aimed at different groups: school-based computer centers and local Internet centers targeted at the youth (from first grade to age eighteen or twenty-four, depending on programs); training and vocational programs in the form of corporate-sponsored certification programs, computer science programs in universities, and creation of technical schools (targeted at ages sixteen to thirty); and technology incubators and "free-trade zones" as means to provide low-wage computer jobs and encourage entrepreneurship for an export market.

In the first group, developers are targeting the largest percentage of Palestinians; more than half of the population is below the age of fifteen, and approximately 60 percent is below the age of eighteen (PASSIA 2004; World Bank Group 2004b). So the youth "market" is the largest in terms of size and assumed to be a "captive" one that will provide good "return on investment." The creation of local Internet centers and computer labs in schools, while certainly framed within the argument of improving education, bridging the digital divide, empowering young girls, and connecting children to a world beyond the West Bank or the Gaza Strip, is perhaps more successful in creating a set of future computer users and video game players. For many children, surfing the web, chatting, e-mailing, and playing video games has become a way to release political and social frustration.

The IT4Youth project is representative here, symbolizing a capitalist project in the heart of the Palestinian Territories, exemplary of the state-building efforts that have emerged since the Oslo Accords. IT4Youth describes itself as a nonprofit project aimed at enhancing the learning skills and employability of Palestinian youth, especially girls and young women, through computer-based information technology. The program is a collaborative mission between two NGOs, the Welfare Association[3] and the International Youth Foundation (IYF),[4] with additional funding through a grant from USAID, the Intel Corporation, Hewlett-Packard, and other corporations and wealthy diasporic Palestinian individuals.

IT4Youth has a twofold strategy: to set up computer labs and training in schools and to build a Regional Information Technology Center (RITC) in rural areas. In pursuing these two components, IT4Youth's goal is to "build a 'digital bridge,' reducing the digital divide and helping to create a level educational playing field for Palestinian youth" (IT4Youth website). By offering opportunities for training and retraining, it hopes to develop a pool of IT-proficient youth and lay a foundation for the development of an IT industry. In its own words, IT4Youth's intended goals are "to create hope among the most disadvantaged, vulnerable young people in Palestine, through improving the learning skills, creativity, and employability of those between the ages of 10 and 24" (IT4Youth website). The program is based on the assumption that addressing young people's needs is central to creating conditions for enduring peace in the region.

IT4Youth is neither unique nor the first project of its kind. The Intel Club House, a program that by 2003 existed in over sixty countries, opened a center in Ramallah in 2002, itself a joint program of the IYF and the Welfare Association, funded in part by Intel Capital, the latter a corporate venture program that invests billions of dollars in technology companies worldwide in order to accelerate market development of the "Internet economy" and the global adoption of the Internet. IT4Youth's RITC is based on the Intel Club House model; however, it differs in that its main target is the underprivileged rural population. Other Western-funded projects exist across the West Bank and Gaza Strip, and Islamic, Arab, and Palestinian NGOs have also followed suit: for example, Islamic Relief has established five computer labs across the territories; Palestinian groups have raised funds for similar endeavors, often getting capital from U.S.-based IT firms; the Jerusalem Fund opened thirteen computer labs; and BirZeit University in Ramallah launched the Across Borders program, aimed at refugee camps in the territories, Lebanon, and Jordan.

While Palestinian youth previous to 1993 had no opportunity to pursue extracurricular activities, post-Oslo kids now have Internet centers. By 2005, more than 40 percent of Palestinians between the ages of six and seventeen had regular access to the Internet (PCBS 2005), a percentage that is likely to grow as more investors make their way into the territories. The creation of and investment in playgrounds, community centers, soccer teams, and art clubs, for example, still lags far behind computer centers, since there are no long-term economic benefits to the investors in creating and sustaining those.

For the population no longer in school or over the age of eighteen, training and vocational programs have been established. This type of Internet development ranges from certification programs for software programs to technical and secretarial training. I also include computer science and IT-related programs at postsecondary schools. By 2004, there were thirteen "Cisco Academies," seven Microsoft certification programs (all created by the Welfare Association), three Oracle certification programs, and five more Cisco certification programs run by universities. While some of these programs have obvious corporate interest—such as "Cisco certification"—even the technical and postsecondary school programs have more often than not been infused with Western corporate investments. The majority of these programs were created in the hope of providing a cheap labor pool of certified workers to Israel's growing high-tech industry.

Programs were also created for students less knowledgeable about computers, and those without hopes of Israeli working permits, as a means to supply and grow an internal Palestinian IT industry. The creation of vocational and technical schools filled this gap. For example, two vocational schools were created in the Gaza Strip specifically for young women to be trained in basic computer and secretarial skills. For the manually dexterous young men, programs in computer and electronics systems maintenance were launched. By 2004, eleven such programs existed across the Territories.

In postsecondary educational institutions computer science departments were created. Since 2000, of the thirteen institutions of higher learning in the territories, more than half have formed new IT departments, ranging from Al Najah University, the largest university in the West Bank, to the Islamic University in Gaza. For example, at Al Quds University the enrollment of students in computer programs has grown to more than half of the total student population between the late 1990s and 2005.

A large part of the "demand" for such education was the perceived belief that Palestine could truly emulate Bangalore, Accra, or other regions positioning themselves as technologically enabled outsourcers.[5] There was not only the successful Israeli high-tech industry across the street, but the burgeoning Gulf market too. No one seemed to recognize that Israel was closing its borders to cheap Palestinian labor (and relying on even cheaper labor from Asia for manual work within Israel, or on labor from Egypt and Jordan for outsourcing needs). Nor did anyone seem to realize that in order to get to Dubai, a Palestinian person, product, or service must first make it through impassable Israeli borders. By 2005, certification and training programs were producing a qualified workforce that had nowhere to work and could only hope to outperform Egyptian or Jordanian counterparts (by charging lower rates). But lest all hope was lost, there was a third sector of Internet development that could incorporate these overqualified, unemployed, technically skilled Palestinians.

In November 2003 the PA announced the establishment of the first "technology incubator" in Ramallah at the cost of $3.2 million (Greenbaum 2003). The Palestinian Information and Communications Technology Incubator's (PICTI) main mission is to "design, develop, implement and promote those initiatives that support the development of entrepreneurial business ventures with high growth potential . . . providing . . . support for the commercialization of ideas and [enhancing] the development and growth of dynamic enterprises" (PITA 2005). A joint project with the PA, USAID, the Palestine Trade Center, PalTel, and PITA,[6] PICTI is modeled not only as a source of support, but also as a free-trade/industrial zone to provide jobs and encourage the creation of products and services for an export market.

The notion of free-trade zones is not new to the territories. The Erez Industrial Estate (EIE) was launched as a joint World Bank, European Investment Bank, USAID, PA, and Israeli government project in the 1970s, based on the concept of export processing zones (EPZs) such as Shenzhen or

Guangzhou in China, characterized by surplus-labor economies with an urgent need for employment creation. Seen as potentially able to generate at least fifteen thousand to twenty thousand direct jobs, and thousands more indirect jobs, this project came to exemplify the short-term, highly visible marketing ploy for "peace" developers were in search of. Here is how it was described: "The issue of time is critical in the short-term, with the overriding need—as articulated by leaders on both sides—to rapidly demonstrate to the local population the potential positive impact of the new political environment on their day to day lives" (EastWest Institute 2005, 7).

While the EIE functioned as an industrial park that sought to increase Israeli-Palestinian joint ventures and provide jobs for Gazans in factories specializing in metals, textiles, carpentry, and garages, it did not prove as successful as developers had hoped. By April 2004, less than five thousand Palestinians were employed among factories of which even numbers were owned by Israelis and Palestinians (two jointly owned), and paid average daily wages of US$18 (EastWest Institute 2005, 7). The mild success of EIE and the changing political atmosphere of the late 1990s made foreign funders eager to attempt other "peace-building projects." The Gaza Industrial Estate (GIE) was launched in 1998 at Karni Crossing in Gaza, with similar investors.[7]

The zones have proved better for Israel than for Palestine, since their viability for investors hinges on the areas' exemption from periodic border closures, which Israel continues to enforce. While the industrial estates are subject to full Israeli responsibility and territorially fall within the security parameter (even after "disengagement"), they are not fully subject to Israeli law—which is helpful to factory owners on issues such as environmental dumping and lax employment regulations. Palestinian businessmen are not the ones benefiting from these arrangements, since the Israeli market is the main destination for finished goods, and over 70 percent of the concessions are Israeli owned or subcontracted. Moreover, regulations (approved by the PA, Israeli government, and the World Bank) entitle investors to full repatriation or removal of invested capital and profits earned from the territories. As one researcher claimed, Gaza's free-trade zones are symbolic of "industrial activity . . . stripped of its contribution to economic growth" (Yanai 2001, n.p.). While the GIE provides proximity and accessibility of workers for Israeli industrialists, the recent trend of Israeli industries relocating to cheaper venues in Jordan and Egypt continues (see Bouillon 2004). In the meantime GIE factory workers are unprotected, without contracts, benefits, or minimum wages.

No matter the disappointing results of the industrial zones in the past, there is, especially after Israel's "disengagement" from Gaza, resurging interest, expressed as follows: "The revitalization of the estates, which represent scarce and readily useable industrial land and supporting infrastructure, could make a substantive contribution to the alleviation of current massive unemployment in Gaza. They are the focus of local and foreign investor interest, which can in turn be translated into support for the long-term development of the area" (EastWest Institute 2005, 6). There is still no recognition that these projects are unlikely to help Palestinians economically, and certainly not politically. In order to remain competitive, these projects must maintain low production costs, that is, low wages. The Palestinian estates have the further stipulation of having to compete with Israeli-Egyptian and Israeli-Jordanian zones where products must contain at least 11.5 percent Israeli-made materials in order to qualify for trade benefits with the United States (Bouillon 2004). "So while the [estates are] promoted as a means of increasing Palestinian prosperity, [their] success depends on precisely the opposite" (Yanai 2001, n.p.). Furthermore, incentives favoring large capital investments squeeze out smaller Palestinian enterprises, often forcing Palestinian business owners into subcontracting for Israeli companies, further deepening dependence on Israel.

PICTI is partly modeled after the "technology incubators" of Bangalore, and built on the premise that the digital economy will be enough to propel Palestinians out of poverty; that digital products and services will increase trade; and that providing cheap labor to Israel, the Arab world, and beyond should suffice for the Palestinian worker. The incubator's mission is to design, develop, implement, and promote initiatives that will grow the IT sector by providing assistance (not necessarily financial) for entrepreneurs who have "innovative products . . . with strong regional and/or international market potential" (USAID 2005). Never mind that the sheer number of Indian outsourcers outstrips all of Palestine's population; the success of technology incubators rests on Israel relinquishing control of Palestinian import and export markets—a measure unlikely to happen in the foreseeable future. PICTI is also modeled after the industrial estates, and as such its success is predicated on worker exploitation and continued dependence on Israel, not strengthening the Palestinian economy.

PICTI, IT4Youth, and the Cisco Academies are part and parcel of Internet development, all professing similar benefits and results to Palestinians. Not only are these programs born of the same ideology (premised on the liberatory possibility of technology, modernization as emulation of the West's success, economic gains as the means for political and social gains, etc.), but they share similar organizational structures. Exemplary of development programs in the 1990s, especially those directed by USAID, they receive funding from governmental and corporate sources, from within, and mostly from outside, Palestine. They are organized by what Howell and Pearce (2001) call "sponsorships," and share a goal similar to what Morris-Suzuki (2000) calls "bongos," business-oriented or business-organized NGOs, establishing parallel structures to (and/or structures that further support) the market. Thus they exemplify how Internet development is driven by capitalistic orientations, where access to communication, skills, and the public sphere are deemed as commodities rather than fundamental elements of social organization. This is very much in line with the mainstream discourse on technology, development, and civil society, where economic vitality becomes the means by which to establish peace and build a modern state. I offer a critical evaluation of this discourse in the next section.

TECHNOLOGICAL INNOVATION, CAPITALIST EXPANSION, AND THE PITFALLS OF DEVELOPMENT

Modern Western technology has been profoundly shaped by capitalist enterprise, privileging narrow goals of production and profit over genuine human and social development (Leiss 1990; Davis, Hirschl, and Stack 1997; Feenberg 1991, 1999; Robins and Webster 1999; Webster 2001). With respect to Palestinian Internet development, two issues are essential to consider: first, that technology growth, and the growth of the Internet specifically, has become a "cause and effect" of capitalist expansion (D. Schiller 1999; Webster 1995, 2001); and second, that economic strategies are always implemented by hegemonic social blocs in which the interests of those dominant in society (regionally and globally) at a particular time find expression.

The Internet and new communications technologies are usually privileged elements in accounts of recent global changes. They are presented as main motors of change, innovations that are bringing about radical social transformation, as embodied in the rhetoric used by developers and those at PICTI or IT4Youth. But the Internet is also a leading edge in the epic transnationalization of economic activity, with cyberspace being colonized by the logic of the market system, and comprises nothing less than the central production and control apparatus of an increasingly supranational market system. Dan Schiller (1999) describes this process as "digital capitalism," whereby the Internet is one element of an emerging telecommunications order and the expanding zone of liberalized development. In Schiller's words, "the Internet is only a leading element in the hurricane of destructive creativity that has cascaded through global telecommunications. At stake in this unprecedented transition to neoliberal or market-driven telecommunications are nothing less than the production base and the control structure of an emerging digital capitalism" (37). The boom of digital capitalism—manifested in the Palestinian case under the rubric of Internet development—represents the direct and massive interlock between U.S. trade policies, U.S. corporate domination of global information markets, and the needs of transnationalizing (American, Israel, Palestinian, and other) capital. As such, digital capitalism and Internet development strengthen two long-standing features of the market system: inequality and domination, two economically inhibiting realities already present in the territories due to Israeli policies and PA corruption.

The lesson to be taken from theorists such as Schiller is that technology must be understood as being developed and spread with certain purposes and practices already in mind to which the technology is not marginal but central. To assess the Internet's role in Palestinian society, then, is to consider the implications of the victory of technological reason and to recognize the underside of "progress": the enslavement of humans to machines, the creation of an alienated society controlled from above, the exploitation of workers whose status is further undermined by defining human beings according to their location in the mode of production and consumption. As shown in the example of technology incubators, their success depends precisely on exploiting Palestinian workers, integrating them in the global economy as cheap outsourcers, and making them dependent not only Israel but on technology as well. Or, to use the words of Robins and Webster (1999), Internet development in Palestine will likely result in "the degradation and destruction of much employment, the further concentration and consolidation of corporate capital, and the imposition of its criteria and priorities on the nation state, the aggravation of existing inequalities in our society, the perpetuation of consumerist ethics, and an increasingly atomized society" (303). One must recognize that in its reifying embrace of technology, a society being "modernized," as development agencies and elite groups claim to be doing in Palestine, suffers as much from economic exploitation as from technical domination, imprisoning Palestinians in an inescapable "iron cage." While such an account may be overly pessimistic, and implicitly assumes "direct" media effects, it makes us aware of the implications of Internet development. Because of their history, ITs are simultaneously commodities and artifacts, creators and purveyors of capitalist ideology—the repercussions of which on the Palestinian future are dire. If we recognize the extent to which technology driven by capitalist interests has problematic consequences as noted above, then we ought to recognize the results as even more problematic in the Palestinian case of neoliberal Internet development, doubly exploited as a stateless territory and as a source of cheap labor in the global economy.

It is necessary here to make a distinction between the reality of capitalism and the concept of development. Development should not be confused with the realities of the modern world, which is geared not to "development" but to the expansion of capitalism. As Samir Amin (1997) remarks, "the fact that the gurus, politicians and managers playing the current development game routinely blur this crucial distinction merely underlines their commitment to a latent capitalist design" (141). The danger of such rhetoric is that it masks the undemocratic and "unmodernizing" aspects of uneven and unequal development—or in the extreme case, de-development.

These projects should be scrutinized as development produced by and shaped in response to the larger process of global capitalism, and development embedded in the political economy of peace and state building. Thus they are part of the establishment of capitalist social relations in Palestine, which seeks to further subordinate the working class as a (sub)periphery in the global economy. This process of unequal development and the new spatial divisions of labor it creates permanently disadvantage "the majority of those citizens in comparison with the majority of citizens in wealthier countries from which foreign direct investments are initiated" (Calabrese 1995, 235–36). What results is that the condition of "peripheral" states is dictated in large part by the emergence of new local and national elites who use their affluence, their access to information and capital, and their mobility to dominate the majority of the population, who comprise a cheap, abundant (and, in the case of Palestinians, desperate) labor pool. Since 1993, the newly risen post-Oslo elite class, which has adopted capitalist values, as symbolized in the Internet development projects they manage and direct, has sought to integrate itself in the global capitalist system in at least two ways, through global capital accumulation and continued exploitation of the Palestinian working class.[8]

Reducing human beings to the status of the commodity of labor power is an integral part of the destructive dimension of capitalism and its accompanying form of modernity. Global polarization induced by capital accumulation means that the majority of human beings, usually in the "peripheries," have, in the words of Samir Amin (2003), "no prospect for satisfying the needs that modernity has promoted, and hence of enjoying even the degraded democracy practiced in the heartlands of the system. For most of humanity, capitalism is a hateful system, and the modernity accompanying it a tragic farce" (50). The "development" of the Palestinian Territories will not put an end to the polarization inherent in existing global capitalism. And, like Third World industrialization in general, it does "not reproduce social evolution in the image of the developed West" (Amin 1997, ix). In other words, Internet development projects will not result in "development."

The strategy of development in general, and of development based on the Internet in particular, produces its opposite: underdevelopment and impoverishment; exploitation and oppression; a growth in dependence, not independence. The society in question may no longer be dominated by classical colonialism. But this does not mean that "autonomy" is suddenly achieved or achievable. Rather the structure of dependency has changed, so that a society is dominated by global capitalism and relegated to the status of the periphery. The successful future for Palestinian workers and youth is thus to be realized in Internet skills, Microsoft Academies, and technology incubators, there to serve the interests of core countries and corporations, not local needs.

The choice for those in the periphery becomes one between a dynamic renegotiation of dependency—one that may allow Palestinians to accede to the production of *some* of the new technologies—or further marginalization from the world economy. What results for Palestinians is to become more and more subjected to types of economic integration that are coupled with greater social disintegration, which brings with it sociocultural "perversion" and political disarticulation. Moreover, it is naïve to assume that the creation of a market economy, were it really "allowed" in the Palestinian case, would benefit Palestinians politically, for "there is nothing inherently democratic about the formation of market economies. . . . In fact, 'a market economy is set in motion only under predemocratic conditions. In order to promote it, democratic rights must be held back in order to allow for a healthy dose of original accumulation'" (Claus Offe quoted in Calabrese 1995, 249). This logic also negates some of the promises made by Internet development agencies, that concomitant with economic growth, the Internet is an inherently democratizing agent, affording its users a public sphere—as if freedom and democracy in the cyber-realm can be translated into freedom and democracy in the political realm without larger structural changes.

The result of Internet development as part of capitalism's expansion and elite power is to subsume Palestinians into the global workforce as alienated, cheap labor. Economically, a country's position in the global hierarchy is defined by its capacity to compete in the world market. This competitiveness is a complex product of many economic, political, and social factors and cannot be understood as merely enabling a technological society or workforce. While Palestinians may produce an IT industry and create a technologically enabled workforce, this guarantees neither improved economic conditions, the creation of a more democratic and secular populace, nor a nation-state—sovereign or not. And, as the above discussion demonstrates, Internet development promises more repression than freedom.

THE IMPOTENCE OF CIVIL SOCIETY

The pervasiveness of neoliberal values has reached into the spaces that should be opposed to them. Internet development projects should be understood as exemplary of a larger trend (not only in the Palestinian Territories but globally and particularly in the "Third World") of foreign aid marginalizing indigenous civil society. Thus, they provide fodder for revisiting the concept of civil society and its relationship to state building.

The institutional base of a civil society has been defined as created by voluntary unions outside the realm and control of the state, in organizations such as churches, cultural associations, sports clubs, independent media, labor unions, and the like (Habermas 1989). Scholars argue that civil society can facilitate "Third World" countries' changes toward capitalist development while alleviating some of the painful economic and political pains that come with such change. If, conceptually at least, civil society is to be outside the influence and realm of the state as an alternative space, then empirically this is a problematic space within Palestinian society. First, the Palestinian "state" only has the working apparatus of a state without any of its benefits—sovereignty, protection of citizens, international recognition, control over borders or economic policies, and so on. For example, the political party Fateh, which could be considered a form of civic institution, attempted to restore its past legitimacy as a national liberation movement through the militarization of the Intifada and not through the incorporation and mobilization of Palestinian civil society (see Frisch 1998; Roy 2001; Brown 2003). Second, Palestinian civil society itself is in shambles—in great part due to the marginalization occurring because of funding patterns discussed below. Alternative institutions' civic work is shrinking every day; for example, women's movements and the grassroots institutions represented by the GUPCS, which have had a long history in the formation and maintenance of Palestinian civil society, are shriveling up (Robinson 1997; Brown 2003; Jamal 2004).

Since the Second Intifada, it is difficult to envision a process of reconstruction or reassertion, be it political, social, or economic. There is no governing institution in the Palestinian Territories that can protect its citizens or engage in meaningful public service in any form. Therefore, given the history of occupation and lack of a "state," many civic institutions in the Palestinian Territories have had to act in lieu of a national government (Robinson 1997; Frisch 1998; Brynen 2000; Roy 1996, 2001; Brown 2003). Civil society is said to exist where associations can determine or redirect the course of state policy, representing the space for possible and necessary social, political, and economic changes. But when national issues stand in the forefront, one has to take into account all the entities in civil society and all movements that promote a national agenda—which means including oppositional institutions and those not governed by Western funding (such as Hamas). Finally, because of the rise of foreign funding, oppositional groups such as Hamas and Islamic Jihad, have been economically marginalized by the West. And yet it is Hamas that has succeeded at creating a civil society, not the slew of Western-funded projects supposedly there to promote or strengthen civil society (albeit an American- or Western-style one, not one ruled by Islamic ideology).

Even though the concept of civil society itself is problematic, it can be conceived in a radically different manner. One could understand civil society as an intellectual space in which individuals through their diverse associations and organizations have the right to contribute to discussions about how to organize their society, deal with its problems, and ultimately define what kind of development is desired. Or, it might be the source of a regenerated public sphere, where communications might place the public interest on the agenda without suppressing pluralities and differences. Hence, civil society could be the source of new and constructive thinking about the "state" and "development," a source of critique of current development efforts. Conceived this way, Internet development projects are not establishing such a space. Rather, civil society is reified by the developers and NGOs as a needed component of a capitalist, "developed" society. According to this view then, civil society creates inequalities and exploitative relations that weaken or strengthen some groups at the expense of others. It becomes the space where the post-Oslo elites, such as the executives of Palestinian corporations and heads of development projects, exercise their social and economic power, turning it into an arena driven by the inequalities and exploitation generated by capitalism.

Western/Westernized NGOs posit themselves as taking over the role of civil society and central players in this arena, creating further conceptual and empirical problems, especially in the realm of Internet development. There is an explicit promise among Internet development projects that although the primary reason to pursue these projects is economic growth, other benefits will trickle down into the sociopolitical realms. Such a belief stems from the conceptualization of the Internet as a democratic public sphere, of technology as the great enabler of Palestinian political and economic freedom.

In the realm of Internet development in the territories, USAID is the largest player, and as such, an important organization to analyze. Its aid framework gives priority to countries according to two criteria, namely the possibility of achieving change and U.S. interests—the latter a shorthand euphemism for the promotion of a particular ideology and set of values. Aid is directed to those local civil society organizations that are in accord with the dominant U.S. vision of economic and political development (Howell and Pearce 2001), making it clear from the onset that the recipient's role is partially to benefit the U.S. USAID follows the model of forging "partnerships" with businesses and NGOs—pursuing the practical approach of the consensus triadic model of the state, market, and civil society, which has been at the center of mainstream development thinking since the early 1990s. Such a model assumes shared notions of the public good and a common vision between organizations such as USAID, the multinational corporations, the local NGOs, and the society in question. These partnerships cannot be neutral but are very much political, and they show how both the "state" and civil society serve as arenas in which the power of capital and concomitant hegemonic ideas are reproduced and circulated (see Meiskins Wood 1990), and simultaneously serve to marginalize local organizations such as Hamas.

Equally problematic, the role of external actors in promoting "development" becomes one of marginalizing grassroots movements and actors of civil society. Given the funding patterns and the creation of Internet development by foreign interests, this results in economically disempowering local

movements. New hierarchies emerge where grassroots and oppositional movements are no longer funded. New realities are formed where "development"
takes on an imitative aspect of the West. Thus, NGOs contribute to the status
quo of the Western mainstream discourse of development. Thus, they do not
engage with Palestinian society or respond to its needs. The reason why
Hamas has succeeded is in great part due to its focus on precisely those realms
where the PA and foreign aid organizations have not: actual local needs.

Moreover, the marginalization that results is problematic. First, it creates
animosity and tension between the grassroots movements and Westernize'¹
Palestinian NGOs (such as the Welfare Association) or Western NGOs (such
as the IYF), as well as between the latter and the society in question. Second,
the lack of collaboration present in the territories, due to political chaos, is
compounded by a competitive relationship between institutions vying for international funding. The logic of capitalism is manifested on the sectoral level
as well: even the "nonprofit" sector has to respond to market forces, where
the logic of competition becomes built in to funding patterns.

Looked at in this way, NGOs represent a Western "threat": agents of foreign political and economic interests with a mission to democratize, secular-
ize, and modernize "Palestine" on their own terms. Consequently, NGOs are
not necessarily democratic benevolent entities, but are attempts by the West
to control Palestinian state building. In this way, NGOs are no different than
other "colonial" attempts by the United States to control, civilize, reform, and
discipline Middle Eastern states. These organizations become an arm of a
Western colonizing project, as is the entire NGO-ization process in the Territories, where NGOs have a distinctly political function of being aligned with
the West (or the United States).⁹ Performing a kind of missionary function on
behalf of the West, NGOs are far from transcending politics, but are rather in
the midst of it, as part of the strategy to further cement global inequality.

With their capitalist definition of economic growth, Internet development
projects mark a new trend in the NGO-ization of the territories, as the pro-
tomarkets, or market-boosters, not just protostate actors. One of IT4Youth's
executive member's words are enlightening here. When asked specifically
about the project's role in civil society, he responded thus: "Of course our
project is an integral part of it [civil society] . . . because we are helping build
both a state and a market. We have neither in a complete form in Palestine, so
every one of our efforts in the NGO sector is to bolster our nation through our
economic strength." His statement exemplifies the "politics of civil society"
as a normative idea guiding action, reifying it as a natural and historically inevitable component of a capitalist economy. But the market is not a freely
formed association: participation is mandatory on the terms required by the
system. This notion of civil society, fixed in a neoliberal approach that celebrates capitalism as the only route to economic development, should concern
us, because it fails to account for the ability of the capitalist system to affect

the exercise of personal freedom as significantly as the unbridled exercise of state power.

It is helpful here to return to Gramsci (1971), who viewed civil society as an extension of the bourgeois state, as a sphere in which the ruling elites "struggle" for the establishment of cultural hegemony. The tripartite schema proposed by Gramsci and elaborated by Cohen and Arato (1992) distinguishes civil society from the market and from the state. In other words, civil society flourishes where free associations exist that are under the tutelage of neither the state nor the market, but where they can redirect state policy (Taylor 1995). Gramsci shifted civil society from the sphere of economic necessity to the sphere of social superstructure, away from its liberal eighteenth-century roots to a distinct and normative concept by the end of the twentieth century. The Gramscian perspective on civil society detaches it from the economy and the state, and recognizes it as the realm where consent could be manufactured and at the same time challenged. For Gramsci and others after him (Meiskins Wood 1990; Cohen and Arato 1992; Taylor 1995), civil society is valuable *precisely* because it is a level of defense against the type of power wielded by the state *and* the capitalist free market.

Civil society could then be the site on which the hegemony of capital is challenged and where dominant values are contested. As such civil society offers an agency for such contestation in the form of grassroots movements, social organizations, and certain types of NGOs such as GUPCS. Just as importantly, then, civil society as "agency" ought to preserve its autonomy not only from the state and from the market but also in terms of the right to put forward propositions about different kinds of development.

Modern or mainstream conceptions of civil society, as with its appropriation by Internet development projects, ignore Gramsci's conceptualization, which was "unambiguously intended as a weapon against capitalism, not an accommodation to it" (Meiskins Wood 1990, 63). Rather than act as a space of opposition against the power of the market, Internet development projects are explicitly attempting to help the market grow (whether specifically by building an IT industry in the Palestinian Territories, or generally by adopting a neoliberal approach to development), establishing structures that further support the market. Thus, in their model, civil society organizes hegemony by consent in support of the elites that profit most by the maintenance of the capitalist state. Just as other NGOs have historically had to act in lieu of a "state," IT4Youth, PICTI, and the Cisco Academies are acting in lieu of a market—or at the least in aid of the market. As such it becomes problematic to posit these new institutions as representing Palestinian civil society at the interstices of the state and the market, when they are more like a pseudoreplacement of the two. Hence, what Internet development epitomizes is not simply neutral development projects aimed at increasing Internet literacy, jump-starting an IT industry, and shrinking the digital divide on the road to peace, but a manifestation of the influences of global market forces over local Palestinian interests, with "development" as the means through which to do so.

CONCLUSION

The Palestinian experience in Internet development and the ensuing marginalization of civil society by Westernized and Western NGOs challenge the notion that market, state, and civil society are three autonomous spheres, and that civil society ought to emerge as a way of resolving the contradictions and tensions of capitalism, especially its atomizing, unequalizing, and exclusionary effects. The notion of society as made up of three separate entities—the state, the market, and civil society—needs to be further contested. The boundaries in the tripartite scheme are not clear-cut, undermining the acclaimed autonomy and separateness of civil society. To simply reduce civil society to the arena of "nonprofit" or Westernized NGOs weakens the political function of civil society as a critical eye on both the state and the market. The political success of Hamas in the Palestinian legislative elections of January 2006 demonstrates the strength of opposition to both the state (in the form of the Fateh-controlled PA) and the market (in pursuing its own domestic development projects).

Hamas has been a major contributor to the establishment of contemporary Palestinian civil society and ought not to be considered as a "degenerate" form of civil society because it has not followed the models or rules of the West. If anything, Hamas symbolizes how an oppositional organization, with no support from mainstream "development" groups, has played a significant role in state building; and now, with legitimate (i.e., democratically gained) political power, it can play a role in further state formation—the consequences of its shunning by the global community and whether it will continue to be shunned remain to be seen. Furthermore, the reactions by Western donor agencies and governments to reshuffle, withdraw, or block aid to Palestinians because of Hamas's success are a testament to how "development" is used for political purposes and influence by the West. The tensions that will certainly rise between Hamas and foreign funders will offer much to further debate and analysis that challenges mainstream notions of civil society and state building. Arguably the Palestinian case is not unique, but extreme, and serves as an example of what happens when the state, the market, and NGOs become subsumed by global capitalism, giving rise to an oppositional institution that will itself be eschewed by global politics and economics because it refuses to play by the rules.

The trends discussed throughout this chapter are of concern because of the precarious situation Palestinians find themselves in—lacking a state, an indigenous economic market, or a body that can fight for their interests and fend for their rights on a global scale. Society is at its most vulnerable when its constitutive elements are atomized, when associational life becomes dire or nearly impossible—as is the case in the Palestinian Territories, not only because of fragmentation due to Israeli policies, but also because of capitalism's production of difference and fragmentation (Harvey 2000), and the Internet's atomic associations (Tawil 2005). Without Hamas, Palestinians are left atomized, fragmented, differentiated, with no power to resist the ambush of Internet development, and no choice but to think that integrating into the global economy—even as the cheapest labor pool—is the only alternative left. These Internet development projects, which promise to integrate Palestinians into the global economy as subperipheries, serve the transnational elite interests of "digital capitalism." They have also served as a platform to address the disintegration and impotence of both the Palestinian "state" and Western notions of civil society in the face of globalization.

NOTES

1. Sara Roy (2001, 10) describes three kinds of closures: general closure refers to overall restrictions placed on the movement of labor, goods, and the factors of production between the West Bank and Gaza, and between them and Israel. Total closure is the complete banning of any movement, usually placed before the threat of or after an attack on Israeli soil. Internal closure restricts movement between Palestinian localities within the West Bank (and the Gaza Strip), which was facilitated by the 1995 Oslo II agreement, which turned the West Bank into a series of 227 separate cantons. Israel controls all of the areas in between, effectively turning Palestinian areas, most of which are no bigger than two square kilometers, into incongruous Bantustans. Also see Hass 2002.

2. Poverty rates have climbed, depending on calculations, from 20 percent in 1995 to over 50 percent by 2004 (PASSIA 2004; PCBS 2005; World Bank Group 2004a). Similarly unemployment has risen from 16 percent in 1995 to 36 percent by 2005 (World Bank Group 2004a; PCBS 2005). This has resulted in almost half of Palestinian families living on less than $2.50 a day, with a quarter of the families living on less than a dollar a day (World Bank Group 2004a; 2004b). In that time span GDP per capita also dropped from $150 in 1995 to $650 by 2005 (PASSIA 2004; PCBS 2005).

3. The Welfare Association has become the premier Palestinian funding agency/NGO. A "Westernized" agency, both in terms of its professionalization and its ideological belief in neoliberal values, the Welfare Association is a Swiss-based, private, nonprofit foundation established in 1983 by a group of Palestinian diaspora leaders, joined by leading Palestinian and Arab philanthropists, to build a $100 million endowment to support Palestinian development in the territories. The WA draws on Palestinians in the diaspora and other Arabs to contribute their intellectual and financial resources toward development in the territories. The WA is the largest Palestinian NGO in terms of budget, employees, presence, and number of projects. By 2000 it emerged as a leading Palestinian development organization (by which time it had disbursed approximately $100 million).

4. The International Youth Foundation (IYF) runs programs in sixty countries with the aim of improving the conditions and prospects of young people through the networking of companies, foundations, and civil society organizations to "scale up" existing programs in education

and technology. IYF's programs provide support and services in such areas as vocational training, health education, recreation, cultural tolerance, environmental awareness, and the development of leadership, conflict resolution, and decision-making skills. Most of the IYF's funding
and the majority of its projects are tailored to the needs of the project's corporate partners, creating a "branded program that matches a company's giving interests and core business needs"
(See www.ifynet.org).

5. For a critical analysis of Bangalore as an IT center and the complex political and social
consequences, see Nair 2005. Bangalore is examined also in chapter 14 of this volume.

6. PITA, the Palestine IT Association of Companies, is a member-based organization that
supports local IT companies, advocates business-enabling policies to the PA, attempts to locally
and globally promote Palestinian IT firms, and assists in human resources for IT firms. PalTel,
a public shareholding company in which the PA has a 10 percent stake, became the Palestinian
telecommunications national provider in 1997. At the time of writing PalTel was the sole non-
cellular telecommunications provider in the territories, as well as one of the largest and finan-
cially most successful Palestinian firms of the 1990s and 2000s. It is noteworthy to note that
PalTel's founders and largest shareholders are also the founders/shareholders of Palestine's
other successful large corporations and represent the largest notable (i.e., elite) family in the territories.

7. The Palestinian role would be played not by the PA this time, but by one of the largest local corporations, PADICO, founded and owned by the same family that runs PalTel, the Palestinian telecommunications firm.

8. The owners of PalTel and PADICO serve as an example of the rise of post-Oslo elites in
Palestinian society, who have relied on strategies of continuous cheap local labor and capital accumulation on a global scale. For example, between 2000 and 2005, the two most successful
companies on the Palestine Stock Exchange have been PalTel and PADICO, whose share price
has risen more than 400 percent. In late 2005, PalTel shares were also traded on the larger and
more accessible Dubai stock exchange.

9. As the reaction by the United States to stop aid funding in response to Hamas winning the
January 2006 elections shows, aid is also used as a political tool in the reverse manner, not just
in disbursing it, but in preventing it.

14

Labor In or As Civil Society? Workers and Subaltern Publics in India's Information Society

Paula Chakravartty

The relationship between class formation and political transformation has been at the heart of Marxist political economic analysis and debate since the publication of the Eighteenth Brumaire and Marx's writings on the distinction between a class in and for itself. Marx, as polemic critic of the liberal concept of civil society and nationalism, was dismissive of civil society as nothing more than the organized expression of self-interest and appeals of the bourgeois liberal nation-state as constituting the elevation of particular interests over the general.[1] In the twenty-first century, it is surely not enough to debate whether workers are engaging in economism as part of a privileged labor aristocracy, but the relationship of organized as well as unorganized labor to civil society in the emancipatory sense needs further examination. In this chapter, I examine the complex relationship between the state and the stratified categories of both workers and civil society in India's deeply uneven information society.

Critical scholars in media and information studies have reclaimed and reinterpreted Marxist and later more historically nuanced Gramscian propositions about organized labor in relation to civil society and nationalism, particularly in the Eastern European context (Splichal et al. 1994; Sparks 2005). If this work draws distinctions between liberal, pluralist, and Marxist class-based understandings of civil society, a parallel literature takes into account discussions about the role of technologies—community radio, mobile media, and the rise of the Internet—in consolidating or challenging neoliberal economic integration from "below" alongside or at the center of social movements, both old and new. These discussions about transnational networks of civil society actors draw our attention to the new stakes of political struggle around "material and immaterial labor" (Dyer-Witheford 1999), and new forms of participatory and "tactical" movements that blur divisions between labor and "community" struggles (Downing 2001; Lovink and Schneider 2004; Rodríguez 2001). Within the field of communication and media studies, the relative paucity of research on labor and work has led to a renewed urgency for research in these areas, especially in the context of expanding global integration of information and culture-related industries (Mosco and McKercher 2006; Maxwell and Miller 2005)

In considering the possibilities for political transformation of the global information economy, scholars of labor and class more broadly, and of workers and trade union movements more specifically, have had to engage with the expansive literature on global civil society. Despite the range of political and theoretical variation in these important works, one central assumption that runs across much of the analysis has to do with the evaluation of the emancipatory potential of workers in the "new" economy—whether understood as digital capitalism (Mosco 2004; D. Schiller 1999), a variation of post-Fordism (Dyer-Witheford 1999; Miller et al. 2005), or as network society (Castells 1996). Associated with each of these formulations are distinct arguments about how we make sense of the new international division of labor and its articulation in terms of transnational collective identity in reproducing or resisting unequal relations between transnational capital and labor.

Marxists have long questioned the separateness of civil society from the influence of private capital. However, there remain in current discussions about information and communication workers in civil society less nuanced reflections on the specificities of the stratification of civil society formations, including in the framing of organized workers as civil society.[2] Given the relatively privileged symbolic and economic position of "knowledge" workers within uneven information economies, it becomes important to recognize the ways in which workers are excluded from gaining access to formal employment—based on considerations of nationality, gender, caste/race, and ethnicity, among other categories. It would not be too much of a generalization to argue that in the "developing world" access to employment in the formal economy, especially in high-tech sectors like information technology (IT) is restricted largely to the already privileged sectors of any given society. Recognizing these deep structural inequalities, scholars of technology and globalization differing in political perspective from Castells (1996, 2000) to Dyer-Witheford (2004) have argued that those too marginalized from the global economy to be worth exploiting from the perspective of capital—the "immiserated" masses—are in a sense external to the logic of change that shapes the information economy or network society.

Although India, where some 40 percent of the nation's billion-plus citizens continue to live in conditions of extreme poverty, certainly appears to fit this characterization, it is sub-Saharan Africa that is seen as the "black hole of the network society" (Castells 2000). In Dyer-Witheford's (2004) Agambem-inflected reading,

> The sovereign power of the market decrees that most of the inhabitants of sub-Saharan Africa are excluded from anything that the liberal citizenry would consider as a properly human existence, becoming the "homo saucer" of human capital. (27)

The polemic pessimism of such analyses exposes a Eurocentric vantage point, and as James Ferguson (2006) in his fierce retort of "Afro-pessimism" points out, this same logic then tends to romanticize an authentic, local grass-roots civil society in the face of globalizing forces from "above." The problem with such stark characterizations has to do with the rigid separation of modern liberal citizenry from the vast (and perhaps unknowable) masses of the poor, who are seen as outside of modern forms of claims making, whether as aspiring consumers or as citizens making demands of the state.

In some sense, these arguments echo similarly stark distinctions between "political" and "civil society" as formulated by Partha Chatterjee (2004). Chatterjee contends that we need to make a distinction between the bureaucratized version of civil society, which in the Indian context is largely captured by urban middle-class citizens who see themselves as rights-bearing individuals, and the "denizens" of "political society," whose relationship to the state is largely defined through illegal practices. Political society encompasses social movements that are often at odds with the narrow development agendas found in civil society in more recognizably modern institutional forms of associational life, including trade unions, NGOs, and civic politics. For Chatterjee, claims made by those in political society—which might mean informal migrant workers squatting on public land or residents of slums in legal battles over access to electricity or telecommunications—are necessarily outside of the legal domain.

Chatterjee's intervention is useful in considering the limits of an idealized model of associational life in the context of neoliberal "development," and resonates with the ways in which middle-class NGOs have to a large extent captured the space of civil society as discussed earlier in this volume by Aginam and Tawil Souri. However, if we accept that much of what we recognize as civil society has been captured by a minority of middle-class interests, recent cross-national empirical research on the political practices of poor urban citizens in Brazil, India, and Mexico suggests that electoral or party politics is "generally, oriented toward the denizens of political society, rather than the middle class citizens of civil society" (Harriss 2006, 454; Harriss 2005). I have argued elsewhere (Chakravartty 2001, 2004), that the domain of politics and the politicization of the technocratic neoliberal reform in India are recognized by policy elites as an obstacle to the nation's potential to "leapfrog" development. As we will see in subsequent sections, in the Indian context, this has meant the consistent rejection of a "high-tech" neoliberal development agenda at both the national and regional levels.

What we can take from Chatterjee's formulation then is the argument that the postcolonial state is embedded in differentiated relationships with multiple publics on distinct terms. Today, this includes a highly differentiated but nevertheless minority of workers in the formal urban economy and a much larger majority of workers whose formal class position is more difficult to categorize and who I refer to here as subaltern publics. A stark picture of the world of work between the information haves and have-nots that fails to take the dynamic and variegated context into account invariably reproduces assumptions about the antithetical interests between those employed by formal and informal labor markets, long a topic of debate in development and policy circles.[3]

In sub-Saharan Africa, as well as in many parts of India where poverty is as acute, this assumed dichotomy of experience, between the small minority of workers in the modern formal urban sectors and the majority of the working poor, simply fails to hold up to extensive empirical scrutiny (Agarwala 2006).[4] Although the experiences of the latter heterogenous group are no doubt extremely varied (across but also within national contexts), aspirations to the benefits of modern society are central to political struggles in virtually all emerging "information societies." Thus if critical studies of cultural globalization have established the limits of linear temporal narratives of development, we must also pay attention to what Ferguson has compellingly argued is an equally important aspirational dimension of modernity "to rise in the world, in economic and political terms." In India this has meant "specific aspirations to such primary "modern" goods as improved housing, health care and education" (Ferguson, 2006, 32), as well as the aspiration for work in the modern "knowledge" or information society.

In the last two decades, the mobility and precariousness of work and workers within and across national borders have become central to transnational debates about the merits and costs of global integration. In Northern nations, particularly the United States, concerns about losses in traditional manufacturing sectors have been somewhat displaced by public debates about the potential and threats associated with immigration and the outsourcing of service-related work, including "high-skilled" white-collar jobs in areas like information technology. But in many parts of the "developing" world, most obviously in India, access to modern employment opportunities in the IT and IT-related industries carries significant symbolic power for both advocates and critics of high-tech modernization strategies.

My argument in the subsequent sections is that current debates about IT or "knowledge" workers and their relationship to civil society have to take into account new modes of exclusion and new claims for citizenship that have parallels across "emerging" economies spanning Brazil, China, and South Africa, to name the most obvious examples. If we look closely at the political economic debates over high-tech modernization in the Indian context, we see contests and claims for cultural competence allowing entry into the modern workforce that represent at least partially distinct issues at stake from the familiar (to Western audiences) debate about the costs and benefits of "outsourcing" of white-collar work from nations like the United States to those like India and the weakening of the power of organized labor in relation to transnational capital. The experiences of the U.S. information society cast a long shadow in shaping our analyses of global integration, given the historical dominance of the United States' IT industry and the significance of Silicon Valley models of economic and technological development. Given the relative marginalization of workers as political subjects in the U.S. scenario, I suggest this makes it an especially poor case on which to base global assumptions about the role of workers in contemporary debates about civil society.[5] In the Indian context, I examine the distinct claims made by workers as part of a larger subaltern public in political society versus those made by formally employed IT workers in civil society. In the next section, I turn first to elaborate my theoretical discussion about labor in civil society in the postcolonial context, before examining the specificities of the politics of high-tech work in India.

THE LABOR–CIVIL SOCIETY NEXUS AND THE POSTCOLONIAL STATE

With a few piece-meal exceptions, China is a gaping hole in the global communications network that links the multitude of trade Unions and Social Movements unions, NGOs, and movement activists who are forging cross-border cooperation on labor and environmental standards. . . . From the perspective of the movement for alternative globalization, China is still closed for business. (Ross 2006, 263)

Andrew Ross suggests that it makes little sense to theorize the possibilities of workers challenging the terms of neoliberal globalization without taking the case of the Chinese global workforce into account. The visible absence of Chinese civil society in transnational arenas of global governance can be seen as particular to its positioning outside of liberal democratic institutions of governance, as elaborated by Zhao in this volume. As she argues (Zhao and Duffy, 2007), the massive spontaneous protests and everyday mobilization by workers in globalized China remain largely outside of discussions of the transformative potential for a "global civil society." When it comes to discussions specific to the global information society, for example within the context of the World Summit on the Information Society (WSIS) (held between 2003 and 2005), questions of the role of labor and work are virtually absent within what constitutes official global civil society (Chakravartty 2007; Chakravartty and Sarikakis 2006).

Examining the African context, Aginam in this volume offers a compelling critique of the idealized liberal concept of civil society as a "neutral" political space of volunteer associational life, embodied in the form of the NGO as representative of the public interest. The limitations of this model of civil society are as apparent in neoliberal Africa, where most societies are seen as subject to "weak" or "predatory" states, as they are in the politically authoritarian Chinese context. Most relevant for my arguments here are the problematic assumptions in debates about the emancipatory potential of global civil society that take for granted a "boundedness" of civil society as a separate sphere from the state (Mamdani 1996) and what James Ferguson (2006) has called the "vertical topography of power" that positions the state on top versus civil society below. In this section, I argue that these conceptual limitations fail to account for the labor–civil society nexus in relation to the workings of the postcolonial state. In addition, I argue that the inability of the state in both the previous developmentalist and the current neoliberal era produced specific forms of "claims making" from organized workers, as well as the vast majority of marginalized publics engaged in daily modes of popular struggle, often, but not always, around access to the fruits of the modern state—education, healthcare, housing, land, and jobs (Cooper 2005, 234–35; Ferguson 1996; Harriss-White 2002; Harriss 2006).

The distinct relationship between the postcolonial state, organized labor, and social movements, encompassing what historians have identified as "subaltern publics," has challenged Eurocentric narratives of working-class identity, nationalism, and social reform (Chakrabarty 2000a; Cooper 2005). For our purposes, it is useful to consider how historians have located the vast majority of nonformal workers who make up subaltern publics in postcolonial societies. Amin and Van der Linden (1997) have argued that the "intermediary forms of wage labor"—the urban unemployed, the underemployed, the migrants who move between city and village—are not outside of the "true working class," but are in fact constitutive of a "worldwide segmentation of the labor force." In the post–Cold War context they contend that

> in this labor force, some workers (mostly in the core countries) are relatively free, well paid and secure, while other workers especially along the periphery, are less free, poorly paid and "floating." The boundaries between the two segments are vague and constantly shifting. (4–5)

In India, these subaltern publics, also referred to as the "working poor" or the "informal working class," possess the least cultural capital and "come disproportionately from the historically lower castes . . . and are generally poorer, not necessarily in terms of income but certainly of vulnerability" (Harriss 2006, 447).

The relationship between the postcolonial nation state and the "floating" or "semi-proletarianized" subaltern subjects has historically been ambivalent at best and violent and punitive at worst (Mahmood 1996). In contrast, the relationship between the postcolonial state and organized labor has a more cooperative if politically contested history, which began to change its course drastically as governments implemented aggressive liberalization policies beginning in the 1980s. This is essentially the basis for arguments about social movement unionism, when the state's retrenchment from corporatist or populist models inadvertently forced trade unions in strategic sectors, particularly in the South, to seek allies with social movements more widely (Waterman and Wills 2002). Ronaldo Munck (2004) has argued that while the neoliberal variant of capitalism can "unmake or de-proletarinise vast swaths of the global working class," especially in the North, the expansion of wage labor associated with export-led development has led to novel attempts to link economic and political struggles between organized labor and the "floating" workers, or working poor, described above. The possibilities for progressive alliances are documented in research on social movement unionism (Munck 2002) as well as in feminist interventions on labor and globalization (Kabeer 2002; Sassen 1999). These works recognize and caution, the relationship between trade union movements and the semiproletarianized "floating" classes, young migrant women workers, and all those who remain on the margins of organized labor, continues to be ambivalent. As such, in looking at the "more hopeful" Latin American context, or at the perhaps less inspiring African or South Asian labor–civil society landscape, it seems crucial to question the "taken-for-granted spatial mapping" of workers in the information economy as located in an "authentic" civil society from below challenging state power and "imperial capitalism" from above (Fergusson 2006, 106–9).

To illustrate my argument, and situate my analysis specifically in the Indian context, I turn to labor anthropologist Jan Breman's (1996) rich ethnographic study of what he terms "footless laborers." These are landless agrarian workers—mostly men but also women—seeking employment as temporary or casual workers in urban Gujarat during India's first phase of economic liberalization (1986–1994). Breman, like most labor scholars of India, argues that the trade union leadership has played an ambivalent role in relation to these workers, largely absent from organizing the growing casualized workforce across all sectors of the economy. He argues that the footless laborers occupy "zones of employment" that are "fluid and merge into one another" (247), between what both the World Bank and critical scholarship posit as the "formal" and "informal economy." Breman recognizes that the obstacles for workers like these to gain entry to formal work (much less to formal work in the IT industry discussed below) are virtually nonexistent. However, his study of the working poor or what Harriss (2006) calls the "informal working class" is premised on the fact that by the time of India's first phase of global integration in the mid-1980s, the increased casualization of work at the bottom of the Indian economy was "accompanied by increased labor mobility"—meaning migration from village to city, and also across states—with former agrarian workers escaping often much harsher conditions of economic and social inequality (10).

In his careful assessment of the location of these workers in relation to the state and economic reforms, Breman argues that along with their new geographic mobility, "the ideology of inequality, presumably the hallmark of Hindu civilization," has, in his thirty years of research in Gujarat, "lost social legitimacy" among these workers. In other words, these forms of "existential inequalities," associated with the denial of the recognition of human beings as individuals through slavery, patriarchy, religious difference, and in India, through caste (Therborn 2006), were beginning to lose social legitimacy among these more mobile but vulnerable workers. This is an important finding, especially given the concurrent rise of right-wing Hindu nationalist electoral politics both in the national arena and in the the state of Gujarat. Breman finds that "new claims for dignity" based on the assertion of caste, communal, regional, and linguistic identity inflect both spontaneous and organized efforts in areas ranging from housing, education, and access to employment. Breman describes the potential for communal violence in this context given the neoliberal mode of governance through a form of political apartheid, the distancing and exclusion of those in informal sector serving as a "no-go zone" for policy makers (1996, 263).

As the horrific Gujarat genocide against Muslim minority communities in February of 2002 would reveal, Breman's study was prescient in its chilling prediction about the potential for explosive communal violence, given the segregation of disenfranchised migrant working poor in a self-consciously globalizing region of India. These examples of the resurgence of ethnonationalism and communal violence within civil society should not then be seen as a "return" to or even a renewal of primordial identities, and a rejection of modern modes of claims making, since the claims to the benefits of modern market society were systematically left ignored by the state at the regional and national levels.

The violence that exploded in Gujarat has not reoccurred in urban India on a comparable scale since the events of 2002, and in 2004, the Hindu nationalist Bharatiya Janata Party (BJP) lost to a Congress-led center-left coalition, heralding a new era of globalization that is more responsive to questions of social inequity. As I noted in the introduction, more recent studies of political transformations in India have shown that it is precisely this category of footless laborers and migrant workers—the subaltern publics whom Chatterjee

(2004) characterizes as the "denizens" of political society—who engage in political activity, whether simply through the act of voting or in having "mediated" or ("brokered") and direct relationships to the state (Harriss 2006, 452). Paralleling changes in political discourse in China (Zhao, forthcoming) and much of the "developing" world in the "post–Washington Consensus" era, Indian national and regional political leaders promise policy interventions in key social development areas, including education and employment. In the next section, I turn to the emerging Indian information society, in order to locate workers both in and as civil society, in light of the renewed commitment by the nation-state to meet the claims of those left behind by uneven globalization.

CASTE, CLASS, AND HIGH-TECH MODERNITY

In this section, I provide a very broad overview of the complex history of organized and informal labor and their relationship to the postcolonial state.[6] As I suggested above, the neoliberal transformation of the state in much of the South (including India) intensified the processes of casualization and informalization, which already existed under state-led forms of economic development in India. The marginal location of the "floating" working classes in relation to the organized sectors of the workforce existed therefore prior to the World Bank–inspired reforms in India in 1991. But as Breman and others have argued, the pervasiveness of the casualization of work coincided with the geographic mobility of this intermediate category of workers, and the waning of the social legitimacy of "traditional" forms of inequality like caste also saw the rise of Hindu nationalism (Deshpande 2003). It is important to highlight the importance of political mobilization and middle-class backlash around caste-based access to higher education, employment, and political representation as embedded in the Indian constitution and supported through the judiciary. While the constitution mandates that the state take "special measures for the social advancement of the historically oppressed groups at the bottom of traditional India's case society," it was not until the 1990s that caste-based political parties like the Bahujan Samaj Party (BSP) in Uttar Pradesh, and a social movement around Dalit (untouchable) rights, became important regional and national players pushing to expand reservation-based access to higher education, political office, and both public and private sector employment.[7]

Keeping this set of important changes in mind, we turn to the location of workers in civil society as it relates to the more rarefied world of India's national information society. In order to better understand the struggles around work, we move our discussion from the industrial belt in Gujarat to the first and most famous high-tech center in India: Bangalore. In this section, I trace how claims for redistribution through inclusion—in the enormous economic gains of the jarringly unequal information societies in urban centers—are articulated around access to education and employment on the one hand, and around wages and work conditions in the IT and IT-enabled sectors on the other hand.[8] Demands for greater access to educational and employment opportunities in the Indian context, as evident in current debates over reservation policy in higher education and access to jobs in the private sector, are significant because the claims being made are ostensibly not for a marginalized minority, but rather for an "underprivileged" majority that includes Dalit ("untouchable" castes identified as Scheduled Castes) and Adivasi (indigenous communities identified as Scheduled Tribes) as well as the larger group that falls under the category of "Other Backward Classes" (OBC): "about 70 per cent of the Indian population may come under the rubric of the state's special treatment provisions in keeping with the constitutional mandate" (Vij 2006).

Regional governments in "cybersavvy" states like Andhra Pradesh and Karnataka as well as successive national governments in power since the 1990s have deployed IT-based development growth rates as well as stunning projections for future employment as marketing tools promising rapid economic and social transformation. The promise of transformative growth based on job projections in the tens of millions is fundamental for the IT and IT-enabled services (including call centers or business process outsourcing centers, or BPOs) that have throughout the 1990s employed a tiny fraction of the overall working population, even if we take only urban India into account. Throughout the last decade, much of the English-language media in the country has been only too eager to embrace what Vincent Mosco (2006) has described as the mythic nature of the hype around the potential of the "new" economy. In the Indian case, as I have argued before (2001, 2004), the self-consciously meritocratic IT industry represents an egalitarian vision of modernization overturning previous premodern inequalities and hierarchies in terms of access to employment, education, and welfare. The IT industry, through a variety of trade and industry associations; its close relationship with the news media; and partnerships with governance initiatives at local, regional, and national levels, juxtaposes a vision of a merit-based modernization agenda against the failed model of development associated with the bureaucracy-raj.

In this environment, the strategically placed National Association of Software and Service Companies (NASSCOM) became the legitimate national voice in reporting the gains and projected gains in terms of employment in the larger IT sector, consistently projecting wildly optimistic numbers while serving as the national industry lobby group for the IT sector. The most current figures show approximately 1.5 million workers in both IT and ITES services, with the most rapid expansion in employment being in the ITES sector and growth projected to reach five million directly employed in the industry by 2012.[9] Although there is little doubt that the IT-based industry's rapid expansion has generated impressive export revenue in the last decade, gains in overall employment and future employment are less firmly accepted by critics, in no small part due to the fact that NASSCOM provides the only nationally available data on IT-based employment.

Labor organizations and critical researchers alike have contested NASSCOM's employment projections and assessment.[10] If India's comparative advantage in the global IT-based industry stems from its relatively lower-paid, English-speaking skilled workforce, then in addition to statistics about employment, higher education becomes a key variable in predicting these optimistic rates of sustained growth. If we keep in mind the fact that half of India's citizens are nonliterate (61 percent of women), this only slightly clouds the picture for NASSCOM projections about how the nation produces an estimated one million university graduates per year, in addition to over 500,000 technically trained and other engineering graduates. As Upadhya and Vasavi have pointed out, industry-commissioned studies on India's manpower projections show that only some 10–25 percent of all graduates are qualified to work in the IT-based industry (2006, 26). NASSCOM also claims that the "knowledge professionals" in the IT-based sectors are supplemented by an estimated three million workers who are indirectly employed through the sector: "Indirect employment includes expenditure on vendors including telecom, power, construction, facility management, IT, transportation, catering and other services. Induced employment is driven by consumption expenditures of employees on food, clothing utilities, recreation, health and other services" (NASSCOM 2006, 2).

Questioning NASSCOM's projections about future employment opportunities raises one of the central political concerns that continue to haunt the overall high-tech development mandate: the skewed redistributional gains and growing rates of inequality associated with the rapid expansion of the transnational IT industry. Nowhere in India have these political economic as well as spatial differences played out as sharply as in the case of Bangalore. In her carefully documented study of the history of the city's rise to its status as high-tech metropolis, Janaki Nair (2005) argues that the Nehruvian state's attempts at planned development in the 1950s and 1960s both created jobs and housing for the industrial working class and led to a parallel unplanned expansion of slums and work in the informal sector. Bangalore is described in this period as the "public sector city par excellence" (81), serving as the base for telephone manufacturing and domestic electronics manufacturing on one hand while becoming an increasingly important site of national scientific research on the other hand. While the public sector industries provided jobs to hundreds of thousands of workers in the formal economy, Nair reinforces the fact that parallel informal sectors thrived alongside, over the decades, accounting for anywhere between 50 to 70 percent of the city's total workforce.

By the mid-1990s, when the success of the IT sector in Bangalore began to register in the United States and East Asia, one-fifth of the city's population lived in slums and some 70 percent of its labor force was engaged in the informal economy (Nair 2005). The relationship between this floating labor force and the formal sectors of the economy, including the prized IT economy, is dynamic in the modes of engagement suggested above by Breman. If we are to locate the relationship between labor and civil society in Bangalore since the 1990s, we must then take into account the role of the vast majority of its working citizens and their claims for access to the gains of the export-oriented IT economy.

We can situate the local context of Bangalore in the major shift in overall national development strategy from a largely state-led development model toward privatization and liberalization of the overall economy starting in earnest in 1991, resulting largely from a balance of payments crisis and the intervention of the World Bank and IMF. The origins of India's relative early lead in the area of information technology can be traced back to the 1984 Rajiv Gandhi Congress government's initial efforts at economic reforms and the deregulation of the domestic computer industry (Chakravartty 2004). The importance of the informal economy has only grown, as private sector investment has outstripped the state-led development model (Benjamin 2000). Bangalore was targeted by the national government in the mid-1980s as the first of multiple high-tech development zones, and has evolved to become the transnational symbol of successful globalized capital and labor flows.

The financial and symbolic success of transnational Indian entrepreneurs based in Silicon Valley and beyond, as well as the growing prominence of key domestically based transnational IT firms like WIPRO and Infosys, among others, transformed the role of the private sector in entering, in many cases directly shaping discussions about both regional and national development (Chandrashekar 2000; Upadhya 2004). As the national global IT center of the twenty-first century, Bangalore boasted new institutional alliances toward urban and regional governance efforts, whereby a newly appointed IT ministry, along with urban planners and civic organizations, sought to "depoliticize" development priorities, often at the direct expense of the urban poor and marginalized.[11] For the purposes of my argument, I would draw attention to how transformations in governance reformulated the specific relationships between corporate actors, the state, and a newly invigorated category of "civil society."

Bangalore would become then a new model of technocratic modernization for similar regional initiatives across India to "leapfrog" development by luring IT and biotech investment and research. As Soek-Fang Sim's chapter in this volume suggests, the "model" of Bangalore was itself designed with the hopes of creating a "Singapore of South Asia." There has been a substantial amount of research documenting the growing spatial inequalities or "splintered urbanism" that characterizes global Bangalore, from privatized access to infrastructure to the expansion of gated communities and shopping malls.[12] Beginning in the mid-1980s, city and state officials have increasingly made it more difficult for the urban poor and workers to demonstrate and occupy public spaces. Beyond the curtailing of overt political acts, Nair (2005) argues that middle-class municipal reform movements have deployed aesthetic rationales to control "a range of plebian practices" seen as disruptive to public life, from the display of wall posters and cinema culture to the zoning away of slums and chaotic street traffic.

Following the insights of Chatterjee's distinction of "political society," Nair points to the gulf that separates the "social municipalism" of the new consuming middle-class citizen focusing on "quality of life" concerns—saving a local park or keeping the neighborhood clean—from wider political struggles. These forms of middle-class "activism" are seen increasingly by social scientists in India today as a definitive feature of elite middle-class identity and distinction in urban India, clearly demarcated from the lumpen "dirty" world of mass mobilization and electoral politics (Deshpande 2003; Fernandes 2006; Fernandes and Heller 2006; Harriss 2006). In Bangalore, struggles over land, housing, and education and employment opportunities have been structured by incidents of communal violence as well as linguistic and caste-based politics. In a city of migrants—from the neighboring states of Tamil Nadu and Kerala and well beyond—local or Kannada regional identity has mobilized both spontaneous demonstrations and social protest over the access to the benefits of Bangalore's "shining" IT industry. In this way, the spatial regulation of distinct zones of the city's globalized enclaves led to popular protest by the communities of semiproletarianized workers described in the previous section. As in the case of the footless workers in Gujarat, the subaltern publics in Bangalore did not accept their position in established social hierarchies. However, as ethnographic research on the subaltern publics in globalizing India has shown (Hansen 2001), the outcome of these struggles based on caste alliances, linguistic nationalism, or ethnic and religious communal identities can fall outside of the progressive versus reactionary spectrum that might be suggested by emancipatory definitions of civil society from below.

In terms of electoral politics, both regionally (in the Southern States of Karntaka and Andhra Pradesh) and at the national level, mass popular opposition to the narrow gains of newly globalized India—represented in no small part by the urban IT-based economy and society—led to a series of unexpected losses for politicians and parties too closely associated with this new development mandate, when the Hindu chauvinist BJP coalition was ousted from national power in 2004. The new centrist coalition government led by the former architect of liberalization, Prime Minister Manmohan Singh, announced a series of proposed reforms to directly address the growing inequalities in India, including those outlined in the its National Common Minimum Program and the setting up of a "high-level advisory body" to the prime minister under the title of the National Knowledge Commission,[13] with the daunting task of "transforming India into a knowledge society." The reforms announced as a result of these programs include the very controversial measure of expanding caste-based reservation of seats in both vocational educational and the elite higher educational institutions, including the IITs (Indian Institutes of Technology); extending caste-based reservation to the private sector; and implementing the historic National Rural Employment Guarantee Act, meant to address the enormous needs in livelihood generation in rural India, which is still home to over 60 percent of India's citizens.[14]

Unlike the period between 1991 and 2004, which witnessed the unrestrained liberalization of the IT-based sector in particular, with states and cities competing for high-tech tapes down free trade zones and boasting tax holidays and loosened labor laws, the period since 2004 has seen both state and corporate actors engaged in broader development concerns more proactively. This helps explain the national context for the growing number of public-private partnerships (PPPs) promoting the benefits of IT for rural development in a variety of areas from e-governance to health and education. Many prominent CEOs of Indian IT giants, like Azim Premji from WIPRO, have committed foundation funding to basic primary education through partnerships with state governments, NGOs, and "educational entrepreneurs."[15]

What should be apparent from the previous discussion is that jobs in the modern IT sector are desirable because of their higher relative salary, as well as the symbolic power associated with these jobs and how they have redefined what it means to be part of the Indian globalized middle class (Deshpande 2003; Fernandes 2006).[16] Although the salaries of software professionals in India are estimated to be anywhere between one-third and one-fifth of those in the United States (Chandrashekar 2005), Indian IT professionals are likely to emphasize the vast difference in income, their ease of access to foreign travel, and their much higher consumption power, relative to their parents' generation (Chakravartty 2005). The temporal distinction between generations places these workers in a self-consciously transnational workforce with new forms of cultural capital and modes of access and competence in global consumer society, including critiques of the "excesses" of globalized culture in relation to "traditional" values of gender norms, family, and community.

As an extensive study by Upadhya and Vasavi (2006) of work conditions and work culture in the export-oriented IT-based industry in Bangalore reveals, the relative homogeneity of the IT-based workforce contradicts the industry's claim to employ a much broader cross-section of Indian society (43). In examining the recruitment practices of human resource managers as well as interviewing workers, the researchers of this study found that unintentional processes of exclusion tend to "weed out those who lack the requisite cultural capital, such as communication and social skills" (184). This only reinforces the filtering that goes on as companies target graduates from a small number of colleges, which are much more likely to draw students from privileged metropolitan households.

Whereas it might be expected that the "higher-skilled" jobs in the IT sector are likely to reproduce caste inequality, it is equally true that extant empirical studies on the caste composition of "lower-skilled" call center workers also show a "deep division" between the higher castes and historically marginalized OBC, Dalit, and Adivasi communities.[17] This fact supports the finding across various studies that IT-enabled workers in call centers, medical transcription services, and other related areas are much more educated in India as compared to their "developed"-country counterparts. In addition, the vast majority of these workers have studied in English-medium schools— which itself is a marker of privilege and private education in most cases. For example, a "typical" call center employee in the United States or medical transcription worker in the UK is likely to have 1.5 years of college and high school or at most an undergraduate degree respectively. In India, a comparable worker in a call center is likely to have a minimum of five years of college education, or a postgraduate degree in the case of medical transcription services (CWA 2006, 51).

While it is beyond the scope of this chapter to go into any meaningful detail on working conditions, the Indian IT industry, like its counterparts in Silicon Valley and beyond, promotes self-regulation, firmly opposing the introduction of labor laws and legislation specific to the industry. I will note that the qualitative research on the changing subjectivity of the workforce and the modes of organizational control of the workplace suggests long work hours and high rates of attrition and stress, the latter phenomena especially common in the second-tier BPO sector that depends on a younger and more feminized workforce (Ramesh 2004). Upadhya and Vasavi (2006) have argued that despite differences in education, status, and salary between the IT and ITES sectors, employers in both rely heavily on cultural forms of control, including the promotion of "fun at work" and "empowerment" and instilling the normative values of entrepreneurial individualism (163). The self-disciplining modes of control are of course global management practices, and workers in the North would also be familiar with some of the central concerns in the IT sector, including the use of contract labor and the lack of job security. Questions of sexual harassment of women workers (an issue of growing importance in the BPO sector) and the practice of working long hours (especially in the IT industry) are perhaps more distinct to some extent in the Indian or post-colonial context.[18]

Only very recently have new and established sections of the organized labor movement targeted the IT workforce, who are often categorized under the nation's Essential Service Act and therefore restricted from participating in

strikes or bandhs (Noronha 1996). It is not surprising that in the IT sector itself, nascent efforts, often by IT professionals themselves, to form informal
workers' associations face an uphill battle. However, based on the earlier discussion of the particular relationship between the urban middle classes and
civil society engagement, I would argue that it is also important to consider
the ways in which IT professionals are a core part of urban civic and associational life in cities like Bangalore. I would argue that the elite from the relatively homogenous (upper-caste, upper- and upper-middle-class, urban) IT
professional workforce locates itself as civil society through online activities
and networks as well as through offline involvement and civic participation.[19]

For the purposes of this chapter, I would draw attention to the role of Bangalore's IT professionals in founding or simply volunteering in the various
NGOs involved in both civic and developmental imperatives as a redefinition
of civil society in high-tech urban centers like Bangalore. It is from the ranks
of these workers and their upwardly mobile families that Nair (2005) traces
the emergence of volunteer organizations, self-help groups, cultural associations, and development-based NGOs following what appears to be a classic
liberal model of tough associational life and political engagement. In his recent study, Harriss (2006, 461–63) argues that the range of urban middle-class
civil society organizations, whether they speak in the language of consumer-
citizens or human rights, are deeply "anti-political."

On a parallel front alongside the rise of the "anti-political" new politics of
middle-class civic associationalism, we see that since 2004, both the party-
affiliated labor movement and newer efforts at independent unions with ties
to transnational unions have begun to gain momentum in the area of organizing BPO workers, gaining legitimacy in a sector that defines itself as antiu-
nion (Bhattacharjee and Azcarate 2006). As we have seen above, the worlds
of the more privileged IT and second-tier ITES workforces are not so rigidly
separated, so the distinction I am making here is somewhat overly general. I
would argue, however, that it is in this self-identified second tier of the IT industry where we see a slightly more heterogeneous mix of castes and class
(upper but also middle castes, and middle but also lower middle class). Here,
we also see a more feminized workforce demonstrating the attributes of a
"pink-collar" professional identity and gendered class formation (Freeman
2000). Finally, workers in the lower echelons of the IT industry are more
likely to come from smaller towns that have less access to the established professional and social networks in urban metropolitan areas like Bangalore
(Chakravartty 2005). As is evident in the recent momentum toward unioniz-
ing efforts among this set of workers, claims making here is more likely to include worker rights and potentially eventual larger-scale unionization.[20]

In contrast to both of these categories of workers, the informal working
classes or subaltern publics on the margins of Bangalore's formal information
society are much more likely to be from lower-caste groups, including OBC,

Dalit, and Adivasi communities. They are likely, if at all, to work as casualized and contract labor in related industries like construction, food, custodial services, and a range of other services. For this reason, I would argue that for this much larger group of workers and more importantly for these communities at large, we see very separate kinds of claims in relation to both the private IT industry and the state. In the local context of Bangalore, these include the popular claims (most often deemed illegal) over access to infrastructure, land, and housing, articulated through a politics of language, community, and caste, as documented by Nair (2005) and Solomon (2000). As Harriss (2006) argues, these claims are distinct from the "anti-political" claims made by urban middle-class elites who have increasing access to governance through civil society. They are also distinct from the claims "directed against capital" (464) made by formal workers through trade unions and other less formal associations for wages that we saw in our discussion of "second-tier" IT workers, like those employed in the BPO sector.

These are claims for citizenship directed at the state (Chandhoke 2002; Harriss 2006), as demonstrated through the recent legislative efforts to significantly expand caste-based reservation to institutions of higher education and to job opportunities in the private sector. The current debates can be traced back to 1989, when the coalition government headed by V. P. Singh implemented the Mandal Commission recommendations, extending the domain and extent of reservation to include private educational institutions and "high-end" government jobs. The targets of these reforms included not only the marginalized minority communities of Dalits and Adivasis, but also the larger category of OBCs, leading to dramatic mass upper-caste student demonstrations that found sympathetic support in the media. In this period, the elite institutions of higher scientific and managerial education, particularly those training the most powerful members of the workforce in the IT-related sectors in the twenty universities making up the Indian Institute of Technology (IIT), the Indian Institute of Management, and the All India Institute of Medical Sciences (AIIMS), were minimally implementing the quota system and doing so on a clearly "two-track" basis.[21]

It was not until 2004 that the left-coalition parties began demanding reservation for jobs in the private sector, including the much-coveted IT-based sector, and more expansive reservation in the elite higher educational institutions. In 2005, the new centrist coalition government led by Manmohan Singh promised to implement the quota system more rigorously, including greater access to Dalit, Adivasi, and OBC and minority communities (i.e., Muslim minorities and women). This required drafting an amendment to the constitution, and in May of 2006 the government announced the reservation of 27 percent of seats run by the central government, including the twenty elite IITs, IIMs, and AIIMs. The political upheaval in response to this decision has been intense, with protests and hunger strikes as well as threats of suicide by upper-caste students and professionals, provoking tremendous media interest in the story (Vij 2006).

Given the political volatility of the expanding caste-based reservation and quota debate, the IT industry mobilized quickly and vocally, arguing against these measures to an already outraged urban middle-class public and deploying arguments familiar to U.S. critics of affirmative action policies. Kirin Karnik, the president of the IT trade association NASSCOM, wrote the following in an editorial in the nation's leading financial paper:

> If one is to use a single parameter for identifying the truly disadvantaged, it would not be caste but class. The wealthy, irrespective of caste, are unfairly advantaged. If they are not meritorious enough to get into IIT, they go to MIT or Stanford in the U.S. It is in this overall context that one needs to devise means of providing equal opportunity to each individual on a non-discriminatory basis. Those truly interested in the welfare of the disadvantaged would agree that the most desirable objective is to enable them to compete with others on an equal footing. Thus, the focus must be on developing competency, not lowering standards; on creating capabilities, rather than crafting crutches. Quotas and reservations do not achieve this; if any thing, they serve to engender permanent dependency, and brand beneficiaries as "second class." (Karnik 2006)

The argument presented above that these are problems associated with class rather than caste, by one of the leading voices of corporate India, is consistent with the ways in which upper-caste communities have responded more positively to the plight of the Dalits, whose economic marginalization cannot be denied, as opposed to the larger constituency of OBCs, who are in fact a majority and thereby pose a much more direct challenge to the established power of the middle of the established and new economic elite (Jafferlot 1998). Having to recognize the vast inequalities in Indian society, industry advocates like Karnik promote instead private-sector "partnerships" aimed at expanding the education system, improving schools in rural and "backward areas," introducing special training in math and sciences as well as in "soft" skills including English, and fostering general educational reform based on market incentives. While all these measures are reasonable and a welcome shift in discourse for activists and scholars alike because they certainly address current redistributional imbalances in the IT-based development vision (Radhakrishnan 2004), they are clearly aligned with the "anti-politics" stance of urban middle-class civil society opposition to state-regulated intervention or in this case, monitoring of industry practices of recruitment. The problem in framing the issue as one of class as opposed to caste has to do with the fact that caste continues to play a pivotal structuring role in compounding these inequalities, a fact that the IT industry, which has historically defined itself against the state-based cronyism and corruption of the preliberalization era, is deeply opposed to recognizing.

Market-led reforms and IT-led development have failed to erase these inequalities, and have in fact reinforced the degree and extent of inequality both within urban high-tech centers like Bangalore and between these centers and rural peripheries. I have tried to argue that within this new geography of inequality, especially in urban areas, subaltern publics can be seen as making distinct claims for citizenship based on the spectacular benefits of India's fractured information society. The reservation issue challenges the "antipolitical" solutions offered by middle-class activists in civil society, and highlights the aspirational dimension of modernity and inequality in contemporary India. A final example to illustrate my point comes from the Dalit-Bahujan Freedom Network, an organization that argues that the Indian information economy fails to provide access to quality English-medium education, crucial for participation in an increasingly globalized India:

> Thus far, Dalit children (and large sections of the Backward Castes) have had no access to such quality education. English-medium education is the preserve of the moneyed upper caste and middle-class elite. This movement rejects the hypocrisy of the elitist castes whose children are educated in English, while the children of the oppressed castes are encouraged to study in the "vernacular" in the name of culture and extremist nationalism (Dalit-Bahujan Freedom Network 2005).

For this Dalit Rights organization, the cultural capital associated with competence in the English language, along with representation in higher education, is seen as vital to any meaningful redistributive reform of the skewed Indian IT-based economy. In this case, claims for citizenship through access to the linguistic proficiency of globalized urban elites exemplify the changing political landscape of India's information society. As I have tried to show in this section, jobs in the IT-based industry are widely coveted by young aspiring youth beyond Bangalore, across metropolitan, small-town, and even sections of rural India, while employment opportunities remain extremely skewed by class and gender, but also clearly by caste and community.

THE FRICTION OF GLOBAL SOLIDARITY

In this chapter, I have argued that in studies of global communications there is a need to more carefully consider the historically complex relationship between the state, workers, and civil society in the postcolonial context. Not only is there an urgent need to turn our attention to the context of production in the "global information economy," but as this chapter tries to demontrate, in so doing, we must engage with the ways in which the market is embedded within distinct information societies. In terms of the emerging information society in India, I have tried to account for the ways in which subaltern publics make distinct claims for access to education and the jobs themselves, along with protests, occupations, and claims to public goods and services through the state. The politicization of caste and the issue of reservation of educational seats and access to jobs in both the public and private sector then become crucial areas of struggle for this much wider category of subaltern publics in civil society, whose actions and claims are often deemed illegal or illegitimate by the neoliberal state and condemned as "dirty politics" by newly empowered middle-class social actors who define themselves as civil society.

In contrast, workers in both the formal IT and ITES sectors in India can be seen as having a very distinct relationship to the officially recognized category of civil society. For urban middle-class IT professionals with the most cultural capital, volunteering through the NGO and civic sectors has meant a direct channel to governance and development through civil society organizations in cities like Bangalore and well beyond. For the second-tier ITES workers, as part of a pink-collar workforce at a relative disadvantage as compared to the former group, we see a new focus on collective action and bargaining rights directed at the IT industry and initial calls for increased state regulation of the industry. Efforts by both researchers and activists to build stronger networks between workers across Southern and Northern locations address the limitations of nationalist and xenophobic debates about the outsourcing of work in expanding transnational industries like IT (CWA 2006). However, in thinking about commonalities and differences in terms of the wider political stakes, it becomes imperative to consider, as I have here, the complex relationship between the much larger section of subaltern publics in civil society and the relatively privileged workers employed by the IT-based economy, who position themselves as civil society.

This chapter began by considering the role of organized labor in current discussions about digital capitalism, or the network society. As the chapters by Arthur-Martins Aginam and Helga Tawil Souri in this volume vividly attest, the boundedness of civil society as well as the assumed topography of power, with the state positioned on top and civil society below, fails to capture the lived realities in contemporary postcolonial societies. Moreover, the vantage point of (in this case) workers and working peoples in the South makes a difference in assessing universal theories of globalization, including theories that might suggest a globalization from "below."

This chapter shows that there is no "authentic" or "local" overarching perspective shared by Indian workers both within and at the gates of the much-prized IT economy. It also shows that the seemingly separate worlds inhabited by subaltern publics and IT professionals occasionally overlap, as seen in both the "anti-politics" interventions in managing political society and the distinctly political claims for citizenship as in the case of caste-based reservation targeting the IT industry. If we are to speculate on the role of workers in potentially challenging, much less transforming, India's unequal information society, we have to acknowledge the complex relationship between the much larger section of subaltern publics in civil society and the tiny fraction of relatively more privileged workers who might position themselves as civil society. More carefully locating how the politics of work are embedded in societies where the semiproletarianized workforce—the floating or footless laborers—are an engaged and dynamic part of the global information economy changes our assumptions about what is at stake between the "information haves and have-nots." If the Indian case provides any clues to make sense of similar potential struggles elsewhere, then we must pay greater attention to claims to overcome existential inequalities like those based on caste, and to the significance of access to cultural capital such as competence in English. As we have seen with the Indian case, employment generation and its respective corollary, greater democratic access to higher education, represent hotly contested political claims for redistributive justice in response to the narrow gains of global integration and high-tech modernization.

NOTES

1. Theoretical discussions about Marx and civil society are too lengthy to cite meaningfully here (See Cohen and Arato 1992 and their interlocutors). Marx discussed the limitations of civil society in much of his writing; for example, "On the Jewish Question" (1844) contends: 'The perfect political state is, by its nature, man's species-life, as opposed to his material life. All the preconditions of this egoistic life continue to exist in civil society outside the sphere of the state, but as qualities of civil society." See www.marxists.org/archive/marx/works/1844/jewish-question/index.htm.

2. For instance, in the most recent academic debates about the role of civil society within the emerging global information society that surrounded the World Summit on Information Societies (WSIS), there was little to no emphasis on the role of organized labor and workers' associations as part of or separate from civil society. In the Southern context, the employment-generating potential of ICTs (or the lack thereof for the vast majority of citizens) is central to local and national public debates and struggles over the future of what are always fractured information societies. For more elaboration on this issue, see Chakravartty and Sarikakis (2006).

3. Two recent ethnographic studies provide stimulating theoretical insights on the dynamic and yet distinct sites of the politics of such global integration; see Ong 2005 and Tsing 2005.

4. There is an ongoing highly politicized debate about the relationship between India's neoliberal economic reforms and the overall poverty rate, which the World Bank and other sources argue has declined overall because of the 1991-initiated reforms. Political economists have argued that this overall picture ignores the concentration of poverty within specific regions, with growing gaps between urban and rural sectors. Specifically, while the decline in poverty rates has been steady since the 1980s, regional inequality between the faster-growing western (like Gujarat discussed below) and southern (like Karnataka discussed below) states, against slower-growing states in the North and East of the country. Most studies concur that the rates of inequality overall have increased significantly, especially between urban and rural areas as well as within urban areas (Deaton and Drèze 2003). For more on the pervasiveness of rural poverty, see Patnaik 2007 at www.networkideas.org/featart/jan2007/fa08_Neo-Liberalism.htm.

5. I have argued elsewhere that the strategic role of organized labor based in the North is fraught with the pitfalls of xenophobic nationalism (2005, 2006), an argument reinforced by progressive labor organizers in the recent report on binational labor conditions in India and the United States (CWA 2006). In a combination of online discussions and offline activism, which I have followed closely in the last seven years, class interest of workers are generally trumped by appeals to a "middle-class sensibility" and national unity against what Hashmi (2006) has called "barbarians at the gate." The resonance of nationalist appeal against the image of a vast army of "techno-coolies" fuelled public opposition to outsourcing, allowing former staunch conservatives like CNN news personality Lou Dobbs to successfully reinvent themselves as the voices of the newly recognized "victim of globalization": the white-collar American worker (Hashmi 2006, 244).

6. A recent issue of Critical Asian Studies (2006) provides a much more thorough and empirically grounded overview of organized labor, informal working-class formation, and middle-class civil society organizations. See in particular the articles by Agarwala (2006) and Harriss (2006). The author wishes to thank Patrick Heller for bringing this special issue to her attention.

7. The reservation system in India shares some features with affirmative action in the United States as discussed in great detail by Weisskopf (2005), who also provides a useful overview of the Indian scenario. However, it is perhaps more useful to begin our discussions by recognizing that in the Indian case, it is the majority as opposed to the minority whose interests are at stake. It is beyond the scope of this chapter to discuss the complexities of this debate, and suffice it to say that there are many contradictory aspects to caste-based politics that do not provide a unified front against upper-caste domination in any coherent way. However, there have been growing alliances and calls for caste-based reservation around education and employment that we can see since 2004. In addition to caste, the role of underprivileged religious minorities, most notably the Muslim community, is also an important component of these debates. For a thoughtful discussion of the political alliances around caste and community see Jafferlot (1998). In terms of the particular constitutionally recognized categories that demarcate caste, they include the following categories:

OBC (Other Backward Classes), who are heterogeneous communities from the traditionally marginalized castes (Shudras) at the bottom of the Hindu caste system who use the term Bahujan, and who make up the largest community in numbers, with estimates of anywhere between 20 and 40 percent of the population.

SC (Scheduled Castes or "untouchables"), whom the social reformer and activist Ambedkar called Dalit ("the broken and the oppressed") and who fall outside the Hindu caste system, making up approximately 17 percent of the population.

ST (Scheduled Tribes), also referred to as Adivasis, who are hundreds of indigenous groups and who make up approximately 8 percent of the population.

8. In this chapter I focus on the faster-growing software side of the IT sector, making a distinction between employment in IT services (programmers, system analysts, computer scientists, and engineers) and IT-enabled services (including a range of IT-enhanced occupations ranging from the Business Processing Operators—call center workers, animators, data processors, and medical transcription service workers).

9. See www.nasscom.in/upload/5216/NASSCOM%20Knowledge%20Professionals%20Factsheet%202006.pdf.

10. For a detailed assessment of NASSCOM's projections about the IT labor force in India (drawing extensively from a much-publicized study by private consulting firm McKinsey), see Chandrashekar (2005). The recent Bi-national Report published by workers organizations in India and the United States also highlights this problem, as did labor-rights organizers whom I interviewed in Bangalore in July 2006.

11. This was most obvious in the Karnataka state government's failed efforts at urban renewal through the Bangalore Agenda Taskforce (BATF) in 2001. This was a high-level policy

group made up of corporate leaders and civil society organizations that failed to gain public support. For more see Nair (2005) and www.alf.org.

12. Bangalore in many ways typifies the characterizations made in Graham and Marvin's (2001) work on "splintered urbanism" that connects and disconnects translocal urban nodes of the information economy. For more on Bangalore itself, see Nair (2005) and "urban studies" at the Alternative Law Forum's website: www.altlawforum.org/RESEARCH_PROJECTS.

13. Sam Pitroda, who was one of the architects of the mid-1980s reform "missions" around information and development, heads the Knowledge Commission, which includes a high-profile advisory body made up of experts who are either academics or industry leaders. Differences in opinion over the reservation policy led to the recent resignation of two of these high-profile members. See knowledgecommission.gov.in/about/members.asp.

14. See pmindia.nic.in/cmp.htm.

15. See, for instance, azimpremjifoundation.org.

16. As I have argued elsewhere (Chakravartty 2005), there are internal hierarchies of class, caste, and gender that shape the mobility and "flexibility" of IT workers within the higher echelons of the transnational IT economy. However, for the purposes of this chapter, I am distinguishing this relatively privileged group from both workers in the ITES sector and the larger urban workforce in high-tech centers like Bangalore.

17. The most recent, and one of the most extensive, empirical studies on call center workers found that 94.4 percent of all call center workers identified in the general caste category, in contrast to the bottom segments of the caste hierarchy (CWA 2006, 50).

18. This is a very broad-brush overview of details provided in the extensive report by Upadhya and Vasavi (2006).

19. This is based on initial and ongoing fieldwork in Bangalore and Kolkata (July 2006), which has involved interviews with IT professionals who both operate and volunteer in various NGOs and civic organizations in both cities.

20. Labor activists whom I interviewed in Bangalore (July 2006) argued that this was especially true for sections of the ITES industry that were focused on the domestic sector as opposed to export-based sectors.

21. For a more detailed discussion of the ways in which the quota system was implemented in the specific case of the IITs, see the report by the Dalit Media Network at www.pucl.org/reports/National/2001/dalits.htm.

References

Abbas, Akbar, and Jon Nguyet Erni, eds. 2004. *Internationalizing cultural studies*. Malden, Mass.: Blackwell Publishers.

Abercrombie, Nicholas, Stephen Hill, and Bryan S. Turner. 1980. *The dominant ideology thesis*. London: George Allen & Unwin Ltd.

Abu-Lughod, Lila. 1993. Finding a place for Islam: Egyptian television serials and the national interest. *Public Culture* 5(3): 493–513.

———. 2004. *Dramas of nationhood: The politics of television in Egypt*. Chicago: University of Chicago Press.

Acuña, Rudolfo. 1988. *Occupied America: A history of chicanos*. New York: Harper and Row.

Adams, David. 2002. Embarassed pro-coup media silent as Chavez returns. *Times* (London). April 15.

Adekson, Adedayo O. 2004. *The "civil society" problematique: Deconstructing civility and southern Nigeria's ethnic radicalization*. New York: Routledge.

Adeoye, Adewale (chairman, Journalists for Democratic Rights [JODER], Lagos, Nigeria). 2004. Personal interview. June 20.

African Charter for Popular Participation in Development and Transformation, 1990. www.un.org/issues/docs/documents/a-45–427.asp (accessed January 18, 2005).

African Charter on Broadcasting. 2001. *Media Development* 3 (200): 53–54.

African Women's Media Center. 1999. *A handbook for media leadership*. www.awmc.com.

Afshar, Haleh, ed. 1996. *Women and politics in the Third World*. London and New York: Routledge.

Agarwala, Rena. 2006. From work to welfare: A new class movement in India. *Critical Asian Studies* 38 (4): 419–44.

Aginam, Arthur-Martins. 2005a. Media in "globalizing" Africa: What prospect for democratic communication? In *Democratizing global media: One world, many struggles,* ed. Robert H. Hackett and Yuezhi Zhao, 121–42. Lanham, Md.: Rowman and Littlefield.

———. 2005b. Democratization and the politics of freedom of information in Africa. Paper presented at the European Institute for Communication and Culture (EURICOM) international colloquium—"The MacBride Report: 25 Years Later," Fiesa, Slovenia, September 15–17.

Aglietta, Michel. [1979] 2000. *A theory of capitalist regulation. The US experience*. London, New York: Verso Books.

Ahmed, Leila. 1992. *Women and gender in Islam*. New Haven, CT, and London: Yale University Press.

Akingbolu, Akin (executive director, Institute for Media and Civil Society [IMS], Lagos, Nigeria). 2004. Personal interview, Lagos, Nigeria. June 10.

Akinola, Richard (chairman, Center for Free Speech [CFS], Lagos, Nigeria). 2004. Personal interview, Lagos, Nigeria. May 30.

Aksoy, Asu, and Kevin Robins. 1992. Hollywood for the 21st century: Global competition for critical mass in image markets. *Cambridge Journal of Economics* 16:1–22.

Alexeyeva, L. 1983. *Istoria inakomysliya v SSSR* [History of dissidence in the USSR]. www.memo.ru/history/diss/books/ALEXEEWA/index.htm.

Alhassan, Amin, 2004. *Development communication policy and economic fundamentalism in Ghana*. Tampere: Tampere University Press.

Ali, Tarik. 2006. When NGOs are more of a bane than a blessing. *Taipei Times*. www.taipeitimes.com/News/editorials/archives/2006/04/2003301976.

Althusser, Louis. 1969. *For Marx*. London: NLB.

Altvater, Elmar. n.d. What happens when public goods are privatised? www.rosalux.de/cms/fileadmin/rls_uploads/wemgehoertdiewelt/altvater_0312.pdf (accessed January 30, 2006).

Amin, Samir. 1993. Social movements in the periphery. In *New social movements in the South: Empowering the people,* ed. P. Wignaraja, 76–100. London: Zed Books.

———. 1997. *Capitalism in the age of globalization*. New Jersey: Zed Books.

———. 2003. *Obsolescent capitalism: Contemporary politics and global disorder*. New York: Zed Books.

Amin, Shahid, and Marcel Van der Linden. 1997. *"Peripheral" labour: Studies in the history of partial proletarianization*. Cambridge: Cambridge University Press.

Amoore, Louise, and Paul Langley. 2004. Ambiguities of global civil society. *Review of International Studies* 30:89–110.

Amos, Valerie, and Pratibha Parmer. 1984. Challenging imperial feminism. *Feminist Review* 17 (Autumn): 3–20.

Anderson, Benedict. 1991. *Imagined communities: Reflections on the origin and spread of nationalism*. New York: Verso.

Anderson, Kathleen, and Marla Matzer Rose. 2004. Hispanic TV ad growth seen waning. *Hollywood Reporter,* June 17.

Ang, Ien. 1995. *Living room wars: Rethinking media audiences for a postmodern world*. London: Routledge.

Ang, Ien, and Jon Stratton. 1996. Asianizing Australia: Notes toward a critical transnationalism in cultural studies. *Cultural Studies* 10 (1): 16–36.

Anzaldúa, Gloria. 2004. Linguistic terrorism. In *Tongue-tied: The lives of multicultural children in public education,* ed. Otto Santa Ana, 270–71. Lanham, Md: Rowman and Littlefield.

Appadurai, Arjun, ed. 1986. *The social life of things: Commodities in cultural perspective*. Cambridge: Cambridge University Press.

———. 1996. *Modernity at large: Cultural dimensions of globalization*. Minneapolis: University of Minnesota Press.

Appiah, Kwame A. 1992. The postcolonial and the postmodern. In *In my father's house: Africa in the philosophy of culture*. New York: Oxford University Press.

Armstrong, Sally. 2002. *Veiled threat: The hidden power of the women of Afghanistan*. Toronto: Penguin/Viking.

Arogundade, Lanre (coordinator, International Press Center [IPC], Lagos, Nigeria). 2004a. Personal interview, Lagos, Nigeria. June 15.

———. 2004b. Introduction: A step towards a charter. In *Issues in professional and union rights of women journalists,* ed. L. Arogundade and T. Aremu, ii–iii. Lagos, Nigeria: International Press Center.

Artz, Lee. 2003. Globalization, media hegemony, and social class. In *The globalization of corporate media hegemony,* ed. Lee Artz and Yahya R. Kamalipour, 3–32. Albany: State University of New York Press.

Artz, Lee, and Yahya R. Kamalipour, eds. 2003. *The globalization of corporate media hegemony.* Albany: State University of New York Press.

Asante, Molefi Kete. 1996. The principal issues in Afrocentric identity. In *African intellectual heritage: A book of sources,* ed. M. K. Asante and A. S. Abarry, 256–61. Philadelphia: Temple University Press.

Aufderheide, Patricia. 1999. *Communications policy and the public interest: The Telecommunications Act of 1996.* New York: Guilford Press.

Axtmann, Roland. 2004. The state of the state: The model of the modern state and its contemporary transformation. *International Political Science Review* 25 (3): 259–79.

Bailey, David A., and Gilane Tawadros, eds. 2003. *Veil: Veiling, representation and contemporary art.* London: Institute of International Visual Arts and Modern Art Oxford.

Bailie, Moshoed, and Dwayne Winseck, eds. 1997. *Democratizing communication: Comparative perspectives on information and power.* Cresskill: Hampton Press.

Baker, Gideon. 2002. *Civil society and democratic theory: Alternative voices.* London: Routledge.

Bakhtin, Mikhail. 1981. *The dialogical imagination: Four essays.* Ed. M. Holquist, trans. C. Emerson and M. Holquist. Austin: University of Texas Press.

Balve, Marcelo. 2004. The battle for Latino media. *NACLA Report on the Americas* 37 (4): 20–26.

Barahona, Diana. 2005. The corporate media vs. Chavez: Uneasy standoff in Venezuela's media wars. *Counterpunch.* www.counterpunch.org/barahona08162005.html (accessed September 15, 2005).

Barghouti, Mustafa. 1994. *Palestinian NGOs and their role in building a civil society.* Jerusalem: Union of Palestinian Medical Relief Committees.

Barmé, Geremie. 1999. *In the red: Contemporary Chinese culture.* New York: Columbia University Press.

Basu, Indrajit. 2006. Unions woo Indian call centers. *Asia Times.* www.atimes.com/atimes/South_Asia/GJ25Df03.html.

Baum, Richard, and Alexei Shevchenko. 1999. The "state of the state." In *The paradox of China's post-Mao reforms,* ed. M. Goldman and R. MacFarquhar, 333–60. Cambridge, Mass.: Harvard University Press.

Bayart, Jean-Francois. 1986. Civil society in Africa. In *Political domination in Africa: Reflections on the limits of power,* ed. P. Chabal, 109–25. Cambridge: Cambridge University Press.

BBC News. 2001. Cherie Blair attacks Taleban "cruelty." November 19. news.bbc.co.uk/1/hi/uk_politics/1663300.stm

Beale, Alison. 1999. From "Sophie's Choice" to consumer choice: Framing gender in cultural policy. *Media, Culture & Society* 21:435–58.

Beales, Gregory. 2001. The Birth of Asiawood. *Newsweek.* May 21, 52–56.

Benjamin, Solomon. 2000. Governance, economic settings and poverty in Bangalore. *Environment & Urbanization* 2 (1): 35–56.

Bernstein, Richard, and Ross H. Munro. 1998. *The coming conflict with China.* New York: Vintage.

Bettig, Ronald. 1996. *Copyrighting culture: The political economy of intellectual property.* Boulder, Colo.: Westview Press.

Bhattacharjee, Anannya, and Fred Azcarate. 2006. India's new unionism. *New Labor Forum* 15 (3): 64–73.

Billig, Michael. 1991. *Ideology and opinions: studies in rhetorical psychology.* London: Sage.

Blevins, Jeffrey Layne. 2002. Source diversity after the Telecommunications Act of 1996: Media oligarchs begin to colonize cyberspace. *Television and New Media* 3 (1): 95–112.

Boateng, Boatema. 2004. African textiles and the politics of diasporic identity-making. In *Fashioning Africa: Power and the politics of dress,* ed. J. Allman, 212–26. Bloomington: Indiana University Press.

Borkhurst-Heng, Wendy. 2002. Newspapers in Singapore: A mass ceremony in the imagining of the nation. *Media Culture & Society* 24 (4): 559–69.

Boucher, Geoff. 2005. FCC rules may force Indie 103.1 FM to change its tune. *Los Angeles Times.* February 24.

Bouillon, Markus E. 2004. The failure of big business: On the socio-economic reality of the Middle East peace process. *Mediterranean Politics* 9 (1): 1–28.

Bourdieu, Pierre. 1999. Rethinking the state: Genesis and structure of the bureaucratic field. In *State/culture: State-formation after the cultural turn,* ed. George Steinmetz, 53–75. Ithaca, N.Y.: Cornell University Press.

———. 2007. *Distinction: A social critique of the judgment of taste.* Cambridge, Mass.: Harvard University Press.

Bourgault, Louise M. 1995. *Mass media in sub-Saharan Africa.* Bloomington: Indiana University Press.

Bowman, Betsy, and Bob Stone. 2006. Venezuela's cooperative revolution: An economic experiment is the hidden story behind Chávez's "Bolivarian Revolution." *Dollars and Sense* 266 (July–August). www.dollarsandsense.org/archives/2006/0706bowmanstone.html.

Boyd-Barrett, Oliver. 1997. International communication and globalization: Contradictions and directions. In *International communication and globalization,* ed. A. Mohammadi, 11–26. Thousand Oaks, CA: Sage.

———. 1998. Media imperialism reformulated. In *Electronic empires: Global media and local resistance,* ed. D. K. Thussu, 157–76. London: Arnold.

Boyer, Robert. 2000. The political in the air of globalisation and finance focus on some regulation school research. *International Journal of Urban and Regional Research* 24 (2): 274–322.

Boyle, James. 1996. *Shamans, software and spleens: Law and the construction of the information society.* Cambridge, Mass.: Harvard University Press.

Breman, Jan. 1996. *Footloose labour: Working in India's informal economy.* Cambridge: Cambridge University Press.

Breslin, Shaun. 2006. Serving the market or serving the party: Neo-liberalism in China. In *The neo-liberal revolution: Forging the market state,* ed. Richard Robison, 114–34. New York: Palgrave.

Bright, Martin. 2001. Heartbroken of Kandahar. *Observer.* November 4.

Brown, Michael. 2003. *Who owns native culture?* Cambridge, Mass.: Harvard University Press.

Brown, Nathan J. 2003. *Palestinian politics after the Oslo Accords: Resuming Arab Palestine.* Berkeley: University of California Press.

Brubaker, Rogers, and Frederick Cooper. 2000. Beyond "identity." *Theory and Society* 29 (1): 1–47.

Brynen, Rex. 1996a. Buying peace? A critical assessment of international aid to the West Bank and Gaza. *Journal of Palestine Studies* 25 (3): 79–92.

———. 1996b. International aid to the West Bank and Gaza: A primer. *Journal of Palestine Studies* 25 (2): 46–53.

———. 2000. *A very political economy: Peacebuilding and foreign aid in the West Bank and Gaza.* Washington, DC: United Institute of Peace Press.

Bulard, Martin. 2006. China breaks the iron rice bowl. *Le Monde Diplomatique.* January. Mondediplo.com/2006/01/04china (accessed February 8, 2006).

Burawoy, Michael. 2003. For a sociological Marxism: The complementary convergence of Antonio Gramsci and Karl Polanyi. *Politics & Society* 31 (2): 193–261.

Burgess, Katrina. 2004. *Parties and unions in the new global economy.* Pittsburgh: University of Pittsburgh Press.

Bush, Laura. 2001. Radio address. Crawford, Texas. November 17. www.whitehouse.gov/news/releases/2001/11/20011117.html.

Business Environment Risk Intelligence. 2002. All figured out of productivity digest. *Spring Singapore*. www.spring.gov.sg/portal/newsroom/epublications/pd/2002_06/index10.html.

Buxton, Julia. 2001. *The failure of political reform in Venezuela*. Aldershot: Ashgate.

Calabrese, Andrew. 1995. Local versus global in the modernization of central and eastern european telecommunications: A case study of US corporate investments. In *Democracy and communication in the new Europe: Change and continuity in East and West*, ed. F. Corcoran and P. Preston, 233–56. Cresskill, N.J.: Hampton Press, Inc.

——. 2004. Toward a political economy of culture. In *Toward a political economy of culture: Capitalism and communication in the twenty-first century*, ed. Andrew Calabrese and Colin Sparks, 1–12. Lanham, Md.: Rowman & Littlefield.

Calabrese, Andrew, and Colin Sparks. 2004. *Toward a political economy of culture: Capitalism and communication in the twenty-first century*. Lanham, Md.: Rowman & Littlefield.

Campo-Flores, Arian. 2004. The Latino Radiohead. *Newsweek*. December 27, 106.

Canache, Damarys. 2004. Urban poor and political order. In *The unravelling of representative democracy in Venezuela*, ed. Jennifer L. McCoy and David J. Myers, 33–49. Baltimore: Johns Hopkins University Press.

Castañeda Paredes, Mari. 2003a. The transformation of Spanish-language radio in the United States. *Journal of Radio Studies* 45 (2): 10–36.

——. 2003b. Television set production at the US-Mexico border: Trade policy and advanced electronics for the global market. In *Critical cultures studies: A reader*, ed. J. Lewis and T. Miller, 272–81. Oxford: Blackwell Publishing.

——. 2003c. FCC Rules Translate Poorly. *Newsday*. June 23, A19–20.

Castells, Manuel. 1988. *The developmental city-state in an open world economy: The Singapore experience*. Working Paper No. 31, Berkeley Roundtable on the International Economy, University of California, Berkeley.

——. 1996. *The rise of the network society*. Cambridge: Blackwell Publishers.

——. 2000. *End of millenium*. Boston: Blackwell Press.

Catia TVe Collective. 2006. Catia TVe, Television from, by and for the people. July 19. www.venezuelanalysis.com/articles.php?artno=1780.

Chabal, Patrick. 1992. *Power in Africa: An essay in political interpretation*. London: Macmillan.

Chakrabarty, Dipesh. 2000a. *Rethinking working class history: Bengal 1890–1940*. Princeton, N.J.: Princeton University Press.

——. 2000b. *Provincializing Europe: Postcolonial thought and historical difference*. Princeton: Princeton University Press.

Chakravartty, Paula. 2001. Flexible citizens and the Internet: The global politics of local high-tech development in India. *Emergences: Journal for the Study of Media and Composite Cultures* 11 (1): 69–88.

——. 2004. Telecommunications, development and the state: A post-colonial critique. *Media, Culture and Society* 26 (2): 227–49.

——. 2005. Weak winners of globalization: Indian H-1B workers in the American information economy. *AAPI Nexus* 3 (2): 59–84.

——. 2007. Governance without politics: Civil society, development and the postcolonial state. *International Journal of Communication* 1. ijoc.org/ojs/index.php/ijoc.

——. Forthcoming. India, Brazil, South Africa: Tracing the History of South-South Alliances. In *Communications rights and social justice: Reflections on the short history of a social movement*, ed. Andrew Calabrese and Claudia Padovani. Boulder, Colo.: Rowman & Littlefield.

Chakravartty, Paula, and Katharine Sarikakis. 2006. *Media policy and globalization*. Edinburgh: Edinburgh University Press.

Chan, Joseph M. 2003. Administrative boundaries and media marketization: A comparative analysis of the newspaper, TV and Internet markets in China. In *Chinese media, global contexts*, ed. L. Chin-Chuan, 159–76. London: Routledge/Curzon.

Chan, Joseph M., and Eric Ma. 2002. Transculturating modernity: A reinterpretation of cultural globalization. In *In search of boundaries: Communication, nation-states and cultural identities*, ed. Joseph M. Chan and Bryce I. McIntyre, 3–18. Westport, Conn.: Ablex.

Chan, Joseph M., and Bryce T. McIntyre, eds. 2002. *In search of boundaries: Communication, nation-states and cultural identities*. Westport, Conn.: Ablex.

Chandhoke, Neera. 2002. The limits of global civil society. In *Global civil society*, ed. Marlies Glasius, Mary Kaldo, and Helmut Anheier, 35–53. Oxford: Oxford University Press.

Chandrashekar, C. P. 2000. ICT in a developing country context: The Indian case. Background paper for human development report. New York: UNDP.

———. 2005. T-services as locomotive. *Frontline* 1 (July 5): 120–21.

Chatterjee, Partha. 1986. *Nationalist thought and the colonial world: A derivative discourse?* London: Zed Books.

———. 2004. *The politics of the governed: Reflections on popular politics in most of the world.* New York: Columbia University Press.

Chavez, Hugo, and Marta Harnecker. 2005. *Understanding the Venezuelan revolution: Hugo Chavez talks to Marta Harnecker.* Trans. Chesa Boudin. New York: Monthly Review Press.

Chavez, Leo R. 2001. *Covering immigration: Popular images and the politics of the nation.* Berkeley: University of California Press.

Chen, Kuan-Hsing. 1998. *Trajectories: Inter-Asia cultural studies.* London: Routledge.

Chen, Feng. 1999. An unfinished battle in China: The leftist criticism of the reform and the third thought emancipation. *China Quarterly* 158 (June): 447–67.

Chin, Yik-Chan. 2003. The nation-state in a globalising media environment: China's regulatory policies on transborder TV drama flow. *The Public/Javnost* 10 (4): 75–92.

Choices Video Inc. n.d. cjoicesvideo.net/html/awards/daughtersreviews.html.

Christiansen, Thomas, and Knut Erik Jørgensen. 1999. The Amsterdam process: A structurationist perspective on EU treaty reform. *European Integration Online Papers* 3 (1). eiop.or.at/eiop/texte/1999–001a.htm.

Christiansen Thomas, Knut Erik Jørgensen, and Antje Wiener. 1999. The social construction of Europe. *Journal of European Public Policy* 6 (4): 528–44.

Chua, Amy. 2004. *World on fire: How exporting free market democracy breeds ethnic hatred and global instability.* New York: Anchor Books.

Chua, Beng-Huat. 1995. *Communitarian ideology and democracy in Singapore.* London: Routledge.

Cisneros, Oscar S. 2001b. The trouble with wiring Palestine. *Wired News.* www.wired.com/news/print/0,1294,41134,00.html (accessed February 8, 2006).

Clarke, John. 1997. The state, popular participation and the voluntary sector. In *NGOs, states and donors: Too close for comfort?* ed. D. Hulme and M. Edwards, 43–58. London: Macmillan.

Cocks, Peter. 1980. Towards a Marxist theory of European integration. *International Organisation* 34 (1): 1–40.

Cody, Edward. 2004. China declares a people's war against porn. *Vancouver Sun.* August 21, A13.

Cohen, Jean-Louis, and Andrew Arato. 1992. *Civil society and political theory.* Cambridge, Mass.: MIT Press.

Colas, Alejandro. 2002. *International civil society: Social movements in world politics.* Cambridge: Polity Press.

Collon, M. 2002. *Neft, PR, Voina: Globalny kontrol nad resursami planety* [War: Global control over the planet's resources]. Moscow: Krymsky Most-9D, Forum.

Committee for the Protection of Journalists. 2002. Attacks on the press in 2002 in Venezuela. www.cpj.org/attacks02/americas02/ven.html (accessed May 16, 2004).

Comor, Edward. 2002. Media corporations in the age of globalization. In *Handbook of international and intercultural communication, second edition,* ed. W. B. Gudykunst and B. Mody, 309–24. Thousand Oaks, Calif., and London: Sage.

Constitution of the Bolivarian Republic of Venezuela. 1999. www.gobiernoenlinea .ve/docMgr/sharedfiles/059.pdf (accessed September 14, 2004).

Coombe, Rosemary. 1998. *The cultural life of intellectual properties: Authorship, appropriation and the law.* Durham, N.C.: Duke University Press.

Cooper, Frederick. 2005. *Colonialism in question: Theory, knowledge, history.* Berkeley: University of California Press.

Copps, Michael J. 2003. Press statement: Dissension regarding shareholders of Hispanic Broadcasting Corporation (Transferor) and Univisión Communications, Inc. (Transferee). Washington, DC: Federal Communications Commission. hraunfoss.fcc.gov/edocs_public/attach match/DOC-239081A3.doc.

Crandall, Robert W. 2005. *Competition and chaos: U.S. telecommunications since the 1996 Act.* Washington, DC: Brookings Institute Press.

Curran, James. 2002. *Media and power.* London: Routledge.

Curran, James, and Myung-Jin Park, eds. 2000. *De-Westernizing media studies.* London and New York: Routledge.

CWA [Communications Workers of America]. 2006. *Bi-national perspective on offshore outsourcing: Collaboration between Indian and US Labour.* files.cwa-union.org/National/What sHot/061017_full.pdf (accessed October 26, 2006).

Dalit-Bahujan Freedom Network Webpage. 2005. www.dalitnetwork.org/go?/dfn/who_ are_the_dalit/c102/ (accessed October 15, 2006).

Dávila, Arlene. 2001. *Latinos, Inc.: The marketing and making of a people.* Berkeley: University of California Press.

Davila, Luis Ricardo. 2000. The rise and fall of populism in Venezuela. *Bulletin of Latin American Research* 19 (2): 223–38.

Davis, Fred. 1979. *Yearning for yesterday: A sociology of nostalgia.* New York: The Free Press.

Davis, Jim, Thomas A. Hirschl, and Michael Stack, eds. 1997. *Cutting edge: Technology, information capitalism and social revolution.* New York: Verso.

Davis, Mike. 2000. *Magical urbanism.* New York: Verso.

De Veaux, Alexis. 2004. *Warrior poet: A biography of Audre Lorde.* New York: W. W. Norton.

Deaton, Angus, and Jean Drèze. 2003. Poverty and inequality in India: A re-examination. *Economic and Political Weekly.* Reprinted in IDEAS Network: see ideas.repec.org/ p/cde/cdewps/107.html.

Dedman, Martin J. 1996. *The origins and development of the EU 1945–1995.* London: Routledge.

Dehousse, Renaud. 1998. *European institutional architecture after Amsterdam: Parliamentary system or regulatory structure?* Robert Schuman Centre, EUI working paper RSC No 98/11. San Domenico, Italy: European University Institute.

Denning, Michael. 1996. *The cultural front: The laboring of American culture in the twentieth century.* London and New York: Verso.

Deshpande, Satish. 2003. *Contemporary India: A Sociological View.* New Delhi: Penguin.

Diamond, Larry. 2002. Thinking about hybrid regimes. *Journal of Democracy* 13 (2): 5–21.

Diaz, David R. 2005. *Barrio urbanism: Chicanos, planning, and American cities.* New York: Routledge.

Dicklitch, Susan. 1998. *The elusive promise of NGOs in Africa.* London: Macmillan Press.

Dinan, Desmond. 1994. The European Community, 1978–93. *Annals of the American Academy of Political and Social Sciences* 53 (January): 10–24.

Dinges, John. 2005. Soul search. *Columbia Journalism Review* 44 (4), www.cjr.org/issues/2005/4/dinges.asp (accessed September 14, 2005).

Dirlik, Arif. 1991. Culturalism as a sign of the modern. In *The nature and context of minority discourse,* ed. A. R. Jan-Mohamed and D. Lloyd, 394–431. New York: Oxford University Press.

———. 1994. *After the revolution: Waking to global capitalism.* Hanover, Conn.: Wesleyan University Press.

———. 2003. Empire: Some thoughts on colonialism, culture and class in the making of global crisis and war in perpetuity. *Interventions: International Journal of Postcolonial Studies* 5 (2): 207–17.

———. 2004. *Marxism in the Chinese revolution.* Lanham, Md.: Rowman & Littlefield.

Domowitz, Susan. 1992. Wearing proverbs: Anyi names for printed factory cloth. *African Arts* 25 (2): 82–104.

Donnell, Alison. 2003. Visibility, violence and voice? Attitudes to veiling Post–11 September. In *Veil: Veiling, representation and contemporary art,* ed. D. A. Bailey and G. Tawadros, 122–35. London: Institute of International Visual Arts and Modern Art, Oxford.

Downing, John D. H. 1996. *Internationalizing media theory: Transition, power, culture: Reflections on media in Russia, Poland and Hungary, 1980–95.* Thousand Oaks, Calif.: Sage.

———. 2001. *Radical media: Rebellious communication and social movements.* London: Sage.

Downing, John D. H., and Cao Yong. 2004. Global media corporations and the People's Republic of China. *Media Development* 4, 18–26.

Drahos, Peter, and John Braithwaite. 2002. *Information feudalism: Who owns the knowledge economy?* New York: New Press.

Du Boff, Richard B. 2001. NAFTA and economic integration: Regional or global? In *Continental order: Integrating North America for cybercapitalism,* ed. V. Mosco and D. Schiller, 35–63. New York: Rowman and Littlefield.

Duany, Jorge. 2003. *Reconstructing racial identity: Ethnicity, color, and class among Dominicans in the United States and Puerto Rico.* Lanham, Md.: Rowman and Littlefield, Inc.

Dubitskaya, Viktoriya. 1998. *Televideniye: mifoteknologii v eletronnih sredstvah massovoi informatsii.* Moscow: RAS Institute of Sociology Press.

Dunford, Michael. 2000. Globalization and theories of regulation. In *Global Political Economy: Contemporary Theories,* ed. R. Palan, 143–67. London and New York: Routledge.

Dyer-Witheford, Nick. 1999. *Cyber-Marx: Cycles and circuits of struggle in high-technology capitalism.* Urbana-Champlain: University of Illinois Press.

———. 2004. Species being and the new commonism: Notes on a new interrupted cycle of struggles. *The Commoner* 11:15–32.

EastWest Institute. 2005. The Erez and Gaza industrial estates: Catalysts for development. New York: EastWest Institute.

Economist. 2000. Sins of the secular missionaries. January 27.

———. 2002a. Coup and counter-coup. April 12.

———. 2002b. Chavez redux—In democracies, bad leaders are voted out not deposed. April 20.

———. 2005. Oil, missions and a chat show. May 12.

Eimer, Charlotte. 2004. Venezuela's war of the airwaves. BBC News Online. March 19. news.bbc.co.uk/go/pr/fr/-/1/hi/world/americas/3524760.stm (accessed April 11, 2004).

El-Haddad, Laila. 2003. Intifada spurs Palestine Internet boom. Al-Jazeera. December 11. english .aljazeera.net/NR/exeres/3707F879–1FB0–41BD-AC75-AF49B2F9F87A.htm (accessed June 27, 2004).

Ellner, Steve. 2001. The radical potential of Chavismo in Venezuela: The first year and a half in power. *Latin American Perspectives* 28 (5): 5–32.

———. 2003a. Venezuela on the brink. *Nation.* January 13. www.thenation.com/doc/20030113/ellner (accessed March 20, 2004).

———. 2003b. Introduction: The search for explanations. In *Venezuelan politics in the Chavez era: Class, polarization, and conflict,* ed. S. Ellner and D. Hellinger, 7–26. Boulder, Colo.: Lynne Reiner.

Ellsworth, Brian. 2002. The "radical" thesis on globalization and the case of Venezuela's Hugo Chavez. *Latin American Perspectives* 29 (6): 88–93.

———. 2004. The oil company as social worker. *New York Times.* March 11. www.nytimes.com/2004/03/11/business/worldbusiness/11pdvsa.html?ex=1394427600&en= 179f03b724d3dcc9&ei=5007&partner=USERLAND (accessed May 23, 2005).

Enzensberger, Hans Magnus. 1962. *Einzelheiten I. bewusstseins-industrie.* Frankfurt: Suhrkamp Verlag.

Ermert, Monika, and Christopher R. Hughes. 2003. What's in the name? China and the domain name system. In *China and the Internet: Politics of the digital leap forward,* ed. Christopher R. Hughes and Gudrun Wacker, 127–38. London: RoutledgeCurzon.

Escalante, Virginia. 2000. The politics of Chicano representation in the media. In *Chicano renaissance: Contemporary cultural trends,* ed. M. Herrera-Sobeck, I. D. Ortiz, and D. R. Maciel, 131–68. Tucson: University of Arizona Press.

Esedebe, P. Olisanwuche. 1994. *Pan-Africanism: The idea and movement, 1776–1991.* 2nd ed. Washington D.C.: Howard University Press.

European Community. 1997. Directive 97/36/EC of the European Parliament and of the Council of 30 June 1997 Amending Council Directive 89/552/EEC on the Co-ordination of Certain Provisions Laid down by Law, Regulation or Administrative Action in Member States Concerning the Pursuit of Television Broadcasting Activities, OJ L 202, 30.07.97/ 60–71.

Fanon, Frantz. 1965. *A dying colonialism.* New York: Grove Press Inc.

Fardon, Richard, and Graham Furniss, eds. 2000. *African broadcast cultures: Radio in transition.* Oxford: James Currey.

Featherstone, Mike. 1995. *Undoing culture: Globalization, postmodernism and identity.* London: Sage.

Federman, Joseph. 2003. Palestinians turn to Internet to cope with Israeli restrictions. *USA Today.* November 18. www.usatoday.com/tech/news/2003–11–18-palestine-online_x.htm (accessed May 16, 2004).

Feenberg, Andrew. 1991. *Critical theory of technology.* New York: Oxford University Press.

———. 1999. *Questioning technology.* New York: Routledge.

Feld, Stephen. 2000. A sweet lullaby for world music. *Public Culture* 12 (1): 145–71.

Ferguson, James. 1994. *The anti-politics machine: "Development," depoliticization and bureaucratic power in Lesotho.* Minneapolis: University of Minnesota Press.

———. 2006. *Global shadows: Africa in the neoliberal world order.* Durham, N.C.: Duke University Press.

Fernandes, Leela. 1997. *Producing workers: The politics of gender, class and culture in the Calcutta jute mills.* Philadelphia: University of Pennsylvania Press.

Fernandes, Leela. 2006. *India's new middle class: Democratic politics in an era of political reform.* Minneapolis: University of Minnesota.

Fernandes, Leela, and Patrick Heller. 2006. Hegemonic aspirations: New middle class politics and India's democracy in comparative perspective. *Critical Asian Studies* 38 (4): 495–522.

Fernandes, Sujatha. 2005. Growing movement of community radio in Venezuela. *Znet.* December 24. www.zmag.org/content/showarticle.cfm?ItemID=9393.

Fewsmith, Joseph. 2001. *China since Tiananmen: The politics of transition.* Cambridge: University of Cambridge Press.

Fiske, John. 1986. Television: Polysemy and popularity. *Critical Studies in Mass Communications* 3 (4): 391–408.

Fitzgerald, Mark. 2002. Under siege in Caracas. *Editor & Publisher* 35 (5): 28.

Fletcher, Bill Jr. 2004. A new chapter in Venezuela? TransAfrica Forum Website. www.transafricaforum.org/documents/AnewchapterinVene.oct2004_002.pdf (accessed September 17, 2005).

Flores, Juan. 2000. *From bomba to hip hop: Puerto Rican culture and Latino identity.* New York: Columbia University Press.

Flores, Juan, and George Yúdice. 1993. Living borders/buscando América: Languages of Latino self-formation. In *Divided borders,* by Juan Flores, 199–224. Houston: Arte Público Press.

Flores, William V. 1997. *Citizens vs. citizenry: Undocumented immigrants and Latino cultural citizenship.* Boston: Beacon Press.

Florini, Ann M., ed. 2000. *The third force: The rise of transnational civil society.* Washington, D.C.: Japan Center for International Exchange and Carnegie Endowment for International Peace.

Forbes. 1999. Gustavo Cisneros and Family. Forbes Billionaires. www.forbes.com/finance/lists/10/2001/LIR.jhtml?passListId=10&passYear=1999&pasListType=Person&uniqueId=GX8F&datatype=Person (accessed July 22, 2004).

———. 2000. Gustavo Cisneros and Family. Forbes Billionaires. www.forbes.com/finance/lists/10/2000/LIR.jhtml?passListId=10&passYear=2000&passListType=Person&uniqueId=GX8F&datatype=Person (accessed July 22, 2004).

———. 2001. Gustavo Cisneros and Family. Forbes Billionaires. www.forbes.com/finance/lists/10/2001/LIR.jhtml?passListId=10&passYear=2001&passListType=Person&uniqueId=GX8F&datatype=Person (accessed July 22, 2004).

———. 2002. Gustavo Cisneros and Family. Forbes Billionaires. www.forbes.com/finance/lists/10/2002/LIR.jhtml?passListId=10&passYear=2002&passListType=Person&uniqueId=GX8F&datatype=Person (accessed July 22, 2004).

———. 2003. Gustavo Cisneros and Family. Forbes Billionaires. www.forbes.com/finance/lists/10/2003/LIR.jhtml?passListId=10&passYear=2003&passListType=Person&datatype=Person&uniqueId=GX8F (accessed July 22, 2004).

———. 2006. Gustavo Cisneros and Family. Forbes Billionaires. www.forbes.com/lists/2006/10/GX8F.html (accessed January 4, 2007).

Forero, Juan. 2004. Caracas journal: Pirate radio as public radio, in the President's corner. *New York Times.* March 8.

Foucault, Michel. 2000. Governmentality. In *Power,* Vol. 3 of *Essential Works of Foucault,* ed. J. Faubion, *1954–1984.*

Fox, Claire. 1999. *The fence and the river: Culture and politics at the U.S.-Mexico border.* Minneapolis: University of Minnesota Press.

Freedom of Information Bill. 1999. *Federal Republic of Nigeria Official Gazette* 86(91) (December).

Freeman, Carla. 2000. *High-tech and high heels in the global economy: Women, work and pink-collar identities in the Carribean.* Durham: Duke University Press.

Frere-Jones, Sasha. 2005. Qué caliente: A Latin genre gets bigger. *New Yorker.* December 19, 96.

Friedman, Andrew. 2000. Microregulation and post Fordism: Critique and development of regulation theory. *New Political Economy* 5 (1): 59–76.

Friedman, Thomas. 2005. *The world is flat: A brief history of the twenty-first century.* New York: Farrar, Straus and Giroux.

Frisch, Hillel. 1998. *Countdown to statehood: Palestinian state formation in the West Bank and Gaza.* New York: State University of New York Press.

Fukuyama, Francis. 1992. *The end of history and the last man.* New York: The Free Press.

Fung, Anthony. 2006. "Think globally, act locally": China's rendezvous with MTV. *Global Media and Communication* 2 (1): 71–88.

Gable, Dawn. 2004. Civil society, social movements, and participation in Venezuela's fifth republic. Venezuelanalysis.com. www.venezuelanalysis.com/articles.php?artno=1103 (accessed February 9, 2004).

García Canclini, Néstor. 1989. *Culturas híbridas: Estratgegias para entrar y salir de la modernidad.* Mexico City: Grijalbo. Trans. by S. López and E. Schiappari, 1995, as *Hybrid cultures: Strategies for entering and leaving modernity.* Minneapolis: University of Minnesota Press.

———. 1990. *Consumidores y ciudadanos: Conflictos multiculturales de la globalizacíon.* Mexico City: Grijalbo.

———. 1995. *Hybrid cultures: Strategies for entering and leaving modernity.* Minneapolis: University of Minnesota Press.

———. 2001. *Consumer and citizens: Globalization and multicultural conflicts.* Trans. G. Yúdice. Minneapolis: University of Minnesota Press. (Original work published 1990).

García Danglades, Antonio Guillermo. 2003a. Another viewpoint. Venezuelanalysis.com, June 16. www.11abril.com/index/articulos/DINR16june03.asp (accessed July 22, 2004).

———. 2003b. The dark side of the Venezuelan opposition. Venezuelanalysis.com, October 24. www.venezuelanalysis.com/articles.php?artno=1042 (accessed June 26, 2004).

Garnham, Nicholas. 1990. *Capitalism and communication.* Thousand Oaks, Calif.: Sage.

Geiss, Immanuel. 1974. *The pan-African movement: A history of pan-Africanism in America, Europe and Africa.* New York: Africana Publishing Co.

Georgiou, Myria, and Eugenia Siapera, eds. 2006. Multiculturalism. Special issue. *International Journal of Media and Cultural Policy* 2 (3).

Gerbner, George. 1976. Living with television: The violence profile. *Journal of Communication* 26 (2): 173–99.

Giddens, Anthony. 1990. *The consequences of modernity.* Palo Alto, Calif.: Stanford University Press.

———. 1994. *Beyond left and right.* Cambridge: Polity.

Gilley, Bruce. 2001. Jiang's turn tempts fate. *Far Eastern Economic Review,* August 30, 18–21.

———. 2004. *China's democratic future: How it will happen and where it will lead.* New York: Columbia University Press.

Ginsburg, Faye, Lila Abu-Lughod, and Brian Larkin (eds.) 2002. *Media worlds: Anthropology on new terrain.* Berkeley: University of California Press.

Global Information Infrastructure Commission. 2004. Commissioner Gustavo A. Cisneros. www.giic.org/commissioners/bio/bio_cisneros.asp (accessed July 22, 2004).

Godfrey, Brian J. 2004. *Barrio under siege: Latino sense of place in San Francisco, California.* Austin: University of Texas Press.

Golding, Peter. 1974. Media Role in National Development. *Journal of Communication* 24 (3): 39–53.

Golding, Peter, and Phil Harris. 1997. *Beyond cultural imperialism: Globalization, communication and the new international order.* London: Sage.

Golding, Peter, and Graham Murdoch. 1978. Theories of communication and theories of society. *Communication Research* 5 (3): 339–56.

Gole, Nilufer. 2002. Islam in public: New visibilities and new imaginaries. *Public Culture* 14 (1): 173–90.

Golinger-Moncada, Eva. 2003a. The proposed law of social responsibility in radio and television. Venezuelanalysis.com, September 10. www.venezuelanalysis.com (accessed September 16, 2003).

———. 2003b. New media giant raises ethical concerns. Venezuelanalysis.com, September 25. www.venezuelanalysis.com (accessed September 26, 2003).

Goltung, Johan, 1999. State, capital, and civil society: A problem of communication. In, *Towards equity in global communication: MacBride update,* ed. Richard C. Vincent, Kaarle Nordenstreng, and Michael Traber, 3–21, Cresskill, N.J.: Hampton Press.

Gómez, Luis. 2005a. An interview with the Aporrea.org Collective, pt. 1: The new voice of the Venezuelan people. Venezuelanalysis.com, May 17. www.venezuelanalysis.com/articles .php?artno=1451.

———. 2005b. An interview with the Aporrea.org Collective, pt. 2: Media constructed from below. Venezuelanalysis.com, May 18. www.venezuelanalysis.com/articles.php?artno=1452.

Gong, Yang, ed. 2003. *Sichao: Zhongguo xinzoupai jiqi yingxiang* [Intellectual trends: China's new left and its influence]. Beijing: China Social Sciences Press.

Gonzales Rodríguez, Sauro. 2002. Cannon fodder. Venezuela special report, Committee for the Protection of Journalists. www.cpj.org/Briefings/2002/ven_aug02/ven_aug02.html (accessed July 24, 2004).

Goodman, David S.G. 1981. *Beijing street voices: The poetry and politics of China's democracy movement*. London: M. Boyars.

Gott, Richard. 2005. *Hugo Chávez and the Bolivarian Revolution*. London: Verso.

———. 2006. Venezuela's Murdoch. *New Left Review* 39 (May–June 2006): 149–58.

———. 2007. Revolutionary leadership. *Guardian Online*. January 9, 2007. commentisfree .guardian.co.uk/richard_gott/2007/01/post_888.html (accessed January 10, 2007).

Gramsci, Antonio. 1971. *Selections from the prison notebooks*. London: Lawrence and Wishart.

Greenbaum, Lior. 2003. Palestinians set up first technology incubator. *Globes: Israel's Business Arena,* November 6.

Gregor, Alison. 2003. What's Spanish for "big media"? A controversial merger ignites the diversity of voices issue. *Columbia Journalism Review*. 42 (3): 62.

Gries, Peter Hays. 2004. *China's new nationalism: Pride, politics, and diplomacy*. Berkeley, Calif.: University of California Press.

Grioni, Raul, and Donatella Iacobelli. 2004. Venezuela's diario vea: A new way to do journalism; interview with Servando Garcia Ponce. Venezuelanalysis.com. www.venezuelanalysis .com/articles.php?artno=1206 (accessed June 26, 2004).

Grover, Ron. 2004. The heavyweight on Latin American airwaves. *Business Week* 62, August 9. www.businessweek.com/magazine/content/04_32/b3895109_mz016.htm.

Grushin, B., and L. Onikov. 1980. *Massovaya informatsiya v sovetskom promishlennom gorode* [Mass information in a Soviet industrial city]. Moscow: Politizdat.

Guadalupe, Patricia. 2003. A merger mired in controversy. *Hispanic Business,* July/August, 62.

Guardian Newspapers (Nigeria). 2005. Zimbabwe threatens NGOs, blocks mercenaries release. March 12. www.ngrguardiannews.com/africa/article02.

Gudkov, L. 2004. *Negativnaya identichnost. Statyi 1997–2000 godov* [Negative identity. Articles from 1997–2000]. Moscow: Novoye Literaturnoye Obosreniye—VCIOM-A.

Gupta, Akhil. 1998. *Postcolonial developments: Agriculture and the making of modern India*. Durham, N.C.: Duke University Press.

Haas, Ernst B. 1948. The United States of Europe. *Political Science Quarterly* 63:528–50.

Habermas, Jurgen. 1989. *The structural transformation of the public sphere: An inquiry into a category of bourgeois society*. Cambridge, Mass.: MIT Press.

———. 1996. *Between facts and norms: Contributions to a discourse theory of law and democracy*. Trans. William Rehg. Cambridge, Mass.: MIT Press.

Hackett, Robert, and Yuezhi Zhao. 1998. *Sustaining democracy? Journalism and the politics of objectivity*. Toronto: Garamond Press.

———. 2005. *Democratizing global media: One world, many struggles*. Lanham, Md.: Rowman & Littlefield.

Halbert, Deborah. 1999. *Intellectual property in the information age: The politics of expanding ownership rights*. Westport, Conn.: Quorum Press.

Hall, Stuart. 1980. Encoding/Decoding in television discourse. In *Culture, media, language,* ed. S. Hall, D. Hobson, A. Lowe, and P. Willis, 128–38. London: Hutchinson.

———. 1991. The local and the global: Globalization and ethnicity. In *Culture, globalization, and the world-system,* ed. A. King, 19–39. London: Macmillan.

———. 1997. The work of representation. In *Representation: Cultural representations and signifying practices,* ed. S. Hall, 13–64. London: The Open University.

Hallin, Daniel C. 2000. Media, political power and democratization in Mexico. In *De-Westernizing media studies,* ed. J. Curran and M. J. Park, 97–110. London: Routledge.

Hannerz, Ulf. 1996. *Transnational connections: Culture, people, places.* London: Routledge.

Hansen, Thomas Blom. 2001. *Wages of violence: Naming and identity in postcolonial Bombay.* Princeton, N.J.: Princeton University Press.

Hara, Yumiko. 2004. Import and export of Japanese television programs. Paper presented at 13th JAMCO Online International Symposium, Japanese TV Dramas that Go Beyond "Japan": Their Transnational Significance and Influence. www.jamco.or.jp/2004_symposium/en/.

Hardt, M., and Antonio Negri. 2000. *Empire.* Cambridge, Mass.: Harvard University Press.

———. 2005. *Multitude, war and democracy in the age of empire.* London: Hamish Hamilton.

Harriss, John. 2005. Political participation, representation and the urban poor: Findings from Delhi. *Economic and Political Weekly* 11 (11): 1041–54.

———. 2006. Middle-class activism and the politics of the informal working class: A perspective on class relations and civil society in Indian cities. *Critical Asian Studies* 38 (4): 445–66.

Harriss-White, Barbara. 2002. *India working: Essays on society and economy.* Cambridge: Cambridge University Press.

Hart-Landsberg, Martin and Paul Burkett. 2005. *China and socialism: Market reforms and class struggle.* New York: Monthly Review Press.

Harvey, David. 2000. *Spaces of hope.* Berkeley: University of California Press.

———. 2003. *The new imperialism.* London: Verso.

———. 2005. *A brief history of neoliberalism.* Oxford, N.Y.: Oxford University Press.

Hass, Amira. 2000. *Drinking the sea at Gaza: Days and nights in a land under siege.* New York: Owl Books.

———. 2002. Israel's closure policy: An ineffective strategy of containment and repression. *Journal of Palestine Studies* 31 (3): 5–20.

He Weifang Xishan huiyi fayan jilu [Transcript of He Weifang's speech at the Xishan Conference]. 2006. *Kaifang,* June, 64–67.

Held, David, and Anthony McGrew. 2002. *Globalization/anti-globalization.* Cambridge: Polity.

Herman, Edward, and Noam Chomsky. 1998. *Manufacturing consent: The political economy of the mass media.* New York: Pantheon Books.

Herman, Edward S., and Robert W. McChesney. 1997. *The global media: The missionaries of global capitalism.* London and Washington, D.C.: Cassell.

Herman, Eric. 2004. Competition spurs action at La Raza. *Chicago Sun Times.* March 15.

Hibou, Beatrice, ed. 2004. *Privatizing the state.* Trans. Jonathan Derrick. New York: Columbia University Press.

Hicks, Kyra. 2003. *Black threads: An African American quilting sourcebook.* Jefferson, N.C.: McFarland & Company, Inc.

Hill, Mike, and Warren Montag. 2000. What was, what is, the public sphere? Post–Cold War reflections. In *Masses, classes and the public sphere,* ed. M. Hill and W. Montag, 1–10. London: Verso.

Hills, Jill. 2002. *The struggle for control of global communication.* Urbana: University of Illinois.

Hirst, Paul, and Grahame Thompson. 1996. *Globalization in question: The international economy and the possibilities of governance.* Cambridge: Polity Press.

Hobsbawm, Eric J. [1990] 2004. *Nations and nationalism since 1780: Programme, myth, reality.* Cambridge: Cambridge University Press.

Holloway, John. 2004. Power and the state. www.redpepper.org.uk/Nov2004/x-Nov2004 -Holloway.html (accessed January 20, 2005).

Hoodfar, Homa. 1993. The veil in their minds and on our heads: The persistence of colonial images of Muslim women. *Resources for Feminist Research* 22 (3–4): 5–18.

Hopkins, Mark. 1970. *Mass media in the Soviet Union.* New York. Pegasus.

——. 1983. *Russia's underground press: The chronicle of current events.* New York: Praeger.

Horwitz, Robert B. 2001. "Negotiated liberalization": The politics of communications reform in South Africa. In *Media and globalization: Why the state matters,* ed. N. Morris and S. Waisbord, 37–54. Lanham, Md.: Rowman and Littlefield.

Howell, Jude, and Jenny Pearce. 2001. *Civil society and development: A critical exploration.* Boulder, Colo.: Lynne Rienner Publishers.

Hu, Andy. 2006. *Swimming against the tide: Tracing and locating Chinese leftism online.* MA thesis, School of Communication, Simon Fraser University, Canada.

Hu, Angang, Zhou Ping, and Li Chunbo. 2001. 1978–2000 nian: Zhongguo jingji shehui fazhan de dique chaju [1978–2000: Regional differences in China's economic and social developments]. In *2001 nian Zhongguo shehui xingshi fenxi yu yuce* [China social situation analysis and forecast], ed. Ru Xin, Shan Tielun, and Lu Xueyi, 167–84. Beijing: Shehui kexue wenxian chubanshe.

Hu, Hsing-chi. 2004. Chinese re-makings of pirated Japanese VCD TV dramas. In *Feeling Asian modernities: Transnational consumption of Japanese TV Drama,* ed. K. Iwabuch 205–26. Hong Kong: University of Hong Kong Press.

Huang, Ping, Yao Yang, and Han Yuhai. 2006. *Women de shidai* [Our times]. Beijing: Central Compilation and Translation Press.

Hueva, William, Keyan Tomaselli, and Ruth Tomaselli. 2004. The political economy of media in Southern Africa, 1990–2001. In *Who owns the media? Global trends and local resistances,* ed. P. N. Thomas and Z. Nain, 97–117. Penang, Malaysia: Southbound.

Huff, Richard. 2001. Networks co-operating on news at record level. *The Province* (Vancouver, B.C.). October 12.

Hughes, Christopher R., and Gudrun Wacker. 2003. *China and the Internet: Politics of the digital leap forward.* London: RoutledgeCurzon.

Hulme, David, and Michael Edwards. 1997. NGOs, states and donors: An overview. In *NGOs, states and donors: Too close for comfort?* ed. D. Hulme and M. Edwards, 2–22. London: Macmillan Press.

Human Rights Watch. 2003. Venezuela: Official press agency distorts Human Rights Watch position. October 28.

Humphreys, Peter. 2007. The EU, communications liberalisation and the future of public service broadcasting. In Media and cultural policy in the European Union, ed. Katharine Sarikakis, special issue of *European Studies: An Interdisciplinary Series in European Culture History and Politics* 24: 91–112.

Huntington, Samuel P. 1996. *Clash of civilizations and the remaking of the world order.* New York: Simon & Schuster.

Hutchinson, John, and Anthony D. Smith, eds. 1996. *Ethnicity.* Oxford: Oxford University Press.

Iacobelli, Donatella, and Raul Grioni. 2004. Interview with Communication and Information Minister Jesse Chacon, pt. 2. Venezuelanalysis.com. www.venezuelanalysis.com/print.php ?artno=1106 (accessed March 14, 2004).

IFJ [International Federation of Journalists]. 2002. *Missing links in Venezuela's political crisis; How media and government failed a test of journalism and democracy, Report of IFJ mission to Caracas.* June 10–12, 2002. www.ifj.org/pdfs/venezuelajuly02.pdf (accessed June 26, 2004).

——. 2006. Few investigations into deaths of journalists. www.ifj.org/default.asp?Index =2903&Language=EN.

Ihnen, Hans J. 1995. *Grundzüge des Europarechts* [Fundamental characteristics of European Law]. München: Vahlen.

Intel Club House. www.computerclubhouse.org/.

Intellectual Property Watch 1 (1), November 2004.

InterAction Newsletter. 2004. Interaction member ICT success stories: IT4Youth: Creating hope for Palestinian youth. January 2004. www.interaction.org/ict/success_ict.html (accessed March 25, 2004).

Internet World Stats. 2004. Internet usage in the Middle East. September 30. www.internet -worldstats.com/stats5.htm (accessed October 3, 2004).

Ismael, T. Y., and J. Measor, 2003. Racism and the North American media following 11 September: The Canadian setting. *Arab Studies Quarterly*. 25 (1–2): 101–37.

IT4Youth [Information Technology for Youth]. www.it4youth.com.

Ito, Mamoru. 2004. The representation of femininity in Japanese television drama of the 1990s. In *Feeling Asian modernities: Transnational consumption of Japanese TV drama*, ed. K. Iwabuchi, 25–42. Hong Kong: University of Hong Kong Press.

Ivy, Marilyn. 1995. *Discourses of the vanishing: Modernity, phantasm, Japan*. Chicago: University of Chicago Press.

Iwabuchi, Koichi. 1998. Pure impurity: Japan's genius for hybridism. *Communal/Plural: Journal of Transnational and Cross-cultural Studies* 6 (1): 71–86.

——. 2001. Becoming culturally proximate: A/Scent of Japanese idol dramas. In *Asian media productions*, ed. B. Moeran, 54–74. London: Curzon.

——. 2002. *Recentering globalization: Popular culture and Japanese transnationalism*. Durham, N.C.: Duke University Press.

——. 2004a. Feeling glocal: Japan in the global TV format business. In *Television across Asia: TV industries, programme formats and globalization*, ed. A. Moran and M. Keane, 21–35. London: Routledge, Curzon.

——. 2004b. How "Japanese" is Pokemon? In *Pikachu's global adventure: The rise and fall of Pokemon*, ed. J. Tobin, 53–79. Durham, N.C.: Duke University Press.

——. Forthcoming. When Korean wave meets resident Koreans in Japan: Intersections of the transnational, the postcolonial and the multicultural. In *East Asian pop culture: Approaching the Korean Wave*, ed. B.-H. Chua and K. Iwabuchi. Hong Kong: Hong Kong University Press.

IYF [International Youth Foundation]. www.iyf.org.

Jachtenfuchs, Markus, Diez Thomas, and Jung Sabine. 1998. Which Europe? Conflicting models of a legitimate European order. *European Journal of International Relations* 4 (4): 409–45.

Jackson, Robert H. 1990. *Quasi-states: Sovereignty, international relations and the third world*. Cambridge: Cambridge University Press.

Jafferlot, Christopher. 1998. The Bahjan Samaj Party in North India: No longer just a Dalit party? *Comparative Studies of South Asia, Africa and the Middle East* 17 (1): 35–52.

Jamal, Manal. 2004. The limits of civil society in Palestine: "Bringing politics back in." Paper presented at Middle East Studies Association Annual Conference, San Francisco, CA., November 20–23.

James, Caryn. 2005. Beyond comforting the afflicted. *New York Times*. September 12.

James, Meg, and Jeffery Leeds. 2002. Regulators face a bilingual conundrum. *Los Angeles Times*. November 24.

Jardim, Claudia, and Jonah Gindin. 2004. Venezuela: Changing the world by taking power. Interview with Tariq Ali. Venuezuelanalysis.com. www.venezuelanalysis.com/articles.php ?artno=1223 (accessed December 21, 2006).

Jaszi, Peter, and Martha Woodmansee. 2003. Beyond authorship: Refiguring rights in traditional culture and bioknowledge. In *Scientific authorship: Credit and intellectual property in science,* ed. M. Biagioli, 195–224. New York: Routledge.

Jayasuriya, Kanishka. 2000. Authoritarian liberalism, governance and the emergence of the regulatory state in post-crisis East Asia. In *Politics and markets in the wake of the Asian crisis,* ed. R. Mark Beeson, K. Jayasuriya, and H. R. Kim, 315–330. London, Routedge.

Jenkins, Rob. 2001. Mistaking "governance" for politics: Foreign aid, democracy, and the construction of civil society. In *Civil society: History and possibilities,* ed. S. Kaviraj and S. Khilnani, 250–68. Cambridge: Cambridge University Press.

———. 2003. The ideologically embedded market: Political legitimation and economic reform in India." In *Markets in historical contexts: Ideas and politics in the modern world*, ed. Mark Bevir and Frank Trentmann, 305–35. Cambridge: Cambridge University Press.

Jessop, Bob. 1997. Survey article: The regulation approach. *Journal of Political Philosophy* 5 (3): 287–326.

Jhally, Sut. 1997. *Stuart Hall: Representation and the media.* Video produced for the Media Education Foundation.

Jiang, Xueqin. 2001. Fighting to organise. *Far Eastern Economic Review.* September 6, 74.

Jimenez, Marina. 1998. Ontario sharia plan protested. *Globe and Mail.* September 9.

Johnson, Chalmers. 2007. Republic or empire: A national intelligence estimate on the United States. *Harper's.* January, 63–69.

Kabeer, Naila. 2002. *The power to choose: Bangladeshi women and labor market decisions in London and Dhaka.* London: Verso.

Kachkaeva, A. 2001. Desyat let post-sovietskih SMI. Paper presented at the annual conference of the journalism faculty, Moscow State University, January 22.

Kahn, Joseph. 2006a. A sharp debate erupts in China over ideologies. *New York Times.* March 12. *New York Times.* www.nytimes.com/2006/03/12/international/asia/12china.html?page wanted=2&_r=1&th&emc=th (accessed March 12, 2006).

———. 2006b. China, shy giant, shows signs of shedding its false modesty. *New York Times.* December 9. www.nytimes.com/2006/12/09/world/asia/09china.html (accessed December 11, 2006).

Kaitatzi-Whitlock, Sophia. 2006. *Europe's political communication deficit.* Bury St. Edmunds, Suffolk: Arima Publ.

Kangwa-Wilkie, Sampa (program officer, freedom of expression, MISA). 2006. (E-Mail communication, December).

Karim, Karim H. 2003. *Islamic peril: Media and global violence.* Montreal: Black Rose Books.

Karnik, Kirin. 2006. Create competencies not quotas. *Economic Times.* July 6. economc times.indiatimes.com/articleshow/msid-1708838,curpg-2.cms.

Katz, Elihu, and George Wedell. 1977. *Broadcasting in the Third World: Promise and performance.* Cambridge: Harvard University Press.

Kaufer, Enrique. 2004. Press release: La Opinión/Lozano family and CPK Media announce creation of first national Latino newspaper company. *Impremedia.*

Keane, John. 1998. *Civil society: Old images, new visions.* Cambridge: Polity Press.

———. 2003. *Global civil society?* Cambridge: Cambridge University Press.

Keane, Michael. 2006. Once were peripheral: Creating media capacity in East Asia. *Media, Culture & Society* 28 (6): 835–55.

Kelliher, Laurie. 2003. Emerging alternatives: Low power, high intensity. *Columbia Journalism Review* 42 (5).

Kelly, Janet, and Pedro A. Palma. 2004. The syndrome of economic decline and the quest for change. In *The unravelling of representative democracy in Venezuela,* ed. J. L. McCoy and D. J. Myers, 152–80. Baltimore: Johns Hopkins University Press.

Kettman, Steve. 2001. Deep thinking on the "Inter-Fada." *Wired News.* www.wired .com/news/politics/0,1283,44919,00.html (accessed August 2, 2003).

Khalil, Joe. 2006. Inside Arab reality television. *Transnational Broadcasting Studies* 2 (1). www.tbsjournal.com.

Kien, Grant. 2004. Culture, state, globalization: The articulation of global capitalism. *Cultural Studies, Critical Methodologies* 4 (4): 472–500.

Kirchner, Henner. 2001. Internet in the Arab world: A step towards "information society"? In *Mass media, politics and society in the Middle East,* ed. K. Hafez, 137–58. Cresskill, N.J.: Hampton Press.

Klein, Naomi. 2003. The media against democracy. *Guardian.* February 8. www.guardian .co.uk/comment/story/0,3604,897769,00html (February 21, 2003).

Koltsova, Olessia. 2001. News production in contemporary Russia: Practices of power. *European Journal of Communication* 16 (3): 315–35.

———. 2006a. *News media and political power in Russia.* London: RoutledgeCurzon.

———. 2006b. Whose war? The Chechen conflicts on Russian television. *Kultura (Russian cultural review).* March, 3–7.

Kozloff, Nikolas. 2005. Chávez launches hemispheric, "anti-hegemonic" media campaign in response to local TV networks' anti-government bias. Council on Hemispheric Affairs. www.coha.org/2005/04/28/chavez-launches-hemispheric-"anti-hegemonic"-media-campaign-in-response-to-local-tv-networks-anti-government-bias/ (accessed September 27, 2005).

Kraidy, Marwan M. 1999. The local, the global and the hybrid: A native ethnography of glocalization. *Critical Studies in Media Communication* 16 (4): 456–77.

———. 2002a. Ferment in global media studies. *Journal of Broadcasting and Electronic Media* 46 (4): 630–40.

———. 2002b. Arab satellite television between globalization and regionalization. *Global Media Journal* 1(1). lass.calumet.purdue.edu/cca/gmj/new_page_1.htm.

———. 2004. From culture to hybridity in international communication. In *Frontiers in international communication theory,* ed. M. Semati, 247–62. Laurel, Md.: Rowman and Littlefield.

———. 2005. *Hybridity, or the cultural logic of globalization.* Philadelphia: Temple University Press.

———. 2006a. Reality television and politics in the Arab world—Preliminary observations. *Transnational Broadcasting Studies* 2 (1): 7–28.

———. 2006b. Hypermedia and governance in Saudi Arabia. *First Monday* 11 (9). firstmonday .org/issues/special11_9.

———. 2007. Saudi Arabia, Lebanon, and the New Arab Information Order. *International Journal of Communication* 1 (1). ijoc.org/ojs/index.php/ijoc/article/view/18/22.

Kraidy, Marwan M., and Joe F. Khalil. 2007. The Middle East: Transnational arab television. In *The media globe: Trends in international mass media,* ed. L. Artz and Y. Kamalipour, 77–98. Lanham, Md.: Rowman & Littlefield.

———. Forthcoming. Children, young people and the media in the Arab world. In *International handbook of children, media and culture,* ed. Sonia Livingstone and Kristin Drotner. London: Sage.

Kramer, Martin. 2002. The camera and the burqa. *Middle East Quarterly.* Spring, 69–76. www.meforum.org/article/177.

Laclau, Ernesto. 1977. *Politics and ideology in Marxist theory.* London: New Left Books.

———. 2005. *On populist reason.* London: Verso.

Laclau, Ernesto, and Chantal Mouffe. 1985. *Hegemony and socialist strategy: Towards a radical democratic politics.* London/New York: Verso.

Leary, J. P. 2004. Caracas's barrio newswire. *Z Magazine.* March, 17–20.

———. 2006. Untying the knot of Venezuela's informal economy. *NACLAnews.* December. news.nacla.org/2006/12/06/untying-the-knot-of-venezuela's-informaleconomy (accessed December 24, 2006).

Lebowitz, Michael A. 2006. *Build it now: Socialism for the twenty-first century.* New York: Monthly Review Press.

———. 2007. Why aren't *you* in a hurry, comrade? *MR Zine.* January. mrzine.monthlyreview .org/lebowitz010207.html (accessed February 1, 2007).

Lee, Chin-Chuan, ed. 2000. *Power, money, and media: Communication patterns and bureaucratic control in cultural China.* Evanston, Ill.: Northwestern University Press.

———. 2003. *Chinese media, global contexts.* London and New York: RoutledgeCurzon.

Lee, Chin-Chuan, Zhou He, and Yu Huang. 2006. "Chinese Party Publicity Inc." conglomerated: The case of the Shenzhen Press Group. *Media, Culture & Society* 28 (4): 581–602.

Lee, Dong-Hoo. 2004. Cultural contact with Japanese TV dramas: Modes of reception and narrative transparency. In *Feeling Asian modernities: Transnational consumption of Japanese TV drama,* ed. K. Iwabuchi, 251–74. Hong Kong: University of Hong Kong Press.

Lehrer News Hour. 2004. PBS. June 16.

Leiss, William. 1990. *Under technology's thumb.* Montreal: McGill-Queen's University Press.

Lemoine, Maurice. 2002. Venezuela's press power. *Le Monde Diplomatique.* August 10. mondediplo.com/2002/08/10venezuela (accessed June 21, 2004).

Lerner, Daniel. 1958. *The passing of traditional societies: Modernizing the Middle East.* Glencoe, Ill.: Free Press.

Lepage, Mark. 2004. The Bush-whacker. *Globe and Mail* (Toronto). April 7.

Lessig, Lawrence. 2002. *The future of ideas: The fate of the commons in a connected world.* New York: Vintage Books.

———. 2004. *Free culture: How big media uses technology and the law to lock down culture and control creativity.* New York: Penguin Press.

Levinson, A. 2000. Zhenschina kak tsel i sredstvo v otechestvennoi reklame [Women as target and means in national advertising]. In *Zhenschina i Visualniye Znaki* [Women and visual signs], ed. A. Alchuk, 43–64. Moscow: Ideya-Press.

Lewis, Bernard. 1994. *The shaping of the modern Middle East.* New York: Oxford University Press.

Leys, Colin. 1990. Still a question of hegemony. *New Left Review* 181:119–28.

Li, Liang, and Tonghui Xu. 2006. 2004–2006 "Disanci gaige zhenglun" shimo [The beginning and end of the "Third Debate on Reform," 2004–2006]. *Nanfang zhoumo,* March 16. www.nanfangdaily.com.cn/zm/20060316/xw/tb/200603160002.asp (accessed March 17, 2006).

Liberman, S. 1999. Yugoslavskiy konflikt—tema nome odin. [The Yugoslav conflict—theme number one]. *Sreda* 5 (11).

Library Media Connection. 2005, March.

Liechty, Mark. 1995. Media, markets and modernization: Youth identities and the experience of modernity in Kathmandu, Nepal. In *Youth culture: A cross-cultural perspective,* ed. V. Amit-Talai and H. Wulff, 166–201. London: Routledge.

Lifsher, Marc. 2002. Government drill: In under 48 hours, Venezuelans have enough of a coup. *Wall Street Journal.* April 15, A1.

Lin, Chun. 2006. *The transformation of Chinese socialism.* Durham, N.C., and London: Duke University Press.

Lin, Gang. 2003. Ideology and political institution for a new era. In *China after Jiang,* ed. G. Lin and X. Hu, 39–68. Washington, D.C.: Woodrow Wilson Centre Press.

Lin, Min, and Maria Galikowski. 1999. *The search for modernity: Chinese intellectuals and cultural discourse in the post-Mao era.* New York: St. Martin's Press.

Lionnet, Françoise, and Shu mei Shih. 2005. Introduction. In *Minor transnationalism,* ed. Lionnet Françoise and S. Shih, 1–26. Durham, N.C.: Duke University Press.

Liu, Bo. 2006. Africa looks east: From the "Washington Consensus" to "the Beijing Consensus." news.sina.com.cn/c/2006-11-07/121311448833.shtml.

Liu, Kang. 2004. *Globalization and cultural trends in China.* Honolulu: University of Hawai'i Press.

Llorente, Elizabeth. 2003. Read all about it, en Español: The Spanish-language business is booming. *Hispanic.* December 31, 16.

Lloyd, Christopher. 2000. Globalisation: Beyond the ultra-modernist narrative to critical realist prospective on geopolitics in the cyber age. *International Journal of Urban and Regional Research* 24 (2): 258–73.

Lock, Peter. 2006. *Ökonomie der "neuen Kriege"; Kalte Friedenskonsolidierung durch Kriminalisierung?* [The economy of new wars: Cold consolidation of peace through criminalization?]. www.libertysecurity.org/IMG/doc/Schlaining2005.doc.

Logan, Harriet. 2002. *Unveiled: Voices of women in Afghanistan.* New York: Regan Books, Harper Collins.

Lovink, Geert, and Florian Schneider. 2002. A virtual world is possible: From tactical media to digital multitudes. *Nettime Post.* www.cyberaxe.org/04/pdf/lovink_schneider.pdf (acccessed August 2, 2005).

Lu, Ding, and Chee Kong Wong. 2003. *China's telecommunications market: Entering a new competitive age.* Cheltenham, UK: Edward Elgar.

Lu, Xinyu. 2006. Yish, dianshi he guojia yishixingtai — zaidu 2006 nian chunjiewanhui [Ritual, television and state ideology: Another reading of the 2006 Spring Festival Gala]. http://www.wyzxsx.com/Article/Class10/200608/8917.html (accessed January 18, 2007).

Lugo, Jairo, and Juan Romero. 2003. From friends to foe: Venezuela's media go from consenual space to confrontational actor. *Sincronia* (Jalisco, Mexico). Spring 2002. sincronia.cucsh.udg.mx/lugoromeroinv02.htm (accessed June 21, 2004).

Lyon, Fergus. 2003. Trader associations and urban food systems in Ghana: Institutionalist approaches to understanding urban collective action. *International Journal of Urban and Regional Research* 27 (1): 11–23.

MacDonald, Gayle. 2001. The war on terror: The new world order media fear censorship as Bush requests caution. *Globe and Mail* (Toronto). October 11.

Macdonald, Laura. 1997. *Supporting civil society: The political role of non-governmental organizations in Central America.* New York: St. Martins Press.

MacKenzie, Tyler. 2004. The best hope for democracy in the Arab world: A crooning TV "idol"? *Transnational Broadcasting Studies* 13. www.tbsjournal.com/Archives/Fall04/mackenzie.html.

MacLeod, Ian. 2001. Bin Laden statements could be coded: U.S. fears TV videos contain orders for agents. *Ottawa Citizen.* October 11.

Madsen, Richard. 2003. One country, three systems: State-society relations in post-Jiang China. In *China after Jiang,* ed. G. Lin and X. Hu, 91–114. Washington, D.C.: Woodrow Wilson Center Press and Stanford, Calif.: Stanford University Press.

Magnusson, Lars, and Jan Ottosson. 2000. State intervention and the role of history — State and private actors in Swedish network industries. *Review of Political Economy* 12 (2):191–205.

Mahajan, Rahul. 2002. *The new crusade: America's war on terrorism.* New York: Monthly Review Press.

Majone, G. 1996. Which social policy for Europe. In *Adjusting to Europe. The impact of the European Union on national institutions and policies,* ed. Y. Meny, P. Muller, and J.-L. Quermonne, 123–36. London and New York: Routledge.

Malkin, Elizabeth. 2005. Relations sour between two Hispanic media giants. *New York Times.* May 17, C5.

Mamdani, Mahmood. 1995. Introduction. In *African studies in social movements and democracy,* ed. M. Mamdani and E. Wamba-dia-Wamba, 1–34. Dakar, Senegal: CODESRIA.

———. 1996. *Citizen and subject: Contemporary Africa and the legacy of late colonialism.* Princeton, N.J.: Princeton University Press.

————. 2004. *Good Muslim, bad Muslim: America, the Cold War and the roots of terror.* New York: Pantheon Books.

Mani, Lata. 1998. *Contentious traditions: The debate on sati in colonial India.* Berkeley: University of California Press.

Mansfield, Peter. 1991. *A history of the Middle East.* New York: Viking.

Manthorpe, Jonathan. 2006. Communist party divided on dealing with dissidents. *Vancouver Sun.* January 31, E3.

Marks, Gary, Hooghe Liesbet, and Blank Kermit. 1996. European integration from the 1980s: State-centric v. multi-level governance. *Journal of Common Market Studies* 34 (3): 341–378.

Martín-Barbero, Jesús. 1993. *Communication, culture and hegemony: From the media to mediations.* London & Newbury Park, Calif.: Sage.

Mather, Steven. 2007. Venezuelan government announces $5 billion for communal councils in 2007. Venezuelanalysis.com. www.venezuelanalysis.com/news.php?newsno=2188 (accessed January 2, 2007).

Mattelart, Armand. 1979. *Multinational corporations and the control of culture.* Atlantic Highlands, N.J.: Humanities Press.

————. 1994. *Mapping world communication: War, progress, culture.* Minneapolis: University of Minnesota Press.

————. 1998. Généalogie des nouveaux scénarios de la communication. In *L'Après-Télévision: Multimédia, virtuel, Internet. Actes du Colloque '25 Images/seconde,* ed. J. Berdot, F. Calvez, and I. Ramonet, n.p. Valence, France: CRAC.

————. [1996] 2000. *Networking the world 1794–2000.* Trans. Liz Carey-Libbrecht and James A. Cohen. Minneapolis: University of Minnesota Press.

————. 2002. *Mapping world communication: War, progress, culture.* Minneapolis: University of Minnesota Press.

Maxwell, Richard, and Toby Miller. 2005. The cultural labor issue. *Social Semiotics* 15 (3): 26–266.

Mazzarella, William. 2003. *Shoveling smoke: Advertising and globalization in contemporary India.* Durham: Duke University Press.

McCaughan, Michael. 2004. *The battle of Venezuela.* London: Latin American Bureau.

McChesney, Robert W. 2000a. The political economy of communication and the future of the field. *Media, Culture & Society* 22:109–16.

————. 2000b. *Rich media, poor democracy: Communication politics in dubious times.* New York: The New Press.

McLeod, Kembrew. 2001. *Owning culture: Authorship, ownership, and intellectual property law.* New York: Peter Lang.

Means, Gordon. 1996. Soft authoritarianism in Malaysia and Singapore. *Journal of Democracy* 7 (4): 103–17.

Media Institute of Southern Africa (MISA), *Annual Report* (April 2004–March 2005). www.misa.org/documents/annualreport2005.pdf.

Meehan, Eileen, and Ellen Riordan. 2002. Introduction. In *Sex and money: Feminism and political economy in the media,* ed. E. Meehan and E. Riordan, ix–xii. Minneapolis: University of Minnesota Press.

Meehan, Eileen R., and Ellen Riordan, eds. 2002. *Sex and money: Feminism and political economy in the media.* Minneapolis: University of Minnesota Press.

Meiskins Wood, Ellen. 1990. The uses and abuses of "civil society." In *Socialist register 1990: The retreat of the intellectuals,* ed. R. Miliband and L. Panitch, 60–84. London: Merlin Press.

Melendez, Luis. 2005. Personal interview, Northampton, MA. August 25.

MENA Business Reports. 2003. Palestinian high tech grows 88 percent despite intifada. November 10.

Meyer, Mike. 2005. The world's biggest book market. *New York Times*. March 13. www .nytimes.com/2005/03/13/books/review/013MEYERL.html?ex=1150862400&en=b8d8d5f1 12d6f249&ei=5070 (accessed March 15, 2005).

Mickiewicz, Ellen. 1997. *Changing channels: Television and the struggle for power in Russia*. New York and Oxford: Oxford University Press.

Miller, Mark. 2002. U.S. Latino capitals in flux: Immigration patterns are changing the culture of some of the largest Hispanic markets. *Multichannel News*. October 28.

Miller, Mark Crispin. 2002. What's wrong with this picture? *Nation*. January 7, 18.

Miller, Scott. 2002. Media's role in crisis becomes big story in Venezuela. *Washington Post*. April 17, A08.

Miller, Toby, Nitin Govil, John McMurria, and Richard Maxwell. 2001. *Global Hollywood*. London: British Film Institute.

Miller, Toby, Nitin Govil, John McMurria, Richard Maxwell, and Ting Wang. 2005. *Global Hollywood 2*. rev. ed. Berkeley: University of California Press.

Milward, Alan S. 1992. *The European rescue of the nation state*. London: Routledge.

Mirza, Hafiz. 1986. Multinationals and the growth of the Singapore economy. London: St. Martin Press.

Mitnick, Joshua. 2004. To reach past curfews, Palestinians go online. *New York Times* February 18, W-1. dotlrn.org/press/2004–02-the-new-york-times-to-reach-past-curfews-palestinians -go-online/ (accessed April 6, 2004).

Mohanty, Chandra. 1991. Under Western eyes: Feminist scholarship and Western discourses. In *Third World women and the politics of feminism*, ed. C. T. Mohanty, A. Russo, and L. Torres, 51–80. Bloomington: Indiana University Press.

———. 2003. *Feminism without borders: Decolonizing theory, practicing solidarity*. Durham, N.C.: Duke University Press.

Molina, José E. 2004. From party rule to personalistic politics and deinstitutionalization. In *The unraveling of representative democracy in Venezuela*, ed. J. L. McCoy and D. J. Myers, 152–80. Baltimore: Johns Hopkins University Press.

Monga, Celestine. 1996. *The anthropology of anger: Civil society and democracy in Africa*. Boulder, Colo.: Lynne Rienner.

Moore, David B. 1995. Development discourse as hegemony: Towards an ideological history— 1945–1955. In *Debating development discourse: Institutional and popular perspectives*, ed. D. B. Moore and G. J. Schmitz, 1–53. London: Macmillan Press.

Morales, Magaly. 2004. Global appeal: Spanish-language TV eases cultural tensions, promotes international fare. *Broadcasting and Cable*, March 22, 28–30.

Moran, A. 1998. *Copycat TV: Globalisation, program formats and cultural identity*. Luton, UK: University of Luton Press.

Moravcsik, Andrew. 1993. Preferences and power in the European Community: A liberal inter-governmentalist approach. *Journal of Common Market Studies* 31: 473–524.

Morley, David. 1980. *The "nationwide" audience: Structure and decoding*. London: British Film Institute.

Morley, David, and Kevin Robins. 1995. *Spaces of identities: Global media, electronic land-scapes and cultural boundaries*. London: Routledge.

Morris, Nancy, and Silvio Waisbord, eds. 2001. *Media and globalization: Why the state matters*. Lanham, Md.: Rowman & Littlefield.

———. 2002. Introduction: Rethinking media globalization and state power. In *Media and globalization: Why the state matters*, ed. N. Morris and S. Waisbord, vii–xiv. Lanham, Md.: Rowman & Littlefield.

Morris-Suzuki, Tessa. 1998. Invisible countries: Japan and the Asian dream. *Asian Studies Review* 22 (1): 5–22.

———. 2000. For and against NGOs. *New Left Review* 2 (March–April): 63–84.

Mosco, Vincent. 1982. *Pushbutton fantasies: Critical perspectives on videotext and information technology.* Norwood, N.J.: Ablex Publishing.

———. 2004. *The digital sublime: Myth, power and cyberspace.* Cambridge, Mass.: MIT Press.

Mosco, Vincent, and Catherine McKercher. 2006. Convergence bites back: Labour struggles in the Canadian communication industry. *Canadian Journal of Communication* 31 (3): 733–51.

Mosco, Vincent, and Vanda Rideout. 1997. Communication policy in the United States. In *Democratizing communication? Comparative perspectives on information and power,* ed. M. Bailie and D. Winseck, 81–104. Cresskill, N.J.: Hampton Press.

Mosco, Vincent, and Dan Schiller. 2001. *Continental order? Integrating North America For cybercapitalism.* Lanham, Md.: Rowman and Littlefield.

MRA (Media Rights Agenda). 2003. *Campaigning for access to information in Nigeria: A report of the legislative advocacy programme for the enactment of Freedom of Information Act.* Lagos, Nigeria: Media Rights Agenda.

Munck, Ronaldo. 2002. *Globalization and labor: The new great transformation.* London: Zed Books.

———. 2004. Globalization, labor and the "Polanyi problem." *Labor History* 45 (3): 251–69.

Murdoch Calls Beijing Paranoid. 2005. www.newsmax.com/archives/ic/2005/9/20/201726.shtml (accessed May 25, 2006).

Murphy, Patrick D., and Marwan M. Kraidy, eds. 2003. *Global media studies: Ethnographic perspectives.* London and New York: Routledge.

Muslih, Muhammad. 1995. Palestinian civil society. In *Toward civil society in the Middle East? A primer,* ed. J. Schwedler. Boulder, Colo.: Lynne Rienner Publishers.

Nack, David, and Jimmy Tarlau. 2005. The Communications Workers of America experience with "open-source unionism." *Working USA* 8 (6): 721–32.

Nair, Janaki. 2005. *The promise of metropolis: Bangalore's twentieth century.* New York: Oxford University Press.

NASSCOM. 2006. *Knowledge Professionals Factsheet.* www.nasscom.in/Nasscom/templates/NormalPage.aspx?id=2374 (Accessed December 5, 2006).

Ndegwa, Stephen. 1996. *Two faces of civil society: NGOs and politics in Africa.* West Hartford, Conn.: Kumarian Press.

Negron-Muntaner, Frances. 2004. *Boricua pop: Puerto Ricans and the Latinization of American culture.* New York: New York University Press.

Nelson, Paul J. 1995. *The World Bank and non-governmental organizations: The limits of apolitical development.* New York: St. Martins Press.

Nentwich, Michael, and Albert Weale. 1998. *Political theory and the European Union: Legitimacy, constitutional choice and citizenship.* London: Routledge.

NEPAD (New Partnership for African Development). 2005. www.nepad.org/2005/files/inbrief.php (accessed March 10, 2006).

New York Times. 2000. Univision workers in 4th week of hunger strike. March 15, A20.

Nordenstreng, Kaarle, and Herbert I. Schiller. eds. 1979. *National sovereignty and international communication.* Norwood, N.J.: Ablex.

Noronha, Ernesto. 1996. Liberalisation and industrial relations. *Economic and Political Weekly* 31 (8): 114–20.

Noronha, Ernesto, and Premilla D'Cruz. 2006. A necessary evil: The experience of managers implementing downsizing programmes. *Qualitative Report* 11 (1): 88–112. www.nova.edu/ssss/QR/QR11–1/noronha.pdf (accessed October 5, 2006).

Norris, P., M. Kern, and M. Just, eds. 2003. *Framing terrorism: The news media, the government and the public.* New York and London: Routledge.

Norton, Augustus Richard. 1996. The virtue of studying civil society. In *The civil society debate in Middle Eastern studies*. Los Angeles: UCLA Near East Center Colloquium Series. http://www.international.ucla.edu/cnes/publications/article.asp?parentid=14546

Nowell-Smith, Geoffrey. 1977. Gramsci and the national-popular. *Screen Education* 22:12–15.

NTIS (National Technical Information Service). 2003. Report on Palestinian study on use of Internet service, information technology. October 5.

Nugent, Neil. 1999. *The government and politics of the European Union*. London: St. Martin's Press.

O'Brien, Kevin J., and Lianjiang Li. 2006. *Rightful resistance in rural China*. Cambridge: Cambridge University Press.

O'Leary, Michael K., and William D. Coplin. 1983. *Political risks in thirty-five countries*. London: Euromoney Publications Ltd.

Obi, Cyril I. 2001. *The changing forms of identity politics in Nigeria under economic adjustment: The case of the oil minorities movement of the Niger delta*. Uppsala, Sweden: Nordiska Afrikainstitutet.

Ofuatey-Kodjoe, W. 1986. *Pan Africanism: New directions in strategy*. Lanham, Md.: University Press of America.

Ojo, Edetaen (executive director, Media Rights Agenda [MRA], Lagos, Nigeria). 2004. Personal interview, Lagos, Nigeria. June 7.

Oldenberg, Veena Talwar. 2002. *Dowry murder: The imperial origins of a cultural crime*. Oxford: Oxford University Press.

Ong, Aihwa. 1999. *Flexible citizenship: The cultural logics of transnationality*. Durham, N.C.: Duke University Press.

——. 2006. *Neoliberalism as exception*. Durham, N.C.: Duke University Press.

Onimode, Bade, ed. 2004. *African development and governance strategies in the 21st century*. London: Zed Books.

Oslo Agreements. 1995. The Israeli-Palestinian interim agreement on the West Bank and the Gaza Strip. Washington, D.C., Agreement Text. www.jewishvirtuallibrary.org/jsource/Peace/interimtoc.html (accessed June 27, 2004).

Ottaway, Marina. 2000. Social movements, professionalization of reform, and democracy in Africa. In *Funding virtue: Civil society aid and democracy promotion*, ed. Marina Ottaway and Thomas Carothers, 77–103. Washington, D.C.: Carnegie Endowment for International Peace.

Oushakine, S. 1999. Kolichestvenniy stil: Potrbleniye v usloviyah simvolicheskogo deficita [Qualitative style: Consumption during symbolic deficit]. *Sociologichesky zhurnal* [Sociological Journal], 3–4. knowledge.isras.ru/sj/sj/sj3–4-99ush.html.

Pan, Zhongdang. 2006. Enacting the family-nation on a global stage: An analysis of the CCTV's spring festival gala. Paper presented at the Re-Orienting Global Communication: India and China beyond Borders Conference, University of Wisconsin-Madison, April 21–22.

Panitch, Leo, and Sam Gindin. 2003. Global capitalism and American empire. In *Socialist register 2004: The new imperial change*, ed. Leo Panitch and Colin Leys, 1–42. London: Merlin Press.

Parenti, Christian. 2005. Hugo Chávez and petro populism. *Nation*. April 11. www.thenation.com/doc/20050411/parenti (accessed August 20, 2005).

PASSIA (Palestinian Academic Society for the Study of International Affairs). 2004. Palestine facts. www.passia.org/index_pfacts.htm (accessed June 2, 2004).

Paxman, Andrew, and Alex M. Saragoza. 2001. Globalization and Latin media powers: The case of Mexico's Televisa. In *Continental order: Integrating North America for cybercapitalism*, ed. V. Mosco and D. Schiller, 64–85. New York: Rowman and Littlefield.

PCBS (Palestinian Central Bureau of Statistics). 2003. *Palestinians at the end of year 2003*. Ramallah: PCBS.

———. 2005. *Palestinians at the end of year 2004*. Ramallah: PCBS.

Pearce, Jenny. 1997. Between co-option and irrelevance? Latin American NGOs in 1990s. In *NGOs, states and donors: Too close for comfort*, ed. David Hulme and Michael Edwards, 257–74. London: Macmillan.

Pendakur, Manjunath. 1991. A political economy of television: State, class and corporate confluence in India. In *Transnational communications: Wiring the third world*, ed. Gerald Sussman and John A. Lent, 234–62. Newbury Park, Calif.: Sage.

———. 2003. *Indian popular cinema: Industry, ideology, and consciousness*. Cresskill, N.J.: Hampton Press.

Peng, Lun. 2003. Gongli minjian ziben chanyu chubanye jingzheng, *"erqudao" chengwei ying quxiao* [Encourage private capital to participate in publishing, canceling the "second channel" notation]. www.booktide.com/news/20030114/200301140004.html (accessed January 15, 2007).

Perez, Maclovio. 2003. Do we need Hispanic journalists? *La Prensa*. August 17, 4A.

Perry, Elizabeth J., and Mark Selden, eds. 2003. *Chinese society: Change, conflict and resistance*. 2nd ed. London and New York: RoutledgeCurzon.

Petrulevich, I. 2004. Informatsionnoye prostranstvo Severnogo Kavkaza: Osobennosti stanovleniya i sovemennoye sostoyaniye [Informational space of the Northern Caucasus: Specifics of formation and current state]. Rostov-na-Donu: unpublished manuscript.

Pinney, Christopher. 1998. Adorno at WOMAD: South Asian crossovers and the limits of hybridity talk. *Postcolonial Studies: Culture, Politics and Economy* 3 (1): 401–26.

PITA (Palestinian Information Technology Association). 2005. *Palestine IT directory 2005*. Ramallah: PITA.

Podur, Justin. 2004. Venezuelan community TV: Interview with Blanca Eekhout, director of Vive. *Znet*. September 6. www.zmag.org/content/showarticle.cfm?ItemID=6174 (accessed January 21, 2005).

Polakoff, Claire. 1980. *Into indigo: African textiles and dyeing techniques*. New York: Anchor Books.

Polanyi, Karl. [1944] 1957. *The great transformation: The political and economic origins of our time*. New York: Beacon Press.

Porter, Tim. 2003. Dismantling the language barrier. *American Journalism Review*, October/November, 48–55.

Price, Monroe E. 2000. *Television, the public sphere, and national identity*. Oxford: Oxford University Press, 1996; Russian translation by S. Anikeyev, Moscow University Press, 2000.

Privacy International and European Digital Rights. 2005. Briefing for members of the European Parliament on data retention. www.statewatch.org/news/2005/jul/05eu-data-retention.htm.

Project for Excellence in Journalism. 2004. The state of the news media 2004: An annual report on American journalism. www.stateofthenewsmedia.org/narrative_ethnicalternative_intro.asp?media=9.

Qiu, Jack Linchuan. 2005. Through the prism of the Internet café: Managing access in an ecology of games. *China Information* 19 (2): 261–97.

Radhakrishnan, P. 2004. Job quotas in the private sector. *Economic and Political Weekly*, October 2. www.epw.org.in/showArticles.php?root=2004&leaf=10&file.

Rajagopal, Arvind. 2005. *Politics after television: Hindu nationalism and the reshaping of the public in India*. Cambridge: Cambridge University Press.

Ramesh, Babu. 2004. "Cyber-coolies" in BPOs: Insecurities and vulnerabilities of non-standard work. *Economic and Political Weekly*. January 31. www.epw.org.in/showArticles.php?root=2004&leaf=01&filename=6784&filetype=html (accessed December 15, 2005).

Ramo, Joshua Cooper. 2004. *The Beijing consensus*. London: The Foreign Policy Centre. fpc.org.uk/fsblob/244.pdf (accessed April 18, 2007).

Ramos, Jorge. 2005. *The Latino wave: How Hispanics are transforming politics in America.* New York: Rayo.

Rantanen, Terhi. 2002. *The global and the national: Media and communications in post-communist Russia.* Lanham, Md., Boulder, Colo., New York, and Oxford: Rowman and Littlefield.

Rashid, Ahmed. 2001. *Taliban: Militant islam, oil and fundamentalism in Central Asia.* New Haven, Conn.: Yale University Press.

Ray, Larry. 2001. Civil society and the public sphere. In *The Blackwell companion to political sociology,* eds. Kate Nash and Alan Scott, 219–29. Oxford: Blackwell Publishers.

Razack, Sherene. 1998. *Looking white people in the eye.* Toronto: Toronto University Press.

———. 2000. Your place or mine? Transnational feminist collaboration. In *Anti-racist feminism: Critical race and gender studies,* ed. G. S. Dei and A. Calliste, 39–54. Halifax: Fernwood Publishing.

———. 2004. Imperilled Muslim women, dangerous muslim men and civilised Europeans: Legal and social responses to forced marriages. *Feminist Legal Studies* 12: 129–74.

Reid, Angus. 2003. Wave the flag or be silenced. *Vancouver Sun.* May 3.

Release of Kandahar film in London. Islam for Today. November 16, 2001. www.islamfortday.com/kandahar.htm

Remesh, Babu P. 2005. *Dynamics of service work in the information society: Work organization, controls and "empowerment" in call centres.* Bangalore, India: National Institute of Advanced Studies.

Renato, Rosaldo. 1997. Cultural citizenship, inequality, and multiculturalism. In *Latino cultural citizenship: Claiming identity, space, and rights,* ed. W. V. Flores and R. Benmayor, 27–38. Boston: Beacon Press.

Renne, Elisha. 1997. "Traditional modernity" and the economics of handwoven cloth production in southwestern Nigeria. *Economic Development and Cultural Change* 45 (4): 773–92.

Reporters sans Frontieres. 2002. La Prensa ausente de los kioscos [The press is absent at the newsstands]. April 14. www.rsf.fr/article.php3?id_article=1110\ (accessed July 14, 2004).

Reporters without Borders. 2005. Criminal code amendments pose threat to press freedom. March 23. www.rsf.org/article.php3?id_article=12973 (accessed October 1, 2005).

———. 2007. Government looking at three options for privately-owned broadcaster. January 2. www.rsf.org/article.php3?id_article=20218 (accessed January 2, 2007).

The revolution will not be televised. 2003. Directed by Kim Bartley and Donnacha O'Briain. Bord Scannán na hÉireann/Irish Film Board.

Rhodes, Martin, and Bastiaan Van Apeldoorn. 1997. *The transformation of West European capitalism?* EUI working paper RSC No. 97/60. San Domenico, Italy: European University Institute.

Rios, Diana I. 2000. Chicana/o and Latina/o gazing: Audiences of the mass media. In *Chicano renaissance: Contemporary cultural trends,* ed. M. Herrera-Sobeck, I. D. Ortiz and D. R, Maciel, 169–90. Tucson: University of Arizona Press.

Rivero, Yensi. 2003. Alternative media to receive state support. *Inter Press Service.* November. www.venezuelanalysis.com/articles.php?artno=1049 (accessed March 19, 2004).

Robertson, Roland. 1992. *Globalization: Social theory and global culture.* London: Sage.

———. 1995. Glocalization: Time-space and homogeneity-heterogeneity. In *Global modernities,* ed. M. Featherstone, S. M. Lash, and R. Robertson, 25–44. London: Sage.

Robins, Kevin. 1997. What in the world's going on? In *Production of culture/cultures of production,* ed. P. du Gay, 11–47. London: Sage.

Robins, Kevin, and Frank Webster. 1999. *Times of technoculture: From the information society to the virtual life.* New York: Routledge.

Robinson, Glenn E. 1997. *Building a Palestinian state: The incomplete revolution.* Bloomington: Indiana University Press.

Robison, Richard. 2006. Preface. In *The neo-liberal revolution: Forging the market state,* ed. Richard Robison, vii. New York: Palgrave.

———. ed. 2006. *The neo-liberal revolution: Forging the market state.* London: Palgrave.

Rodan, Garry. 1997. The Internet and political control in Singapore. *Political Science Quarterly* 113 (1): 63–89.

———. 2003. Embracing electronic media but suppressing civil society: Authoritarian consolidation in Singapore. *Pacific Review* 16 (4): 503–24.

———. 2004. Neoliberalism and transparency: Political versus economic liberalism. Murdoch University, Working Paper No. 112. www.arc.murdoch.edu.au/publications.wpapers.shtml.

Rodríguez, Clemencia. 2001. *Fissures in the mediascape: An international study of citizens' media.* Creskill, N.J.: Hampton Press.

Rofel, Lisa. 1999. *Other modernities: Gendered yearnings in China after socialism.* Berkeley, Calif.: University of California Press.

Romero, Simon. 2002. Coup? Not Cisneros's style. But power? Oh, yes. *New York Times.* April 28.

———. 2007a. Chávez moves to nationalize two industries. *New York Times.* January 9.

———. 2007b. Killings and threats rattle journalists in Venezuela. *New York Times.* November 19.

Ross, Andrew. 2006. *Fast boat to China: Corporate flight and the consequences of free trade.* New York: Pantheon.

Ross, Doran. 1998. *Wrapped in pride: Ghanaian kente and African-American identity.* Los Angeles, CA: UCLA Fowler Museum of Cultural History.

Roy, Sara. 1993. Gaza: New dynamics of civic disintegration. *Journal of Palestine Studies* 22 (4): 20–31.

———. 1994a. "The seed of chaos, and of night": The Gaza Strip after the agreement. *Journal of Palestine Studies* 23 (3): 85–98.

———. 1994b. Separation or integration: Closure and the economic future of the Gaza Strip revisited. *Middle East Journal* 48 (1): 11–30.

———. 1996. U.S. economic aid to the West Bank and Gaza Strip: The politics of peace. *Middle East Policy* 4 (4): 51–76.

———. 1999. De-development revisited: Palestinian economy and society since Oslo. *Journal of Palestine Studies* 28 (3): 64–82.

———. 2001. Palestinian society and economy: The continued denial of possibility. *Journal of Palestine Studies* 30 (4): 5–20.

Ryan, Michael. 1998. *Knowledge diplomacy: Global competition and the politics of intellectual property.* Washington, D.C.: Brookings Institution Press.

Said, Edward. 1978. *Orientalism: Western conceptions of the Orient.* London: Penguin Books.

———. 1981. *Covering Islam: How the media and the experts determine how we see the rest of the world.* New York: Pantheon Books.

Sakr, Naomi. 2002. *Satellite realms: Transnational television, globalization and the Middle East.* London: I. B. Tauris.

Samad, Yunus. 1998. Media and Muslim identity: Intersections of generation and gender. *Innovation* 11 (4): 425–38.

Sanchez, Martin. 2004. Venezuela opposition plan promises return to free market and elimination of referenda. Venezuelanalysis.com. www.venezuelanalysis.com (accessed July 14, 2004).

Sandholtz, Wayne, and Alec Stone Sweet. 1998. *European integration and supranational governance.* Oxford: Oxford University Press.

Sandhu, Amandeep. 2006. Why unions fail in organising India's BPO-ITES industry. *Economic and Political Weekly.* October 14, 4319–22.

Sangari, Kumkum, and Sudesh Vaid, eds. 1989. *Recasting women: Essays in colonial history.* New Delhi: Kali for Women.

Sarikakis, Katharine. 2004. *Powers in media policy. The challenge of the European Parliament.* Oxford/Bern/New York: Peter Lang.

———. 2005. Defending communicative spaces: The remits and limits of the European Parliament. *International Communication Gazette* 67 (2): 155–72.

———. 2006. *"Making" security: Citizenship, public sphere and the condition of symbolic annihilation.* www.libertysecurity.org/IMG/doc_challengepaper.doc.

———. 2007. Mediating social cohesion: Media and cultural policy in the European Union and Canada. *European Studies. An Interdisciplinary Series in European Culture, History and Politics,* 24.

Sassatelli, Monica. 2002. Imagined Europe: The shaping of a European cultural identity through EU cultural policy. *European Journal of Social Theory* 5 (4): 435–51.

Sassen, Saskia. 1999. *Globalization and its discontents: Essays on the new mobility of people and money.* New York: New Press.

Schiller, Dan. 1996. *Theorizing communication: A history.* New York: Oxford University Press.

———. 1999a. *Digital capitalism: Networking the global market system.* Cambridge, Mass: The MIT Press.

———. 1999b. The legacy of Robert A. Brady: Antifascist origins of the political economy of communication. *Journal of Media Economics* 12 (2): 89–101.

———. 2003. The telecom crisis. *Dissent,* Winter, 66–70.

———. 2005. Poles of market growth? Open questions about China, information and the world economy. *Global Media and Communication* 1 (1): 79–103.

———. 2007. *How to think about information.* Urbana: University of Illinois Press.

Schiller, Herbert I. 1976. *Communication and cultural domination.* White Plains, N.Y.: International Arts and Sciences Press.

———. 1989. *Culture, Inc.* New York: Oxford University Press.

———. 1991. Not yet the post-imperialist era. *Critical Studies in Mass Communication* 8 (1): 13–28.

———. 1992. *Mass communications and American empire.* Boulder, Colo.: Westview.

Schlesinger, Phillip. 2002. "Identities: traditions and news communities"—a response. *Media, Culture and Society* 24 (5): 643–48.

Schmitz, Gerald J. 1995. Democratization and demystification: Deconstructing "governance" as development paradigm. In *Debating development discourse: Institutional and popular perspectives,* ed. D. B. Moore and G. J. Schmitz, 54–90. London: Macmillan Press.

Scholte, Jan A. 2000. Global civil society. In *The political economy of globalization,* ed. N. Woods, 173–201. London: Macmillan.

Schramm, Wilbur. 1964. *Mass media and national development: The role of information in the developing countries.* Stanford, Calif.: Stanford University Press.

Schwedler, Jillian, ed. 1995. *Toward civil society in the Middle East? A primer.* Boulder, Colo.: Lynne Rienner Publishers.

Seah, Chiang Nee. 2001. Socialism revisited. *Little Speck.* October 20. www.littlespeck .com/content/economy/CTrendsEconomy-011020.html.

Sell, Susan. 1998. *Power and ideas: North-South politics of intellectual property and antitrust.* New York: State University of New York Press.

———. 2003. *Private power, public law: The globalization of intellectual property rights.* Cambridge: Cambridge University Press.

Semati, Mehdi, ed. 2004. *New frontiers in international communication theory.* Lanham, Md.: Rowman and Littlefield.

Sharpe, Jenny. 1993. *Allegories of empire: The figure of woman in the colonial text.* Minneapolis: University of Minnesota Press.

Shiva, Vandana. 1997. *Biopiracy: The plunder of nature and knowledge.* Boston: South End Press.

Shlapentokh, V. 2000. Pochemu rushatsya kolossy? Popitla obyektivnogo analiza [Why do giants collapse? An attempt at an objective analysis]. *Sociologicheskiye issledovaniya* [Sociological Research], 2.

Sim, Soek-Fang. 2001. Not the end of history: Authoritarianism in defense of capitalism. *Javnost/The Public* 8 (2): 45–66.

———. 2005. Social engineering the world's freest economy: Neo-liberal capitalism and neo-liberal governmentality in Singapore. *Rhizomes* 10 (Spring). www.rhizomes.net/issue10/sim.htm.

———. 2006. Hegemonic authoritarianism in Singapore: Economics, ideology and the Asian economic crisis. *Journal of Contemporary Asia* 36 (2): 143–59.

Sinclair, John. 1992. The decentering of cultural imperialism: Televisa-ion and globo-ization in the Latin world. In *Continental shift: Globalisation and culture,* ed. E. Jacka. Double Bay, Australia: Local Consumption.

———. 1997. The business of international broadcasting: Cultural bridges and barriers. *Asian Journal of Communication* 7 (1): 137–55.

Sinclair, John, Elizabeth Jacka, and Stuart Cunningham, eds. 1996. *New patterns in global television: Peripheral vision.* Oxford: Oxford University Press.

Sinha, Pravin. 2004. Dilemma of organizing IT workers—The case of India. Paper presented at the Australian Labour Market Research Workshop, the University of Western Australia, Perth.

Skaine, Rosemarie. 2000. *The women of Afghanistan under the Taliban.* Jefferson, N.C., and London: McFarland and Co. Inc.

Sklair, Leslie. 2001. *The transnational capitalist class.* Oxford: Blackwell Publishers.

Smythe, Dallas W. 1981. *Dependency road: Communications, capitalism, consciousness and Canada.* Norwood, N.J.: Ablex Publishing.

Sokolov, M. 2005. Vremya politiki. Radio Liberty. April 25. www.svoboda.org/programs/tp/2005/tp.042505.asp.

Sparks, Colin. 2003. Are the Western media really that interested in China? *The Public/Javnost* 10 (3): 93–108.

———. 2005. Civil society as contested concept: Media and political transformation in Eastern and Central Europe. In *Democratizing global media: One world, many struggles,* ed. Robert Hackett and Yuezhi Zhao, 37–56. Boulder, Colo.: Rowman & Littlefield.

Spivak, Gayatri C. 1990. *The post-colonial critic,* ed. Sarah Harasym. New York: Routledge.

———. 1992. Acting bits/identity talk. *Cultural Inquiry* 18:770–803.

Splichal, Slavo, Andrew Calabrese, and Colin Sparks, eds. 1994. *Information society and civil society: Contemporary perspectives on the changing world order.* Purdue, Ind.: Purdue University Press.

Sreberny-Mohammadi, Annabelle. 1991. The global and the local in international communications. In *Mass media and society,* ed. J. Curran and M. Gurevitch, 118–38. London: Edward Arnold.

Sreberny-Mohammadi, Annabelle, and Ali Mohammadi. 1994. *Small media, big revolution: Communication, culture and the Iranian Revolution.* Minneapolis: University of Minnesota Press.

Sreberny-Mohammadi, Annabelle, Dwayne Winseck, Jim McKenna, and Oliver Boyd-Barrett. 1997. *Media in global context: A reader.* New York: St. Martin's.

State Council of PRC. 2005. *Guowuyuan guanyu feigongyouzhi zizben jinru wenhua chanye de ruogan jueding* [State council decision on the entry of non-public capital in the cultural industries]. new.xinhuanet.com/fortune/2005–08/08/content-3325932-htm (accessed August 20, 2005).

Statistical and UN Economic Commission for Europe (UNECE). 2005. *Counting immigrants and expatriates in OECD countries. A new perspective.* www.unece.org/stats/documents/2005/03/migration/wp.7.e.pdf.

Stavans, Ilan. 2001. *The Hispanic condition.* New York: Harper Collins.

Steet, Linda. 2000. *Veils and daggers: A century of National Geographic's representation of the Arab world.* Philadelphia: Temple University Press.

Stein, Laura. 2001. Access television and grassroots political communication in the United States. In *Radical media: Rebellious communiation and social movements,* ed. J. Downing, 299–324. London: Sage.

Steiner, Christopher B. 1994. *African art in transit.* Cambridge: Cambridge University Press.

Stephens, Bret. 2007. China's gift. *Wall Street Journal.* January 23, 13.

Stewart, Susan. [1984] 1993. *On longing: Narratives of the miniature, the gigantic, the souvenir, the collection.* Durham, N.C.: Duke University Press.

Stiglitz, Joseph E. 2002. *Globalization and its discontents.* New York: W.W. Norton.

Stoller, Paul. 2002. *Money has no smell: The Africanization of New York City.* Chicago: University of Chicago Press.

Strategy Research Corp. 1998. *U.S. Hispanic market: 1998.* Miami: Strategy Research Corporation.

Straubhaar, Joseph. 1984. Brazilian television: The decline of American influence. *Communication Research* 11 (2): 221–40.

——. 1991. Beyond media imperialism: Asymmetrical interdependence and cultural proximity. *Critical Studies in Mass Communication* 8 (1): 39–59.

Sun, Liping. 2003. *Duanlie: Ershishiji jiushi niandai yilai the Zhongguo shehui* [Fractured: Chinese society since the 1990s]. Beijing: Shehui kexue wenxian chubanshe.

——. 2004. *Shiheng: Duanlieshehui de yunzhou luoji* [Imbalance: The operational logic of a fractured society]. Beijing: *Shehui kexue wenxian chubanshe.*

Sun, Wanning. 2002. *Leaving China: Media, migration, and transnational imagination.* Lanham, Md.: Rowman and Littlefield.

Sussman, Gerald. 1995. Transnational communications and the dependent-integrated state. *Journal of Communication* 45 (4): 89–106.

——. 2001. Telecommunications after NAFTA Mexico's integration strategy. In *Continental order: Integrating North America for cybercapitalism,* ed. V. Mosco and D. Schiller, 136–62. Lanham, Md: Rowman and Littlefield.

Sussman, Gerald, and John A. Lent, eds. 1991. *Transnational communications: Wiring the third world.* Newbury Park, CA: Sage.

Swyngedouw, Erik. 1996. Reconstructing citizenship, the re-scaling of the state and the new authoritarianism: Closing the Belgian mines. *Urban Studies* 33 (8): 1499–1521.

Talbot, Karen. 2004. Coup-making in Venezuela: The Bush and oil factors. January 13. www.vheadlines.com/readnews.asp?id=14617 (accessed February 14, 2004).

Tamney, Joseph. 1996. *The struggle over Singapore's soul: Western modernisation and Asian culture.* Berlin: Walter de Gruyter.

Tawil, Helga. 2005. *The denial of development: A critical study of Palestinian Internet center.* PhD diss., University of Colorado, Boulder, 2005.

Tawil Souri, Helga. 2006. Marginalizing Palestinian development: Lessons against peace. *Development* 49 (2): 75–80.

Taylor, Charles. 1995. *Philosophical arguments.* Cambridge, Mass.: Harvard University Press.

Therborn, Goran. 2006. Meaning, mechanisms, patterns, and forces: An introduction. In *Inequalities of the world: New theoretical frameworks, multiple empirical approaches,* ed. Goran Therborn, 1–60. New York: Verso.

Third Tier Cities Project. 2002. *Holyoke: Known challenges, hidden assets.* City of Holyoke, Massachusetts.

Thobani, Sunera. Forthcoming. Imperial longings, feminist responses: Imagining Canadian nationhood after 9/11. In *Reaction and resistance: Feminism, law and social change,* ed. D. E. Chunn, S. B. Boyd, and H. Lessard. Vancouver: UBC Press.

Thomas, Pradip N., and Zaharom Nain, eds. 2004. *Who owns the media: Global trends and local resistances.* London and New York: Zed Books, Penang: Southbound, and London: WACC.

Thompson, Mark. 2001. Whatever happened to Asian values? *Journal of Democracy* 12 (4): 154–65.

Thuermer, Karen F. 2003. Spanish language media not minority TV. *Hispanic Outlook in Higher Education.* February 24, 21.

Thussu, Daya K. 1998. *Electronic empires: Global media and national resistance.* London: Arnold.

——. 2006. *International communication: Continuity and change.* 2nd ed. London: Arnold.

Thussu, Daya, ed. 2006. *Media on the move: Flow and counterflow.* New York: Routledge.

Tian, Hong. 2005. "Zenyang kandai 'huashengtun gongshi' yu 'beijing gongshi'" [How to view "the Washington Consensus" and the "Beijing Consensus"]. June 16 theory.people .com.cn/GB/40553/3473930.html (accessed April 19, 2007).

Tilly, Charles. 1990. *Coercion, capital and European states AD 990–1990.* Oxford: Blackwell.

Tobin, Joseph J. 1992. Introduction: Domesticating the West. In *Re-made in Japan: Everyday life and consumer taste in a changing society,* ed. J. Tobin, 1–41. New Haven, Conn.: Yale University Press.

Tomlinson, John. 1991. *Cultural imperialism: A critical introduction.* Baltimore: Johns Hopkins University Press.

Torres, Joseph. 2002. Press release: NBC purchase of Telemundo. The National Association of Hispanic Journalists. www.nahj.org/media/2003/hmr010603.html.

Torres, Maria de los Angeles. 2003. Transnational political and cultural identities: Crossing theoretical borders. In *Latino/a thought: Culture, politics, and society,* ed. R. D. Torres and F. H. Vasquez, 370–85. Lanham, Md: Rowman and Littlefield.

Torres, Rodolfo D., and Victor Valle. 2003. Class and culture wars in the new Latino politics. In *Latino/a thought: Culture, politics, and society,* ed. R. D. Torres and F. H. Vasquez, 385–408. Lanham, Md.: Rowman and Littlefield.

Tsing, Anna Lowenhaupt. 2006. *Friction: An ethnography of global connection.* Princeton, N.J.: Princeton University Press.

Tunstall, Jeremy. 1977. *The media are American: Anglo-American media in the world.* London: Constable.

——. 1995. Are the media still American? *Media Studies Journal,* Fall, 7–16.

Turow, Joseph. 1997. *Breaking up America: Advertisers and the new media world.* Chicago: University of Chicago Press.

UK Government. 2003. UK government response to the commission consultation on TVWF directive 89/552/EEC as amended by 97/36/EC.

——. 2005a. National statistics international migration. www.statistics.gov.uk/cci/ nugget.asp?id=766.

——. 2005b. Statutory instrument 2005 No. 220. The foreign satellite service proscription order 2005. www.opsi.gov.uk/si/si2005/20050220.htm.

UNDP Focus. 2001. www.papp.undp.org/pub/focus/2001v72.pdf (accessed August 16, 2004).

UNESCO. 1996. *Basic texts in Communication:* 89–95. Paris: UNESCO.

Upadhya, Carol. 2005. Culture incorporated: Control over work and workers in the Indian software outsourcing industry. Paper presented at the International Conference on New Global Workforces and Virtual Workplaces: Connections, Culture, and Control, Bangalore, India.

Upadhya, Carol, and A. R. Vasavi. 2006. *Work, culture, and sociality in the Indian industry: A sociological study* (Final Report). Bangalore, India: Indo-Dutch Programme for Alternatives in Development.

USAID. 2005. Economic growth: Expanded private-sector economic opportunities. www.usaid .gov/wbg/program_economic.htm (accessed November 16, 2005).

U.S. Embassy, Islamabad. n.d. Films premiere highlights Taliban abuse against women. usem bassy.state.gov/islamabad/wwwh03042906.html.

Van der Veur, Paul R. 2002. Broadcasting and political reform. In *Media and democracy in Africa*, ed. G. Hyden et al., 81–105. New Brunswick, N.J.: Transaction Publishers.

Van Kersbergen, Kees. 1997. *Double allegiance in European integration: Publics, nation-states and social policy*. EUI working paper RSC No 97/15. San Domenico, Italy: European University Institute.

Velter, Andre. 2003. Lifting the veil. In *Women of Afghanistan*, ed. I. Delloye, xi–xiv. Trans. Marjolijn de Jager. Saint Paul, Minn.: Ruminator Books.

Venezuela Information Office. 2005. Venezuela's law of social responsibility in radio and television. www.rethinkvenezuela.com/downloads/medialaw.htm (accessed October 2, 2005).

Venezuelanalysis.com. 2003. October 31. Opposition leaders prepare "civil rebellion" with media support—Seek 15 years of post-Chavez dictatorship. www.venezuelanalysis.com (accessed March 20, 2003).

Véron, René, Stuart Corbridge, Glyn Williams, and Manoj Srivastava. 2003. The everyday state and political society in eastern India: Structuring access to the employment assurance scheme. *Journal of Development Studies* 39 (5): 1–28.

Vij, Shivam. 2006. Dalit intellectualising and the other backward classes. *Himal*. September. www.himalmag.com/2006/september/opinion_2.htm.

Villa, Raul Homero. 2000. *Barrio logos: Space and place in urban Chicano literature and culture*. Austin: University of Texas Press.

Vincent, Richard C., Kaarle Nordenstreng, and Michael Traber, eds. 1999. *Towards equity in global communication: Macbride update*. Cresskill, N.J.: Hampton Press.

Vincent, Roger. 2004. California: Spanish papers square off. *Los Angeles Times*. March 2.

Viva, Dario. 2004. Lecture delivered by a member of the Venezuelan National Assembly at Vancouver Public Library, Vancouver, B.C. April 25.

Von Bogdandy, Armin. 1993. The contours of integrated Europe. *Futures: The Journal of Forecasting, Planning and Policy* 25 (1): 22–31.

Vulliamy, Ed. 2002. Venezuela coup linked to Bush team. *Observer*. April 21. www.guardian/co/uk/Archive/Article/0,4273,4398499,00.html (accessed March 20, 2003).

Wacker, Gudrun. 2003. The Internet and censorship in China. In *China and the Internet: Politics of the digital leap forward*, ed. Christopher R. Hughes and Gudrun Wacker, 58–82. London: RoutledgeCurzon.

Wade, Robert. 2004. *Governing the market*. Princeton, N.J.: Princeton University Press.

Waisbord, Silvio. 2002. Grandes gigantes: Media concentration in Latin America. Opendemocracy .net. February 27. www.opendemocracy.net/debates/article.jsp?id=8&debateId=24&article Id=64 (accessed March 20, 2003).

Walby, Sylvia. 2003. The myth of the nation-state: Theorizing society and politics in a global era. *Sociology* 37 (3): 529–46.

Waldman, Amy. 2004. In Afghanistan, U.S. envoy sits in seat of power. *New York Times*. April 17.

Wall Street Journal Americas. 2004. May 24. www.dowjones.com/special.htm (accessed June 14, 2004).

Wallerstein, Immanuel. 1974. *The modern world system I: Capitalist agriculture and the origins of the European world-economy in the sixteenth century*. New York: Academic Press.

——. 1991. *Geopolitics and geoculture.* Cambridge: Cambridge University Press.

Wang, Chaohua, ed. 2003. *One China, many paths.* London: Verso.

Wang, Georgette, Jan Servaes, and Aruna Goonasekara, eds. 2000. *The new communications landscape: Demystifying media globalization.* London: Routledge.

Wang, Hui. 2003. *China's new order: Society, politics and economy.* Ed. Theodore Hunter. Cambridge: Harvard University Press.

Wang, Jing. 2000. Zhongguo dazhong wenhua yanjiuzhong de guojia wenti [The state question in Chinese popular cultural studies]. *Taiwan: A Radical Quarterly in Social Studies* 39: 153–90.

——. 2001a. Culture as leisure and culture as capital. *Positions: East Asia Cultures Critique* 9 (1): 69–104.

——. 2001b. The state question in Chinese popular cultural studies. *Inter-Asia Cultural Studies* 2 (1): 35–52.

Ward, David. 2001. Hispanic outlets, media roundup: Hispanic boom presents plenty of PR opportunities. *PR Week,* November 26, 15.

Warkentin, Craig. 2001. *Reshaping world politics: NGOs, the Internet, and global civil society.* Boulder, Colo.: Rowman and Littlefield Publishers.

Waterman, Peter, and Jane Wills, eds. 2002. *Place, space and new labor internationalisms.* New York: Blackwell.

Watson, James L., ed. 1997. *Golden arches east: McDonalds in East Asia.* Stanford, Calif.: Stanford University Press.

Watson, Peggy. 2000. Politics, policy and identity. *Journal of European Public Policy* 5 (1): 185–213.

Wearden, Graeme, and Karen Gomm. 2005. Entertainment industry "trying to hijack data retention directive." ZDNet UK. November 24. news.zdnet.co.uk/business/legal/0,39020651,39238422,00.htm.

Weber, Max. 1968. *Economy and society: An outline of interpretative sociology.* Vol. 1. New York: Bedminster Press.

Webster, Frank. 1995. *Theories of the information society.* London: Routledge.

——, ed. 2001. *Culture and politics in the information age: A new politics?* New York: Routledge.

Weidenfeld, Werner. 1990. *Europäische Kulturpolitik und europäische Identität in Europäische Kultur: das Zukunftsgut des Kontinents.* Gütersloh: Bertelsmann Stiftung.

Weisbrot, Mark. 2003. A split-screen in strike-torn Venezuela. *Washington Post.* January 12.

Weisbrot, Mark, Luis Sandoval, and David Rosnick. 2006. Poverty rates in Venezuela: Getting the numbers right. Center for Economic and Policy Research Issue Brief, May 2006. www.cepr.net/publications/venezuelan_poverty_rates_2006_05.pdf (accessed December 23, 2006).

Weisskopf, Thomas. 2004. *Affirmative action in the United States and India: A comparative perspective.* London: Routledge.

Weyland, Kurt. 2001. Will Chavez lose his luster? *Foreign Affairs.* November–December. www.foreignaffairs.org/20011101faessay5775/kurt-weyland/will-chavez-lose-his-luster.html (accessed March 20, 2004).

White House. 2003. *President signed U.S.-Singapore free trade agreement.* May 6. www.whitehouse.gov/news/releases/2003/05/20030506–11.html.

White, Robert. 1995. Democratization of communication as a social movement process. In *The democratization of communication,* ed. P. Lee, 92–113. Cardiff: University of Wales Press.

Wilk, Richard. 1995. Learning to be local in Belize: Global systems of common difference. In *Worlds apart: Modernity through the prism of the local,* ed. D. Miller, 110–33. London: Routledge.

Williams, Raymond. 1962. *Communication.* Harmondsworth: Penguin.

Williamson, John. 1990. What Washington means by policy reform. In *Latin America in adjustment: How much has happened?* ed. J. Williamson, 7–20. Washington: Institute for International Economics.

Wilpert, Gregory. 2002. Counter coup. Venezuela: The nation that refused to roll over for the oil barons. *Counterpunch.* April 15. www.counterpunch.org/wilpert0415.html (accessed March 15, 2004).

——. 2003a. Censorship or regulation of the airwaves? The Chavez government vs. Globovision TV. Venezuelanalysis.com. October 9. www.venezuelanalysis.com (accessed December 14, 2003).

——. 2003b. Community media in Venezuela. Venezuelanalysis.com. November 14. www.venezuelanalysis.com (accessed November 16, 2003).

——. 2004. Community airwaves in Venezuela. *NACLA Report on the Americas* 37 (4): 34–35.

——. 2007. Venezuelan government will not renew "coup-plotting" TV station's license. Venezuelanalysis.com. January 3. www.venezuelaanalysis.com/news.php?newsno=2182 (accessed January 3, 2007).

Wood, E. Meiksins. 2002. *The origin of capitalism: A longer view.* London: Verso.

World Bank Group. 2002. West Bank and Gaza update: West Bank and Gaza strategic outlook. April.

——. 2004a. *Four years—intifada, closures and Palestinian economic crisis: An assessment.*

——. 2004b. *News release No. 2005/190/MNA.* www.worldbank.org.

Xinhua News Agency. 2005. Hu: Harmonious society crucial for progress. June 28. www.chinadaily.com.cn/english/doc/2005–06/28/content_455332.htm (accessed August 1, 2005).

Yakovenko, I. (project supervisor). 2000. *Obschestvennaya expertiza: Anatomiya svobody slova* [Community expertise: Anatomy of free speech]. Moscow. www.freepress.ru/win/index1.html.

Yanai, Daniela. 2001. The materiality of subordination in the Israeli occupation of the West Bank and Gaza. www.hrcberkeley.org/download/report_dyanai.pdf (accessed September 22, 2005).

Yang, Taoyuan. 2004. *Zhongguo tisheng ruanshili: Beijing gongshi qudai huashengduan gongshi* [China promotes soft power: the "Beijing Consensus" replaces the "Washington Consensus"]. June 13.

Yankah, Kwesi. 1995. *Speaking for the chief: Okyeame and the politics of Akan royal oratory.* Bloomington, IN: Indiana University Press.

Yoshihara, Kunio. 1988. *The rise of ersatz capitalism in South-East Asia.* Singapore: Oxford University Press.

Yu, Jianrong. 2006. *Zhongguo gongren jieji zhuangkuang* [Conditions of the Chinese working class]. Hong Kong: Mirror Press.

Yúdice, George. 2003. *The expediency of culture: Uses of culture in the global era.* Durham, N.C.: Duke University Press.

Zadorin, I. 1999. Reiting Vladimira Putina dostig absolutnogo maximuma [The rating of Vladimir Putin has reached the absolute maximum]. *Expert,* December 6 (4): 6. www.zircon.ru/russian/publication/1/99120600.shtml.

Zaller, John. 1992. *The nature and origins of mass opinion.* Cambridge: Cambridge University Press.

Zartman, William I. 1995. Introduction: Posing the problem of state collapse. In *Collapsed states: The disintegration and restoration of legitimate authority,* ed. W. I. Zartman, 1–14. Boulder, Colo.: Lynne Rienner.

Zassoursky I. 1999. *Mass media vtoroi respubliki* [Mass media of the second republic]. Moscow: Izdatelstvo MGU.

Zelik, Raul. 2003. Venezuela and the popular movement: An interview with Roland Denis. Trans. Gregory Wilpert. *Z Magazine Online.* October. zmagsite.zmag.org/Oct2003/zelik1003.html (accessed August 20, 2005).

Zhao, Bing. 1998. Popular family television and party ideology: The spring festival eve happy gathering. *Media, Culture & Society* 20:43–58.

Zhao, Suisheng. 2004. *Nation-state by construction: Dynamics of modern Chinese nationalism.* Stanford, Calif.: Stanford University Press.

Zhao, Yuezhi. 1998. *Media, market, and democracy in China: Between the party line and the bottom line.* Urbana: University of Illinois Press.

———. 2000a. Caught in the Web: The public interest and the battle for control of China's information superhighway. *Info* 2 (1): 41–65.

———. 2000b. From commercialization to conglomeration: The transformation of the Chinese press within the orbit of the party state. *Journal of Communication* 50 (2): 3–26.

———. 2003a. Transnational capital, the Chinese state, and China's communication industries in a fractured society. *The Public/Javnost* 10 (4): 53–73.

———. 2003b. Fanlun Gong, identity, and the struggle over meaning inside and outside China. In *Contesting media power: Alternative media in a networked world,* ed. N. Couldry and J. Curran, 209–23. Lanham, Md.: Rowman and Littlefield.

———. 2004a. The state, the market, and media control in China. In *Who owns the media: Global trends and local resistances,* ed. P. Thomas and Z. Nain, 179–212. Penang, Malaysia: Southbound; and New York: Zed Books.

———. 2004b. The Media matrix: China's integration into global capitalism. *Socialist register 2005: The empire reloaded,* 197–217. London: Merlin Press.

———. 2007a. After mobile phones, what? Re-embedding the social in China's "digital revolution." *International Journal of Communication* 1:92–120. www.ijoc.org/ojs/index.php/ijoc/article/view/5/20.

———. 2007b. Marketizing the "information revolution" in China. In *Cultural capitalisms: Media in the age of marketization,* ed. Janet Wasko and Graham Murdock, 189–217. Cresskill, N.J.: Hampton Press.

———. Forthcoming. *Communication in China: Market reforms and social contestation.* Lanham, Md.: Rowman and Littlefield.

Zhao, Yeuzhi, and Robert Duffy. 2007. Short-Circuited? The communication of labor struggles in China. In *Knowledge workers in the information economy,* ed. K. McMercher and V. Mosco. Lexington Books.

Zhao, Yuezhi, and Dan Schiller. 2001. Dances with wolves? China's reintegration with digital capitalism. *Info* 3 (2): 135–51.

Zhang, Junhua. 2003. Network convergence and bureaucratic turf wars. In *China and the Internet: Politics of the digital leap forward,* eds. Christopher R. Hughes and Gudrun Wacker, 83–101. London: RoutledgeCurzon.

Zheng, Yongnian. 2004. *Globalization and state transformation in China.* Cambridge: Cambridge University Press.

Zhou, Yongming. 2006. *Historizing online politics: Telegraphy, the Internet, and political participation in China.* Stanford, Calif.: Stanford University Press.

Ziff, Bruce, and Pratima V. Rao, eds. 1997. *Borrowed power: Essays on cultural appropriation.*

Žižek, Slavoj. 2002. *Welcome to the desert of the real.* London and New York: Verso.

———. 2006. Nobody has to be vile. *London Review of Books* 28 (7). www.lrb.co.uk/v28/n07/zize01_.html (accessed February 1, 2007).

Index

ABC (television network), 241n13
Abu-Lughod, Lila, 230
Access to Information Bill (Nigeria, 1999), 252–53
Acción Democrática (Venezuela), 115
ACHPR (African Commission of Human and Peoples Rights), 249
Across Borders program (BirZeit University), 270
Acuña, Rudy, 206
adinkra cloth production, 163, 170–79; African American consumption of, 170–71; Asantehene and, 172, 173–74, 187n16; commodification of, 12–13, 164; cultural appropriation of, 170–71; gendered division of labor, 170, 173–75, 178–79; global economy, links to, 172; history of, 172–73; intellectual property law and, 175–76, 177–78; local appropriation of, 175–76; modern innovations, 172–73; motifs, 163, 175; traditional-modern divide, 176–77
adinkra cloth production, factory-made: public acceptance of, 175; use of adinkra motifs, 187n18; women traders and, 175–77, 178, 187n20
adinkra motifs, 163, 188n25; local appropriation of, 175
Afghanistan: contemporary representations of, 230–31; and Taliban regime, 231–32.

See also *Daughters of Afghanistan*; *Return to Kandahar*; war on Afghanistan
Africa, sub-Saharan: Chinese relations, 2–3, 38; freedom of the press, violations of, 251; poverty in, 286–87; Structural Adjustment Policies, failure of, 8, 19n5; telecommunications sector, deregulation of, 257–58
African Americans: Africans, historical and political links to, 181–82; African textiles, consumption of, 170–71, 180–81; Black identity, assertion of, 179
African Charter for Popular Participation in Development and Transformation (1990), 248, 259n7
African Charter on Broadcasting (2001), 248–49, 256, 259
African Commission of Human and Peoples Rights (ACHPR), 249
Africans: African Americans, historical and political links to, 181–82
African Union, 259n7
African Women's Media Center (Senegal), 254
Aginam, Arthur-Martins, 5, 6, 8, 290
Aglietta, Michel, 99, 102, 107
Agreement on Trade Related Aspects of Intellectual Property Rights (TRIPS), 165, 167, 186n7

Ahmed, Leila, 223
Akinola, Richard, 250
Al-Arabiya (television network), 193
Al Dia (newspaper), 212
Alhassan, Amin, 2
Al-Hayat (newspaper), 193
Al-Jazeera (television network), 191, 192–93, 226
All About Eve (television program), 161n2
Al Najah University, 271
Alo Presidente (television program), 134–35
Al Quds University, 271
Al-Ra'is (television program), 194, 198
American cultural hegemony, 143–44; decentralization of, 144–45; Japanese media industries and, 149
Amin, Samir, 29, 275, 276, 290
Amsterdam Treaty, Public Service Broadcasting Protocol to, 98
Ang, Ien, 156
anti-Americanism, 36–37, 66, 68
Anzaldúa, Gloria, 206
Aporrea media collective (Venezuela), 128
Appadurai, Arjun, 186n2, 190
Aquino, Corazon, 84
Arab reality television, 189; format acquisition, 194; production advantages of, 191; Saudi-Lebanese link, 198. *See also* Arab satellite television industry; *Star Academy*
Arab satellite television industry, 191–94; growth of, 191–92; liberalization of, 192; networks, transformation into, 192–93; post-Fordist practices of, 193–94. *See also* Arab reality television
Arato, Andrew, 281
Armstrong, Sally, 219, 220, 221, 234–35, 241n6, 241n8; access to power as a Westerner, 233; knowledge producer, authenticity as, 228; and Muslim women as the Other, 227–28, 236; Taliban and, 232. See also *Daughters of Afghanistan*
Asante, 163, 186n10; women, status of, 187n17
Asantehene, 173–74, 187n16
"Asian Capitalism," 77
Asian financial crisis (1997), 7, 8–9, 84
Asokwa (Ghana), 174

asymmetrical warfare, doctrine of, 37, 49n5
Atlanta, Georgia, 207
audience studies, 80–81
AVEX (Japanese music company), 153
Azcarraga family, 211–12

Bahujan Samaj Party (India), 293
Baker, Gideon, 259n2
Bangalore (India), 1–2, 4, 293; formal *vs.* informal economy, 295–96; spatial inequalities in, 296–97; technocratic modernization, model of, 296
Bangalore Agenda Taskforce (India), 306–7n11
Bart (Japanese magazine), 150
Beijing Consensus, 38, 44
Berezovsky, Boris, 72n6
Bettig, Ron, 167
Between Ourselves (Lorde), 180
Bharatiya Janata Party (India), 8, 292, 297
Big Brother (television program), 1
Bin Talal, Al-Waleed, 193, 198
biopiracy, 169
BirZeit University, 270
Blair, Tony, 77, 81
Blevins, Jeffrey Layne, 202
BoA (Korean singer), 152
Boateng, Boatema, 5, 8, 12
bogolanfini fabric, 180
Bolívar, Simon, 116
Bolivarian revolution (Venezuela), 116–17, 118–20, 139–40n1; community media, promotion of, 132–34; economic and social policy reforms, 119–20; participatory and protagonist democracy, 118–19; social base of, 140n2; Venezuealan commercial media system and, 122, 123–24, 124–26
Booth, Cherie, 224
Border Media Partners, 212
Borrero, Gerson, 213
Bourdieu, Pierre, 11
Boutelfiqa, Abdelaziz, 200n7
Braithwaite, John, 167, 168
Brazil, 8
Breman, Jan, 291–92
Budanov, Russian colonel, 68
Burawoy, Michael, 49
Bush, George W., 77, 237

Bush, Laura, 222, 224
Bush doctrine, 233

Cable TV Law (Taiwan, 1993), 150–51
Canadian Broadcasting Corporation (public media), 221, 226, 237
CanWest (television network), 226
capitalism, 6; contradictions of, 75; development and, 275; Internet, shaping of, 274–75; modernity and, 14, 15; polarization inherent in, 275–76. *See also* globalization
Capriles, Miguel Angel, 121
Caracas Municipal Press, 129
Carazao (Venezuelan urban revolt), 115
Carmona, Pedro, 124
Castañeda Paredes, Mari, 5, 9
Castro, Fidel, 213
Catia TVe, 125, 128, 130–32, 133
CBS, 241n13
Center for Free Speech (Nigeria), 244, 250
Central Asian republics, geopolitical importance of, 222–23
Chacon, Jesse, 119, 132
Chakravartty, Paula, 5–6, 8, 15, 34
Chan, Joseph M., 40–41
channel 8 (Venezuelan television station), 125
Chatterjee, Partha, 30, 287
Chávez, Hugo, 1, 8, 113, 116, 117–18. *See also* Bolivarian revolution
Chechnya, 56, 61, 68, 72n2
child pornography, 112n17
China, 1; African relations, 2–3, 38; Asian financial crisis and, 8–9; asymmetrical warfare doctrine of, 37, 49n5; civil society of, 289–90; conflation of state repression and market rationality, 24–25, 28; Internet and, 32–33, 45–46; media ownership in, 39–43; nationalist discourse within, 30, 36; neoliberalism as exception, 9, 25–26, 29–30; and "new left," 48; social inequality within, 43–44
China, state transformation: contradictions of, 23–24; leftist criticism of, 44–47; market regulation and, 32–34; media and, 29–30, 34–37, 39–43; and private property, protection of, 39; rightist criticism of, 46–48; ruling doctrines and,

31–32, 36; and "soft power," strengthening of, 37–39
China Central Television (CCTV), 29, 30, 37
Chinese agency, 26–27
Chinese Communist Party, 28; ruling doctrines, reinvention and rearticulation of, 31–32, 36
Chinese socialism, 23, 44
Chinese textile industry: adinkra cloth, appropriation of, 172, 182
Choueiri, Antoine, 200n2
Cisco Academies (Palestinian Territories), 270, 273, 281
Cisneros Group of Companies, 121
Cisneros Rendiles, Gustavo, 121, 122
civil society, 245, 259n2; bureaucratized version of *vs.* urban middle-class as denizens of political society, 287; in China, 289–90; defined, 277–78; and foreign aid, marginalizing effect of, 277, 279–80; Gramscian perspective of, 281; idealized liberal concept of, 290; within India, 300; Marx on, 285, 305n1; neoliberalism and, 245–46; and Palestinian Territories, 266–67, 278, 281–82; radical conceptions of, 278–79
Clear Channel Communications, 204
CNN, 191, 241n13
Cocks, Peter, 99–100
Cohen, Jean-Louis, 281
colonialism: and European Union, 100; and non-Western woman as victim, trope of, 223
Columbia Journalism Review, 122
Comisión Nacional de Telecomunicaciones (Venezuela), 131
Comite de Organizacion Politica Electoral Independiente (Venezuela), 115
common sense, sources of, 79–82
Commonwealth Parliamentary Association, 259n5
communication, technology and, 107–8
communication research, 10, 11, 202
Communications Rights Agenda (South Africa), 258
community media: African NGO advocacy of, 256–57, 260n28; Venezuela and, 132–34

consciousness industry, 110n1; in the European Union, 97–98, 100, 106–9, 112n7
Convergence Bill (South Africa, 2005), 257–58
Coombe, Rosemary, 168, 169
Coplin, William D., 90
Copyrighting Culture (Bettig), 167
Council of Ministers (EU), 98, 111n10
CPK Media Holdings, 212–13
Crandall, Robert W., 204
Creative and Media Business Alliance (media lobby), 109
critical transculturalism, 189–90
"cross-institutional groups" (CIGs) (Russia), 58–60
cultural imperialism, 15, 202
cultural production, 163–69; appropriation of, 168–69; assimilation of, 168; authenticity, diminished emphasis on, 163–64, 186n2; commodification of, 163–64; Third World's response to commodification of, 165–66. *See also* adinkra cloth production
cultural proximity, notion of, 154–55
Curran, James, 52

Dalit-Bahujan Freedom Network, 303
Dallas Morning News, 212
Daughters of Afghanistan (documentary), 219, 220–21; Afghanistan, representation of, 230–31, 232–33, 234–35; war on Afghanistan, legitimization of, 239. *See also* Armstrong, Sally
Dávila, Arlene, 205
Davila, Luis Ricardo, 214
Davis, Angela, 179
Davis, Mike, 207–8
de Armas, Armando, 121
"Declaration of the Rights of Women and the Citizen" (Olympe de Gouges), 111n11
de Menezes, Jean Charles, 112n20
democracy, defined, 52
Deng Xiaoping, 31, 36, 44, 46
Denis, Roland, 136
Denning, Michael, 127
Department for International Development (UK), 246
De Veaux, Alexis, 180

development, capitalism and, 275
Diaz, David R., 208
digital cable industry, 208–9
digital capitalism, 274–75
digitalization, 111n6
direct-to-home (DTH) satellite technology, 107–8
Dirlik, Arif, 27
Dobbs, Lou, 306n5
Donnell, Alison, 239
Dostum, General, 241n15
Drahos, Peter, 167, 168
Duany, Jorge, 206
Dubai TV, 192
Du Boff, Richard B., 203
Duffy, Robert, 5, 8
Dyer-Witheford, Nick, 287

East Asian media flows: audience reception of, 154–56; collaboration among media firms, 151–52; cultural proximity and, 154–55; glocalization strategies and, 145, 146–48; Japanese consumption of, 157–59; and Japanese popular culture, 148–51; and Korean popular culture, 152–53; and marginalized populations, exclusion of, 160; transnational dialogue, catalyst for, 158, 159–60; unevenness of, 160–61
Eekhout, Blanca, 135, 136
Egypt, 191, 192
Egypt Satellite Channel, 191
El Diario/La Prensa (newspaper), 212–13
El Nacional (newspaper), 121
El Universal (newspaper), 121, 122
Embedded (Robbins), 241n11
embedded neoliberalism, 102
Enzensberger, Hans Magnus, 110n1
EPZs. *See* export processing zones
Erez Industrial Estate, 271–72
Europe: history of integration, 99–100, 111n8; identity of, 100, 101
European Commission (EC) support of African NGOs, 246–47, 252
European Investment Bank, 271
European Parliament, 98, 101, 111n10
European Union (EU): African NGOs, support of, 246; consciousness industry and, 97–98, 100, 106–9, 112n17; cultural

policy initiatives, 104–5; economic integration, 97; identity of, 103–5; human rights and, 104, 105–6, 109; multiculturalism and, 100–1; multilevel governance of, 98–99, 111n10; and Television Without Frontiers Directive, 97, 98, 108
Euroskepticism, 102
Everton, Robert, 5, 8, 18, 139, 140n6
export processing zones (EPZs), 271–72
Extasi TV, 108

Fanon, Frantz, 238
Fateh (Palestinian Territories), 278
Federal Communication Commission (FCC), 121, 211
Federal Trade Commission, 211
Ferguson, James, 15, 19n5, 287, 288, 290
Fiske, John, 80
Flores, Juan, 206
Florini, Ann, 243
footless laborers, 291–92. *See also* subaltern publics
foreign aid: marginalizing effect on civil society, 277, 279–80; and Palestinian Territories, 265–66, 267; as political tool, 284n9
Fort Worth Star Telegram (newspaper), 212
Fox News, 241n13
Fraser, Nancy, 112n12
Freedom of Expression Institute (South Africa), 244, 249–50, 255, 259; and community media advocacy, 256–57, 260n28; Legal Unit of, 251; media pluralism and access advocacy of, 253; policy reform programs of, 252; public broadcasting, safeguarding of, 256; and telecommunications sector, opposition to deregulation of, 257, 258
Freedom of Information Bill (Nigeria, 2006), 253
free trade policy, media institutions, impact on, 203
free-trade zones, 271–72
Fremantle Media, 194
Frere-Jones, Sasha, 210
Friedman, Thomas, 4
funtumfunafu denkyem motif, 188n25
Future Television (FTV), 191, 194

Gandhi, Rajiv, 296
Garcia Canclini, Nestor, 134
GATT/GATS (General Agreement on Tariffs and Trade/General Agreement on Trade in Services), 97, 165
Gaza Industrial Estate, 272
Gender Links, 254
General Union of Palestinian Charitable Societies (Palestinian Territories), 267, 278
Germany, 70; Hartz IV social benefits policy of, 112n21
Ghana: cultural nationalism, 179; folklore, efforts at legal protection for, 165–66, 177–78, 183, 184, 186n5. *See also* adinkra cloth production
Giddens, Anthony, 75
Gilley, Bruce, 28, 31, 32
glasnost, 55
global communications, defined, 10
globalization: cultural diversity *vs.* homogenization, 14; defined, 52; nation-state and, 171; paradigms on the politics of, 4. *See also* capitalism
Globovisión (television network), 120–21
glocalization, 145, 146–48
Gole, Nilufer, 238
good governance, doctrine of, 8
Good Muslim Bad Muslim (Mamdani), 231
Gramsci, Antonio, 281
Granier, Marcel, 124
Great Transformation, The (Polanyi), 5
Gries, Peter Hays, 36
Guangzhou Daily Group, 40–41
Guardian (newspaper), 123
Gujarat genocide (India, 2002), 292
Gussinsky, Vladimir, 59, 62

Habermas, Jürgen, 259n2
Hackett, Robert, 225
Halbert, Deborah, 167–68
Hall, Stuart, 75, 81, 145, 149, 238
Hamas (Palestinian Territories), 278, 280, 282, 284n9
Hana yori dango (comic series), 153
Hanliu phenomenon, 153, 161n3
Haraway, Donna, 112n12
Hardt, Michael, 100, 102, 108, 111–12n12, 243

Harriss, John, 290–91, 300
Hartz IV social benefits policy (Germany), 112n21
Harvey, David, 35, 39–40
hegemony, identification of, 81
Held, David, 4
He Weifang, 47–48
Hewlett-Packard, 269
Hill, Mike, 259n2
Hispanic Broadcasting Corporation, 121, 211
Holyoke, Massachusetts, 206
Hong Kong, 157, 159
Horwitz, Robert, 260n14
Howell, Jude, 273
Hu, Hsing-chi, 151
Huang Jisu, 48
Hueva, William, 258
Hu Jintao, 9, 24, 31, 32, 37, 38, 44
hybrid transcultural forms, 13–14

Illarionov, Andrey, 54, 69
IMF. *See* International Monetary Fund
imperialism: and non-Western woman as victim, trope of, 223. *See also* cultural imperialism
Impremedia (newspaper chain), 212
Independent Broadcasting Authority (South Africa), 257
Independent Communications Authority of South Africa, 257
Independent Journalism Center (Nigeria), 259n5
India: and caste-based reservation system, 1, 293, 294, 297–98, 301–2, 306n7; civil society of, 300; globalization, popular opposition to, 8; Gujarat genocide (2002) in, 292; Naxalite movement in, 19n6; poverty within, 286, 305n4
India, IT industry: and caste-based reservation system, opposition to, 302; growth projections of, 294–95; meritocracy, vision of, 294; organized labor movement and, 299–300; working conditions and culture of, 298–99. *See also* Bangalore
India, subaltern publics: and citizenship claims, 297, 301, 303; geographic mobility of, 291–92; working conditions and culture, 300–1

indigenous peoples, defined, 187n13
Indonesia, 84
Initial D The Movie (2005), 152
Institute for Media and Society (Nigeria), 244, 250, 254
Institute for Press and Society (Venezuela chapter), 137
Intel Capital (corporate venture program), 270
Intel Club House program, 270
Intel Corporation, 269
intellectual property law, 165–66
intercontextuality, 190
Internal Security Act (Singapore), 78
International Association for Media and Communication Research conference (Cairo, 2006), 6
Internationale Kulturpolitik statt Außenpolitik? (Sombart), 104
International Federation of Journalists (Brussels), 254, 259n5
International Monetary Fund (IMF), 19n5, 259n7
International Press Center (Nigeria), 253, 254
international property regime studies, power imbalances and, 166–70
International Women's Media Foundation, 254
International Youth Foundation (IYF), 269, 270, 283–84n4
Internet, 167; capitalism, shaping by, 274–75; China, 32–33, 45–46. *See also* Palestinian Territories, Internet development; telecommunications industry
Iran, 1, 70
Iraq, 1
Islamic fundamentalism, militant, 231–32
Islamic Jihad, 278
Islamic Relief, 270
Islamic University in Gaza, 271
Ismael, T. Y., 225, 241n12
Israel: Palestinian Territories, economic restrictions imposed on, 267, 283n1; West Bank, territorial control of, 264–65
IT for Change (India), 1–2
IT4Youth project (Palestinian Territories), 263, 269–70, 273, 281

Iwabuchi, Koichi, 5, 6, 8, 11
Izarra, Andrés, 123–24

James, Caryn, 241n11
Japan: American popular culture,
    indigenization of, 145–46; East Asian
    media flows, consumption of, 157–59;
    transnational media industries, 145,
    146–51
Jay, Paul, 220
Jerusalem Fund, 270
Jiang Zemin, 31, 45
Jimenez, Marina, 215
Johnson, Chalmers, 49
Jordan, 192
Journalists for Democratic Rights (Nigeria),
    244, 250, 259n5; "unheard voices"
    project of, 254

Kachkaeva, A., 60
Kahn, Joseph, 28
Kandahar (film), 219, 240n1; critical
    acclaim for, 220, 237, 240–41n4, 242n20
Karim, Karim H., 225–26
Karnik, Kirin, 302
Karzai, Hamid, 235
kente fabric, 180
Kenya, 246, 259n1
Koltsova, Olessia, 5, 6, 7
Korean TV Production Company, 151
Korean Wave, 153, 161n3
Korten, David, 243
Kraidy, Marwan, 5, 7–8
Kramer, Martin, 237, 242n19
kuntunkuni cloth production, 173–74
Kwame Nkrumah University of Science and
    Technology, 172
Kwanzaa festival, 179

La Causa Radical (Venezuela), 140n1
Laclau, Ernesto, 116, 140n3
La Estrella (newspaper), 212
Land Acquisition Act (Singapore, 1966),
    76
Lang Xianping, 46–47
La Opinión (newspaper), 212
Lara, William, 140n8
Latino diaspora: cultural influence, growth
    of, 207–8, 210; discrimination against,

205–6; expansion of, 205. *See also*
    Spanish-language media industry
Law on Mass Media, 2001 amendment
    (Russia), 62, 72n8
Lebanese Broadcasting Corporation (LBC),
    191, 193, 194, 197, 200n2
Lebanon, 192, 198
Lenin, Vladimir, 54
Lessig, Lawrence, 167
Lewis, Bernard, 266
Leys, Colin, 81
Liechty, Mark, 157
Lima (Afghani girl), 221
Lin Chun, 14, 23, 27, 47, 49, 49n3
linkage-bargaining, system of, 165
Liu Kang, 31
Liuxing Huayuan (television program), 153
logic of capital, 40
logic of one-party dominance, 77–78
logic of territory, 40
Lorde, Audre, 180
Los Angeles, California, 207–8

Mahathir Mohamad, 84
Maher, Bill, 241n11
Maihofer, Werner, 104
Makhmalbaf, Mohsen, 219
Malaysia, 84
Mamdani, Mahmood, 231
Mandal Commission, 301
Man Sa Yarbah Al-Malyoun? (television
    program), 194
Mansfield, Peter, 266
Mao Zedong Flag (website), 45
Martín-Barbero, Jesús, 11
Marx, Karl, 285, 305n1
Mattelart, Armand, 82
McChesney, Robert W., 202, 204
McGrew, Anthony, 4
Measor, J., 225, 241n12
media: in Africa, 255–56, 257; in China,
    29–30, 34–37, 39–43; defined, 51; free
    trade policy, impact of, 203; public
    knowledge, shaping of, 224–25; in
    Singapore, 82–84, 86–88; in the UK, 108.
    See also East Asian media flows; media,
    Western; Russia, media; Spanish-
    language media industry;
    telecommunications industry; U.S.,

media; Venezuela, post-coup media
   system; Venezuela, pre-coup media
   system
media, Western: liberalization and
   privatization of, 95–96; Russian
   inferiority complex and, 64–66; and war
   on Afghanistan, legitimization of, 225–26
Media Bill (Nigeria, 1999), 252
Media Development and Diversity Agency
   (South Africa), 256–57
media effects, 80, 81
media flows. *See* East Asian media flows
Media for Democracy Program (Nigeria),
   252, 253
Media in Global Context: A Reader
   (Sreberny-Mohammadi), 10
Media Institute of Southern Africa (MISA),
   244, 248, 249, 261n30; Gender and
   Media Baseline Study, 254–55; media
   pluralism and access advocacy, 253, 256,
   257; policy reform programs, 252; SADC
   Journalists under Fire campaign, 251
Media-MOST (media company), 58–59, 62,
   67, 68
media NGOs. *See* NGOs
Media Rights Agenda (MRA), 244, 250, 252,
   259n5
Meehan, Eileen R., 202
"Meteor Garden" (television program), 153
Mexico, 209
Meyer, Mike, 42
Miami, Florida, 208
Middle East Broadcasting Center (MBC),
   191, 193, 194
Midstream (periodical), 45
Miller, Mark Crispin, 204
Milosevic, Slobodan, 72n11
Milward, Alan S., 99, 111n7
"Missiones" (Venezuelan social development
   initiatives), 119
Model Provisions for National Laws on
   Protection of Expressions of Folklore
   against Illicit Exploitation and Other
   Prejudicial Actions (1982), 165–66
modernity, capitalism and, 14, 15
Mohanty, Chandra, 223
Montag, Warren, 259n2
Morocco, 192
Morris-Suzuki, Tessa, 159, 273

Mosco, Vincent, 12, 202, 294
Movimiento Bolivariano Revolucionnario-
   200 (Venezuela), 117
Movimiento V República (Venezuela), 118
Mugabe, Robert, 246
multiculturalism, European Union, 100–1
multitude as singularities acting in common,
   concept of, 111–12n12
Munck, Ronaldo, 291
Murdoch, Rupert, 35, 42

Nair, Janaki, 295–96, 297, 300
nation, defined, 53
National Association of Software and
   Service Companies (India), 294–95
National Association of Women Journalists
   (Nigeria), 254
National Broadcasting Commission
   (Nigeria), 260n20, 260n25, 261n34
National Common Minimum Program
   (India), 298
National Community Media Forum (South
   Africa), 252
National Endowment for Democracy (U.S.),
   246, 259n4
National Knowledge Commission (India),
   298, 307n13
National Rural Employment Guarantee Act
   (India), 298
nationhood, 102–3
nation-state: economic integration as survival
   strategy in, 99; and EU directives,
   implementation of, 106; factors
   transforming role of, 96; globalization
   and, 171; governing philosophy of, 102;
   sovereignty and, 106, 108, 109–10
nation-state, postcolonial: organized labor,
   relationship between, 291; subaltern
   publics, relationship between, 290–91
Naxalite movement (India), 19n6
NBC (television network), 212, 241n13
Negri, Antonio, 100, 102, 108, 111–12n12,
   243
Negron-Muntaner, Frances, 210
neoliberalism, 4–5; in China, 25–26; civil
   society and, 245–46; defined, 25; NGOs
   and, 244, 247; in Venezuela, 115–16
New Partnership for African Development,
   259–60n7

New Policy Agenda, 245–46
"New Singapore Shares," 77
Newspapers and Printing Press Act
    (Singapore), 83
New York Times, 28, 37, 138
NGO Coordination Act (Kenya, 1990),
    246
NGOs (nongovernmental organizations),
    243; abuse of state power, monitors of,
    255; "brief-case," 246, 259n3; civil
    society and, 245–46; criticism of,
    247–48; donors, categories of, 246–47;
    growth of, 259n1; neoliberalism and,
    244, 247; and Palestinian Territories, 266,
    279–80; regulation of, 246. *See also*
    NGOs, African; *individual* NGOs
NGOs, African, 250–57; civic and human
    rights education of, 251–52; community
    media advocacy and, 256–57, 260n28;
    freedom of expression advocacy and,
    251; media deregulation and, 255–56;
    media pluralism and access advocacy,
    253, 254–55, 256–57; media
    professionalization, encouragement of,
    253; policy reform programs and,
    252–53; public broadcasting,
    safeguarding of, 256; South African and
    Nigerian groups, differences between,
    250–51. *See also individual* African
    NGOs
NHK (media company), 153
Nigeria, 244. *See also* NGOs, African
Nigerian Communications Commission, 258,
    261n34
Night Guard (Russian fantasy film), 73n13
9/11 legacy, 110
Nkrumah, Kwame, 179
nongovernmental organizations. *See* NGOs
North American Free Trade Agreement
    (NAFTA), 203
Northern Alliance (Afghanistan), 231, 232
Norton, Augustus Richard, 266
Ntonso, Ghana, 174
NTV (television company), 58–59, 62

O'Leary, Michael K., 90
Olympe de Gouges, 111n11
Omar, Mullah Mohammed, 231
Omed, Hamida, 221

101 Proposal (television program), 151
One TV, 192
Ong, Aihwa, 25–26, 28, 43
organized labor: in India, 299–300; and
    postcolonial nation-state, relationship
    between, 291; xenophobic nationalism of,
    306n5
Orientalism, 225
Oslo Agreements (1993), 264–65, 266,
    283n1
Otero, Miguel Henrique, 121, 124
Ottaway, Marina, 246, 259n3

PAC Ltd. (television production house), 193,
    200n2
PADICO (telecommunications company),
    284nn7–8
Palestinian Authority, 264, 266, 271
Palestinian Information and Communications
    Technology Incubator (PICTI), 263, 271,
    273, 281
Palestinian Territories: and civil society,
    266–67, 278, 281–82; foreign aid to,
    265–66, 267; free-trade zones of, 271–72;
    Internet growth in, 267–68; poverty in,
    283n2; telecommunications industry of,
    263–64, 267–68; territorial division and
    segmentation of, 264–65
Palestinian Territories, Internet development,
    15–16, 269–74; and capitalism,
    implications of, 274, 275, 276–77; civil
    society, erosion of, 281–82; NGOs and,
    279–80
Palestinian Trade Center, 271
PalTel (telecommunications company), 271,
    284n6, 284n8
pan-Africanism, 179, 188n24
Panos Institute, 247
Parents Maintenance Bill (Singapore), 77
Paris Economic Protocol (1994), 265, 266
Park, Myung-Jin, 52
Patria Para Todos (Venezuela), 140n1
Pazira, Nilufer, 219, 221, 227, 240, 241n14;
    access to power as a Westerner, 233;
    Bush doctrine, promotion of, 233–34;
    "Canadian-ness," assertion of, 227;
    knowledge producer, authenticity as,
    228–30; native informant, authenticity as,
    219–20, 227; and the Othering of Muslim

women, 236; Taliban and, 232. See also
    Return to Kandahar
Pearce, Jenny, 273
People's Action Party (Singapore), 7, 75; and
    hegemony, strategies for securing, 82–85;
    legitimacy of, 77–79. *See also* Singapore
People's Daily, 45–46
Perenchio, Jerrold, 211
Pérez, Carlos Andrés, 115
Pérez, Maclovio, 213
Peter the Great, 6, 54
Philip Morris, 67
PICTI. *See* Palestinian Information and
    Communications Technology Incubator
PITA (Palestine IT Association of
    Companies), 271, 284n6
Pitroda, Sam, 307n13
Podur, Justin, 135
Polanyi, Karl, 5, 33
Poleo, Rafael, 121, 124
political economy, defined, 11
Politically Incorrect (talkshow), 241n11
Poplalzai, Imam, 232
populism, 140n3
pornography industry, 107–8, 112n17
poverty: in Africa, sub-Saharan, 286–87; in
    India, 286, 305n4; in Palestinian
    Territories, 283n2
Premji, Azim, 298
Primakov, Yevgheny, 67
Promotion of Access to Information Act
    (South Africa, 2000), 252
public-private partnerships (PPPs), 298
Pursuit of Truth, The (periodical), 45
Putin, Vladimir, 61, 63–64, 68, 69, 72n10

Qatar Television, 192

Radio Alternativa de Caracas, 125
Radio Catia Libre, 125
Radio Perola, 125, 130
Ramírez Pérez, Victor, 125
Ramo, Joshua Cooper, 38, 44
Ramos, Jorge, 201, 207
Rao, Pratima, 168
Rashid, Ahmed, 231
Rather, Dan, 241n10
Ravell, Alberto Federico, 124
Ray, Larry, 259n2
Razack, Sherene, 223, 224

RCTV, 125, 138, 140nn7–8
reggaeton/hip-hop radio stations, 210
Renne, Elisha, 170
Resorte ("Law of Social Responsibility in
    Radio and Television"), 136–38
Return to Kandahar (documentary), 219,
    237, 240nn2–3; aesthetic sensibility of,
    226–27; Afghanistan, representation of,
    230–31, 232; critical acclaim for, 220,
    241n5; veil, image of, 219–20; war on
    Afghanistan, legitimization of, 239. *See
    also* Pazira, Nilufer
Revolutionary Association of the Women of
    Afghanistan, 232
Rhodes, Martin, 102
Rice, Condoleezza, 226
Rich Also Cry, The (television program), 61
Riordan, Ellen, 202
Rise of Great Powers, The (documentary
    series), 37
Robbins, Tim, 241n11
Robertson, Roland, 66
Robins, Kevin, 275
Robison, Richard, 18n4
Rodan, Garry, 83
Rosa Luxemburg Foundation, 247
Ross, Andrew, 289–90
Ross, Doran, 181
rossiysky, 53
Rotana network, 193
Roy, Sara, 283n1
Russia: anti-Americanism in, 66, 68;
    capitalist transition in, 7; diversity within,
    54; economic recovery of, 72n9;
    institutional disintegration of, 57–59, 70;
    national inferiority complex, Western
    media and, 64–66; and nationalism, rise
    of, 66–69, 70; reconsolidation of, 61–63;
    spatial disintegration of, 55–57, 71
Russia, media, 55–63; centralization of,
    61–63; institutional disintegration, role
    in, 57–59; and media wars, 59–61;
    nationalism, role in rise of, 66–69; spatial
    disintegration, role in, 55–57
Russian Union of Journalists, 60
russky, 53

Sachs, Jeffrey, 18n2
Said, Edward, 225
Salinas, Maria Elena, 208

Samar, Dr. Sima, 220–21, 233, 235, 241n7
Sandholtz, Wayne, 99
sankofa motif, 188n25
Sarikakis, Katharine, 5, 9, 34
Saudi Arabia, 192, 198
Schiller, Dan, 27, 202, 274
Schiller, Herbert, 52, 202, 203
Schlessinger, Phillip, 70
Second Intifada (Palestinian Territories), 267–68
Shetty, Shilpa, 1
Shiri (1999), 153
Shiva, Vandana, 168–69, 170
Shi Zongyuan, 42
Siemens AG (engineering company), 67
Sim, Soek-Fang, 5, 7, 75, 77
Singapore: ideological alternatives, absence of, 93–94; media in, 82–84, 86–88; and neoliberalism, model of, 7, 76–77; popular discourse, impact of official ideology on, 89–93; and S21 project, 81, 84–85, 86. *See also* People's Action Party
Singapore Inc., 76
Singapore Press Holdings, 83
Singapore 21 Project (S21), 81, 84–85, 86
Singh, Manmohan, 8, 19n6, 297–98, 301
Singh, V. P., 301
SME (music company), 153
Smythe, Dallas W., 202
social movement unionism, 291
Sogra (Hazara woman), 221
Sombart, Nikolaus, 104
Sony, 147, 149
Souri, Helga Tawil, 5, 15
South Africa, 244; democratization process of, 260n14; and NGO policy reform programs, 252. *See also* NGOs, African
South African Broadcasting Corporation, 256
South African Telecommunications Regulatory Authority, 257
South Korea, 84; and North Korea, perception of, 159; and popular culture, regional circulation of, 152–53
Soviet Union, media obligations, 54–55
Spanish-language media industry, 207–13; advertising revenue of, 213; corporate consolidation of, 210–13; exploitation of workers within, 213; market expansion of, 201, 207, 208–9
Spivak, Gayatri C., 223

Splendors of Thirty Centuries (Mexican art show), 203
Sreberny-Mohammadi, Annabelle, 10
Star Academy (television program), 193–94; censorship of, 200n7; controversy surrounding, 195–96, 197; linguistic markers of foreignness in, 196–97; post-Fordian practices of, 199; promotion of, 195; regional and global factors, interplay between, 199
Starwave (event management company), 193
state, defined, 52–53
State Asset Management Bureau (China), 46
Stavans, Ilan, 206
Stiglitz, Joseph, 18n2
Stoller, Paul, 181
Stone Sweet, Alec, 99
Straits Times (newspaper), 75, 82, 86
Stratton, Jon, 156
"Strengthen the Nation Forum" (online forum), 45–46
Structural Adjustment Policies (SAPs), 8, 19n5
subaltern publics, 290; and postcolonial nation-state, relationship between, 290–91. *See also* India, subaltern publics
Sun Liping, 43
Superstar (television program), 194
Susu groups, 187n21
Syria, 191, 192

Taiwan: Japanese popular culture, consumption of, 150–51, 155–56
Taliban regime, 231–32
Teather, David, 242n18
Telecommunications Act (U.S., 1996), 204, 207
telecommunications industry: Africa, 257–58; Palestinian Territories, 263–64, 267–68. *See also* Internet; media
Telemundo, 212
Telesur (public satellite television station), 134
Televisa (media company), 211–12
television formats, 194
Television Without Frontiers Directive (EU), 97, 98, 108
Thadda Al-Khawf (television program), 200n3

Thobani, Sunera, 5, 9, 13
Times (London newspaper), 125
Times of India (newspaper), 1
TNCs. *See* transnational corporations
Tomaselli, Keyan, 258
Tomaselli, Ruth, 258
Torres, Rodolfo D., 214
traditional knowledge, defined, 186n8
transcultural political economy framework, 10–11
transculturation, 12–14
transnational corporations (TNCs), 101–2, 109, 160. *See also individual* transnational media industries
transnational cultural power, structure of, 148–49
transnational media industries, East Asian, 151
transnational media industries, Japanese: American cultural hegemony and, 149; and Japanese popular culture, regional circulation of, 148–51; localization strategies of, 145, 146–48
TRIPS (Agreement on Trade Related Aspects of Intellectual Property Rights), 165, 167, 186n7
Tsing, Anna Lowenhaupt, 13
Tunstall, Jeremy, 147
Turner, Ted, 62
TV Caricuao, 125

Uganda, 246
UK: Anti-Social Behavior Order (ASBO) notices, 112n21; Department for International Development, 246; and human rights, campaign to devalue, 101; and media censorship, 108; migration in, 110n3; naturalization process in, 103; and public, monitoring of, 112n20
Undesirable Publications Ordinance (Singapore), 83
UNESCO (United Nations Education, Scientific and Cultural Organization), 165, 248, 249
Union Radio, 121, 125
United Arab Emirates, 192
United Nations, 259n7
United States Agency for International Aid (USAID), 246, 247, 259n6, 266, 267, 269, 271, 279

University of Ghana, 175
Univisión (television network), 121, 211–12, 213, 214
Unocal (oil company), 235
Upadhya, Carol, 295, 298–99
U.S.: and child pornography, policing of, 112n17; cultural imperialism of, 202; English Only movement in, 206; Hamas and, 284n9; and Islamic fundamentalism, complicity in rise of, 231; Northern Alliance, support of, 232; war on Afghanistan, objectives of, 222–23. *See also* Latino diaspora
USAID. *See* United States Agency for International Aid
U.S. Department of Justice, 211
U.S., media: deregulation of, 204–5; war on Afghanistan and, 225, 241nn10–11, 241n13. *See also* Spanish-language media industry
U.S. State Department, 239

Valle, Victor, 214
van Apeldoorn, Bastiaan, 102
van der Linden, Marcel, 290
van Kersbergen, Kees, 102
Vasavi, A. R., 295, 298–99
VCD repackaging, illegitimate, 151
VCIOM (All-Russia Center for Public Opinion Research), 51, 64, 66, 71n1
veil, complexities surrounding use of, 238
veilomentaries: and imperial violence, distraction from, 237–38; propaganda value of, 239; and uncritical use of the veil as a signifier, 238; war on Afghanistan, legitimization of, 221–22. See also *Daughters of Afghanistan*; *Return to Kandahar*
Velter, Andre, 230
Venevisión TV, 121, 124, 125
Venezolana de Television, 134
Venezuela: neoliberalism in, 115–16; political history of, 114–16; popular mobilization against media coup, 126–29. *See also* Bolivarian revolution
Venezuela, post-coup media system, 129–38; and commercial media sector, regulation of, 136–38; and community media sector, 129–32, 133; and state support of community media, 132–34

Venezuela, pre-coup media system, 120–26;
    Bolivarian revolution, opposition to, 122,
    123–24; and 2002 coup attempt, 124–26
ViVe (state-funded public television),
    135–36
Vivendi Universal (media company), 14
Vogel, E., 76

Wang, Jing, 24–25, 32
war on Afghanistan: legitimization sources
    for, 221–22, 224, 225–26; U.S. media's
    support for, 241nn10–11, 241n13; U.S.
    objectives in, 222–23
Weber, Max, 52
Webster, Frank, 275
Weidenfeld, Werner, 112n15
Welfare Association, 269, 270, 283n3
Weltgesellschaft, 112n15
"We Walk on a Broad Road" (Huang),
    48
White, Robert, 259n2
Williams, Raymond, 126, 130
Williamson, John, 25
Windhoek declaration (1991), 249, 256
Winter Sonata (television program), 153,
    157, 158

WIPO (World Intellectual Property
    Organization), 165, 186n6; Development
    Agenda, 166, 167
women, Western: tool to legitimize war on
    Afghanistan, 224
Workers Party (Brazil), 8
World Bank, 19n5, 259n7, 265, 271
World Bank Institute, 259n5
World Intellectual Property Organization.
    See WIPO
World is Flat, The (Friedman), 4
World Summit on Information Societies
    (WSIS), 305n2
World Trade Organization (WTO), 165, 167,
    183
Wrapped in Pride (Ross), 181
WTO. *See* World Trade Organization
Wu Shuqing, 38–39

Xinhua News Agency, 32

Yakovenko, I., 56
Yeltsin, Boris, 64, 67
Yúdice, George, 206

Zhao, Yuezhi, 5, 6, 9, 15, 225

About the Contributors

Arthur-Martins Aginam is a doctoral candidate in communication at Simon Fraser University, Canada. Formerly a public-affairs journalist in Nigeria, his research interests cut across civil society, media and democratization (particularly in sub-Saharan Africa), globalization, and the political economy of international communication and social movements and the media.

Boatema Boateng is an assistant professor in the Department of Communication at the University of California, San Diego. Her research interests include the politics of cultural production, particularly its mediations by institutions, location, and identity. Her current focus is on the power implications of the intellectual property protection of "folklore" in Ghana.

Mari Castañeda is an associate professor in the Department of Communication and the Center for Latin American, Caribbean, and Latino Studies at the University of Massachusetts, Amherst. Her fields of study include Spanish-language and Latina/o media, media and cultural policy, digital media, and the political economy of communication. She is currently working on a project that examines the cultural politics and property creation of Latina/o media in the U.S.

Paula Chakravartty is an associate professor at the Department of Communication at the University of Massachusetts, Amherst. She is the author of several articles and book chapters on the political economy and culture of high-tech development in India, as well as on migration, labor and nationalism in India and the U.S. She is the coauthor of *Globalization and Media*

Policy and her current research focuses on the politics of info-development
and civil society in Brazil and India.

Robert Duffy is a master's candidate in the School of Communication at Simon Fraser University, focusing on cultural studies and the political economy
of communication. He is currently writing his thesis, a study of the U.S. government's post-9/11 interventions in transnational Arab media culture.

Robert Everton received his PhD in Communication from Simon Fraser
University in 2003, and lectured in Communication and Latin American
Studies at Simon Fraser University and the University of Windsor. A lifelong
activist, Everton's passion for social justice carried him from revolutionary
Chile in the early 1970s to the global justice movements of the twenty-first
century. Bob Everton passed away in 2004.

Koichi Iwabuchi is professor at the School of International Liberal Studies
at Waseda University, Japan. His recent books include *Recentering Global-
ization: Popular Culture and Japanese Transnationalism*, *Feeling Asian
Modernities: Transnational Consumption of Japanese TV Dramas*, and *Rogue
Flows: Trans-Asian Cultural Traffic* (coedited with S. Mueke and M.
Thomas).

Olessia Koltsova is an associate professor in mass communication in the Department of Sociology of the Higher School of Economics, St. Petersburg,
Russia. During the last ten years she has been researching post-Soviet media
transformation and development. She is the author of *News Media and Power
in Russia* (Routledge 2006).

Marwan Kraidy is an associate professor at the Annenberg School for Communication at the University of Pennsylvania. A former fellow at the
Woodrow Wilson International Center for Scholars, he has authored *Hybridity, or The Cultural Logic of Globalization* and coedited *Global Media Studies: Ethnographic Perspectives*. He is now writing a book on reality TV and
Arab politics.

Katharine Sarikakis is a senior lecturer in communications policy at the Institute of Communications Studies at the University of Leeds. Her research
interests are in the field of international communications and the role of institutions in supra- and international communications policy processes. She is
the author of *Powers in Media Policy*, *British Media in a Global Era*, the
coauthor of *Media Policy and Globalization* (Edinburgh University Press
2006), the coeditor of *Ideologies of the Internet* (Hampton Press 2006), and

the managing editor of the *International Journal of Media and Cultural Politics*.

Soek-Fang Sim is a visiting fellow with the School of Communication at Nanyang Technological University. Her research interests are in the field of global media (East Asia and Middle East) and comparative news, and she serves on the board of the journal *Media and Culture in the Arab and Muslim World*. She has published several essays, including one that was awarded the Top Faculty Paper prize by the International Communication Association.

Helga Tawil Souri is an assistant professor in the Department of Culture and Communication at New York University. Her research focuses on various aspects of Palestinian and Arab media practices and spaces, including analyses of local broadcasting industries and cinema, the relationship between the Internet and national/economic development, and issues around social and political spaces. She is also a photographer and documentary filmmaker.

Sunera Thobani is an assistant professor of women's studies at the University of British Columbia. Her research interests include race and gender relations, globalization, migration and citizenship, and media and the war on terror. She has served as a president of the National Action Committee on the Status of Women, and is a founding member of Researchers and Academics of Colour for Equity. She is the author of *Exalted Subjects*.

Yuezhi Zhao is an associate professor and Canada Research Chair in the Political Economy of Global Communication at the School of Communication at Simon Fraser University. In addition to more than thirty journal articles and book chapters, she is the author of *Media, Market, and Democracy in China: Between the Party Line and the Bottom Line* (1998), coauthor of *Sustaining Democracy? Journalism and the Politics of Objectivity* (1998), and coeditor of *Democratizing Global Media? One World, Many Struggles* (2005). Her forthcoming book is entitled *Communication in China: Market Reforms and Social Contestation* (Rowman & Littlefield).